Research Methods in
PSYCHOLOGY

Third Edition

JEFFREY S. ANASTASI
JESSICA R. LEE

Kendall Hunt
publishing company

Cover image © Shutterstock, Inc.

Kendall Hunt
publishing company

www.kendallhunt.com
Send all inquiries to:
4050 Westmark Drive
Dubuque, IA 52004-1840

Copyright © 2016, 2020, 2022 by Kendall Hunt Publishing Company

ISBN 979-8-3851-1547-1

Published in the United States of America

Contents

Chapter 1

Research Methods in the Real World

Research in the Media

Whether you're planning on attending graduate school in psychology (or some other area) or if you're simply taking a research methods course because it's a required class for your major, research is an extremely important part of psychology and simply surviving in daily life. While you may not really notice, you are bombarded with research on a daily basis. You're presented with research on news programs, magazines, newspapers, talk shows, radio shows, advertisements, at sporting events, by politicians, when making purchases of various products, in addition to any scientific research you might find in research journals. Some research may tell you about the health risks of smoking or eating certain foods or the benefits of certain types of exercise or dietary supplements. There's research on the benefits of breastfeeding, of enrolling your children in certain types of extracurricular activities, or even to encourage you to own your own home. You're presented with research on which car is the best or the safest, which vitamins and foods are the healthiest, which toothpaste or chewing gum is the best, which cleaning product or deodorant or paper towel or toilet paper works best. Research really is everywhere. Pay attention for the next couple of days, and I'll bet you're surprised at how much research you're presented with on a daily basis. And this doesn't even include the research that you're exposed to in your current education.

As you're presented with research, you may notice that the research that is presented in the media isn't presented in the same way as the research that is presented in a scientific journal. Research in the media is typically a very abbreviated version of the research presented in scientific journals. This research is also presented in a way that should make it more accessible to your average person and not include a lot of scientific jargon. At first glance, these two characteristics sound very appealing—and these characteristics are appealing. However, if the research is abbreviated then many of the details will not be included. These details may be extremely important for one to assess the quality of the research or to determine if the conclusions are warranted. When the research is made more accessible, there may be problems where the research may be misinterpreted by the individual summarizing the study. This may be done to make the research sound more fantastic or it could be because the individual describing the research isn't an expert on that topic. Either way the research may be misrepresented.

Another major issue with research as it is presented in the media is that it is important to know research, understand the methods that are used to collect the data, know the type of research approach that was used to collect the data (i.e., experimental vs. nonexperimental approaches), and know the limitations of each research approach. As a consumer of the research that you're presented with, it's really up to you to determine if the research has been conducted well and to determine if the research is really measuring or evaluating what it's supposed to be measuring. Many of these details won't be presented in an abbreviated form of the research as presented by the media. It may also be very difficult to determine which research approach was taken with the research as it is presented in such an abbreviated form, and there are numerous research approaches that can be utilized to investigate certain topics. Some of these approaches are better than others for various reasons, but there are trade-offs for each approach. We'll discuss many of these trade-offs later in this textbook. While the different research approaches will be

1

discussed in greater detail in later chapters of this textbook, it is important to note that only experimental approaches allow one to make causal statements. A **causal statement** is one where it is appropriate for the researcher to say that one variable causes a certain effect. Nonexperimental approaches do not allow one to make causal conclusions. For example, does smoking cause lung cancer in humans?

The obvious answer is yes, of course it does. However, this may not be as simple of a conclusion as one might think. Many years ago I attended a political town hall meeting in South Carolina. Keep in mind that South Carolina is an area of the country where tobacco is a major crop. The presidential candidate made a statement to the tobacco farmers who attended that town hall that there was no scientific evidence that tobacco causes cancer or even emphysema in humans. This statement is clearly a lie, right? Well, it might be somewhat misleading, but *technically* it's not a lie. In order to show that smoking does actually cause cancer, you'd have to conduct a true experiment. This would involve, as a hypothetical example, getting a large group of infants, dividing them into two equal groups, and following them throughout their lives. We'd randomly assign some of those infants to the smoking group; we'll make them smoke each day of their life for 40 years. The other infants will be in the nonsmoking group; they'll not be allowed to smoke for 40 years. After 40 years we'll assess the incidence of cancer in these groups. Since these groups were equivalent and we treated them the same way, if the smoking individuals acquired cancer at a higher rate than the nonsmokers then we can say that smoking causes cancer. So, have they ever conducted this type of study? Of course not! This study would be highly unethical and will never be conducted. However, there have been many similar studies with all kinds of animals, such as cats, dogs, hogs, and monkeys, and these studies consistently show a causal relationship between smoking and cancer in every type of animal tested. Some studies with human cells have shown that the chemicals in cigarettes cause mutations in the cells that cause those cells to become malignant. Still other nonexperimental studies (typically correlational or quasi-experiments) have been conducted with humans that show that individuals who smoke have a much higher rate of cancer and many other ailments compared to individuals who do not smoke. While these human studies are very helpful (and the only ones that can be ethically conducted with humans), one can't make a causal statement based on these nonexperimental human studies. There are numerous potential differences between individuals who choose to smoke and those who chose to not smoke. For example, it may be true that nonsmokers are more interested in their health than smokers. Nonsmokers may exercise more or eat healthier because of this. Thus, the health differences that have been observed in these studies may be because of these differences in exercise and diet, instead of the cigarette smoking itself. It may be the cigarette smoking, but we can never tell because there are numerous potential differences between these groups. Interestingly, because of the very consistent nonexperimental studies with humans and the experimental studies conducted with nonhumans, the Surgeon General's Office has placed a warning on cigarette packs that indicate that the scientific community is very sure that, even though the appropriate studies can't be conducted with humans, smoking does indeed cause cancer and other health issues in humans. You may ask the obvious question, if the Surgeon General's Office is adept at understanding scientific research then why would they make a causal statement based on nonexperimental evidence with humans and experimental evidence with nonhumans to conclude that cigarette smoking causes certain illnesses in humans. I think it's actually a very valid question. The potential answers are 1. The Surgeon General shouldn't be making such claims or 2. That the evidence is clear enough, even though the appropriate experimental evidence can't ethically be conducted, that cigarette smoking is bad for one's health.

The experimental research with various species of animals is pretty clear. The experimental research with human cells is pretty clear. The nonexperimental research with humans is pretty clear. By using what is referred to as **converging evidence**, one can see that all of the research that has been conducted points to the fact that cigarette smoking does cause harm to one's health. As a result, the Surgeon General's Office determined that it was appropriate to first place warnings on cigarette packaging and then later make those warnings somewhat stronger as additional converging evidence came in. The Surgeon General's office first used a very appropriate statement on cigarette packaging starting in 1966 that was appropriate based on the fact that there were no true experiments conducted that, due to ethical reasons, demonstrated that cigarette smoking caused specific illnesses in humans. This statement said that "Cigarette smoking may be hazardous to your health." With additional converging evidence, the statements became somewhat stronger. Here are the different messages that have been placed on cigarette packaging with the year that it started:

Here are some examples of health warnings that the Surgeon General's office has included on cigarette packaging.

- Caution: Cigarette Smoking May be Hazardous to Your Health (1966–1970)
- Warning: The Surgeon General Has Determined that Cigarette Smoking is Dangerous to Your Health (1970–1985)
- SURGEON GENERAL'S WARNING: Smoking Causes Lung Cancer, Heart Disease, Emphysema, and May Complicate Pregnancy. (1985–present)
- SURGEON GENERAL'S WARNING: Quitting Smoking Now Greatly Reduces Serious Risks to Your Health. (1985–present)
- SURGEON GENERAL'S WARNING: Smoking By Pregnant Women May Result in Fetal Injury, Premature Birth, and Low Birth Weight. (1985–present)
- SURGEON GENERAL'S WARNING: Cigarette Smoke Contains Carbon Monoxide. (1985–present)

We've included several examples of research as it is presented in the media at the end of this chapter. Take some time to consider your thoughts on the listed research. As you go through Chapter 2 and discuss some of the different research approaches, consider what types of studies are being described and what kinds of conclusions can be made from such studies. Also, think of alternative explanations for the findings from the various studies.

The Status of Psychology as a Science

Do you think psychology is a science? While this may seem like a pretty simple question, you may get many different answers depending upon who you ask. I've overheard many introductory psychology students say that psychology "is really just common sense." A walk into a bookstore can give you another perspective concerning the views of psychology as a science. You'll typically find many psychology books in the self-help section of the bookstore and many of those books aren't written by psychologists! The majority of self-help books are written not by individuals trained or who are active researchers on the specific topic, but by individuals who have experienced some of these issues and as a result consider themselves to be "experts." While some of these individuals may have something to offer, you'll often find that these self-help books provide recommendations that aren't supported by any science; it's simply one person's beliefs. These unfounded self-help books hurt psychology's image by dispersing unfounded information or personal beliefs to the masses. They also encourage readers to believe that psychology is just common sense since these individuals lack credentials or ideas supported by research. In fact, Cialdini (1997) looked at how the media refers to psychologists. He found that natural scientists are referred to as "scientists" by the media 80% of the time, whereas social scientists are referred to as "authors" 80% of the time.

Additionally, when you ask nonpsychology majors or laypersons to name psychologists, the first response is usually Sigmund Freud or Dr. Phil. The vast majority of psychologists are not big supporters of Freud due to the difficulty in testing his theories. One major problem with many of his theories is that they can't be disproven. For example, in his explanation for why we all experience infantile amnesia (the inability to remember events from our early childhood) he believes it is due to the repression of the memories that we had when we were children. Specifically, the sexual feelings we had towards our opposite sex parent were so bothersome to us that we repressed those feelings and in the process repressed all other memories for this time in our childhood. If one were to argue with Freud that we never had these feelings, he would simply say that that is the evidence that we have repressed them. Your only other option would be to admit to these feelings—either way, Freud would be correct and his theory can't be disproved. As for Dr. Phil, while Dr. Phil may help some individuals, his therapy is more appropriate for a television show than for scientifically-based therapy. Dr. Phil has published numerous self-help books that sell very well, but he has only one scientific publication that was published in 1981 (Achterberg, McGraw, & Lawlis, 1981). This one publication, where he wasn't even the primary author, was evaluating approaches to help with rheumatoid arthritis and was based on his dissertation research. He has no additional scientific publications. Perhaps these individuals aren't the strongest representatives of a scientific psychology.

Rational vs. Empirical Approaches

There are two general ways to try and understand behavior or other things in our world. There's the rational approach and the empirical approach. The **rational approach** is understanding behavior through reason, intuition, and logic. This approach involves sitting back and thinking about why the world is the way that it is. The **empirical approach** involves using direct observation and testing in order to understand behavior. So which does science use? Can you have a science that's based solely on the rational approach? Well, science actually uses both the rational and empirical approaches. And no, you can't have a science that is based solely on the rational approach. The rational approach is used by science in formulating hypotheses or theories. This is the first step in investigating something and is part of the scientific method. No science would generate a hypothesis or theory and then simply stop there. For example, a science could formulate the hypothesis that humans are more likely to receive assistance from others when more people are present than when only one person is present. In other words, if you were choking on some food at a restaurant, this hypothesis would argue that you would be more likely to receive help from someone if there were more people present at your table than if there was only one person at the table. The reasoning would be that if one were choking there would be more individuals who would be able to provide assistance or that there was a better chance that one of these individuals would have the knowledge to help or even that there would be a higher likelihood that one of these individuals would have the right personality to jump up and provide assistance. This hypothesis is very reasonable, intuitive, and logical. However, just because it seems reasonable and logical, doesn't make it true. If we stopped with our hypothesis and assumed that it must be true because it's logical then we'd be using only the rational approach. Clearly no science would do this. The second part of the scientific method would be to actually observe or test what happens in this situation. This topic was a real question asked by psychologists in the 1960s. Darley and Latané (1968) conducted studies in order to determine if this hypothesis was actually correct. Their findings actually showed that the likelihood that someone will help another individual is inversely related to the number of bystanders. In other words, the likelihood of help is much greater if there was only one person sitting at the table with you than when you had 10 others at the table. When other people are around, individuals are less likely to help someone because they believe that someone else will assume the responsibility and help the individual. In the case of a single bystander, that bystander assumes 100% of the responsibility, whereas when there are 10 bystanders, each of these bystanders assumes 10% of the responsibility and is less likely to help. Thus, even if everyone agrees that the

This gentleman was the only person at the table and assumed 100% of the responsibility to help this woman in distress—lucky for her.

rational approach is reasonable, intuitive, and logical, it doesn't make it correct. One must go beyond the rational approach and also utilize the empirical approach in order to find the true answer when using the scientific approach.

Soft Science vs. Hard Science: What Makes Something a Science?

We've all heard the term "soft science," but what does it really mean? Most people are able to determine the "hard" sciences. They include biology, medicine, chemistry, physics, and the like. What is it that makes these hard sciences? The terms hard science and soft science have nothing to do with the difficulty of the topics. The difference is how much these areas rely on the scientific method and the ability to test various theories or hypotheses. Additionally, how well these areas stand up to the scrutiny of the scientific method is also important for sciences in general. As a result, hard sciences are typically seen as more legitimate than soft sciences. So, where does psychology fit in? Is psychology a hard science like biology, chemistry, and physics or more of a soft science like history, sociology, and political science? It's an interesting question and one that I've even heard psychology majors argue about. Let's talk about why people see psychology as a soft science. There are typically two reasons why people sometimes see psychology as a soft science. First, individual differences make it difficult to predict behavior with certainty. One of the goals of psychology is to predict behavior. Since the behavior of individuals varies, it's nearly impossible to predict any particular individual's behavior with certainty. However, our hard sciences have this same problem. For example, most people see biology and medicine as hard sciences. However, these same individual differences are present in those areas of study as well. When you take something as simple as a pain reliever, which pain reliever do you take? Some individuals take aspirin, some take ibuprofen, some take acetaminophen, and others may take naproxen sodium. Why? Well, most of us take the pain reliever that is most effective for us. Because our body chemistry is different (i.e., individual differences), certain pain relievers work better for us. Additionally, how many pills do you take in order to get rid of a headache? Again, this number varies considerably due to how sensitively our bodies respond to certain pain relievers. When your doctor prescribes you with an antibiotic, which one do you receive? This also varies extensively. Some antibiotics may not work very well with you, but are highly effective for others. You may also have an allergic reaction to some medications that others don't experience. These are all individual differences. The same kinds of individual differences that are found in psychology.

Second, we can't see the internal workings or thoughts that accompany behavior in psychology. Due to the fact that we can't observe all of the topics that we study in psychology, people sometimes believe that it isn't scientific. For example, when studying an organism's behavior, we can't observe their thought process. When a clinical psychologist is diagnosing an individual with a certain psychopathology, they do this by looking at the individual's symptoms and then making a diagnosis. Medical doctors do the same thing. When you visit a medical doctor he or she will evaluate your symptoms and come to a specific diagnosis that corresponds with these symptoms. The doctor may not be able to actually see the illness, but they diagnose you based on these symptoms. Much of physics studies things that can't be observed, but we can see the effects of the phenomenon. For example, while we can't actually observe momentum, we can manipulate it and observe its effects on objects. Even in astrophysics, the study of black holes provides an example of studying something that isn't actually seen. Astrophysicists don't actually see black holes. Instead they notice something that appears to have such a strong gravitational pull that even light or x-rays or radiation are unable to escape it. So the existence of black holes is inferred based on the lack of light in an area or the path of a star or other object with mass that may orbit the black hole.

One final note is that individuals argue that in psychology there are sometimes more than one theory that predict a particular behavior. This makes it difficult to determine the truth about what is causing the behavior. While this is sometimes true, I'd argue that you have these same issues in all sciences. A very simple example is in physics and deals with how light travels. Does light travel as a wave or via particles?

Physics says it can't be both, but the evidence shows that it has the characteristics of both. This basic question has plagued physics since the ancient Greeks. All sciences have unanswered questions. While this uncertainty may be uncomfortable for some individuals, this is the nature of anything that we study. We study these things in order to slowly reduce the number of things we don't know. Unfortunately, it may be a slow process.

What about Pseudosciences?

What is a pseudoscience? A **pseudoscience** is an area of study that is thought to be similar to an established science, but doesn't hold up to the scrutiny of scientific testing. For example, astrology has been used quite extensively and is very popular. Astrologists argue that astrology was considered a science in human's early history and that it is simply an extension of astronomy. Astronomy mentions many constellations that are made up by the orientation of the stars. Astrologists use these same constellations, but then make the added assumption that individuals born during certain dates have specific characteristics that are based on these constellations. Many individuals swear by the predictions made by astrologists. In fact, former president Ronald Reagan used astrology to make many foreign policy decisions while he was in the White House (Johnson, 1991). Some police departments in the 1980s used astrology to help investigate certain crimes or criminals (Marshall, 1980). The leading horoscope magazine has a circulation of one-quarter million which is more than most science magazines (Bastedo, 1981).

Can this psychic really tell you your future? It doesn't appear likely.

The support for pseudosciences is typically in the form of testimonials or the publication of a rare finding such that in 100 tests of the phenomenon, one shows the effect. This one finding is the one that is published to support the phenomenon's existence. As you'll see in Chapter 9, one significant finding out of a 100 is easily possible by chance alone and wouldn't indicate true support unless it could be replicated. For example, many individuals are very interested in extrasensory perception (or ESP) or find it fascinating. In fact, two thirds of American adults believed that they had experienced ESP. Here are some signs that you may have ESP:

The telephone rings and you know who it is before you answer it.

You know what someone is about to say to you before they say it.

You get a hunch or know about something and it turns out to be correct.

You get a sudden urge to go somewhere or do something and when you do that thing it turns out to be the right thing that you should have done and you are pleased.

You get a sudden urge to go somewhere or do something and you ignore it or don't do it, and it turns out that you should have and you regret it.

You can understand someone's true inner feelings even though on the outside they are hiding their feelings.

You have a feeling that there is a presence or that someone or something behind the scenes is helping you.

While many individuals may have had these same experiences, do these provide scientific evidence for the existence of ESP? If these claims were tested and then verified then one could believe these claims and conclude that ESP does actually exist. Unfortunately, when ESP is scientifically evaluated, the evidence shows that ESP doesn't actually exist. Like other pseudosciences, when the claims are scientifically evaluated they fail to work. In Chapters 6 and 7 we'll discuss the proper way to test many such claims, but most testing is going to involve some sort of a control condition that rules out any expectations that the participant may have (i.e., a placebo condition). This type of condition becomes very important when testing most phenomena. For example, many studies evaluating homeopathic medicines give participants the homeopathic medicine and find out if they get better. When the individuals do get better, the person administering the homeopathic remedy then concludes that it must have been the homeopathic medicine that cured the individual. But consider what just happened here. Was it the medicine? *Could* it have been because of the homeopathic medicine? Maybe. Maybe not. How can we know? We don't know for sure because there's nothing to compare it to. We don't have another group of individuals who received nothing or received some sort of placebo to compare to the individuals receiving the homeopathic medicine. As a critical evaluator of this researcher, you should be asking about alternative explanations for their

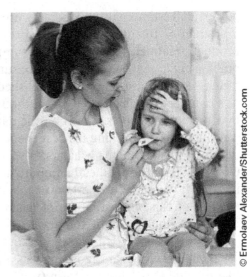

Based on this little girl's fever, it looks like she has the flu . . . or maybe it's a cold . . . either way she'll get better soon.

proof that homeopathic cures worked in this situation. Could the individuals have gotten better on their own, without the homeopathic medicine? For example, many times when you go to the doctor with the flu or even a cold, the doctor's diagnosis is "yep, you have the flu." You ask the doctor what you can do about it and the doctor's response is "nothing, just wait it out. Your body just needs some time to fight the temporary illness. It just needs to run its course." For our homeopathic medicine evaluation, it's very possible that the medicine did nothing at all. The individual might have just got better because the illness ran its course. If you tested the homeopathic remedy by having a placebo group and by having another group that received the homeopathic medicine, you'd know what was going on. If both groups got better then you'd know that it was just the illness running its course. If only the homeopathic group got better and the placebo group was still sick, you'd know that the homeopathic medicine did actually help the individual get better.

Importance of Scientific Study

Examples like testing the effectiveness of drugs or treatments or virtually any other potential claim can be effectively evaluated using the scientific method. Having the proper control groups and evaluating the claims in a critical manner allows one to truly assess those claims. As mentioned previously with our evaluation of homeopathic treatments, one must, at a minimum, include the condition where the individuals receive the treatment and some other comparison group that allows one to determine if the treatment works. Many companies or individuals who "test" their products don't use a proper comparison or control group. They have individuals take their treatment and see if they feel like it worked. As described above, this isn't an effective test of the product. Additionally, various companies use techniques to sell their products that are deemed very vivid. The **vividness effect** is achieved when "evidence" like testimonials are seen as more influential than the actual scientific evidence by individuals. Many companies sell products, such as dietary supplements, weight loss or muscle gaining pills, and hair loss remedies, and use no evidence other than testimonials. In fact, take a look at virtually any product for sale online. The most influential "evidence" that people use in deciding to purchase products are testimonials by people who supposedly tried the products. You'll also see testimonials by individuals who claim to have seen ghosts, big foot, aliens, etc. These eyewitness accounts or individual testimonials are powerful. Testimonials may be very useful in the early stages of investigation in order to determine if a product or treatment might be worth further evaluation, but they can't be used to actually test the product, treatment, or theory. For example, let's say we have a friend named Cory. Cory is interested in purchasing a used car. As a good consumer, he collects extensive data on the prices, gas mileage, safety ratings, etc. He also finds some published data that provides the reliability data on the different cars that he's considering which is based on thousands of individual reliability reports, such as those published by Consumer Reports. Based on the data that he collects, he determines that the best vehicle for him is a Mazda. Upon telling his best friend about his decision to purchase the Mazda, his friend tells him that his cousin bought a Mazda last year and has had nothing but problems with the vehicle. What does Cory do? Does he go ahead and purchase the Mazda because he's collected a plethora of data indicating that it would be the best, most reliable vehicle for him to purchase or would he pick a different car because of this one testimonial? Clearly he should purchase the Mazda, but most of the time we don't. This is an illustration of the power of the vividness of testimonials. As mentioned previously, many products are sold based solely on testimonials. They have individuals who say that the product worked for them. Several years ago there was an Excedrin commercial that really bothered me. First of all, I'd like to state that I use Excedrin (well, actually its generic equivalent) to get rid of headaches. Thus, I guess I'm providing a testimonial here. In this commercial, the individual says that they take Excedrin, not because of any scientific evidence that shows that it might work or any studies that have been done to demonstrate its effectiveness, but because it works for them. In essence, this commercial is coming right out and saying, don't take Excedrin based on scientific studies, just take it because it worked for this actor that we've hired who is providing you with a testimonial that they use it and that it works for them. It seems silly, but it works.

A well-thought-out study that attempts to rule out alternative explanations is typically extremely helpful in allowing one to determine the cause or effectiveness of some treatment or phenomenon. One historically influential example of this is the story of a horse named Clever Hans. The story of Clever Hans is a classic story in the history of psychology and science more generally. Wilhelm von Osten was a retired mathematics teacher in Berlin, Germany. He believed that animals could be as intelligent as humans if they were given a proper education. So he sought out to provide such an education to a horse named Hans. After extensive training von Osten could give Hans various mathematical problems and after extensive training Hans was able to solve these mathematical problems with perfect accuracy by tapping his hoof on the ground. Virtually any mathematical question was answered by Hans perfectly. In 1891, Von Osten displayed his clever horse to many individuals and many people traveled to him to see this amazingly intelligent horse. As word spread of this remarkable animal, a committee (the Hans Commission) was assigned in 1904 to investigate this horse to verify that it was actually making these computations and that there was no sort of trickery being conducted by von Osten. The committee, in its presence, asked von Osten to evaluate Hans so as to find out if von Osten was cheating. They also tested Hans in the absence of von Osten, thinking that perhaps he was somehow giving Hans the answers. After extensively testing Hans, the committee concluded that Hans was indeed a very intelligent horse and that Hans was conducting mathematics as von Osten had claimed. A psychologist by the name of Carl Stumpf who was part of this committee continued to think that something just wasn't right, and assigned one of his graduate students to further evaluate Hans (with the full permission of von Osten). The graduate student's name was Oskar Pfungst. Pfungst also replicated some of the testing that the committee had done. He too was very impressed with Hans. He then tested Hans in an interesting way. He, as the committee had done, tested Hans in the absence of von Osten. Hans still did very well. Additionally, he made it so that the individual evaluating Hans didn't actually know the answer to the mathematics problem. When he did this, Hans' accuracy plummeted to zero. Interesting! He then tested Hans so that the person asking Hans the questions wasn't in Hans' line of vision. When Hans couldn't see the person asking the question, he was unable to correctly answer the question. As it turns out, Hans really had no expert knowledge of mathematics. Instead, he became very sensitive to very slight muscle movements of the individuals who were asking him questions. When individuals asked him a mathematical equation, such as what is the square root of 25, they would look down at this hoof as the horse tapped out 1, 2, 3, 4, and 5. When Hans got to 5, the individual would then look up or make a small muscle movement that indicated Hans to stop. So Hans didn't really understand mathematics, but was detecting these small movements. When these movements were not present, such as the person being out of Hans' sight, he couldn't use these cues. When the questioner didn't know the answer, they made no movements when Hans reached the correct answer. So while Hans wasn't as clever with mathematics as originally thought, he was still clever indeed.

Hans the Wonder Horse studying for his next big test.

The Objectives of Science

There are four primary objectives of science: description, prediction, explanation, and control. Of these objectives, description is the simplest and most basic. **Descriptive observation** involves a systematic and unbiased account of the observed characteristics of behaviors (Myers & Hansen, 2012). Case studies, naturalistic observation, and sometimes surveys are excellent examples of studies that utilize a descriptive approach. In each of these types of approaches the researcher is simply describing a behavior or attitude. A famous case study example is that of Phineas Gage. On September 13, 1848, Gage was working as a railroad blasting foreman. Due to an accidental explosion, a tamping iron was driven through Gage's head, damaging much of this left frontal lobe. Gage survived the accident, although he suffered extensive brain damage. His behavior and personality following the accident were extensively studied and recorded. The observations were simply descriptive in nature as the researchers merely described how Gage acted following the accident. While some of his changes in behavior following the accident were certainly caused by the damage to his frontal lobe, other changes could have been the result of Gage being frustrated with the recovery process or even the way people judged him due to being disfigured by the accident, among other potential explanations.

Phineas Gage is one of the most well-known examples of a case study in psychology.

   Predictive observations are other approaches and are typically used by correlational and quasi-experiments. With predictive observations one tries to predict a specific behavior by using some other data, event, or condition. For example, many high school students take the SAT or ACT tests in order to be admitted to certain universities. Undergraduate psychology students take the GRE test each year in order to score well enough on this standardized test to be admitted into the graduate program of their choice. Why are these important? Well, most universities have data that look at the performance of students in their programs and they can look at the SAT, ACT, or GRE scores of those students. These data demonstrate a moderately strong relationship between Scholastic Assessment Test (SAT) and American College Testing (ACT) scores on undergraduate Grade Point Average (GPA) as well as between Graduate Record Examination (GRE) scores and graduate school GPA. These schools can then use these data to predict the performance of future students. If one were to know the SAT score of a student applying to their program, they could then use these correlational data in order to predict future college GPA.

Explanation (or Explanatory) observations take one's study a step further. In explanatory observations one is attempting to determine what actually causes a certain behavior. As previously discussed in this chapter, if one wanted to determine the cause of a certain behavior, one would need to conduct a true experiment. In this approach, one would randomly assign individuals into two equal groups. For example, if one wanted to determine if watching violent cartoons caused children to behave aggressively, one could form two equal groups of children. One group of children would watch aggressive cartoons for one hour, while the other group would watch nonaggressive cartoons for one hour. Following the cartoon presentations, our children would be allowed to play on the playground. The researchers could then measure how many aggressive actions the children had on the playground. Let's assume that the children watching the aggressive cartoons end up displaying more aggressive actions. If these groups were initially equivalent and if the only difference between them was the presentation of the different types of cartoons, then we can say that the aggressive cartoons caused the children to behave more aggressively. This is an explanation for why the children are behaving more aggressively. A similar study could be conducted in order to test a certain drug's effectiveness. For example, if we developed a drug that was intended to make cats feel loyalty and love towards their owners (we'll call our drug *Catacare*), we would test the drug by sorting our cats into two equal groups. One group would receive injections of *Catacare* and the other group would receive a saline, placebo injection. If our *Catacare* cats showed more affection towards their owners, we would say that *Catacare* was successful in causing the cats' behavior to change.

Clearly this cat has taken a large dose of *Catacare*.

© Happy monkey/Shutterstock.com

Control observations are the final type of observation. Once we have an understanding of the cause of certain behaviors, we can then control or manipulate behavior. Using the *Catacare* example above, we could control the cats' affection by administering *Catacare* to them. With our violent cartoon example, by showing children aggressive cartoons, we could control their behavior by causing an increase in aggression. Of course, we probably wouldn't conduct a study in order to increase aggression in children, but we could have a similar study where we showed the children prosocial behaviors (such as being polite and helping others) in order to help manipulate their behavior in a positive way. Regardless, the idea with control is that one could use the knowledge gained by finding causal relationships in order to manipulate behavior.

Concluding Remarks

The purpose of this textbook and the remaining chapters is to help you to become a critical evaluator of research and a capable research scientist. This textbook will introduce you to all the information that you need in order to become a competent researcher or simply a proficient consumer of research as you're presented with it on a daily basis. Enjoy the journey!

References

Achterberg, J., McGraw, P., & Lawlis, G. F. (1981). Rheumatoid arthritis: A study of relaxation and temperature biofeedback training as an adjunctive therapy. *Biofeedback & Self Regulation, 6*(2), 207–223.

Bastedo, R. W. (1981). Am empirical test of popular astrology. In K. Frazier (Ed.), *Paranormal borderlands of science*. Buffalo, NY: Prometheus.

Cialdini, R.B. (1997). Professionally responsible communication with the public: Giving psychology a way. *Personality and Social Psychology Bulletin, 23*, 675–683.

Johnson, H. (1991). *Sleepwalking through history: America in the Reagan years*. New York, NY: W. W. Norton & Company.

Marshall, E. (1980). Police science and psychics. *Science, 210*, 994–995.

End of Chapter Quiz

___1. Which of the following statements is true of research as it is presented in the media?
   a. The media does an adequate job at presenting the research in an unbiased manner.
   b. The media only presents unbelievable findings to the general public.
   c. Research presented in the media is usually purposely misrepresented to make it more interesting.
   d. Research presented in the media typically doesn't have enough details to be truly evaluated properly.
   e. Only C and D are true

___2. Based upon the correlational data collected thus far, does cigarette smoking cause lung cancer in humans?
   a. Yes   b. No

___3. An explanation is empirical if it is
   a. based on widely held beliefs   c. based on observations
   b. simple and makes few assumptions   d. limited in scope

___4. If you were to make conclusions based upon your own intuition and logical reasoning alone, you would be utilizing the _____ approach.
   a. empirical   c. objective   e. all of the above
   b. rational   d. subjective

___5. According to the research conducted by Darley and Latané (1968), which of the following would be the best number of individuals present if you were choking on your food?
   a 1   b. 5   c. 10   d. 15   e. none of the above

___6. Which of the following individuals was able to show that Clever Hans was picking up on very slight cues, rather than actually knowing the answers to the questions asked of him?
   a. John Watson   c. Oskar Pfungst   e. all of the above
   b. Wilhelm von Osten   d. Carl Stumpf

___7. Which of the following is NOT one of the goals of science?
   a. description   c. explanation   e. control
   b. prediction   d. justification

___8. Colleges using SAT or ACT scores and high school GPA to admit students is an example of which goal of science?
   a. description   c. explanation   e. control
   b. prediction   d. justification

___9. According to Cialdini's (1997) research, psychologists are typically referred to as _____ by the mainstream media.
   a. "scientists"   c. "researchers"   e. "liars"
   b. "Mr. or Ms."   d. "authors"   f. "charlatans"

10. Is psychology a science? Please provide your answer and explain your logic to support your answer.

Homework Assignment #1

#1: Go to a bookstore (not the university bookstore) and find the Psychology Section. Write down the title and author of the first five books that catch your eye. In a sentence or two, describe the general nature of each book. Write down your general opinions/thoughts concerning what you found. In other words, do you think this book adequately represents psychology?

Homework Assignment #2

#2: Research in the Media

Each of the examples below provides real examples of research as it was presented in the media. Some of these are excerpts that came from radio or television commercials, from magazines, from newspapers, or other sources. For each, consider the study, the approach of the study along with the limitations of that approach, and whether you should believe the findings.

A. Music is Good for the Brain

High school music students score higher on SATs in both verbal and math than their peers. In 2001, SAT takers with coursework/experience in music performance scored 57 points higher on the verbal portion of the SAT and 41 points higher on the math portion than students with no coursework/experience in the arts.

B. Where You Sit Matters

Studies show that students who sit in the front and center (middle) of the classroom tend to achieve higher average exam scores (Rennels & Chaudhari, 1988). One study discovered a direct relationship between test scores and seating distance from the front of class: students in the front, middle, and back rows of class score 80%, 71.6%, and 68.1%, respectively, on course exams (Giles, 1982). These findings occur even when students are assigned to these seats by their instructor, which indicates that it is not simply due to the fact that more motivated students tend to sit in the front and center of the classroom.

C. Get Happier, Live Longer

Optimistic women are 30% less likely to die from heart disease, according to a new Women's Health Initiative study, so thinking positively is even more crucial as you get older.

D. Girls Schools Better Prepare Students

A 2000 study of 4,274 girls' school alumnae, conducted for the National Coalition for Girls' Schools by the Goodman Research Group of Cambridge, Massachusetts, examined outcomes at single-sex schools for girls. The girls' school alumnae were overwhelmingly positive in their responses. Ninety-one percent cited preparation for college and academic challenge as very good or excellent. Eighty-eight percent would repeat their girls' school experience. Eighty-three percent perceived themselves to be better prepared for college than their female counterparts from coeducational high schools. Thirteen percent intended to major in math or science, which is significantly more than females and males nationally (which is 2% and 10%, respectively).

E. Homeownership

Home ownership leads to higher self-esteem and better grades in children compared to children who live in a family where the home is not owned.

F. Breastfeeding: The Natural Way to Feed Your Baby

Without a doubt, breastfeeding is the best way for you to feed your baby. Scientific evidence points out that breastfeeding is superior to all other ways of feeding your baby. In fact, breastfeeding increases your baby's IQ with an average increase of about seven points.

Chapter 2
Overview of Research Methods

In this chapter, we'd like to introduce you to the basics of research methods. While the remainder of this textbook is designed to give you all the specifics about various aspects of research, this chapter gives you a general overview of everything you need to know in order to understand the research process. You'll need to know the basic terminology, and you'll need to gain a general understanding so that you can begin the research process and talk intelligently about research.

Two Ways to Understand Behavior

As discussed in Chapter 1, there are two ways that we try to understand behavior or gain knowledge of the world: the rational and empirical approaches. The **rational approach** is where we attempt to understand behavior through logic, reason, and intuition. The **empirical approach** is where we understand behavior through direct observation and testing of ideas. Which of these seems like a better approach to you? Your answer might depend on your formal training and your background. The rational approach is one that is often used by philosophers or some social scientists, whereas the empirical approach is used by individuals with other training (we'll discuss this in more detail shortly). Let's take a look at a research question and compare our two approaches. Imagine you're in the following situation: You are eating dinner at a nice restaurant, when you get some food stuck in your throat. The food is really lodged in your throat such that you can't expel the food and it's stopping you from breathing. You start to panic because you can't breathe and the food seems to be really stuck. In this situation, would you rather be sitting at a table with one other person or ten other people? This might be a pretty simple question, depending upon your background. When people were asked this question, they thought the answer was pretty obvious. Of course they'd rather have ten people. With ten people present the odds of having someone who would know what to do in this situation should be greater. There's also a better chance that someone would help you. With only one other person, the likelihood of this one individual knowing what to do and actually doing it, are much smaller. When a group of psychologists started to investigate this problem, others thought they were idiots. Why would anyone study a problem where the answer is obvious? Using the rational approach, having ten people present is intuitive, and it makes logical sense. Everyone agreed. However, it's not the correct answer. When conducting studies investigating this type of situation (i.e., using the empirical approach) and other situations that involved getting someone to help another individual, researchers found that the likelihood of getting help was inversely related to the number of bystanders. The more bystanders, the less likely the individual is to receive help from any of the bystanders (Darley & Latané, 1968). While there are many other variables that have been evaluated with regard to this bystander effect, the effect is a very robust effect in social psychology. This study provides a nice example of the distinction between the rational and empirical approaches. The rational approach by itself is not an approach that will lead to a true science. A true science does require the use of the empirical approach. Now we're not arguing that the rational approach is useless either. The rational approach is important and it does have a place. In fact, part of the scientific method depends on the rational approach. Here are the basic steps to the scientific process:

1. Determine your question
2. Construct a hypothesis or make a prediction
3. Test your hypothesis
4. Analyze your data and draw your conclusions
5. Communicate your results

Which of the above step(s) depends on the rational approach? Determining your question and constructing your hypothesis both involve the rational approach. You consider the question and make your predictions using intuition, logic, and reasoning. However, if you stopped at this point, you'd never know what the correct answer was. The empirical approach is the critical addition as you test your hypothesis to see what actually happens. As was seen with the bystander effect, the actual findings are sometimes counterintuitive. Therefore, the rational approach is helpful for science, but a true science can't depend on the rational approach alone. It must also utilize the empirical approach.

If you think about each of the sciences, you should be able to assure yourself that they each use both the rational and the empirical approaches. For example, does medicine use only the rational approach? Of course not! Doctors do use the rational approach as they come up with a theory for their diagnosis, but they don't stop there. They then observe the individual, discuss the patient's symptoms, and conduct tests in order to test her diagnosis. All of the other sciences such as biology, chemistry, physics, etc. use both approaches as well.

The different methods that are used in psychology utilize the scientific method; not just the rational approach, but also the empirical approach. The two general categories of study in psychology are nonexperimental and experimental methods. There are numerous nonexperimental methods. We will discuss each of these methods throughout this textbook, providing many details about the pros and cons of each technique. This information will allow you to make an educated decision on which approach makes the most sense for the topic that you're interested in studying. Ultimately, the decision on how to study some issue or topic is entirely up to you, and you have a lot of freedom to decide what's best. Before moving on to provide a brief introduction to each of these techniques, we'd like to point out that each of these techniques utilizes the empirical approach. While some of these techniques are better than others in certain situations or allow you to make firmer conclusions, they all rely on actually observing what happens in our world and testing to see what happens. Thus, they're all empirical in nature.

Nonexperimental Research Methods

As previously mentioned, there are numerous nonexperimental methods that can be used to better understand the world. Each of these approaches has one thing in common that makes each of them nonexperimental: nothing is being manipulated. With the experimental approach, the researcher is using manipulated variables. **Manipulated variables** are those variables that the researcher is able to specifically manipulate or change. With nonexperimental approaches, the researcher is studying topics that aren't manipulated or can't be manipulated or can't be ethically manipulated. As we discuss each of these different nonexperimental approaches, keep in mind that there is no manipulation. Here is a list of the major nonexperimental techniques:

Case Study
Observation
    Naturalistic Observation
    Laboratory Observation

Survey Research
    Interviews, questionnaires, surveys
Correlational Research
Quasi-experiments
Archival Research

Case Study

A **case study** follows a single individual and gathers extensive information about that individual. Case studies are oftentimes used when the individual being studied is rare or special in some way. A very famous case study example is that of Phineas Gage. You may remember Phineas Gage from your introductory psychology class or some other course. Phineas Gage was injured while working for the railroad. While at work, an accidental explosion caused a blasting iron to be propelled through Gage's skull. Gage survived the accident, but suffered severe damage to his frontal lobe. By extensively studying Gage and interviewing individuals who knew Gage, scientists were able to determine how the accident changed Gage's behavior and personality. Keep in mind that nothing was manipulated in this study, as it would obviously be unethical to deliberately cause this type of damage to someone. The main issue with case studies is that, since there's no manipulation, researchers must wait until someone comes along who has the particular, rare issue. A second issue is that case studies typically lack **generalizability** (or **external validity**). In other words, it's difficult to generalize the results of this case to the remainder of the population since this individual is typically being studied simply because they aren't like the rest of the population.

Observation

Observational research is the systematic observing and recording of behavior. There are two main ways to study observation: naturalistic observation and laboratory observation. **Naturalistic observation** is any observational study that occurs in a natural setting (whether it is with humans or nonhuman animals). Naturalistic observation can occur in virtually any setting where the participants can normally be found. If you're interested in studying children, then schools, playgrounds, daycares, homes, etc. would be logical locations to observe them. If you're interested in studying giraffes, then observing them in their natural environment makes sense. **Laboratory observation** is similar to naturalistic observation, but where we control the setting in which we are observing the behavior. Obviously, the easiest location to control the setting would be in the laboratory. Rather than studying our children in a school or playground setting, we could bring them into the laboratory and study them in much the same way. However, in the laboratory we'd be able to control the temperature of the room, the lighting, the sound level, the number of toys, the number of other children, etc. The primary advantage of laboratory observation, compared to naturalistic observation, is this control. Thus, laboratory observation allows for much better **internal validity** (or control) compared to naturalistic observation. However, the children may behave somewhat differently in the laboratory since this environment isn't their normal environment; they may realize that they're being studied or observed. Thus, laboratory observation typically has lower external validity (i.e., generalizability) compared to naturalistic observation. Again, keep in mind that like other nonexperimental techniques, there is no manipulation with either observational technique. You might be wondering about this control that we just discussed with laboratory observation. This control is just that, control. It isn't a manipulation because we're simply controlling the environment in the same way for everyone equally. In order to have a manipulation, we'd need to have two groups or conditions. For example, if we were interested in the effects of room temperature so that some of the children were observed in the laboratory with a room that was 90 degrees F and other children were observed in a room that was 60 degrees F then this would be a manipulation.

Survey Research

Surveys provide us with a snap shot of our opinions, attitudes, beliefs, and reported behaviors, and include interviews and questionnaires. Surveys allow us to ask people questions on a variety of topics and easily compare their results to other individuals. Surveys are an excellent way of obtaining a large amount of information, usually in a short amount of time. There are various ways that surveys can be conducted such as in-person, over the phone, via e-mail or internet questionnaires, or regular mailed questionnaires. When surveys are conducted anonymously, we can obtain honest answers regarding sensitive topics or issues. While surveys can be very effective in obtaining large amounts of data, there is the worry that participants may lie or may not fully understand their own attitudes or beliefs. Additionally, it is crucial that researchers are able to obtain a representative sample of individuals in which to administer their survey. The final issue is the return rates or the low level of participation for individuals selected to complete the various types of surveys.

Correlational Research

Correlations are particularly helpful to study questions that cannot be answered using a true experiment for either ethical or practical reasons. **Correlational studies** allow us to measure the relationship between two behaviors or types of data. Correlations allow us to evaluate both the strength of this relationship as well as the direction of this relationship. Typically, a correlation coefficient is calculated using the data collected or obtained for a correlational study. For example, there is a fairly strong, positive relationship between the number of cigarettes smoked and lung cancer as can be seen in the scatterplot depicted in Figure 2.1. The **correlation coefficient** in the figure is depicted as $r = +.77$. So what does this correlation coefficient mean?

As previously mentioned, this correlation coefficient (as well as the scatterplot) allows one to determine the strength and direction of a correlation. The correlation coefficient varies from -1.0 to +1.0. Of the following correlation pairs shown below, which is the stronger correlation?

#1	$r = +.68$	vs.	$r = +.78$
#2	$r = -.43$	vs.	$r = -.23$
#3	$r = +.87$	vs.	$r = -.73$
#4	$r = +.63$	vs.	$r = -.63$

Try to answer each of these yourself before looking at the answers below.

For #1, the +.78 is the stronger correlation.
For #2, the −.43 is the stronger correlation.
For #3, the +.87 is the stronger correlation.
For #4, the correlations are equivalent.

The *strength* of the correlation is determined by the absolute value of the correlation coefficient. In other words, look at the larger number once you've taken away the + or − signs. As a result, the weakest correlation is a 0.0 correlation and the strongest correlations are at +1.0 or -1.0. So what does the sign in the correlation coefficient mean? The sign indicates the *direction* of the correlation. In Figure 2.1, there was a positive correlation. This indicates that as cigarette smoking increases the likelihood of lung cancer also increases. As smoking decreases, the incidence of lung cancer also decreases. With a positive relationship, one variable is observed to increase or decrease as the other variable increases or decreases. For

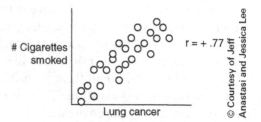

Figure 2.1 A scatterplot diagram that depicts a moderately strong, positive correlation between the number of cigarettes smoked and the incidence of lung cancer.

a negative relationship, as depicted in Figure 2.2, when one variable increases the other variable decreases. For example, Figure 2.2 shows that as the number of cigarettes smoked decreases, predicted grades increase or as the number of cigarettes smoked increases, grades are predicted to decrease.

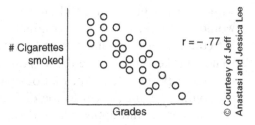

Figure 2.2 A scatterplot diagram that depicts a moderately strong, negative correlation between the number of cigarettes smoked and high school grades.

While the strength of the correlations in these figures is equivalent, the direction is different and the sign informs you of this different relationship.

The major limitation to correlational studies is that they do not allow you to make causal conclusions. Can we say that cigarette smoking causes high school students to have lower grades? Our correlation indicates that the more cigarettes smoked, the lower the students' high school grades. However, few individuals would interpret this to mean that smoking causes the grades to become lower. It may be some other factors such as rebellious activities or being absent from classes or some other factors that lead to this correlation. For example, it may be that students who smoke also are less motivated in school or students who smoke miss information from their classes because they're behind the gym smoking cigarettes. Few individuals would argue that it's actually the smoking that is directly causing these lower grades. This illustrates the idea behind the third-variable problem. In the **third-variable problem** there's some other variable or factor that is related to each of the variables being investigated. This third variable links the variables so that a correlation is observed, even though these variables don't have any direct relationship. Another issue is the directionality problem. With the **directionality problem** we're unsure if variable A is causing variable B or if variable B is causing variable A. For example, we're not sure if smoking is leading to lung cancer (which would make intuitive sense) or if individuals who are more likely to get lung cancer happen to also be genetically predisposed to become addicted to substances such as cigarettes. Due to both of these problems, we're unable to make causal statements with correlational research.

One final warning with correlations is that oftentimes individuals will look at correlational research and, if it makes intuitive sense to them, they will accept those research findings and make causal conclusions. For example, it makes sense that cigarette smoking causes lung cancer in humans. However, there are no studies that have shown that smoking causes lung cancer in humans. It's not that cigarette smoking isn't hazardous to your health, but it's simply due to the fact that a true experiment, the only approach that allows us to make causal statements, cannot be ethically conducted. So, plenty of research shows that cigarette smoking causes lung cancer in virtually every animal that has been tested. Studies also show that the chemicals in cigarettes cause human cells to mutate and become malignant. Further correlational and quasi-experimental studies (which will be discussed shortly) all show a strong relationship between cigarette smoking and lung cancer. So, while cigarette smoking may actually cause lung cancer in humans, we can't make this conclusion based on the nonexperimental studies that have been conducted with humans. When the study doesn't make intuitive sense, such as cigarette smoking directly causing lower grades, most individuals are able to think critically and are quick to generate alternative explanations for the relationship. We'd like you to be a critical thinker in *every* study that you interpret, not just those that don't make intuitive sense to you.

Quasi-experiments

Quasi-experiments are similar to true experiments, except that they lack a researcher manipulated variable. A **manipulated variable** is a variable that the researcher is able to manipulate such that the participants can be randomly assigned to the different conditions by the researcher. Quasi-experiments are particularly useful for investigating variables that cannot be manipulated or cannot be ethically manipulated by the researcher. For example, in our previous smoking studies, it would be unethical for us to manipulate smoking such that some children were randomly assigned to smoke for the next 20 years while another group of children was prohibited from smoking for the next 20 years. Since this study would be unethical for us to conduct, we could conduct a similar study using a quasi-variable instead. We could take individuals who have already chosen to smoke and individuals who have already chosen to not smoke and evaluate them in our study. In this quasi-experiment, everything else can be done like the true experiment, except that our participants have self-selected which group they are in. We aren't randomly assigning them to the different smoking conditions. Because of this self-selection, we have a nonexperimental approach, and we cannot make causal conclusions based on the findings. There may be many other differences between individuals who smoke and individuals who don't smoke that may be causing the difference in incidence rates of cancer other than just the fact that some smoke and some don't. For example, it may be that individuals who smoke care less about their health and have a more unhealthy lifestyle. It may be this generally unhealthy lifestyle or their diet that is causing the higher incidence of cancer in the smoking group, rather than the smoking. Since this isn't a researcher manipulated variable, we can't determine the cause.

There are numerous quasi-variables that are studied in psychology and that are of interest to researchers. Many of the quasi-variables are subject variables. **Subject variables** are characteristics of the participants that cannot be changed or manipulated or cannot ethically be changed or manipulated. Subject variables include things, such as the participants' sex, race, religion, height, hair color, eye color, and intelligence level.

Archival Research

Archival research is research that is conducted with data or data sets that have already been collected. Archival data may include sources such as government documents (e.g., census reports, crime reports, and marriage licenses), the media (e.g., news reports, documentaries, and magazine articles), personal documents (e.g., photographs, letters, and emails), sports statistics, or any other form of preexisting records. A specific type of archival research that is typically very helpful to other researchers who are interested in a particular topic is the meta-analysis. A **meta-analysis** is a procedure in which we statistically combine the data from previous research on a related topic. In a regular experiment, we combine the data from various participants and conduct analyses on those data to see what happens. In a meta-analysis, we combine the group means from various experiments and conduct analyses on those data to see what happens. Just like archival research, a meta-analysis data has already been collected, so there is no direct contact with the participants. The added benefit here is that you will have a summary of the relevant literature for a given topic that is based on all of the experiments that have been conducted on that topic. This summary is extremely helpful to other researchers or individuals who are interested in learning more about the research findings that have been reported on a particular topic.

True Experiments

While each of the nonexperimental approaches have some specific advantages, the primary disadvantage of each of them is that one cannot make causal conclusions for any of them since they are nonexperimental. The only approach that allows you to make causal conclusions is the true experiment. Experiments involve testing at least two groups or conditions and comparing their results. These groups or conditions should be identical other than the specific researcher manipulated variable. The logic then is fairly simple; if these groups or conditions are identical except for the manipulated variable then any differences that we find between these groups or conditions must have been caused by this manipulated variable.

For example, if we wanted to test a drug that we've developed, how would you test it? If you're like most people, you'd have one group that receives the actual drug and another group that receives a placebo. The group that receives the drug is the experimental condition. The **experimental condition** is the group or condition that is exposed to the treatment. The group that receives the placebo is the control condition. The **control condition** is identical to the experimental group, but they are not exposed to the treatment.

Experiments are an excellent way to investigate countless topics. For example, if you wanted to know if violent cartoons make children more aggressive, we could easily construct an experiment to answer this question. We would need to first determine our independent variable and the levels of that independent variable. The **independent variable** is the experimental treatment that the researcher manipulates and the **levels of the independent variable** are the specific manipulations used. For this example, our independent variable might be the type of cartoons that the children watch. The specific levels of these cartoons might be a violent cartoon for the experimental condition and a nonviolent cartoon for the control condition. Thus, we have an independent variable (type of cartoon) with two levels (violent, nonviolent). There's no limit to the number of levels that an independent variable can have, but there must be at least two. So we could have three levels such that we have an extremely violent cartoon, moderately violent cartoon, and nonviolent cartoon.

When looking at independent variables, we also need to determine how we're going to manipulate our independent variable. Each independent variable can be manipulated in one of two ways: between subjects or within subjects. A **between-subjects manipulation** is such that each participant receives only one of the levels of the independent variable. For example, with our type of cartoon, each child would receive either the violent cartoon or the nonviolent cartoon. The exact same experiment could be conducted with the same independent variable and the same levels, but we could manipulate our independent variable within-subjects. If we used a **within-subjects manipulation** of our independent variable then each participant would receive all of the levels of the independent variable. Thus, in our example, each child would be tested after seeing both the violent cartoon as well as after viewing the nonviolent cartoon.

We'd also need to determine our dependent variable. The **dependent variable** is what the researcher measures. In this example, we're interested in aggression and so we'd have some measure of aggression in our children. Perhaps we could measure the number of times the children hit other children on the playground or have the children perform a rating of their current level of aggression following the cartoon. The dependent variable needs to be something that can be easily measured and sensitive enough to detect differences between the groups or conditions.

Experiment Designs

Using our knowledge of the terminology from experiments, we can now take a look at experimental designs. The experimental designs and the issues related to these designs will be discussed in greater detail in Chapters 6 and 7 for each of the different types of designs. Based on how your independent variable(s) is manipulated, you can have three different types of designs. In a **between-subjects design**, all of the independent variables have been manipulated between-subjects or, as discussed earlier, all of the variables are such that participants only receive one of the levels of that independent variable. In a **within-subjects design**, all of the independent variables have been manipulated within-subjects or participants receive all of the levels of each of the independent variables. The third type of design occurs when you have a mix of independent variables. If there's some combination such that some independent variables are manipulated between subjects and others are manipulated within subjects then you have a **mixed-factor design**. Factor is simply another name for an independent variable; thus, there's a mix in how the independent variables have been manipulated.

Additionally, in evaluating our design, we need to determine how many independent variables we have. An experiment must have at least one independent variable with a minimum of two levels, but there's no limit to the number of independent variables that an experiment can have nor is there a limit to the number of levels that an independent variable can have. If we have only one independent variable then we have a **single-factor design**. This single-factor design might have a between-subjects or a within-subjects variable. It would be called a single-factor between-subjects design or a single-factor within-subjects design depending on how this independent variable was manipulated. For example, if we only manipulated the type of cartoon children were exposed to and cartoon type was manipulated between-subjects then we'd have a single-factor between-subjects design.

There are also experiments that have more than one independent variable. These are referred to as factorial designs. Thus, a **factorial design** is simply a study that has more than one independent variable. For example, while we may want to manipulate the level of violence in the programming (violent or nonviolent), we may also want to manipulate the type of show so that the children are exposed to cartoons and live actor shows. So, we would have two independent variables; the first is violence with two levels (violent, nonviolent) and the second is the type of show with two levels (cartoon, live actor). When we write the design of an experiment, we use a specific format for factorial designs. If both of our independent variables were manipulated between subjects then we'd say that we have a 2 (Level of Violence: violent, nonviolent) x 2 (Type of Show: cartoon, live actor) between-subjects design. If both of our independent variables were manipulated within subjects then we'd say that we have a 2 (Level of Violence: violent, nonviolent) x 2 (Type of Show: cartoon, live actor) within-subjects design. And of course, if one variable was manipulated between subjects and the other was manipulated within subjects, we'd say that we have a 2 (Level of Violence: violent, nonviolent) x 2 (Type of Show: cartoon, live actor) mixed-factor design. The numbers prior to the parentheses refer to the number of the levels of the independent variable.

If we had a $2 \times 3 \times 5$ design, then there would be three independent variables. The first independent variable has two levels, the second independent variable has three levels, and the third independent variable has five levels. A 3×4 design has two independent variables with the first independent variable having three levels and the second independent variable having four levels. There are some additional design questions at the conclusion of this chapter to make sure that you're comfortable with these designs.

Extraneous Variables

Another type of variable that we need to discuss are extraneous variables. An **extraneous variable** is some variable, other than the independent variable, that could influence the results. There are three types of extraneous variables:

Subject variables
Task variables
Environmental variables

Subject variables are characteristics of the participants that cannot be changed or manipulated or cannot ethically be changed or manipulated. While these subject variables cannot be manipulated, they can still have an effect on the results. For example, the intelligence level of the participants or their race or their sex could influence the results. More intelligent participants might be expected to do better. **Task variables** are any variable that is related to the task at hand that could have an effect on the results. If participants were asked to solve 100 math problems or 10,000 math problems, this would presumably affect their performance. If participants are strongly encouraged to do their best rather than not given the same level of encouragement, this would be expected to affect their performance. **Environmental variables** are any variable that is related to the environment that participants are being tested in that could have an effect on the results. For example, if participants are tested in a room that is 98 degrees F then we might expect their performance to be poorer since they would be very uncomfortable. While these extraneous variables do exist, the bigger question is, "Are they a problem?"

The short answer is that they're not a problem, as long as they're the same for each of the participants. Extraneous variables exist. You can't eliminate the temperature in the room, but you can make sure that all participants are tested with the same temperature. If participants in the experimental condition are tested in a room that is 98 degrees while participants in the control condition are tested in a room that is 70 degrees, then we have a problem. In this case, we aren't sure if the differences between these conditions are being caused by our independent variable or by the temperature of the rooms. When this occurs, we have a confounding variable or a confound. A **confound** is when we have an extraneous variable that varies with our manipulation. Let's take a look at the example below.

Back in our day, there was a huge advertisement war between Coke and Pepsi where both wanted to be the largest soft drink company. Pepsi came up with a series of commercials where they traveled around the country and gave people a taste test to see which soda individuals preferred. When they conducted their taste test, in order to not confuse the individuals conducting the testing, they put Pepsi in a cup with an "S" on it and Coke in a cup with an "L" on it. What they found is that tasters preferred Pepsi approximately 59% of the time and Coke 41% of the time. Thus, it appeared that Pepsi was preferred over Coke. However, some researchers (Woolfolk, Castellan, & Brooks, 1983) noticed a confound: Pepsi was always in the "S" cup and Coke was always in the "L" cup. While admittedly unlikely, they argued that the letters might be influencing the results. Due to this confound it was impossible for Pepsi to conclude that Pepsi was preferred as it could be that the tasters preferred the letter "S" on the cup. Based on how the Pepsi Challenge was conducted, this was true. So Woolfolk et al. (1983) conducted some additional tests and eliminated or balanced this confound. If they put Pepsi in *both* cups (one cup with an "S" on it and one cup with an "L" on it), tasters still preferred the "S" cup, indicating that tasters were being affected by the letter on cup. While it seemed unlikely that tasters would actually be influenced by the letter on the cup, Woolfolk et al. (1983) showed that they were.

While extraneous variables aren't necessarily a problem, confounding variables are. If you find that you have a confounding variable, there are several techniques that you can use to help control the extraneous variable so that it is not a confounding variable. Most of these techniques or solutions should be done as part of the design of the study. In other words, be aware of confounding variables and control them as you design your study in the first place. First, eliminate the confounding variable. In our Pepsi Challenge example, this would simply involve getting rid of the letters on the cups. Second, hold all extraneous variables constant. In our example, this might involve putting an "S" on both cups. If the letter "S" helps to increase the rating for the sodas then putting the "S" on both cups will ensure that both sodas receive this advantage equally. Third, balance the extraneous variable across conditions. Even if the letter on the cup does make a difference, we could put the "S" on the Pepsi cup and the "L" on the Coke cup for half of the participants tested. For the other half of the participants, test them with the "L" on the Pepsi cup and the "S" on the Coke cup. This way each soda receives the advantage of the "S" an equal amount of the time. The fourth solution is one that can be used if you notice the confound *after* you've already completed the study: rule out the variable as a confound. Woolfolk at al. (1983) attempted to rule out the letters as having an effect. Had they put the same soda in both cups where one cup had the letter "S" and the other cup had the letter "L" and found no taste preferences then this would indicate that the letters made no difference. Thus, the confound, while it may exist, didn't make a difference and the confound has been ruled out.

Developmental Methods

There are two methods that are used to access developmental changes in behavior. The first is a **longitudinal study**. In a longitudinal study, the research assesses the same group at multiple times in order to determine age-related changes in thought and/or behavior. A longitudinal approach is similar to having a within-subjects variable of age. Each participant is assessed when they are of different ages. For example, a researcher in a longitudinal study might assess participants when they are 5, 10, 15, 20, and 25 years of age. Obviously the primary limitation of a longitudinal study is that the study would take a very long time. The alternative would be a **cross-sectional approach**. In a cross-sectional study, different groups of participants who are of different ages are assessed. The cross-sectional approach is similar to having a between-subjects manipulation of age. Thus, a researcher in a cross-sectional study might assess 5-year old, 10-year old, 15-year old, 20-year old, and 25-year old participants, typically around the same time. The main advantage of this approach is that the study can be completed much quicker, but there is a cost. That cost is that individuals of different ages may have different life experiences; thus, these individuals may not be comparable. For example, the educational background and experience of 20-year olds may be very different from that of 70-year olds.

Types of Validity

Validity primarily refers to two factors: (1) are you measuring what you think you're measuring and (2) are the conclusions being drawn by the researcher correct and can they be generalized to others? **Internal validity** looks at the extent to which changes in the dependent variable can be attributed to the manipulation or the independent variable. In essence, internal validity looks at how well controlled your experiment is. **External validity (or Generalizability)** evaluates the extent to which the results can be generalized to other settings and to other participant populations. As you can imagine, laboratory studies provide for better control of the experiment and thus maximize internal validity. Field studies, or studies conducted outside of the laboratory, maximize external validity.

In addition to internal and external validity, there are several other types of validity that are important to keep in mind when conducting research. Each of these additional types of validity are briefly discussed below.

Statistical Validity

Statistical validity is when the researcher, based on the results, makes an incorrect conclusion. As we'll discuss in the statistics chapter, inferential statistics allow one to make decisions based on the data. This decision is essentially if the groups are the same or different from one another and is based on probabilities. Because the decision is made based on probabilities, the researcher should generally make the correct decision; however, there is a small chance that the researcher will make an incorrect decision. Those two errors are cleverly labeled Type 1 and Type 2 errors. A **Type 1 error** is when the decision is to reject the null hypothesis when the null hypothesis is actually true. A **Type 2 error** is when the decision is to accept the null hypothesis when the null hypothesis is actually false. These error types will be discussed in greater detail in Chapter 9, but the main point here is that issues with statistical validity arise when we make the wrong statistical decision due to somewhat unlikely results.

Construct Validity

Construct validity evaluates if the study is measuring what you think it's measuring. For example, Franz Gall developed the "science" of phrenology. You may be familiar with phrenology. Phrenology is where Gall would make determinations about an individual's personality, intelligence, or talents based on the bumps on the person's skull. The idea is that, according to Gall, the brain is like a muscle and that different parts of the brain have different functions. When the individual is really good at something or well practiced at something, that part of the brain is stronger and it physically gets bigger. When it gets bigger it pushes the skull out and causes a bump. A weakness would result in a smaller part of the brain and the skull would have an indentation in this area. How good do you think the construct validity is for phrenology? As you'd expect, it's pretty poor. It didn't do a good job at measuring what it was supposed to measure. Thus, phrenology had very poor construct validity.

Criterion-related Validity

Criterion-related validity evaluates the ability of a measure to produce similar results to another measure. We typically evaluate criterion-related validity by using two other types of validity: concurrent validity or predictive validity. **Concurrent validity** is the extent to which scores on your measurement correspond to scores on from an established measurement that looks at the same construct. For example, if you devised a new IQ test, you might compare the results of your IQ test to other established IQ tests. If your new IQ test correlates well with established IQ tests then your IQ test is said to have strong concurrent validity.

Predictive validity is the ability of a measure to predict some future behavior. A nice example looks at the predictive ability of SAT scores to predict college grades. If the measure does a good job at predicting this other measure or future behavior then the measure is said to be high in predictive ability. Both of these measures, concurrent validity and predictive validity, are used as measures of criterion-related validity.

Face Validity

Face validity is how well a measure seems to evaluate what it's designed to measure. Face validity isn't very difficult to assess, and there really isn't a specific statistical test that evaluates face validity. In order to assess face validity, you simply look at the test to determine if the test seems to measure what it's supposed to measure. For example, if you wanted to develop a test that measures the mathematical ability of individuals, what would you put on the test to do this? Of course, it would be wise to have math problems on the test. This would demonstrate good face validity.

Controlling Experimenter or Subject Bias

Experimenter bias is when the researcher is aware of the experimental hypothesis or which condition the participant is in. Knowing this information can cause the researcher to unconsciously affect the findings of the study by treating participants differently based on the researcher's expectations, thus causing bias. **Subject bias** is when the knowledge that the participant has about the hypothesis affects the study. In other words, if the participant knows what the study is investigating or if they know which condition they are in, it may affect their performance and cause bias. There are a couple of procedures that can be very helpful in eliminating these biases. The first, the **single-blind procedure**, is where the participant is unaware of which condition they are participating in. If the participant doesn't know what condition they are participating in then they can't bias the findings, either consciously or unconsciously. The second technique is the double-blind procedure. In the **double-blind procedure**, neither the participant nor the researcher is aware of what condition the participant is in. Rivers and Webber (1907) first introduced the double-blind procedure in testing the effects of caffeine. This technique is now used in virtually all drug studies because this technique provides a much higher standard of scientific rigor than nonblind or single-blind procedures. Any drug that passes FDA testing was evaluated using the double-blind placebo procedure due to this higher scientific standard.

Replication

One final topic to be discussed is that of replication. **Replication** refers to the ability to reproduce or duplicate scientific findings. Replication is an extremely important aspect of the scientific method. If an experiment finds that a drug works in reducing anxiety levels in patients with anxiety issues then this is, of course, very promising. However, it's possible that the statistical decision being made (i.e., that the drug was effective) was in error. We discussed statistical errors previously and how they are possible, although unlikely, since they are made based on probabilities. It's also possible that the drug only worked with the specific population that was tested. If other groups were evaluated, perhaps the drug wouldn't work. One way to alleviate these issues, is to replicate the findings. Replication is a cornerstone of solid science. In order to replicate scientific findings, there are several ways in which this replication can be carried out. Each method helps to make us more sure that the findings that we obtained are indeed accurate and can be generalized to others. Let's take a look at some of these types of replications.

Types of Replications

Exact replications are fairly straightforward. They are replications where we re-do the experiment again with the same types of individuals and follow the exact same methodology. For example, if we conducted a smoking study where we evaluated the cancer rates for middle-aged, Caucasian nonsmokers compared to 1 pack-a-day smokers, our exact replication would also test middle-aged Caucasians who were nonsmokers and compare their cancer rates to 1 pack-a-day smokers from this same group.

A **conceptual replication** is a replication study that investigates the same conceptual or general topic or hypothesis, but may use different independent or dependent variables. Thus, the idea behind a conceptual replication is to replicate the general idea, but to conduct the study in a slightly different way. For example, perhaps we're still interested in smoking and the negative health effects so we conduct a conceptual replication where we evaluate the cancer rates for middle-aged Caucasians who have been exposed to second-hand smoke and compare them to other middle-aged Caucasians who are 1 pack-a-day smokers. Or perhaps we conduct the same original study, but we look at the incidence of emphysema instead of cancer. Conceptually the study is the same, but it's being carried out in a different way.

A **constructive replication** is another approach where the replicated study investigates the same topic or hypothesis (using either an exact or conceptual replication), but adds an additional independent variable, level of the independent variable, or even an additional dependent variable.

The final type of replication is the **participant replication** where the study is replicated by investigating the same hypothesis, but uses different participants. For our example, we might conduct the same original study but conduct the study with young adults rather than middle-aged adults. Or we may conduct the original study, but evaluate African-Americans rather than Caucasians.

Regardless of which type of replication one uses, the different types of replications allow researchers to rule out various alternative explanations. If the researcher would like to prove that the findings don't only apply to the specific sample being tested then a participant replication would help to clarify this. If the researcher would like to show that her findings aren't simply due to the specific conditions or levels of the independent variable then the researcher can conduct a conceptual or constructive replication. If the researcher wants to show that the same findings occur even with other measures then a conceptual replication with a new dependent variable makes sense. Like many of the choices that researchers have, it's important to know what tools are available to the researcher. With this knowledge the researcher can conduct the best and most effective research studies. The remainder of this text will provide you with additional tools and knowledge so that you can make your own decisions in order to conduct the most effective research studies.

Concluding Remarks

As discussed in this chapter, there are many different research approaches that you can take when you want to investigate some topic of interest. While we simply touched on many of these approaches in this chapter to give you a general overview, later chapters will provide you with more specific information so that you can make an educated decision as to which approach would be best for you and help you to achieve the goals that you have.

References

Darley, J. M., & Latané, B. (1968). Bystander intervention in emergencies: Diffusion of responsibility. *Journal of Personality and Social Psychology, 8,* 377–383. doi:10.1037/h0025589

Rivers, W. H. R., & Webber, H. N. (1907). The action of caffeine on the capacity for muscular work. *Journal of Physiology, 36,* 33–47.

Woolfolk, Castellan, & Brooks (1983). Pepsi versus Coke: Labels, not tastes, prevail. *Psychological Reports, 52,* 185–186. doi: http://dx.doi.org/10.2466/pr0.1983.52.1.185

End of Chapter Quiz

1. The _____ variable is *manipulated* by the experimenter.

2. Please list each of the research methods that allows one to make causal statements.

3. How many IVs are in each of these designs?
   a. 2×3 design?
   b. 3×4 design?
   c. $3 \times 6 \times 2$ design?
   d. $2 \times 3 \times 5 \times 2 \times 8 \times 2$ design?

4. A _____ variable refers to some characteristics of the participant that either cannot be manipulated or cannot be ethically manipulated.

5. What is the name of an extraneous variable that varies with your manipulation?

6. _____ validity evaluates the ability of a measure to produce similar results to another established measure.

7. What technique is oftentimes used to control for the effects of experimenter bias?

8. What are the two primary problems that make it so that we cannot make causal inferences based on the results of correlational studies?

9. When each participant receives all of the levels of the independent variable, what kind of manipulation does this describe?

10. What is the other name for external validity?

Homework Assignment #1

Sample #1

Dr. George wants to conduct an experiment to see if your average college student will severely shock a stranger. In order to conduct this study, she randomly selects psychology intro. students and randomly assigns them to the no instruction group, light compliance group, or the forced compliance group. Dr. George records how much shock the participants give the stranger.

1. **What is/are the DV(s)?**
2. **What is/are the IV(s) and the levels?**
3. **Is/are the IV(s) manipulated between- or within-subjects?**
4. **What's the overall design?**

Sample #2

Dr. George wants to conduct an experiment to see if your average college student will severely shock a stranger. In order to conduct this study, she randomly selects psychology intro. students and randomly assigns them to the no instruction group, light compliance group, or the forced compliance group. Dr. George is also interested in the effects of frustration on aggression, so she places half of the participants in each group into a low-frustration condition and half in a high-frustration condition. Dr. George records how much shock the participants give the stranger.

1. **What is/are the DV(s)?**
2. **What is/are the IV(s) and the levels?**
3. **Is/are the IV(s) manipulated between- or within-subjects?**
4. **What's the overall design?**

Sample #3

Dr. Galton has developed a new drug called Smartex, which should make people smarter. In order to test Smartex, Dr. Galton took 100 individuals and divided them into two groups. Prior to the manipulation, all participants took an IQ test. Half of the participants were then given Smartex every day for 12 months, while the other participants were given a placebo. After 12 months, both groups were then given another IQ test to evaluate their intelligence.

1. **What is (are) the DV(s)?**
2. **What is (are) the IV(s) and the levels?**
3. **How is (are) the IV(s) manipulated?**
4. **What is the overall design of the experiment?**

Homework Assignment #2

Problem #1

Dr. Vishus is conducting a study looking at aggression in children. Dr. Vishus believes that certain television shows lead to violent behavior in children but only when the children are placed in a stressful environment. Dr. Vishus finds 4 classes of students at different elementary schools who are willing to participate in the study. The first group of students is shown a violent television program and is then sent to the gym to perform some low-stress activities. The second group of students is shown the same violent television program and is sent to the gym to perform a high-stress activity. The third group is shown a nonviolent program and is sent to the gym to perform a low-stress activity. The fourth group is shown a nonviolent television program and is sent to the gym to perform a high-stress activity. Dr. Vishus is interested in the number of verbal or physically aggressive actions the children perform during the gym activity.

1. What is (are) the DV(s) of the current experiment?

2. What is (are) the IV(s) of the current experiment?

3. How is each IV manipulated?

4. What is the overall design of the current experiment including how the IV(s) is (are) manipulated?

Problem #2

Dr. Wuree has been asked to test a new drug that is supposed to help individuals who suffer from anxiety disorders. Dr. Wuree decides to test the drug by using some tasks that require different levels of anxiety. He randomly divided his participants into two groups and gave one group the drug and the other group a placebo. After a 30 minute wait to make sure the drug was working, he then tested all of the participants by having them give a short speech on the telephone with no audience, in front of a live audience, and in front of a live audience where the participant's performance was videotaped. He determined how nervous or anxious participants were by the number of times they stumbled on their words.

1. What is/are the DV(s)?

2. What is/are the IV(s)?

3. How is each IV manipulated?

4. What is the overall design of this study (be sure to include how the IV(s) are manipulated)?

Problem #3

Dr. Cuervo is interested in the effects of alcohol on overcoming shyness. She selects 50 individuals who are looking to date and have agreed to use her "dating service." Subjects are asked to drink either a placebo drink, 1 ounce of alcohol, 2 ounces of alcohol, or 4 ounces of alcohol in a 10-minute span. After waiting 30 minutes for the alcohol to have an effect, half of the subjects were asked if they would be interested in making their dating video while the other half were asked if they would be interested in playing a board game. Dr. Cuervo counts the number of individuals in each group who agree to participate in the videotaping or the board game.

1. What is/are the DV(s)?

2. What is/are the IV(s)?

3. How is each IV manipulated?

4. What is the overall design of this study (be sure to include how the IV(s) are manipulated)?

Problem #4

Dr. Reeder is looking at the effects of different ways to teach young children how to read. He has the children learn each of the three reading techniques. He teaches each reading technique for 2 weeks, followed by the second and third reading techniques. In order to determine how the training is working he assesses the children's reading performance prior to each technique, midway through each technique, and at the end of each technique.

1. What is/are the DV(s)?

2. What is/are the IV(s)?

3. How is each IV manipulated?

4. What is the overall design of this study (be sure to include how the IV(s) are manipulated)?

Problem #5

Dr. Kahntext is interested in how our environment affects how we develop. Since it would be unethical to conduct this study with children, she decides to conduct the study on rats and look at their brain development (brain size and neuronal complexity). She raised 10 rats in a normal laboratory cage, 10 rats in a deprived environment, and 10 rats in an enriched environment with lots of toys. She also wanted to see the effects different diets have on the rats so 5 rats in each group were given a vitamin rich food while the other 5 rats in each group were given a vitamin deficient diet.

1. What is/are the DV(s)?

2. What is/are the IV(s)?

3. How is each IV manipulated?

4. What is the overall design of this study (be sure to include how the IV(s) are manipulated)?

Problem #6

Dr. E. T. Ess is interested in the effects of taking an SAT course in order to improve SAT scores for high school students who plan to attend college. He randomly selects 50 high school seniors where 25 of them take the SAT course and 25 do not take the course but are allowed to study on their own. He gives all students a pretest and then gives them all a posttest at the end of the study to see their progress.

1. What is/are the DV(s)?

2. What is/are the IV(s)?

3. How is each IV manipulated?

4. What is the overall design of this study (be sure to include how the IV(s) are manipulated)?

Homework Assignment #3

Imagine that you are a psychological consultant. Your job is to solve problems for different companies and individuals. Below is a list of different problems that certain individuals are having. For each of the following questions below, describe how you would test these ideas. Be sure to provide enough detail so that a reader could understand the general idea behind your study.

1. An animal behaviorist is interested in determining if hamsters have color vision. How could you experimentally test this?

2. The Ford motor company wants to know how bright brake lights should be in order to minimize the time required for the driver of a following car to realize that the car in front is stopping. How could you experimentally test this?

3. Microsoft wants to remodel their offices. They've heard that certain colors help workers to be more efficient and productive. How could you experimentally test this?

4. A social psychologist is interested if the level of pain threshold is different for men and women. How could you experimentally test this?

5. A math teacher has two different math training techniques available to teach her students. However, she wants to teach her students the one that works the best. How could you experimentally test this?

6. Pepsi has approached Special Olympics because they would like to be the "official soft drink for Special Olympics." The Pepsi sales representative says that Pepsi gives the athletes an added boost of energy. How could you experimentally test this?

7. A perfume manufacturer is interested in marketing a perfume with pheromones that is thought to increase sexual attraction between persons of the opposite sex. Before they make this claim in their advertisements the better business bureau says that they have to validate these claims. How could you experimentally test this?

8. Safeway, Albertsons, and H.E.B. all claim to offer what customers want the most out of a grocery store. A neutral marketing firm is going to determine which marketing approach works best but wants to rule out name recognition (people shopping at certain stores because of the name). How could you experimentally test this?

Homework Assignment #4

1. **Devise a 2 × 2 experiment**

   a. Briefly describe the experiment

   b. How are each of your IVs manipulated?

   c. Briefly describe the results of this experiment.

2. **Devise a 3 × 4 experiment**

   a. Briefly describe the experiment

   b. How are each of your IVs manipulated?

   c. Briefly describe the results of this experiment.

3. **Devise a 2 × 2 × 3 experiment**

   a. Briefly describe the experiment

   b. How are each of your IVs manipulated?

   c. Briefly describe the results of this experiment.

4. **Devise a 3 × 2 × 4 experiment**

   a. Briefly describe the experiment

   b. How are each of your IVs manipulated?

   c. Briefly describe the results of this experiment.

Chapter 3

Ethics in Research

One of the more difficult topics to learn (and teach) is research ethics. So much of ethical behavior depends on the specifics of the situation including the intention of those involved. However, the American Psychological Association (APA) does have a fairly specific Code of Ethics. If you'd like to evaluate the APA Ethics Code, go to the following website: http://apa.org/ethics/code. The code of ethics is primarily relevant for therapeutic situations, but much of it can also be applied to conducting research. While there are many reasons for discussing ethics in research, one of the main reasons for discussing ethics is to ensure that all researchers conduct research in a way that upholds the scientific standards that are required by all researchers. These ethical standards ensure that individuals who volunteer or are paid for participating in research studies are treated fairly, are kept safe from harm, and are aware of their rights. Once you've completed this chapter, there are several assignments at the end of this chapter to provide you with further training and that allow you to evaluate what you've learned in this chapter.

Any time you conduct research, you must be sure to uphold the established code of ethics in order to protect participants from any harm, treat them fairly, and make sure that they're aware of their rights as participants.

Plagiarism

The most common type of ethical impropriety is plagiarism. **Plagiarism** is simply using someone else's work or idea and either not giving them credit for it or attempting to pass the work or idea as your own. Students are warned about plagiarism throughout their academic careers. You probably learned about plagiarism in elementary school, high school, and in college. Yet, it still remains a huge problem at all levels of training and even for individuals who are professionals in their field of specialty. Regardless of whether the plagiarism was intentional or not, it would still be plagiarism if you used someone else's words or ideas without giving them proper credit. Giving proper credit in research is usually extremely easy to do, so plagiarism should never be an issue. When you write up or present your research, one of the parts of this presentation is to provide the background literature that led you to the idea that you're investigating. It's expected in this process that you used other people's research or ideas to devise your study. The previous research helped to lead you to the study that you're conducting. This is normal and this is a part of the scientific process. As such, it's absolutely acceptable and expected that you'll be discussing the research that other individuals have completed. You can and should use that research, but you must simply give them proper credit. You can cite any research manuscripts or presentations that you read or attended. You can even cite a conversation that you had with someone. It's easy to do and there's no excuse for failing to do this.

Never use someone's ideas or work without giving them proper credit for their work.

One common misconception that students have is that they need to cite someone else's work only if they're quoting that individual. If you quote someone or use their exact words then you must absolutely cite the source! However, even if you change the words around or paraphrase their words or their idea, you must still cite them! Ignorance isn't a good defense for plagiarizing someone's work; so make sure that you properly cite everything that you use. If you're unsure if you should cite something then cite it just to be sure.

There are several things that you can do to help avoid plagiarism when working on your own research. As we previously mentioned, part of the research process is conducting a review of the literature when you're planning your study and when you're working on writing up the research for dissemination. When you read the other articles that are relevant to your study, try to paraphrase the information by using your own words. We realize that this can sometimes be difficult to put into your own words, but you should do it anyway. The individual's work that you're reading may be someone who has been conducting research on this topic for the past 20 years; the individual may be an expert on this topic. You may even ask yourself, "How am I going to put this in my own words better than this expert?" You may not be able to, but you should try. It will help you to better understand their research or their idea if you're able to put it into your own words. Also, it's easier for you to fit your words into your paper than trying to fit their words into your paper. In other words, your manuscript will read much better if it's all in your own words. As you conduct your literature review, take very complete notes of the ideas that are relevant to your manuscript. Be sure to include all of the citation information so that you know exactly where the idea came from; this helps to avoid inadvertent plagiarism. As you'll see in the chapter on writing APA style, there are many ways to appropriately cite sources. Be sure that you do it correctly and consistently. Also, keep in mind this general rule to successfully avoid plagiarism: When in doubt, CITE!!

Authorship Ethics

Authorship ethics primarily deal with awarding credit to authors in a way that fairly rewards them for the work that they've put into a presentation or publication. The general rule for authorship credit is that the order of authorship should reflect the level of contribution for each of the authors. Therefore, if you collaborated with another individual on a study and you did the majority of the work then you should be the first author and your collaborator should be the second author. This seems pretty simple, right? Well, it *should* be pretty simple, but there are many factors that can make it less clear. In order to help with authorship issues, Smith (2003) published some helpful guidelines in the APA's Monitor. Since this publication is available online at the APA's website, here's the link to this very short article—http://www.apa.org/monitor/jan03/principles.aspx. The first point in this article is an extremely important one: Discuss intellectual property frankly. Discussing who should be the first author is a sensitive subject for nearly everyone. It's very uncomfortable discussing who should be the first author or the second author or the third author. This might be uncomfortable discussing authorship with other collaborators who are at the same standing or academic level as you. For example, for you to discuss authorship with other students can be somewhat uncomfortable to you. Who should get the most credit for doing the most work? What if you think you did the most work and one of your collaborators also thinks that he or she did the most work? Then what? To make things worse, imagine discussing authorship with your research mentor (a faculty member) when you think that you did the most work on the project and therefore that you should be the first author and he or she should be the second author. How would you feel about having that conversation? It would most likely be *extremely* uncomfortable. This conversation can be made much easier if you have this discussion *prior* to starting the research study. With our students, we discuss what is expected of them if they would like to be awarded with first or second authorship prior to starting a study. Furthermore, individuals shouldn't be simply given authorship unless they've earned it, and their contributions should be fairly extensive in order to warrant authorship at all. There have been a few times when I've had this discussion with a student where we agreed what was expected of them in order to be the first author. If that student failed to do the work that they agreed on then I felt justified in not allowing them first authorship since they failed to do what they said they would do. Yes, it's an uncomfortable conversation, but you have to have that conversation.

This professor and student are discussing the work that needs to be completed on a research project that they're working on. Part of this discussion is who will be the primary author on the subsequent manuscript.

There are some other potential issues to deal with that are definitely unethical, but also difficult to deal with. Many years ago, I had a student who approached me to let me know of an authorship predicament that he was in. In order to keep things anonymous, let's call our student Steve. Steve was working in a faculty member's laboratory and had been for the past year or two. Steve had an idea for a research study that he had and had asked my opinion about this study during the previous year. He had presented this idea to his research mentor (i.e., the faculty member whose lab he worked in), but his research mentor thought it wasn't a very good idea. Steve then conducted a literature review on the topic, showed that the study made sense and that no one else had done the study, and told his research mentor that he wouldn't have to do anything but let him use his laboratory to conduct the study. Steve's research mentor finally agreed to let him do the study in his laboratory as long as it didn't interfere with any of the other research that Steve was engaged in for the faculty member. Steve conducted the study, analyzed the data, wrote up the manuscript for publication, and wanted to present the research at a national conference since the study worked out really well. Steve asked his research mentor to take a look at the manuscript and provide him with some feedback. Upon receiving the feedback, Steve noticed that his research mentor had placed his own name as the first author, added one of his friends as the second author, and put Steve as the third author on the manuscript. Unethical? Absolutely!! Steve's research mentor was going up for promotion and needed to have as many publications as possible and, apparently, saw Steve's manuscript as a solution to this. Steve's predicament was what to do about this. You might be saying "Turn in his research mentor so that he gets fired!! His mentor should never get away with this!!" I completely agree with you, and this was the advice that I gave Steve. However, Steve's response shows the seriousness of this situation and how frustrating it can be. It's not always quite that simple. Steve wanted to go to graduate school and was starting to apply to doctoral programs. He said, "I don't think I can turn him in. I need a letter of recommendation from him, and his letter should be my strongest letter."

So is it ethical for a professor to take primary authorship on a student's work that was conducted in his or her laboratory, even if the professor didn't do any work on the project? Of course not. Does it happen? Unfortunately it does. Would it be ethical for the departmental chair to take authorship on any research that was conducted in their department? Of course not. So while this topic of authorship can be very uncomfortable, having this discussion early is always a great idea. The additional aspect of the authors having different levels of status can make this even messier.

This faculty member has a lot of control over this poor student, but it's up to both individuals to make sure that they are behaving ethically when it comes to authorship ethics.

As a scientist, we are often called upon to serve as a reviewer for an article that has been submitted for publication in a journal. As experts on some very specific topic that virtually no one else cares about, it's our duty to review these submitted manuscripts to determine if the research is important and if it's been done well. This is the **peer-review** process. Serving as a reviewer is extra work on top of your already busy schedule, and you don't get paid to serve as a reviewer; this is seen as part of your service to your profession. As a reviewer of a manuscript that has been submitted, you have the opportunity to see research that is currently being conducted. You could read published research in the journals, but published research was probably conducted a year or more ago. Research presented at conferences would be more up-to-date than published research, but it can be of lower quality than research that has been published, it could be a little dated, and it may never get published. Research that has been submitted for publication at a journal has fairly recently been completed and it's of high enough quality to be submitted for publication—at least the author(s) thinks that it was good. So a nice aspect of serving as a reviewer is that you get to see some pretty high quality, up-to-date research. However, you must keep this research confidential. You can't send this manuscript to someone else who you think might be interested in it. You can't cite this research in your own publications without permission from the author. In a sense, it's almost like someone telling you a really great secret that you can't tell anyone else about. While that can be difficult to do, you're ethically bound to keep the manuscript and their findings confidential. Once the research gets published, you can tell everyone about the research and use it in your own publications, assuming that you properly cite them.

In the process of publishing research, mistakes are sometimes made. In the publication process there are several individuals who will be reviewing or proofing a manuscript before it gets published. However, there are times where each of these individuals has missed a mistake or the author could have inadvertently made a mistake or even purposely made a mistake. Obviously, it would be unethical for an author to misrepresent their data or their findings. However, what should you do if you find an error in your research after your article has been published? Are you obligated to say anything? After all, it's gone through the entire publication process and no one noticed the mistake. Unfortunately, you are ethically obligated to let the journal editor know of the mistake. When this happens, the journal will publish an erratum or correction in the same journal. This is embarrassing for you as the author that you missed a mistake, and this is embarrassing for the journal since they also missed the mistake. What if you are a coauthor of a manuscript, and it appears that one of your coauthors has fabricated data or misrepresented your findings?

Clearly, fabricating data that you didn't actually collect would be unethical. Any manipulation of or altering of your data is also unethical. This could happen where the authors deliberately alter their data to make the data look better. If the authors simply changed the data so that their findings looked better, this would clearly be unethical. Perhaps the researchers tested 200 participants, but only report the data from 100 participants whose data were consistent with their theory. Again, this would be manipulating the data. What about something a little less severe? What if you have a theory that you've developed. In order to test your theory, you conduct an experiment. The results of your experiment show that your theory is wrong. Since you think these findings can't be correct, you conduct the experiment again and show again that your theory is incorrect. Are you obligated to report these findings? While you could argue that it's not really your responsibility to destroy your own theory, you are ethically obligated as a scientist and a researcher to report your findings. Yes, someone else will probably show that your theory was wrong in the future, but if you know that your theory is incorrect and you've proven this fact with your own research, you're obligated to report it in some way.

Behaving in an ethical manner is paramount to conducting research in psychology.

Ethics in Selecting a Research Design

In the previous chapter, we discussed the idea that some research can't be conducted as a true experiment. Because of this, you must opt to investigate certain variables using nonexperimental techniques. So while we may be interested in differences between men and women or the viewpoints of individuals who are of different races or religions, we can't ethically manipulate these subject variables. Therefore, we may have to investigate these types of variables using correlational or quasi-experiments. In the previous chapter, we used the example of investigating the effects of smoking on humans. It would be unethical for us to randomly put some individuals into a smoking group and make them smoke for the next 20 years and not allow another group to smoke for the next 20 years. While this *could* be manipulated, we can't *ethically* manipulate this. Therefore, the smoking studies that you see involving humans are typically correlational studies or quasi-experiments.

Basic Ethical Guidelines

When conducting research, there are some very basic ethical guidelines. These ethical guidelines really boil down to two things: As a researcher you must protect the rights of your participants and do your best to protect them from harm. There are federal laws that determine what is against the law or not when conducting research or serving as a therapist. One part of this law is that any institution that conducts research should have an **institutional review board** or **IRB**. This IRB is made up of individuals from various backgrounds to evaluate each study that is to be conducted to ensure that the researchers adequately protect the participants from any potential harm and that their rights are protected. When necessary, this IRB will make a cost/benefit analysis of the proposed research to determine if the importance of the knowledge gained is worth any potential risks. Ultimately, the researcher(s) is legally responsible for any physical or psychological injury to the research participants, and he or she could be sued for damages if participants are harmed in any way. In addition to these federal laws, the APA published their own ethical standards in 2002. Some amendments were added to these standards in 2010 and 2016. While many of these standards deal with the psychologist as a therapist, there are also some specific standards that apply to researchers. Here's the website for the Ethical Principles for Psychologists and Code of Conduct that is published by the APA: http://www.apa.org/ethics/code/. The sections on General Principles and the section on Research and Publication are probably the most relevant to researchers, but all of the ethical principles are relevant. Let's take a look at some of these important guiding principles for researchers.

One of the most important things a researcher must do is to protect the rights of their participants and not put them situations that could be harmful to them.

First and foremost, researchers should protect the rights of their participants; this includes the rights of both human and other animal participants. When conducting a study, it is ultimately up to the researcher(s) to evaluate the amount of risk to the participants and make sure that participants are not at risk of harm and that their rights are being protected; this is true even if the IRB has given approval for the study. The researcher is also responsible for all persons who collaborate in the research. Therefore, the head researchers are responsible not only for their own behavior, but also the behavior of their collaborators, research assistants, or employees. Therefore, all of the individuals involved in the research should protect participants from any potential physical or mental harm. This includes any current and immediate harm as well as any potential future harm. If any harm might be present, the participant must provide consent to participate in the study and must acknowledge that he is aware of this potential harm. The primary way that participants acknowledge their participation is by signing an informed consent document.

An **informed consent** document is given to participants prior to starting a study. This consent document clarifies the role of the researcher and the participants. It must carefully inform the participants about all risks or potential risks of the study. Once the participant is aware of any potential risks, he or she may then indicate his or her consent by signing this form. In order to provide consent, the participant must be of legal age to provide such consent, typically 18 years of age in most states. If the participants are under the legal age, their parent or legal guardian must provide consent. The underage participants (typically between the ages of 7 and 18) would then provide their own **assent** indicating their willingness to participate in the study. In addition to informing participants of any and all potential risks, a critical aspect of this informed consent document informs participants that they may withdraw their consent at any time during the study and that there will be no negative repercussions for doing so. In other words, if they would like to quit the study at any time, they may do so. Researchers are not allowed to coerce them to participate in any way and cannot force individuals to participate. In fact, excessive or inappropriate inducements (such as exorbitant pay for participation) are considered to be a form of coercion.

At the conclusion of the study, the researcher should fully debrief participants about the purpose of the study. **Debriefing** is where the researcher tells the participant about what they did in the study, why their participation was important, and more importantly informs them of the purpose of the study. Additionally, if there was any deception in the study, the researcher must inform the participant of this deception and explain why it was necessary. Also during this debriefing, participants are given the opportunity to ask any questions that they wish about the study. One question that often arises immediately following a research study is, "How did I do in the study?" This debriefing does not involve giving participants feedback concerning their individual performance in the study. Nor can the researcher tell them about the performance of any other participants in the study.

Thus, all data collected in the study should remain confidential. Researchers should never identify a participant or any participant's performance in any kind of dissemination of the data (i.e., conference presentations, publications, etc.) or even in casual conversation. Telling a participant how he performed in the study or informing him how he performed compared to others would be a breach of this confidentiality. So while the participant should be fully debriefed following the study, this debriefing does not include providing feedback as to his performance in the study.

Use of Deception

The use of deception is a touchy subject to many researchers. The general rule is that you should not use deception by lying or misleading your participants. So should all research that involves any kind of deception be abandoned? Of course not! This would eliminate many research questions. However, it may be sometimes necessary to omit a small piece of information or to deceive the participants in order to test the experimental hypothesis, especially if there's no other way to conduct the study since getting informed consent might ruin the study. We're sure that you can think of many studies where this might be the case. For example, if you were interested in seeing what percentage of men wash their hands after using the restroom, you could evaluate this empirical question. But how might it affect your study if you asked each participant as they were entering the bathroom to sign an informed consent document that said that you were interested in looking at their post-elimination hand washing behaviors? Clearly you can't ask participants this and obtain informed consent from them because **subject reactivity**, or when participants alter or change their behavior when they know that they are being observed, would contaminate your study. Since informed consent is supposed to tell the participants about the purpose of the study so that they may make an informed decision on whether to participate or not, how can this be reconciled? If participants don't know everything about the study, can they really provide informed consent? After all, they aren't really being fully informed. The answer to this challenge is fairly simple. Generally, researchers should not deceive participants. However, if there's no other way to answer the experimental question without deception then researchers may be able to use deception if it's deemed acceptable. Typically, the IRB at the institution weighs the costs and benefits of each study that involves deception to determine if the benefits outweigh any potential costs of the study and that deception is deemed necessary. The main caveat is that researchers cannot lie or deceive participants about any potential risks of the study. Thus, the deception must be such that not disclosing the deception at the beginning of the study would not be expected to influence the participant's decision to take part in the study. At the conclusion of a study that uses deception, it becomes even more important to completely disclose or debrief participants about the nature and purpose of the study and allow participants to ask questions regarding the study.

Use of Unobtrusive Measures

As previously mentioned, there are many research questions and topics in psychology where subject reactivity is very likely. Deception is one way to handle the threat of subject reactivity. Another, somewhat related topic is that of unobtrusive measures. An **unobtrusive measure** is where the participants are unaware that they are being observed or studied. The unobtrusive measures provide another tool to use to eliminate or reduce subject reactivity. When using unobtrusive measures, informed consent would be impossible to use. An interesting study by Middlemist, Knowles, and Matter (1976) faced this issue. In this study they looked at the effects that invasions of personal space had on men. Rather than simply observe how men react when another man sits too close to them, this study looked at invasions of personal space at bathroom urinals. They had a confederate use an adjacent urinal or urinals at other distances from the participant. The researchers measured "tension" caused by this personal space invasion by looking at the "start time" to urinate as well as length of their "session." In case you're curious, the start time was 8.4, 6.2, and 4.8 seconds when the confederate was in the adjacent urinal, one urinal away, or when the confederate was absent, respectively. Also, in case you were interested, the researchers had a "periscope" that allowed them to observe the stream of urine of the

Would having another person in an adjacent urinal affect your ability to urinate? Research shows that it does, but would such a study be ethical?

participants. Again, the potential ethical threat caused by a lack of informed consent is again a danger here. As with deception, the IRB would weigh the potential costs and benefits of conducting the study without using informed consent. Another potential concern might be debriefing participants. When we mentioned deception previously, we mentioned the importance of fully debriefing participants to explain the deception. What about with unobtrusive measures? With unobtrusive measures, the participants didn't even know that they were in a study in the first place. Should we now let them know that they were in a study that they didn't know about? In studies where participants are observed in public locations and where there is no manipulation (i.e., in nonexperimental studies), these unobtrusive measures may be less serious. The IRB would still need to evaluate these studies and weigh the costs and benefits of the study, but studies such as this would be less serious. The act of debriefing participants where they didn't know they were even part of a study might be seen as worse than the potential ethical issues related to not debriefing them. Imagine a participant in our hand washing study trying to leave the bathroom and the researcher trying to debrief him. This would probably be extremely uncomfortable. While informed consent and debriefing are always preferred, the researcher and the IRB must carefully determine if the benefits of such research is greater than the potential to cause any kind of mental or physical harm to the participants. As a general rule, if an unobtrusive procedure might embarrass, victimize, or otherwise harm a participant, then explicit prior informed consent and full debriefing is needed.

Confidentiality

Confidentiality and the related issue of anonymity are other tools that researchers use in order to protect the rights of participants and to eliminate subject reactivity. **Confidentiality** is an expectation of the participant that the information that they provide in the course of a study shall not be divulged to any other individuals, except as used by the researchers for the purposes of the study. **Anonymity** is when the participants' data cannot be linked back to the participant. If a study is asking participants about topics, feelings, or behaviors that may be taboo or may embarrass or make the participant uncomfortable, the promise of confidentiality and anonymity can help participants to be more honest and forthcoming in the research. For example, studies asking about participants' sexual orientation, sexual experiences, drug use, medical issues, criminal history, racist attitudes, and many other topics would be more valid with the guarantee of confidentiality and/or anonymity. Without these guarantees, subject reactivity or even participants declining to participate in such a study may be very likely.

Confidentiality and anonymity allow participants to answer truthfully during a research study, particularly regarding topics that are taboo or risqué.

Confidentiality and anonymity are typically fairly easy to ensure by simply removing any identifiers from the data that may link participants with their data. Using a participant number for each participant allows the researcher to keep all of the individual's data together, but does not require identifying the participant. Maintaining confidentiality has many potential benefits. The first would be to protect the rights of the participants from embarrassment or distress. If unlawful behaviors are being disclosed in the course of the study (e.g., drug use or past crimes) then participants may be protected from criminal or civil liability or even the loss of their job.

An additional ethical issue related to confidentiality is whether confidentiality should be upheld in all circumstances. Researchers would be best served by making it clear how confidentiality will be upheld in their studies in the informed consent. Additionally, any circumstances where this confidentiality would be breached must also be clearly provided to the participant prior to agreeing to participate in a study. Generally, if the researcher informs the participant that all information that is disclosed will remain confidential then that information should remain confidential. The purpose of this confidentiality is to protect the participant or others from harm. However, there are mandatory reporting laws at both the local and federal levels. For example, in virtually every jurisdiction, abuse or neglect that is directed toward a child or mentally incapacitated individual must be reported by law. Additionally, if the participant is in imminent risk to harm himself or others then a breach in confidentiality may be warranted. So if the participant communicates an explicit threat of serious physical harm to another individual and has the apparent intent and ability to carry out the threat then the psychologist may take protective actions, which would include contacting the police and/or seeking hospitalization for the participant. Therefore, the threat must be probable, be imminent, and it must involve physical injury. However, the psychologist cannot inform the person who is the subject of the threat. Interestingly, admission of *past* criminal activity without expressing specific intent to engage in future criminal activity that would *physically* harm another individual would typically *not* warrant a breach of confidentiality.

Concluding Remarks

While most ethical situations are clearly laid out, there are some issues that are somewhat less clear. The Code of Ethics published by the APA is an excellent tool as it provides the generally accepted ethical guidelines that psychologists and other scientists use. These guidelines are very useful and will help you to better understand the vast majority of ethical situations, ways to avoid making unethical decisions, and help protect yourself as a researcher. As previously mentioned in this chapter, when proposing a research study, researchers must submit their research proposal to the IRB at their institution. However, the researcher is ultimately responsible for making the ethical decisions regarding his or her research.

There is an ethical dilemma homework assignment at the end of this chapter to help you better understand different ethical situations that may arise in research. There are also other assignments that are designed to provide you with additional information on research ethics.

References

Middlemist, R. D., Knowles, E. S., & Matter, C. F. (1976). Personal space invasions in the lavatory: Suggestive evidence for arousal. *Journal of Personality and Social Psychology*, *33*(5), 541–546. doi: 10.1037/0022-3514.33.5.541

Smith, D. (2003). Five principles of research ethics. *Monitor on Psychology*, *34*(1), 56.

End of Chapter Quiz

1. What organization has a fairly specific Code of Ethics that they publish on their website?

2. True or False: Psychological studies can never use deception since it could be harmful to the participants.

3. What is the most important ethical consideration that should be upheld in all research studies?

4. True or False: Citations are only necessary if you use someone's exact wording.

5. What is the normal order of authors on a research manuscript (i.e, what is the rule to determine who goes first, second, or third as authors on a manuscript)?

6. True or False: In order to participate in a study, participants must always sign an informed consent document so that they know what to expect in the study.

7. What is the name for the term that guarantees that the participants' data cannot be linked back to the participant?

8. What is the name for the part of the study where the researcher tells the participant about what they did in the study, why their participation was important, and more importantly informs them of the purpose of the study?

9. True or False: An unobtrusive study helps to eliminate any effects of subject reactivity.

10. What is the most common ethical impropriety?

Homework Assignment #1

Collaborative Institutional Training Initiative (CITI) Assignment

In order to complete this assignment, you must go to the CITI website—https://www.citiprogram. org/—in order to complete the online training course. Once you've completed the assignment, you will receive a certificate that you can save, print and/or e-mail to your instructor as proof of completion. The assignment will probably take you about an hour to complete. Below are some instructions to help guide you through the process:

1. To begin the assignment, you must first go to the CITI website—https://www.citiprogram. org/—and register. You do this by clicking on the "Register" button in order to Create a New Account.

2. You'll then need to select your university as your participating institution. Typing in the first part of the university name usually helps to find it.

3. Do not select anything in the "Independent Learner Registration" as these would be courses that you would need to pay for.

4. You then need to enter your personal information (name, e-mail, etc.)

5. The next screen will ask for a user name (your university username works well here) and then select your password and security question (in case you forget your password).

6. Identify your gender, ethnicity, etc.

7. On the next screen it will ask if you'd like to participate in the training in order to obtain continuing education credits. Select NO for this, otherwise you'd have to pay to get these credits.

8. You may have to complete some additional information as required by your university. For your "Role in the Research" select "Student Researcher—Undergraduate" or "Student Researcher—Graduate" depending on your educational level.

9. For the next two screens, select "Not at This Time" for the Responsible Conduct of Research option and "No" for the subsequent screens asking about taking the Conflict of Interest course.

10. On the next screen, you should select the "Social-Behavioral-Educational Researchers" Students option for the Human Subjects screen.

11. For the next screen, select "Not at this time" regarding conducing the IRB Chair course.

12. For the next screen, select "Not at this time" regarding Laboratory Animal Welfare.

13. For the next screen, select "Not at this time" regarding CITI US Export Control Regulations course, but click on the "Complete Registration" button.

14. Click on the "Finalize Registration" option and your registration should be complete. You may now select your course and start the training.

Homework Assignment #2

"The Lab: Avoiding Research Misconduct"

In this assignment, you will play the role of a lead character in an interactive movie about research misconduct. Throughout the course of the movie, your character will have to make some tough decisions. These decision will draw on your knowledge of research integrity. You will be able to vicariously experience the long-term, serious consequences of your behaviors (or lack thereof). By the end of the movie you should have gained a deeper understanding of topics, such as research misconduct, mentorship responsibilities, handling of data, responsible authorship, and questionable research practices.

Choose your role:

Kim Park—a third-year graduate student, who questions the use of her data by another researcher.

Hardik Rao—a postdoc researcher, who deals with the competitiveness in an up-and-coming lab while balancing the responsibilities of a home life.

Aaron Hutchins—a principal investigator (PI), whose overwhelming responsibilities as a professor, researcher, & grant writer lead to his decline as a responsible mentor.

Beth Ridgely—a research administrator, who has accepted the role as the university's Research Integrity Officer (RIO) & must quickly learn how to handle allegations of research misconduct.

Your Assignment:

Choose the role you would like to play, then go to https://ori.hhs.gov/content/thelab. Click on the "Play Full Version" icon to begin the movie. The length of the movie varies depending on the decisions you make, but be prepared to give yourself 30–45 minutes to complete the assignment. As you watch the movie and play your role, it would be beneficial for you to take notes regarding the ethical dilemmas your character faces.

After you have finished the movie, write between 1–2 pages (double-spaced, Times New Roman, 12-point font) describing the role you played, the issues you faced, the decisions you made, and the consequences of those decisions. Your paper should also be able to describe what you learned and your personal opinion regarding the importance of exercising scientific integrity.

Homework Assignment #3

Now that you've had a chance to read the chapter, let's test your knowledge of research ethics. For many of the ethical dilemmas below, there could be more than one correct answer. However, your logic or reasoning are a very important part of your answer. For each of the ethical dilemmas, first identify what is the major ethical issue at question. Second, is the situation as described ethical or unethical? Finally, provide a one sentence explanation for your decision (i.e., explain why it's ethical or why you'd consider it to be unethical).

1. You conducted an experiment in which you misled participants about a minor part of the experiment. At the end of the experiment you decided not to fully disclose the purpose of the study so that they couldn't ruin the experiment if they talked with other potential participants in your study.

2. Since you are interested in eyewitness memory in the real world, you go out and stage an armed robbery in a crowded subway station. The person who is the perpetrator and the person being robbed are confederates in your study so that no one is actually being harmed. After the robbery you obtain consent from 80% of the individuals (20% did not want to participate) and ask them questions concerning the robbery. You also have them identify the perpetrator from a photo line-up.

3. You are interested in conducting research on adolescents so you go to a local high school. The study is relatively simple and involves you giving each student a two-page questionnaire to fill out. You approach students during their lunch time so that you do not interfere with their class work and you only take up approximately 10 minutes of their time.

4. Following an experiment, one of your participants wants to know how they did in the experiment. You feel that this is a reasonable request, so you have them wait while you score their data. Once you score their data, you give them their score and let them know how well or poorly they did compared to the other participants that you've tested so far. This participant actually did very well.

5. You conduct an experiment where you measure the amount of personal space different people require. In order to collect your data, you go to the campus library where there are plenty of people who will be sitting down reading/studying. Your confederate approaches different people and sits right up against them (i.e., touching shoulders), 1 foot from them, or 3 feet from them. You measure the subject's reaction to the confederate.

6. You conducted a study which involved having subjects complete a simple questionnaire. You were primarily interested in their attitudes concerning heterosexuals and homosexuals. However, you didn't want to only include questions concerning these topics. Therefore, you included questions on suicide, racism, chauvinism, attitudes toward violence, childhood experiences, etc. During the course of your study, you find one individual who was sexually abused as a child and who has scored extremely high on likelihood of attempting suicide. You decide to call a psychologist and have the psychologist talk with this individual.

7. As a faculty member at a university conducting research, you have undergraduate students conducting research with you. One of your students came up with, what you think, is a great idea for a research study. Thus, you gave the student permission to conduct the study in your lab. Once the study was completed the student writes up the manuscript with your help. Prior to submitting the manuscript to a journal, you have the student add your name to the manuscript as one of the authors since he or she used you lab and you helped mentor the student through the publication process.

8. You are interested in the way people react to helping someone in need. Therefore, a confederate working with you goes to the cafeteria and acts like he's choking on his food. You measure the number of people who actually help the confederate. Your confederate then acts either grateful for the individual's help or laughs at them for being so gullible. You then measure their reaction to the confederate.

9. You have been conducting research in an area for the past 10 years and have a very influential theory. However, in a new study that you've been conducting you replicate four experiments that contradict your theory and show that your theory is wrong. You decide not to publish or present this research since it actually supports the theory of one of your competitors.

10. You are conducting research on a new technique that should help increase the amount of information that people can remember. You have a participant scheduled for your study and know that individual from a class that you're teaching. Since this person isn't very bright, you assign this individual to the control condition which is less likely to see a memory improvement.

11. You have submitted a research manuscript for publication. Although it was done inadvertently, you didn't provide a citation for an idea that you obtained from a well-cited manuscript in your research area. You decide that this information is common knowledge to individuals involved in this research area so you decide not to worry about it if the reviewers don't notice.

12. You have completed a research project and the manuscript that you are interested in publishing. You feel that the research really makes a substantial contribution to the existing literature and you're very excited to submit the manuscript for publication. However, you're having some difficulty trying to determine which journal would be the most likely to publish your manuscript. So, you decide to submit it to the top two journals and one moderately good journal at the same time in hopes that it will be accepted by one of the top journals. The third journal is your backup.

13. In the process of a study, you interview numerous individuals concerning their attitudes toward the police and crime. One of your participants admits to raping a woman and getting away with it approximately 6 months ago. You decide that this information was gathered in your study and you had told your participants that any information would be kept confidential. Thus, you do not report this person to the authorities.

14. You are conducting a study evaluating invasions of personal space. Thus, you observe men at public restroom urinals and have a confederate stand in the adjacent urinal or with one urinal between the subject and your confederate. Using a measuring device at the bottom of each urinal, you measure the time to urinate and the volume of urine in your subjects. Since the subjects do not know that they are in a study, you do not obtain informed consent or debrief them.

15. You ran a drug study with rats and completed it. As you evaluated the data, you realized that the sex of the rat might be an important variable, but never collected this data at the time of data collection. However, based on the rat's weight, you could determine with 95% certainty the sex of the rat. You decided to add the sex of the rats to your data set based on their weight.

Chapter 4
Nonexperimental Methods: Part I

As you learned in Chapter 2, there are two broad types of research approaches; nonexperimental methods and experimental methods. For the next two chapters, we are going to focus on the nonexperimental approaches to research. As we discuss each, we'll identify the approach and discuss the strengths and weaknesses of each approach. Each approach has some inherent value, but there are limitations to each of these approaches. In order to make an educated decision concerning which approach you'd like to use in your own research, you'll need to know what the advantages and limitations of each approach are. Additionally, as a consumer of research, you'll need to know the limitations of each of these nonexperimental methods so that you'll know what you can and can't conclude from the various studies using these approaches.

A General Overview of Observation

There are several types of observation available to you; knowing the different types of observation can help you when you are deciding what type of research study you want to conduct. Once you've identified your research question (i.e., your hypothesis), you then need to determine if you'd like to describe the behavior (i.e., descriptive explanations), look for a relationship between multiple behaviors (i.e., relational explanations), or if you want to explain or determine the cause of the behavior (i.e., explanatory explanations). Your choice will determine what type of research options are available to you. When we look to describe a behavior or relate behaviors to each other, we ask questions that are answered by conducting nonexperimental research.

Research in psychology can take many forms (as can all research). Sometimes we want to be able to *explain* the cause of a behavior; in this case, we are using the experimental approach (which we discuss in detail in Chapters 6 and 7). When you use the explanatory approach, you are in control of the variables that your participants receive because you are able to manipulate the variables. As you can imagine, being able to explain the cause of a behavior is an important aspect of research. However, you may not always be able to manipulate your variables or be interested in the specific cause of the behavior. Sometimes we're actually more interested in describing the behavior or simply understanding how variables relate to one another. In these cases, we are going to use nonexperimental methods.

Nonexperimental Methods

Before we delve into the specific types of nonexperimental designs, let's first look at what exactly makes a nonexperimental study nonexperimental. There are two questions to ask yourself when determining if a study is experimental or nonexperimental:

1. Are you able to manipulate the variable(s) of interest?
2. Are you able to randomly assign your participants to their respective groups or conditions?

If you can answer "yes" to both of these questions, you are looking at a true experiment; however, if you are not able to randomly assign your participants to the different conditions and/or you are not able to manipulate the variable you are interested in, then you will need to conduct a nonexperimental study.

Let's think about a classic drug study in which a participant is given either a drug or a placebo to show how each of these approaches might work. Imagine that you have created a new drug that will increase your participants' IQ. You have 100 participants in your study and you are able to randomly assign half of them to receive the placebo and the other half to receive your new IQ drug. In this way, not only does each participant have an equal chance of getting into your experimental condition (IQ drug group) or the control condition (placebo group) but you are able to manipulate your independent variable (the IQ drug) so that some get a drug and some get a placebo. If this is how your study is set up, you will be able to conduct a true experiment and therefore determine the cause of the behavior changes. In the case of your drug, you would hope that you increased the IQ in those taking your drug and that no change occurred in those who received the placebo. So how does this differ from a nonexperimental design? Well, remember that in the case of the nonexperimental design, you are not able to manipulate the variables and/or randomly assign your participants to the groups. So, if you are interested in the differences in males and females who have taken the drug, you would not be able to randomly assign participants to their groups (i.e., male or female) simply because you are interested in sex differences. Try as you might, it would probably be very difficult to get your participants to agree to undergo sexual reassignment for the purposes of your study or for the extra credit that they might receive. This doesn't mean that we can't evaluate the differences between males and females. We can compare the scores of the males and females who have taken the drug, but we cannot manipulate their sex, even though this is the variable that is of interest to us. In this case, we would have to rely on a nonexperimental approach in order to understand if there were sex differences with regard to the drug.

So, now that you have a somewhat better idea of how the two types of experimentation work, let's look closer at nonexperimental methods. In this chapter we will look at the *Case Study, Observational Research,* and *Survey Research.* In the next chapter (Chapter 5) we will look at *Correlations, Archival Research* (including *Meta-analyses*), and *Quasi-experiments.*

Before we begin, answer each of the four questions below: Can you determine what type of research is being conducted if you know where it was conducted?

1. Can nonexperimental methods be conducted in the field?
2. Can nonexperimental methods be conducted in the lab?
3. Can true experiments be conducted in the lab?
4. Can true experiments be conducted in the field?

The answer to each of these four question is Yes. Why, you ask? Simple, where we choose to conduct our study can affect many things, such as our generalizability and control, but it doesn't tell us anything about the type of research that was conducted. Field studies just provide us with more external validity while lab studies provide us with more internal validity. The real question here is what is the goal your research- to describe, predict, or explain behavior as it occurs in a natural environment (field studies) or to have greater control over the variables in the study to draw clearer conclusions (lab studies).

Case Studies

H. M. was born in 1926 in Connecticut. Around the age of 7, he was struck by a child riding a bicycle hard enough that he ended up falling down and smashing his head on the pavement. Though he appeared fine after regaining consciousness, some days later he started to have seizures. The initial seizures began as relatively mild and infrequent, however, eventually, these focal seizures grew in intensity and frequency. Following his 16th birthday, these seizures progressed to tonic-clonic (or grand mal) seizures. By 1953, at the age of 27, he was no longer able to function in his everyday life. (He averaged 1 to 2 tonic-clonic seizures per day). He was referred to Dr. William Scoville, a neurosurgeon in Hartford. Scoville, after determining that his seizures were located in his left and right temporal lobe, recommended an experimental treatment that included the removal of two-thirds of H.M.'s hippocampus (the seahorse-shaped structure in the brain) and some of the neighboring structures (his amygdala, entorhinal cortex, and the perirhinal cortex). On September 1, 1953, Scoville performed a bilateral medial temporal-lobe resection on H.M.

After his surgery, H.M.'s seizures dramatically reduced (he would only experience 1 to 2 seizures a year!). But that is where the good news ends. It became apparent rather quickly that H.M. was suffering from profound anterograde amnesia (i.e., the inability to form new memories) as well as partial retrograde amnesia (i.e., the ability to remember past events). Eventually, he was able to remember nothing past his 16th birthday . . . 11 years *before* his surgery. While these areas were diminished, his working memory and his procedural memory were unaffected. It was only his ability to form new explicit memories that was reduced; he could not commit new information to long-term memory, he could not remember current events, and he could not remember the events that made up his everyday life. To him, he would never remember a face that he hadn't seen prior to surgery (it was always new to him), he would forever be lost in unfamiliar territory, Harry Truman would always be president (who was the 33rd president and H.M. would live long enough to see the election of Barack Obama, the 44th president), and he would forever have to live in shock at his own aging when he saw himself in the mirror as well as the fact that others had aged. Additionally, he had to relive the news of his parents' death each time he was informed.

At the time of his surgery, there was no real understanding of the function of this area of the brain, in particular, the function of the hippocampus. After showing such a profound memory deficit, Scoville reached out to Brenda Milner (a neuropsychologist out of Montreal) to try to understand just what happened. It was through the work of Milner, and her long working relationship with H.M., that we begin to understand the full extent of H.M.'s loss. According to Milner, there would likely never be a case of amnesia more severe than H.M.'s. While they saw each other almost every day for 30 years, H.M. always treated Milner as if he was meeting her for the first time. Amazingly, H.M.'s cheerful character remained, and those who met him described him as a pleasant individual that was quick with a smile. For 30 years, researchers investigated H.M. and his profound memory loss. They were amazed to learn that while he couldn't remember if he ate lunch just 20 minutes earlier, his short-term memory while working on various tasks (such as a digit-span task) remained intact. In fact, if you were to give him the same crossword puzzle that he just finished, he would see it as new, but give him seven numbers to recite back to you and he did just fine. He was the ideal participant, always eager and he never tired of the task (because it was always a new task for him, even if he had done it a hundred times). He could also retain procedural memories for tasks that he had completed but not be able to explicitly remember that he had done it (i.e., he had no declarative memory). In one task, they would have him do a mirror-drawing task. The researchers would have H.M. trace the outline of a 5-pointed star from the reflection in the mirror (a very difficult task for anyone). At the outset, just like any other participant, H.M. struggled with the task, finding it hard to draw the shape that was reflected in the mirror. Nevertheless, after repeatedly doing the task, he was actually quite good at it (a similar pattern can be seen for most participants who engage in this task). However, while he seemed to retain this procedural memory, his ability to recall that he had ever done the task was gone. To him, the task was always new.

H.M. was a man who was forever in his early 20s even though he lived for another 55 years. He never understood that the old man in the mirror was him. Through his loss, we have gained an incredible understanding of not only memory but of our brains. His case showed us that our short-term and long-term memories are not located in the same area; that they function, in part, independently from each other. That our memories for our personal histories isn't stored with our knowledge of language or our motor skills. He also showed us that individuals can have severe cognitive deficits, but these deficits may not affect our intelligence. In fact, his IQ showed no change after the surgery. That the hippocampus is important in transferring information from our working memory into our long-term memory. It isn't an exaggeration to say that H.M. is one of the most important cases in neuropsychology and memory.

The aforementioned represents a case study. A **case study**, as you might have noticed, follows a single individual and gathers extensive information about that individual. When a particular disorder or behavior is rare (as is the case with H.M.), case studies are often the only option available to us. You will find that case studies are presented in various ways. You will find case studies reported in a journal through a single research article or find whole books devoted to a single or several different case studies. A great example of this is the work of Oliver Sack. I personally recommend the book *The Man who Mistook His Wife for a Hat and other Clinical Tales* (1985).

Case studies have been used throughout the history of psychology and medicine. Many of the psychological disorders you will study throughout your academic career will have started with case studies; *Freud and Little Hans, Breuer and Anna O, Wilbur and "Sybil Dorsett"* all represent famous case studies that went on to have a substantial impact (for better or worse) on the field of psychotherapy. You are familiar with Phineas Gage from chapter 1, who provided an excellent case study on the effects of damage to the left frontal lobe when he had a railroad blasting iron shot through his skull and survived. This case study helped us to understand that different parts of the brain have specific contributions to our complex personalities.

If you decide to conduct a case study, you will need to gather information in multiple forms and from multiple sources. The information that you gather from the individual you are interested in studying will probably not be complete enough. You will need to get information from others who have some type of interaction with that person, such as teachers, friends, family, and coworkers. You will also likely give your participant various tests. As you recall, H.M. took numerous psychological tests, such as the digit span test, personality inventories, and intelligence tests. Just asking H.M. what his memory capabilities were would not have been particularly useful due to his severe memory deficits. For over 30 years, Milner and others gathered extensive data on H.M. Thus, numerous tests were used to not only determine how severe his memory impairment was, but also identify what kind of memory impairment he had (i.e., short-term, long-term, procedural, episodic, etc.). In addition to running memory tests like those used with H.M., you may want to include psychophysiological tests, brain imaging, and physiological measures. You will also need to observe the individual in various settings, like your office, their school, at home, and work.

Case studies, regardless of why they are being conducted, provide us with vast amounts of information. They offer us a unique view of the person's behavior and the issues that they are experiencing. They provide a rich narrative of what is happening in the psychological world of an individual. One of the benefits of case studies is that it may lead us to an understanding of the cause of a behavior or symptom, even though the case study cannot do this itself. In the case of H.M., through an extensive amount of additional work with other individuals and animals, scientists were able to ascertain that the damage to the hippocampus and surrounding areas was the cause of his profound amnesia. Another example of this is the case of Tan, a man that was unable to produce language but was able to understand it. Tan's case was studied by Pierre Paul Broca. Broca created a detailed case study that he and other doctors at the time were able to compare with other patients with similar symptoms. This eventually led researchers to recognize that damage to a specific area of the brain (part of the frontal lobe now known as Broca's area) would produce similar language deficits. This in turn led researchers to understand not only the impact that strokes could have on the brain, but also that language production was localized to a specific part of the frontal lobe and that language comprehension was localized to a nearby part of the temporal lobe (called Wernike's Area following similar case studies with other individuals). As you can see, case studies can often serve as a starting point in our understanding of a particular issue or topic. With the advancement in our understanding (and advances in technology), we can turn the information gathered in case studies into testable theories.

Potential Concerns with Case Studies

At this point you might be asking yourself why we do not always rely on case studies for our research if they provide us with so much information. There are three major problems with case studies:

1. generalizability
2. observer bias
3. inability to make causal claims

Let's start with the issue surrounding generalizability. As you learned in Chapter 2, **generalizability** (or **external validity**) is when you are able to relate the findings of your research to the general population outside of the study. Generalizability can always pose a concern, but with a case study, where we are only observing a single person or behavior, we need to be especially careful in claiming that what we are seeing is an accurate reflection of how the behavior appears in the general population. Additionally, we're typically studying individuals using the case study approach *because* they aren't like the rest of the population. Freud was notorious for using a single case to explain how everyone developed. Take for instance the case of Little Hans. Little Hans and his phobia of horses had a great impact on the development of Freud's psychosexual development theory, especially in regards to the phallic stage of development and the Oedipal complex. Freud believed that Han's phobia of horses actually was a projection of his fear of his father (his father was represented by the horse) and his fear that his father would castrate him (his fear that the horse would bite him) for his incestuous wishes to be with his mother. Freud saw this phobia as a form of the Oedipus complex. Now, is it possible that Hans did indeed desire to be with his mother and also fear that his father would castrate him? Sure, it's possible. However, even if this is true and Freud's interpretation of Hans' behavior is correct, it does not tell us just how prevalent the Oedipal complex is in the general population. Due to this logic, case studies have their own limitations in their usefulness.

The next issue surrounding case studies deals with observer bias. **Observer bias** is when the expectations of the observer (or the researcher) distorts his or her observations; it influences what they see. This is a concern with all research, but in the instance of a case study, the concern lies in how, why, and what they attend to when observing their patient. Returning to the case of Little Hans, we now know that there was a bias when it came to the observation of his behavior. Freud did not initially meet Hans (in fact, he spent very little time over the years of his treatment with the boy) and instead discussed his case through letters with Hans' father. Now, this alone may not seem like a problem, after all, Hans' issues began when he was just 3 years old, so he may not have been able to articulate his thoughts and feelings. The problem is that Hans' father was familiar with Freud's work and wrote to Freud with the belief that Freud would find the case of his son interesting. It was Hans' father that provided Freud with much of the information surrounding Hans' behaviors. Since Hans' father was already familiar with Freud's work and his concept of the Oedipus complex, it is likely that he interpreted his son's behavior in light of this knowledge. It is equally likely that he also influenced Hans' behavior and thoughts to fit in with the theory, possibly even suggesting to his son that he wanted to marry his mother. When we conduct research, we must always be aware of the influence of our biases or at least be aware that these biases could exist. With case studies, where just one person is being observed, it is difficult to see if our behavior and biases are affecting the interpretation of the behaviors since we don't have anyone else to compare our participant with. Related to this idea is the fact that in case studies the researcher interacts with the participant extensively. As the researcher interacts more with the individual, the researcher may become less objective about the individual case.

Our final concern has to do with making **causal claims**. While case studies provide us with a great deal of information, they fail to provide us with the causes of the behavior or disorder. Think back to Little Hans and his phobia of horses. While Freud did make an assumption (or maybe more accurately, a rather large leap) that Hans' fear was due to the Oedipal complex, we cannot make a causal claim with a case study. Remember, you can only claim to understand the cause of a behavior when you have controlled the manipulation of the variables and the antecedent conditions; in other words, when you have conducted a true experiment (see Chapters 6 & 7 for more information on this). As is true for all nonexperimental techniques, one cannot make causal statements based on case studies.

Observational Research

Our next type of nonexperimental research method is observational research. Often, everyday people think that if you are conducting observational research that you are basically just "people watching." This is a very simplistic and inaccurate view of scientific observation. **Observational research** is the systematic observing and recording of behavior. It is much more than just watching a person or animal passively. As you will see shortly, it takes a lot more time, planning, and energy to systematically observe behavior.

Now before we go any further, you may be asking yourself why you would want to conduct this type of research or you may be asking how the observation here is different from the observation used in a case study. Well, just like in a case study, observational research is an excellent tool to help us describe behavior. But, it differs from a case study in that it doesn't just observe a single person or animal; instead, it will observe multiple subjects and will typically require less time for each individual being observed. The real benefit with observational approaches is that since you have more subjects, you will be able to generalize your findings to other members of the population more easily, whereas in a case study you would not be able to do so. Observational research allows us to see if our participants are acting in a unique way compared to other individuals within the study. If I want to see if girls use more aggressive language than boys do, it wouldn't make sense for me to just study one boy and one girl. This particular boy and girl might be very different from the average boy and girl or from the general population. By observing multiple children, I would be able to determine if the behavior I am observing is consistent among other boys and girls. Of course, just like all nonexperimental research, we will not be able to draw causal conclusions about our observations, but observational research may be able to point us in the right direction so that we can find the cause of a behavior in subsequent experimental studies. Observational research may also be conducted when there are ethical concerns that make conducting a true experiment impossible. For example, we cannot randomly put our participants into the boy and girl groups. Since this would be a subject variable, we cannot manipulate the sex of our participants. Thus, conducting a study with the sex of our participants cannot be conducted using a true experiment.

There are several types of observational research methods to choose from which fall into two main categories: Naturalistic and Laboratory observation. Let's explore these further.

Naturalistic Observational Research

Naturalistic observation is any observational study that occurs in a natural setting where the researcher is observing the behavior as it naturally occurs (whether it is with humans or nonhuman animals). We can observe children in a classroom or bonobos (a type of chimpanzee) in the Democratic Republic of the Congo; as long as the observation occurs in their natural setting and the behavior is being observed as it naturally occurs, it falls within the broad category of naturalistic observation.

As you can see, there are many distractions in a kindergarten classroom.

The biggest strength in using naturalistic observation is your ability to generalize your findings (i.e., external validity). This high external validity makes it a very desirable option if you value generalizability, but it comes at a cost; this cost is a lack of control (i.e., internal validity). Since you are observing your participants in their natural environment, you cannot control the environment; you take the environment as it is without manipulating anything. This means that there is a greater chance that the behavior you are seeing may be due to some variable you are not aware of or that you are ignoring. For instance, if you were to enter a kindergarten classroom, you may find that your participants are constantly bombarded with displays of construction paper, bright and busy posters, educational toys, and noise from their classmates. This is typical of an elementary classroom, but if you choose to observe in this setting, you must be aware that any of these things (as well as others that we have not listed) could be influencing the behavior of the children you are observing. Since you want to observe these children in their natural classroom setting, removing any of these things can hurt your ability generalize your results outside of that particular classroom, school, or grade.

Jane Goodall is known for her naturalistic observation of chimpanzees in their natural habitat in Tanzania.

Laboratory Observational Research

As we just saw, you can have high external validity with naturalistic observation, but you will lose your control of the environment or internal validity. If you value this control and would like to maximize your internal validity, there is another type of observational research approach that you can utilize. This type of observation is *laboratory observation*, or analogue observation. **Laboratory observation** is when we bring our participants into a controlled setting in which we are observing the behavior. Don't let the name fool you, it doesn't have to occur in an actual laboratory. In fact, clinicians will often use this method in their offices, such as with children.

In the case of a therapist working with children, they will control what the child will be able to use or play with as well as what is displayed in the office. Everything is meticulously set up so as not to interfere with the observation. Likewise, animal research conducted in a laboratory setting will control what the researcher thinks might interfere with the animal's behavior. This could be the type of bedding, cage, visibility of other animals, etc.

The greatest advantage of using this method over other types of observational research is the greater control and efficiency. Since the researcher does not have to wait for a behavior to occur naturally (as they would need to in a naturalistic observation study), this type of research often takes less time. Here is an example to help you better understand this approach:

> Imagine that you are interested in observing how a married couple deals with conflict; it's a useful topic as many marriages end in divorce and many more married couples are unhappy. Now, you can set up cameras in their home to observe them and wait for a conflict to occur (which will eventually occur), but, depending on the couple, that might take days or even weeks, and that would be a lot of video for you to go through. Plus, couples don't always experience conflict at home in the exact location that you set up your video camera. Instead, you could set it up for them to discuss a prior conflict or give them a scenario that they need to act out (role-playing) or discuss what would lead to a conflict. In this way, you can have the conflict occur at a specific time and in a specific place. Additionally, if you bring your couples into your laboratory and out of their own home, you can control for distractions that might occur, like a phone ringing or the kids coming home from school.

The main disadvantage for this type of observation is the fact that it is only an analogue to real life (it's similar, but not the same as real life). As we have already discussed, this will limit your ability to generalize your research outside of your laboratory setting. Let's go back to our married couples, do you think that how they handle a conflict in a laboratory setting in front of the researcher when it has been planned by the researcher is equivalent to how they would handle it in their normal everyday life? Why or why not? Have you even gotten into a fight with your significant other on the way to a party, but when you get there, you act as though everything is fine? Couples coming into a laboratory setting to discuss their issues with each other and their relationship often act like you do; they are often nicer to each other than they would be if they didn't think anyone was watching them. This type of impression management is quite common in all aspects of our lives. However, this shouldn't dissuade you from using this type of research or thinking that it can't have practical, real-life uses. In a classic research study by Gottman and Levenson (1992), they observed couples revisiting an old argument and coded each partner's behavior toward the other as positive (e.g., showing warmth or humor) or negative (e.g., showing anger or using sarcasm). What Gottman and Levenson found was that those couples that showed greater contempt for each other, failing to maintain a ratio of 5:1 positive to negative exchanges, were at a greater risk of divorce or separation just 4 years later (56% of these high risk couples compared to only 24% of couples able to maintain the 5:1 ratio). Remember, this observation was conducted in a lab setting, on a normal afternoon, at the prompting of a researcher. So, while it lacked ecological validity (i.e., it didn't occur where and how it normally would have), it still proved to be useful at understanding the interactions of married couples.

Obtrusive or Unobtrusive Observation

Regardless of whether you decide to conduct your observation research in the laboratory or in the natural environment, you have the option of making your observations covert (or secret) or overt (or known). This involves answering the question concerning whether your participants know that you are observing them. Thus, you'll need to decide between using either an obtrusive (overt) or unobtrusive (covert) observation method. In this case, we are talking about how much you, as the researcher, blend into the background. Your participants may know that they are being observed (so it is overt) but you can still be unobtrusive in that you don't get in the way (as opposed to being obtrusive where you are interacting with them or asking them questions throughout the study). Unobtrusive measures have the benefit of decreasing the chance that the researcher will contaminate their study with their involvement. Obtrusive measures, on the other hand, will mean that your participants are aware that you are recording them and their behavior. This may make your participants act in a way that is no longer natural. This issue is referred to as **subject reactivity**. Let's take a look at the following example from your days in elementary school. I'm sure many of you remember a time when your principal would come to your classroom to observe your teacher. Not surprisingly, even though they probably were trying to be unobtrusive, the notes they were taking (which were obvious) inevitably had an impact on the teacher and the classroom behavior. The principal's presence may have made you sit up straighter and raise your hand more. Your teachers probably also changed their behavior; some may have become more nervous, others becoming much nicer, but either way, when the principal would write something down on their form, the teacher and the students all were aware of it and it changed everyone's behavior. In fact, if your participants are aware that you are taking notes on them (therefore you are conducting an overt observation), it wouldn't be unheard of for them to ask to see your notes or ask you not to write something down. This isn't necessarily a bad thing. After some time, participants may become disinterested in your note taking, forget that you are there, or even come to enjoy it and make suggestions as to what you should take note of. This will likely only happen if you have told them you are observing their behavior (overt observation), but in the case of obtrusive covert observation, you may find yourself in some trouble when people demand to know what you are doing and why you are writing down what they say and do. So, always be sure you are weighing the risks and the benefits of each type of observation.

Participant Observation

While the other forms of observation typically involve the researcher(s) avoiding interacting with their participants, **participant observation** is when the observer actually becomes part of the group or environment they are studying. This may seem to go against our warnings of reactivity stated earlier, but these types of observations can be conducted covertly. When participant observation is conducted covertly, the researcher may become part of the group such that the group members are not aware that they are being observed; they believe the researcher is one of them.

In a classic study by Leon Festinger and his colleagues back in 1956 (Festinger, Riecken, & Schacter, 1956), they joined a cult that believed that there was going to be a great flood on December 21, 1954 in which most of North America would be devastated. Led by Mrs. Keech, who had been visited by aliens who had warned her about the disaster, some members of the small cult sold off all of their earthly belongings and quit their jobs as preparation of their inevitable rescue by these altruistic aliens. Festinger et al. decided to observe the cult using participant methods because they knew that if they revealed themselves not only as researchers but nonbelievers as well, that the members would not allow them access to their meetings or allow them to be observed. This was especially true if Festinger revealed that the purpose for the study was to observe real-life situations in which *cognitive dissonance* occurs. Cognitive dissonance proposes that when we have two opposing cognitions (or thoughts), that we experience a type of distress or tension. When faced with the reality that our cognitions are incorrect, we can either change our thinking or become more steadfast in our original belief. For Mrs. Keech and her followers, December 21 came and there was no great devastating flood and the aliens never showed up. According to Festinger, this created a state of cognitive dissonance; the belief that aliens existed and would save them from disaster with the reality that the prophecy failed. So, how should they respond when the evidence was contrary to their cognition? Well, logically they should have just accepted the truth and broken up the cult, but in reality what they did was reduce their dissonance by changing their cognitions; essentially, they doubled down. After waiting for hours for the aliens to arrive Mrs. Keech received a new message that the flood had been called off because "The little group, sitting all night long, had spread so much light that God had saved the world from destruction." The following day, the group began to recruit new members and grant interviews (something they were opposed to prior to the failed prophecy), all in hopes to spread the message.

As you can see, participant methods allow us to gain an inside look at groups that we normally wouldn't get access to. But there are concerns with this type of research. For one, while they were acting as members of the group, we cannot rule out that their behavior and their presence affected the group in some way. Perhaps by adding three new members to their group (our researchers), it provided evidence for the members that their beliefs had merit. Could these new members have made the groups' beliefs stronger just by their presence? There is no way to know for sure. Another issue to keep in mind concerns the ethics of this type of research. Did you notice that the members of the cult did not provide their consent for their involvement in the researchers' study? Additionally, the researchers used deception in order to infiltrate the group. As you saw in Chapter 3, both these issues violate ethical guidelines set up by the American Psychological Association. One last concern to keep in mind is that the researcher may become biased in their observations and interpretations. Since joining the group, in order to fit in, they would have to interact with the members. It is likely that they may come to like some, if not all, of the individuals they are observing. Why would this be a bad thing? Why would any personal connection, positive or negative, be an issue with the findings?

Final Notes about Observational Research

It's harder than you think! If you think you will be able to pick your research topic and just start observing people right away, you will be deeply disappointed. When you embark on your observational research, the first thing you will need to do is to determine what exactly you are trying to observe. Take a look at the image below; is the boy in the picture acting in an aggressive way or is he flirting with this girl? To ensure the reliability of your observations, you will need to make sure that you and your fellow observers agree on the answer, otherwise the data that you collect will be worthless.

Is this aggression or flirting? When conducting observational research, it is important that all of your researchers agree on the answer.

Let's look at an example. If you are trying to determine if boys or girls are more aggressive on the playground, you will need to decide prior to observation what you are considering aggressive behavior. Sure, most of us will see hitting, punching, shoving, and slapping as aggressive, but what about language (e.g., "you have cooties!")? What about a child who chooses to exclude another child from a group (e.g., "you can't play with us because Susie doesn't like you")? Do these count as aggressive behavior? This may seem easy, but as we have found there is often disagreement in our classes. To use our earlier example, let's say you are observing 5 and 6 year olds on the playground, and you see a little boy run up to a girl, pull her hair, and run away giggling. Do you consider this aggressive behavior or childhood flirting? If you saw this same behavior in a 15-year-old or a 25-year-old, would your answer change? When we have presented this question to our classes in the past, we find that there is not a group consensus on if this behavior in kindergarten-aged children is aggressive, but our students are always concerned when an adult engages in hair pulling. So, is it a big deal if you don't agree? Yes, it is! When conducting observational research, you need to make sure that all of your observers (because it would be foolish to rely on just you) agree with what they are measuring and seeing. This is known as interrater reliability. Simply put, **interrater reliability** is the extent to which your observers agree with each other on their observations. In order to ensure that you obtain interrater reliability, you will need to develop a *coding system* (or some other way to measure the behavior) with clear operational definitions for the behaviors you wish to observe. This is not something you can do in a night, and some researchers will take months or years to develop and refine their system to ensure they are using the best possible measures. Your observers need to have clearly defined guidelines to follow and extensive training so that they are practiced at observing. Your coding system should provide them with these clear guidelines when observing specific behaviors. It should ensure that there is no overlap between your categories, that every category and every behavior within each category is clearly defined, such that each behavior that you are observing is reflected in your coding system (because leaving something off not only might confuse your observers, but also will affect your interpretation of the data). By setting up a clear system, you should (hopefully) avoid confusion and disagreement among your observers. But you also want to make sure that your coding system isn't too complex or too long, as your observers can become fatigued easily or can miss behaviors if they are overwhelmed with labeling the behavior to your coding system. This is particularly important if you are observing behavior as it occurs (as opposed to reviewing videotapes). Having a long and tedious coding system will make it more likely that you will miss potentially important behaviors. This means that there is a fine balance that must be met here; to have your coding system exact enough but not be too complex that it's impossible to effectively use. Finally, you are going to have to train your observers to your system in order to ensure that you maintain a higher interrater score. Training is going to take time, in some cases weeks or months. A typical observer is likely to be someone like you (an undergraduate or graduate student). During your training, you will be given tests of your ability to observe the behavior and code it. This will be compared with other trained observers. If you are able to meet the minimum standard score set by your researcher (i.e., a certain standard of interrater reliability), then you can begin making observations that will be used for data interpretation. Even after you have been approved to be an observer, you should continue to be periodically checked to ensure that you are not slipping, which may occur when you become fatigued or bored.

Another issue with observational research is one we have encountered before: **observer bias**. Remember that observer bias is the preconceptions and expectations of the observer that alters their observations. Let's go back to our example of aggression in children. What if I go into it thinking that little boys are just naturally more aggressive than little girls? This might change the way I see the same behavior depending on whether it is a boy or girl who is displaying it. These expectations I hold will shape the way I interpret the behavior I see and thus affect my data and interpretation. Observer bias can occur in other ways as well, such as when I decide which grade to observe, what schools, and which classes (advanced or regular). But don't fret, we can minimize observer bias using the guidelines we have already discussed. First, set up a clear coding system. As we have already discussed, this will help us to

Do you think that being observed has changed this leopard's behavior? What about these students?

minimize uncertainty on which behavior to record and how to classify the behaviors. Secondly, be rigorous in your training of your observers. The more training they receive, the better they will use your coding system and the better they can observe the relevant behavior. Finally, reassess your observers' skills to ensure that they continue to use the coding system correctly and reliably. Doing these three things can help save you from bias in your observation and ensure that you locate bias quickly in your study.

One final concern to keep in mind when it comes to observations is one that we have already touched on, *reactivity*. As you should recall, reactivity occurs when the person or animal being observed alters their behavior due to the observation. So if you are observing animals, they may perform differently if they know that you are there (they may see you as a threat, for instance, and not eat or hide). Humans are no different. When we sense that others are watching us, we tend to change the way we act. Reactivity is a problem in research because it has altered a naturally occurring behavior, which is what we are trying to study. It affects our ability to accurately describe behavior and therefore our interpretation of the data. (Keep in mind that reactivity is a concern in all types of psychological research, not just observational research.) Reactivity won't always be a concern in your observational research, and there are certainly ways to minimize it, such as using video recordings or using covert observation methods. One thing that you can do when covert measures are not an option is to rely on habituation. *Habituation* is when repeated exposure to a stimulus decreases the impact it has on the person. Think about reality TV shows. Have you ever thought "wow, how can they act this way? Don't they realize they are on TV?" Well, they have become habituated to the cameras and camera crews; they are so used to seeing them that their presence no longer affects their behavior. As a researcher, you can also use this principle to minimize the impact that your presence has on your participants.

The below figure represents data from survey research. **Surveys** provide us with a snap shot of our opinions, attitudes, beliefs, and *reported* behaviors. We emphasize "reported" behaviors here because

Survey Research

Beliefs About Evolution, by Demographic Group
% of U.S. adults in each group saying that (humans/animals) and other living things have existed in their present form since the beginning of time, or (humans/animals) and other living things have evolved over time

	Humans have ...				Animals have ...			
	Evolved over time	Existed in present form	Don't know		Evolved over time	Existed in present form	Don't know	
All adults	60	33	7	=100	63	32	5	=100
Men	65	28	7	=100	66	29	5	=100
Women	55	38	8	=100	60	35	5	=100
18–29	68	27	4	=100	73	25	2	=100
30–49	60	33	6	=100	64	32	4	=100
50–64	59	35	6	=100	62	33	5	=100
65 and older	49	36	15	=100	50	39	11	=100
College grad+	72	24	4	=100	77	21	2	=100
Some college	62	33	5	=100	64	32	3	=100
H.S. grad or less	51	38	11	=100	52	39	8	=100

Source: Pew Research Center survey March 21-April 8, 2013. Q54, Q56. Figures may not sum to 100% due to rounding.

PEW RESEARCH CENTER

"Public's Views on Human Evolution," Pew Research Center, Washington, DC (December, 2013)

people often think that their attitude matches their behaviors, but our behaviors often betray our implicit attitudes, which we are not always aware of. Because surveys are fairly easy to conduct and because they are able to give us a quick view of how a population feels, thinks, and acts, they are used not only by social scientists but also by advertisers and the media. You're probably very accustomed to participating in surveys in your everyday life and/or given the results from surveys that have been conducted. From political polls (Joe Biden vs. Donald Trump) to polls on your favorite TV show (The Walking Dead vs. Game of Thrones) to your shopping experience on Amazon, we seem to be bombarded with surveys, probably to the point that we barely notice that our opinion is being surveyed. In this section, we are going to look at how surveys are constructed (what makes for a good survey versus a poor survey), the various types of surveys, and the challenges that survey researchers face. We'll also discuss the two primary ways that you can conduct a survey: interviews and questionnaires.

Constructing Your Survey

Whether you want to conduct an interview or administer a questionnaire, you will need to start by actually constructing the survey. Now this may seem easy, but as you'll see, it's actually quite challenging.

Have you ever answered a questionnaire that asked you a leading question? For example, "A recent survey of college students found that the best students spend approximately 17 hours a week studying. How much do you study per week?"; or maybe it asked you an ambiguous question ("What do you like to do?")? So what is wrong with these questions? Well, the first question is a leading question since it implies that if you don't spend at least 17 hours a week studying then you aren't a good student. It leads you to answer the question a certain way, to respond "yes." The second question is vague; just what exactly does the question refer to? What do you like to do for fun? To relax? On a date? As you can see, developing your research questions will take more thought than just writing some questions down on a page. However, as you get some practice at making good survey questions, the process gets quite a bit easier. Let's discuss a few of the things that you'll need to consider as you develop your survey.

First, what exactly are you trying to research? This needs to be exceptionally clear to you. Just stating that you want to understand parent–child relationships won't get you very far in your research. What *specifically* are you trying to investigate? How they cope with stress? Or maybe how they communicate during a disagreement? Or maybe you're interested in how they share good news with each other. Whatever the case may be, you'll need to decide what your ultimate goal is before you start developing your questions. Each question you develop should clearly assess that topic.

Second, as you start to develop the questions for your survey, you will also need to decide if the questions will be open-ended or closed-ended questions. An **open-ended question** is one in which the participant is free to answer however they choose. An example of an open-ended question might look like this:

"When you are stressed, what do you do to relax?"

A **closed-ended question** does not allow the participants to respond freely, instead you provide them with choices for answers. An example of a closed-ended question might look like this:

"When stressed, which of the following do you do to relax?
☐Meditate   ☐Read   ☐Sleep   ☐Watch TV"

As I am sure you've already guessed, both of these have their advantages and disadvantages. With open-ended questions, you have the benefit of depth of details. Participants are able to provide you with their own views and go into detail about their answers to specific questions. These questions allow you to have a more complete understanding and may fill in bits of information that may be lost with a closed-ended question. They also give your participant a lot of freedom in how they interpret and answer the questions. But there is a cost to this freedom. As a researcher, you will need to find a way to compare the responses of your participants with each other. With open-ended questions, this is often a difficult task as you may have several participants that answer in ways that are completely different from their peers. Now, while this is a limitation to the open-ended question, this is not a problem for the closed-ended question format. Since you have provided the answer choices for your participants, you can easily compare how many of your participants responded with "meditate" versus how many responded with "read", and so on. So comparing your data is not a problem with closed-ended questions, but you do end up losing the richness of detail that you can get with the open-ended responses. Maybe you have a participant who respond that they read, but to them that feels like a meditative state. Since you have only allowed them to choose from your options, you may be missing some details that would better explain their behavior. Maybe they like to read and meditate, but you've only allowed them to provide one answer. You may also leave off options that they would have chosen had they been included. You may have thought to yourself that when you are stressed you actually like to work out; you aren't alone in this. But since the researcher didn't provide that for an option, the researcher may be missing out on information or may obtain biased data since certain options were left out.

Third, you'll need to determine if you'd like your survey to be structured or unstructured. While we typically think of this dichotomy to be relevant only to interviews, it is also relevant to questionnaires. In a **structured interview**, the interview questions appear in a fixed, or standardized, order and each participant receives identical questions. If you have ever been on a job interview and seen them reading from a list of prepared questions, they were conducting a structured interview. Clinical researchers often use structured interviews when they first meet a new client. From a structured interview they can learn basic information about the client which can easily be compared to their other clients; "What is your age?", "Have you ever been in therapy before?", "Do you have a family history of mental illness?" As you can see, these are closed-ended questions. As you can probably tell, this information is relatively quick to gather. But, just like with our closed-ended questions mentioned earlier, these interviews are less flexible. You cannot ask an impromptu question based on what your client says which means that you are likely lacking details that could be important. For these reasons, some clinicians will opt for unstructured interviews to initially assess their clients. **Unstructured interviews** can be thought of as informal interviews; they do not follow a specific list of questions, questions can be asked in any order, and, as the interview progresses, some questions may be excluded (deemed not useful) while other questions will be added. Asking a client an open-ended question ("what brings you here today?") will allow you to gain a better sense of the needs, opinions, beliefs, etc. of your client (or participants), while also providing you with some flexibility. Of course these interviews tend to be much more time consuming and much harder to compare your client's responses to that of other clients.

Administering Your Survey

There are basically four main ways to distribute your survey; face-to-face interviews, over-the-phone interviews, through the mail, and electronically (via email and websites). Each of these has their advantages and their drawbacks.

Face-to-face interviews

One type of survey administration that you have probably seen at your local mall or when interviewing for a job is the face-to-face interview. Another term you may hear used for this type of interviewing is *"in-person interviews,"* both terms are correct and can be used interchangeably. As you can gather from the names, these interviews take place face-to-face. This may require you to meet at an office, travel to a person's home or place of work, or, in the case of a convenience sample, wherever groups of people are, like the mall.

There are many advantages to conducting your interview in-person. For starters, you will typically get a much higher response rate compared to the other survey types. There may be a simple reason for this (besides the fact that you can chase participants down); in an in-person interview you can build better rapport with your interviewee. When someone says that he or she has "good rapport" with another person, what they mean is that they have a friendly relationship with them. This is an important part of the interview process. Building rapport with your participants can mean that they are more likely to participate in your study, be more open and honest with you (especially about sensitive topics), and it can actually motivate them to complete your interview (even if it is long and somewhat boring). Another big advantage with in-person interviews is that it allows you (the interviewer) to evaluate your participants better. Any good instructor will tell you that it's not really about *what* a student is telling you, but *how* they tell you. I'm sure you are all familiar with your instructor asking "Does anyone have any questions?" But have you ever had an instructor keep explaining something, even when no one raised their hand? This is probably because they were reading the body language and facial expressions of you and your classmates. Oftentimes people don't want to admit that they are confused or just plain lost when it comes to a topic, so they do what a lot of us do . . . keep their mouth shut, avoid eye contact, and maybe even contort their face. By reading the cues given by the class, your instructor *should* be able to tell if they are completely lost on the topic or if they really do understand the material. As an interviewer, you will need to do this, too. Does your interviewee really understand the question? If not, you may need to clarify what a term means or what you are asking them. You may also get an answer from your interviewee that you know is a lie based on their body language or facial expression. Does your interviewee look bored? Fatigued? Agitated? Emotional? And so on. All of these can influence the results of your interview, so you need to be aware of them.

Just as there are advantages with face-to-face interviews, there are also several drawbacks. One that you may not have thought of is that they are very expensive to conduct. One of the big costs is the effort that goes into training each of your interviewers. It will be important that they are able to administer their surveys in the same way every time they give it. They also need to be able to remain neutral with responses given; not an easy task and one that takes training to accomplish. In the case of consumer report surveys (such as the type you see at the mall), you may need to pay your interviewers. If they are traveling to a specific location, such as a person's house, then you will need to provide them with transportation costs. In fact, a recent report put the cost of face-to-face interviews in the United States at close to $1,000 dollars each if you wanted to conduct an in-home, 1-hour survey (Ball, 2007, March 5). As you can imagine, this can very quickly add up. In the world of academia, you will find that you may not be able to afford to conduct your surveys in this way, even if you feel that it might be the better approach.

Another major drawback to the face-to-face interview is that you may bias the results in unintended ways. One such way is through **interviewer bias.** Simply put, you, as the interviewer, may act or behave in a way that alters the responses of your participants. Your tone of voice, the inflections in your voice, the facial expression you give, . . . these are often unintentional and done without your conscious awareness, but they can have a strong effect on the responses that you receive in the interview. Let's say that you ask your participant "Do you use condoms 100% of the time?" and they respond with "No, I would say it is closer to around 70% of the time." How do you feel about their response? Well your participants shouldn't be able to tell how you feel, but you may have given it away with your facial expression or your "hmmm." This can alter the way they will respond to you in the future. We have an innate need to be liked by others and if someone appears to dislike our responses, we may alter our behavior to fit more in line with what we believe they want to hear. This does us no good in research, where our goal is to get a snapshot of THEIR opinions, beliefs, and reported behaviors. Another response you may get from your participant is that they just shut down, they don't want to participate anymore, and they may even become antagonistic with you and your survey. As you can see, it is vitally important that you don't influence your respondents, but it is also very hard to control what we automatically do. This is where some of that training that we mentioned earlier comes in. Another aspect of the interviewer that may affect the way your participants respond to you is something that is much harder to control, and that is your personal characteristics. *Interviewer characteristics* are the characteristics that make you you (your age, gender, race, etc.) and that may influence the way that your participants respond. Why would it matter if the interviewer was Black or White? Well, it may not, but if you are asking about race issues, you may find that the race of your interviewer can influence the responses of your participants (Campbell, 1981). Interviewees might be more honest about their feelings or attitudes, particularly with less socially acceptable answers, if the interviewer is of their same race. Why do you think this might be?

Face-to-face interviews are the standard when it comes to surveys (Ball, 2007, March 5), but as we have seen, they are not perfect and may not be the best option for your research.

Over-the-phone interviews

As the name implies, over-the-phone interviews are conducted over the phone. Similar to face-to-face interviews, those conducted over the phone have a similar "human touch" factor that can be beneficial. This allows us to help clarify any confusion that the participants might have about a word or the way in which a question is asked. It can also allow us to develop some rapport, though you must do this quickly in our quick-to-hang-up-the-phone world. While training of your interviewers will still be necessary, you will find that you have more control and easier monitoring of your interviewers (you can easily sit next to them or listen in on the line or even record the interview for later playback). In addition to this, the cost of conducting your interviews over the phone is much cheaper than in-person interviews are (Cotter, Cohen, & Coulter, 1982). Finally, given the greater feeling of anonymity that your participants may feel over the phone (versus in-person), you may receive more honest answers from them.

Sometimes, in order to get a random sampling of participants, phone interviews can be conducted using what is known as a *random digit dialing (RDD)* system. Essentially, this is a computer program that will randomly dial phone numbers, even if these numbers are unlisted. This bit is actually quite important as those with listed versus unlisted numbers might be different in some meaningful way, so if we could only rely on listed phone numbers for our research we might end up with a biased sample.

Another advantage of the over-the-phone interview is that these are usually administered using a structured interview (remember from our earlier discussion that these will be easier for researchers to compare answers to one another). While the interviewer is asking the questions, they will likely be typing the responses into a computer, which will also speed up the data collection and make it easier to store and later analyze.

However, there are some rather big drawbacks to over-the-phone interviews. One common problem that occurs is that, while you are able to establish rapport with your participants, you will find that it is not as "deep" as the rapport that you can develop in face-to-face interviews. You may also run into the issue of interviewer bias and the interviewer characteristics, just as you do with face-to-face. The way in which you respond to the participants' answers; a sigh, a yawn, an audible "hmmm," can still influence participants' subsequent responses. You will also likely be judged by the interviewee (interviewer characteristics). While they may not be able to look at you and make a judgment, they can certainly determine (or at least think they can) certain things about you over the phone. Your gender, age, ethnicity, and even where you live (such as in the south or up north) can be given away just by your voice, accent, or dialect (Cotter et al., 1982). As with face-to-face interviews, though, these will usually only be an issue if the question(s) relate to that factor (so a female asking about equal pay for women may elicit a different response from a male respondent than a male interviewer asking the same question). You will also find that it is harder for you to evaluate your interviewee; are they bored, tired, confused, as opposed to a face-to-face interview where you can read their nonverbal cues, particularly facial cues, more easily.

One issue that is relatively new is probably sitting next to you right now . . . your cell phone. The National Center for Health Statistics (NCHS) estimated that in 2008, around 20% of American homes are cell-phone-only homes and another 24% of homes are mostly wireless, receiving almost all of their calls on their cell phones (Boyle, Lewis, & Tefft, 2013). There is no reason to believe that these numbers are not increasing today. The reason that this has become a problem is actually twofold. For one, cell phones and landlines have caller ID these days, something that we didn't have in the heyday of phone interviews back in the 1970s and 1980s. Caller ID has made it very easy to avoid unsolicited calls from individuals trying to conduct a survey via the phone (Kempf & Remington, 2007). The other half of this problem stems from the RDD system, which is not as adept at finding working, personal cell phones as it is at finding groups of landline phone numbers belonging to private residences (as opposed to businesses).

In addition to these issues, research has also found that homes with only cell phones differ on a key demographic; they tend to be younger. In one study, the researchers found that 60% of young adults (25–29 years of age) lived in a cell-phone-only home compared to just 9% of older adults (65+ years of age). This means that surveys using the over-the-phone technique have a greater chance of bias in their sampling by underrepresenting young adults (Blumberg et al., 2012). As you can tell, cell phones have made phone interviewing techniques troublesome, and this may lead researchers to use alternative methods in the future.

Written Questionnaires

Unlike the other two types of surveys we have already discussed, written questionnaires do not require the presence of a researcher (or interviewer) for data collection. In fact, you can easily mail out your survey (e-mail or regular mail) or post your survey online, using one of the many survey sites available to you, such as SurveyMonkey. Sounds easy, right? Well in some ways, it certainly is. In general, written questionnaires will be much cheaper than an in-person or over-the-phone interview. There is less chance that you will have any interviewer bias (as the interviewer in this case is a piece of paper or a computer screen and would be less likely to provide biasing cues to the interviewee). This isn't to say that there is no bias in written surveys, in fact, it is quite possible to bias participants' responses with your language choice. Both of your authors are from Texas, and here in Texas we use a word that is quite common around here, but if you were to use it in some parts of the United States, you might be considered just some "dumb redneck". Any ideas what it is? The word is "y'all" (for any of you reading this that aren't from the south, this word is a combination of the words "you" and "all," and, quite honestly, makes a whole lot of sense to use!—not that we're biased). But it isn't just about your regional word choices, you can also bias your participants by using language that is too advanced or too simplistic. You also have to worry about the clarity of your questions and word choices. Unlike with face-to-face or over-the-phone interviews, if your respondents don't understand the question or a word you have chosen to use, you aren't there to clarify it for them.

However, your lack of a presence may provide you with an advantage, especially when asking about sensitive topics (such as the participants' sex lives and drug use). I'll give you an example of this from my own experiences with surveys.

> While in graduate school, I received an email from another university's psychology program asking for participants in an online survey to help someone with their dissertation. As a graduate student, a part of you believes in karma and thinks that if you help this graduate student out that other individuals will in turn help you out in your time of research need. So, I open the survey which contains a disclaimer that it would be asking about "your sex life and experiences." It started off pretty standard, nothing that I would necessarily have difficultly answering in person (e.g., "are you in a relationship," "have you had sex"). Then came the following question: "What is the most embarrassing thing that has ever happened to you while having sex." Now I want you to think about that for a second. Can you imagine answering that question in a face-to-face interview? If you start to cringe at that thought, you aren't alone. Not only does it ask about an actual sexual experience, but it asks about an embarrassing experience. As a rule, I try not to discuss those, because, well, they're embarrassing. But in a written survey, administered online, there was a greater sense of anonymity.

This is why written questionnaires can be preferable over in-person interviews. The greater sense that they truly are anonymous can help them to open up and be more honest. But, with this anonymity comes the risk of lying, because people do lie, and unlike with our interviews, we won't be able to judge the respondents using nonverbal cues to determine if they may be fibbing. In fact, we don't really have any cue that they are lying, just a sheet of paper or a computer screen where they have marked off their responses.

In general, the cost of a written questionnaire will be much cheaper than the other two types we have already discussed. Moreover, if you choose to administer your questionnaire online (as opposed to mailing it out through regular mail), it will be even cheaper. This is because you don't have to worry about training costs or supply costs. This makes them a desirable alternative to interviews. Also, given the way our world has become so connected via the internet, a researcher can easily disseminate their survey online to targeted groups; for instance, through support groups, blogs, and fan pages. These convenience samples can be useful when examining certain topics; however, you need to be concerned about using these groups for generalizing the findings to the population as a whole as they may not be representative of the population. You must always keep in mind that when you use a convenience sample, they may differ markedly from the general population in important ways. If you use a sample on a food blog about family meals and ask them how often they cook meals for their family, it is completely possible that their responses would be unrepresentative of the general population. Men and women who

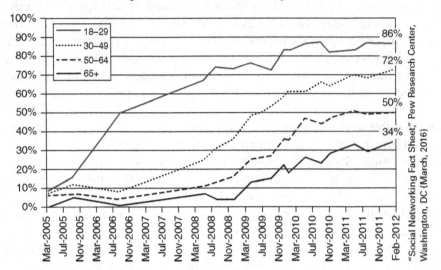

Social networking site use by age group, 2005-2012

% of adult internet users age 18+ who use social networking sites

Notice that younger individuals are more likely to use social networking sites than other age groups. If you are using a social networking site to recruit participants then you will likely not get a representative sample of the general population.

follow food blogs that are designed to help you plan family dinners are likely more concerned about having family dinners than those individuals who choose not to follow these blogs. Also, while it seems that all of us are plugged into the Internet and social media, we aren't. So when we use an online survey measure, we have to keep in mind that those who use the Internet differ in important ways from those who do not. In addition, for those of us that use the Internet, we do so for different reasons. Studies have found that Internet users, particularly those on social networking sites (see Figure below) tend to be younger (Zickuhr & Madden, 2012), and that those using the Internet for product information and news score higher on measures of Need for Cognition and lower on measures of Neuroticism (Tuten & Bosnjak, 2001)

There is still one issue we haven't talked about yet, and it's probably the biggest issue . . . return rates. Whether it is in your mailbox or your inbox, we tend to dislike junk mail. Anything that looks like junk mail is usually sent to the trash bin right away. Even if you do open the survey that is sent you, estimates on return rates are dismal (the average response rate is typically between 10% and 20%), especially when we compare them to our interviewing rates, which can reach upward of 80%. There are things you can do to increase your mailed response rate, such as sending reminders, but your response rates will be lower nonetheless. In addition, you will have to consider that there are differences between those who responded to your survey and those who didn't. Just as we discussed earlier, you will need to question if they are different in a meaningful way, and if so, it will affect your ability to draw conclusions using their data.

Final Thoughts on Surveys

So, why would we use surveys over one of the other research techniques? It seems that no matter how we conduct a survey, we are going to run into problems that can affect our data. Well this is true of all types of research, but we still need to do it and do our best to select the most appropriate research approach. Surveys allow us to ask people questions on a variety of topics and easily compare their results to other individuals. Surveys are an excellent way of obtaining a large amount of information, usually in a short amount of time. At our university, as well as others around the world, we have faculty members, graduate students, and even some undergraduate students conducting research. Some of that research involves studies where participants come into the laboratory to complete and some utilize online surveys. Which studies do you think undergraduate students are most likely to participate in? Yep, online surveys. We've seen online survey studies collect data from over one thousand individuals in one week! Compared to some of the other techniques used in research, surveys are relatively inexpensive (with online surveys usually being the cheapest). Surveys allow us to better understand how our participants are thinking, what they believe, and how they think they behave. This information can be useful on its own but can later be used in other types of research (such as in determining your groups for a quasi-experiment).

A survey won't always be the right choice for your research. You always need to decide what your ultimate goal is and which approach will allow you to reach that goal most effectively. If you are wanting to get a snapshot of a population, then a survey (whether it be in-person, over-the-phone, or written) may be the best option for you.

Concluding Remarks

As we've seen from this chapter, there are several nonexperimental methods that can be used to evaluate whatever behavior or issue that you'd like to study. Each of these techniques provides different information and approaches the study of that behavior in different ways. Due to these differences, there are certain advantages that each of these methods provide. Further, there are certain weaknesses that each of these methods possess as well. As a competent and knowledgeable researcher, it's up to you to carefully weigh these advantages and disadvantages along with the ultimate goals that you have. As mentioned throughout this chapter, each of these nonexperimental techniques allows you to describe or better understand certain behaviors. In the next chapter, we'll be describing some additional nonexperimental techniques. The techniques discussed in the next chapter will also allow us to describe and better understand the studied behaviors or topics, but they will also allow us to make predictions based on the findings of the studies. However, keep in mind, none of the nonexperimental techniques allows us to make causal statements; experiments will be discussed in subsequent chapters.

References

Ball (2007, March 5). Available from http://www.news.cornell.edu/stories/2007/03 despite-allure-internet-surveys-face-face-interview-best

Blumberg, S. J., Luke, J. V., Ganesh, N., Davern, M. E., & Boudreauz, M. H. (2012). *Wireless substitution: State-level estimates from the National Health Interview Survey, 2010–2011.* National health statistics reports; no 61. Hyattsville, MD: National Center for Health Statistics. Retrieved from: http://198.246.124.22/nchs/data/nhsr/nhsr061.pdf

Boyle, J. M, Lewis, F., & Tefft, B. (2013, August) Cell phone mainly households: Coverage and reach for telephone surveys using RDD landline samples. *Survey Practice, 2*(9). ISSN 2168-0094. Retrieved December 20, 2015, from http://www.surveypractice.org/index.php/SurveyPractice/article/view/202

Campbell, B. A. (1981). Race-of-interviewer effects among Southern adolescents. *Public Opinion Quarterly, 45*(2), 231–244. doi: 10.1086/268654

Cotter, P. R., Cohen, J., & Coulter, P. B. (1982). Race-of-interviewer effects in telephone interviews. *Public Opinion Quarterly, 46*(2), 278–284. doi: 10.1086/268719

Festinger, L., Riecken, H. W., & Schachter, S. (1956). *When prophecy fails.* Minneapolis, MN, US: University of Minnesota Press. doi: 10.1037/10030-000

Gottman, J. M., & Levenson, R. W. (1992). Marital processes predictive of later dissolution: Behavior, physiology, and health. *Journal of Personality and Social Psychology, 63*(2), 221–233. doi: 10.1037/0022-3514.63.2.221

Kempf, A. M., & Remington, P. L. (2007). New challenges for telephone survey research in the twenty-first century. *Annual Review of Public Health, 28,* 113–126. doi: 10.1146/annurev. publhealth.28.021406.144059

Pew Research Center (2013). Retrieved from http://www.pewforum.org/2013/12/30/publics-views-on-human-evolution/?utm_medium=App.net&utm_source=PourOver

Tuten, T. L., & Bosnjak, M. (2001). Understanding differences in web usage: The role of need for cognition and the five factor model of personality. *Social Behavior and Personality, 29*(4), 391–398. doi: 10.2224/sbp.2001.29.4.391

Zickuhr, K., & Madden, M. (2012) *Older adults and Internet use.* Retrieved from http://www.pewinternet.org/files/old-media//Files/Reports/2012/PIP_Older_adults_and_internet_use.pdf

End of Chapter Quiz

___1. Which of the nonexperimental techniques utilizes an empirical approach?
   a. observation   c. case study   e. only b and c
   b. survey research   d. all of the above   f. only a and b

___2. A social psychologist who observes the aggressive behavior of children on the school playground is using:
   a. content analysis   d. participant observation
   b. naturalistic observation e. structured interview
   c. deviant case analysis

___3. Experimenters use unobstrusive measures to:
   a. assess behavior without subject knowledge
   b. conceal the true purpose of the interview questions
   c. count behaviors as they occur
   d. obtain more accurate self-reports

___4. When Anastasi and Lee (2016) investigated drug use in professional soccer players by acting as members of a local community team, they were utilizing the _____ method.
   a. archival study   c. field experiment   e. none of the above
   b. ex post facto study d. participant-observer

___5. Researchers conduct experiments in laboratories to achieve the greatest degree of:
   a. generalizability   c. objectivity   e. none of the above
   b. control   d. realism

___6. Which type of survey approach allows the researcher to most easily compare responses from participants?
   a. open-ended   c. structured   e. only A & C
   b. closed-ended   d. unstructured   f. only B & D

___7. In a(n) _____ interview, the same questions are asked of participants in the same order.
   a. unstructured   c. directed
   b. structured   d. undirected

___8. What types of information are surveys NOT good at getting information about?
   a. opinions   c. observed behaviors   e. beliefs
   b. attitudes   d. reported behaviors   f. all of the above

___9. Each of the following was discussed as a way to conduct survey research EXCEPT:
   a. face-to-face   d. through the mail
   b. written questionnaire   e. online
   c. over-the-phone   f. all of the above were discussed

___10. Each of the following are important problems that one might expect to face when using surveys EXCEPT:
   a. lying   c. return rates   e. answering truthfully
   b. interviewer bias   d. biased responses

Homework Assignment #1

For each of the following studies, your task is to evaluate each and determine which of the nonexperimental techniques is being used. While some of these could be conducted in different ways, try your best to evaluate the most likely nonexperimental approach and provide a brief explanation for why you've selected the option that you opted. Select from the following options for each study:

Case study   Naturalistic observation   Laboratory observation   Survey

1. Research indicates that the average American is sleeping less than the recommended 8 hours of sleep per night. On average, Americans are only sleeping 7.2 hours per night.

2. A young man with severe epilepsy had his corpus collosum severed, making it so that the right and left hemispheres of his brain were no longer able to communicate with each other. In order to better understand his capabilities, an in-depth study was conducted to evaluate what tasks he was able to still engage in as well as those that he had difficulty with. Additionally, his friends and family members were also asked about any personality changes or other changes that may also be relevant to better understand how he may have changed following the surgery.

3. A recent study found that the older we get, the quieter we are in social situations. Participants were invited to several social get-togethers at a local community outreach center. The number of times that they spoke as well as the number of words that they used was recorded. The study found that the older the participants were, the fewer times they spoke with other individuals and the fewer words that they used.

4. Although fruits and vegetables can be rich sources of antioxidants, recent research indicates that coffee is the primary source of antioxidants for most Americans.

5. Mary is an older woman who was approximately 64 years old and working as a nurse prior to her automobile accident. She was having minor memory issues, which was normal for women of her age. Following the severe automobile accident, she suffered some brain hemorrhaging that was undiagnosed. As a result of the accident and the undiagnosed hemorrhaging, her memory issues and subsequent dementia became progressively more severe. This study evaluated Mary every 6 months for the next 10 years to document her progression.

6. Although 90% of the students indicated they did not like wearing uniforms, various benefits to wearing uniforms were reported in a recent study, including decreases in discipline, gang involvement and bullying; and increases in safety, ease of going to school, confidence, and self-esteem.

7. A researcher is interested in better understanding how many times parents speak to 2-year-old children when the children are playing. Therefore, the researcher brings the children and adults into a controlled, playground environment equipped with many toys to measure the number of interactions between the adult and child.

8. Recent research shows that higher dietary fiber intake in young women may reduce the risk of breast cancer.

9. A group of researchers wished to evaluate the ability of high schoolers to effectively verbally communicate information in a professional manner. Each high school student was given a page of fairly complex information to look at and then was asked to provide a brief summary of the information. The number of pauses, breaks, or filler words (i.e., "um") were recorded to indicate their fluency. Their responses were also evaluated for their clarity.

10. A recent study evaluated the impact of weather and aggressive behavior in children playing on playgrounds. The study found that children were more likely to behave aggressively toward other children when the temperatures were extremely hot (i.e., above 95°F), but not when the temperature was cold or moderately hot.

Homework Assignment #2

Think about a research problem that you could investigate using a nonexperimental approach. First, describe the research question (hypothesis). Second, describe how you could answer this research question using each of the following nonexperimental research approaches. If you don't think this approach can be used to answer this question, explain in detail why the approach cannot be used.

1. Case study

2. Laboratory observation

3. Naturalistic observation

4. Survey

Chapter 5

Nonexperimental Methods: Part II

In Chapter 4, we looked at some of the various nonexperimental techniques employed by researchers. In this chapter we will continue with four other types of nonexperimental research used in psychology: *correlational research, quasi-experiments, archival research*, and *meta-analyses*. Just as with the other techniques discussed in the last chapter, these approaches will not have manipulated variables. They also will not allow for random assignment to the research groups.

Correlational Research

In psychology you hear the word "correlation" a lot, but what exactly does a correlation look at? **Correlational research** allows us to look at how two or more variables are related to each other (their association to one another). These variables are naturally occurring events that we can measure (not something that we manipulate). While it doesn't allow us to make a causal statement (if X then Y will happen), it does allow us to predict the probability that something will happen. Correlations are all around us, a quick look at the news or even on your Facebook page tells us that late-night snacking may have an effect on your memory (Howard, 2016); drinking soda as a child is linked to violent behavior (Associated Press, 2011); that yoga is better for your mood than other types of exercise (Chavis, 2010), and that football players are more likely to develop neurodegenerative disease (Kounang, 2012). But with the abundant amount of correlational research available to us at the touch of a button these days, there are concerns about how they are interpreted. As you learned in Chapter 1, it is important to be a smart consumer of scientific research, but sadly, a lot people are not, and so they see a news story or a shared post like the ones just mentioned and they take it as a fact; that giving your child soda will make them violent or that playing football will give you a neurodegenerative disease. Correlational research doesn't provide us with enough information to say that these things will happen, only that they are linked. They also inform us that we can predict the likelihood of one event occurring if we know about the other event. Let's now take a look at how we do that. To begin with, let's look at a simple explanation of how a correlation works.

> Let's say I have behavior X and behavior Y, and I want to see if they are related to one another. I begin by measuring behavior X and then measuring behavior Y. I then compute my correlational statistics to determine if there is a relationship between the two behaviors (see Chapter 8 for more on the statistics used for correlational research).

Notice that I am not actually manipulating anything; the behaviors are naturally occurring, and I am just measuring them. Don't let this make you think it isn't research or scientific, because it is (and psychology is by no means the only science that uses this technique). So, how does this look in the real world? Well, most universities use correlational research to determine how you will perform in college. They have examined prior students' Scholastic Assessment Test (SAT) scores and their performance in college. Using correlational research, they found a relationship between these scores and have used the information on incoming students. This is one reason why you take the SAT; the correlational research tells us that we can (somewhat) predict how well you will do in college by looking at your SAT score (with around 10—20% of the variation explained by your score; Paulos, 2015). But, knowing two variables are related doesn't really give you the whole picture. As with the SAT scores, the variance explained is actually pretty low, but if you aren't aware of how to read correlations, you may not realize that. So now, let's look more closely at correlations and how to interpret them.

Understanding the Correlation

When you see a correlation written out, it will range from -1 to +1. The most common type of correlation is the Pearson product moment correlation and it is represented by the letter r (known as a **correlation coefficient**). Each correlation provides us with two pieces of information: the direction and the strength.

First, the direction of the relationship is determined by the positive or negative sign before the number. A **positive correlation** will be marked with a plus sign (+) and means that the variables move in the same direction. This means that as one variable increases in their score, so does the other. It also means that as one of the variable's score decreases, the other variable's score decreases. For example, there is a positive correlation between smoking and alcohol. This means that as your smoking increases, so does your drinking.

A **negative correlation** will be marked with a minus sign (-) and means that the variables move in opposite directions. As one variable's score increases the other variable decreases on their score. As an example, there is a negative correlation between the number of days you skip class and your grade in the class. This means that the higher the number of days of class you miss, the lower your grade will be.

Now, I'm sure you have thought of instances in both of the examples provided that "disprove" these correlations. For instance, maybe you drink alcohol but you never smoke, or maybe you skip class but it has no effect on your grade (you're still making an A). Remember, correlations do not equal causation, we are merely describing a relationship between variables. This relationship may not hold for each individual, but it does describe the general trend when the data from our sample is put together. To determine just how well we can predict an outcome, then, we need to look at the *strength of the relationship*.

So how do we determine strength? The number given in a correlation provides us with this information. When viewing a correlation coefficient, you are given a number along with the sign. As we already learned, the sign tells us the direction of the relationship, but the number, viewed as an absolute value (just looking at the number), tells us how strongly the variables are related to each other. So a $r = +0.29$ and a $r = -0.29$ are equal in strength, but "move" in different ways.

So remember that it is the number of the correlation that determines the strength of the relationship, not the sign of the correlation (which gives of the direction). Regardless of the direction, if the absolute value of the correlation is closer to 1, it is stronger; so $r = -0.85$ is stronger than $r = +0.75$. A correlation of 0, then, means that there is a zero relationship between the variables. A perfect correlation would be a +1 or a −1, but those rarely occur in nature, so most correlations will fall somewhere in between.

One last note about strength, when reading a study, you will likely see the words "weak," "moderate," or "strong" to describe a correlation. This is meant to describe how strong the relationship is, but there is not a standard index for these terms, so be cautious when you see them. One of the more commonly used guidelines for determining the strength of a correlation was provided by Cohen (1988). Cohen uses the terms small ($r = .10–.29$), medium ($r = .30–.49$), and large ($r = .50–1.00$) to describe a relationship between variables. Just remember that these terms are subjective and they fail to capture the true meaning of the data.

Scatterplots

A **scatterplot** is a visual depiction of a correlation using graphs. A scatterplot graphs each data point along the X and Y axis of your graph. The X axis represents values for one of your variables and the Y axis represents values for the other variable, with each dot representing the point where they intersect. From a scatterplot you can determine the direction of a relationship and how strong it is, even without knowing the actual correlation coefficient.

Figure 5.1 shows examples of scatterplots. As you can see in the examples, the closer the dots are to each other, the stronger the relationship is between the variables. In statistical analyses, we would draw what is known as the *line of best fit*. This line can be imagined as running through the middle of our dots. The closer the dots cluster to that line, the stronger the relationship, regardless if it is a positive or negative relationship. As you can see in our last example in Figure 5.1, no matter where you draw your line, you will not see a relationship. The time of the exam and the grade on the exam are not related to each other. Some students do well if the time is early, some when it is late. Conversely, some students do very poorly when the time of the exam is early, while others do poorly when the time is late. Remember, a correlation coefficient of 0 means that there is zero relationship between the variables. No matter your anecdotal evidence, there is still no relationship between these variables. The first two scatterplots in Figure 5.1 allow us to determine the direction by looking to see if the variables move in the same direction. By looking at the first one, we can see that as your scores on the SAT increase, so does your Grade Point Average (GPA), thus showing a positive correlation between SAT scores and GPA. Conversely, the second scatterplot shows us a negative relationship between variables. As your hours spent watching TV increase, your GPA decreases. Note that the data points on this one are not nearly as tightly clustered as with our first scatterplot. This indicates that while there is a relationship, it is not as strong. So yes, the actual correlation coefficient is important and can tell you how your variables are related, but a scatterplot can visually depict the relationship and provide the same outcome.

You have probably heard this before even reading this book, but correlations do not equal causation. This is one of the most important pieces of information to keep in mind as you read through research. Studies have demonstrated that children watching violence on television show more violence later on in their teenage and young adult lives (Anderson et al., 2003). But what exactly does this research show? Well, in the case of Anderson et al., it shows a correlation, meaning that there is a relationship but that we cannot claim that television violence causes the later aggression in teenagers and young adults. Remember, since this is a correlation, nothing has been manipulated and we haven't assigned any participants to groups; we are just observing two variables as they naturally occur. In fact, two of the issues with correlations is something that we have already discussed in Chapter 2—*directionality* and *the third variable problem*. As you may recall, the problem with **directionality** is that we cannot determine which variable is influencing the other. So it could be that violence on television has led to higher displays of aggression in adulthood, or it could be that those who are prone to aggression are more likely to watch aggressive television when they are children. It is also possible that the two variables influence each

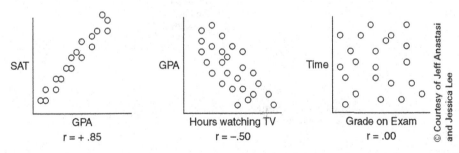

Figure 5.1 Note that even without the correlation coefficient provided, you would be able to determine whether the relationship between the variables were positively or negatively correlated as well as how strongly they are correlated.

Correlations ≠ Causation

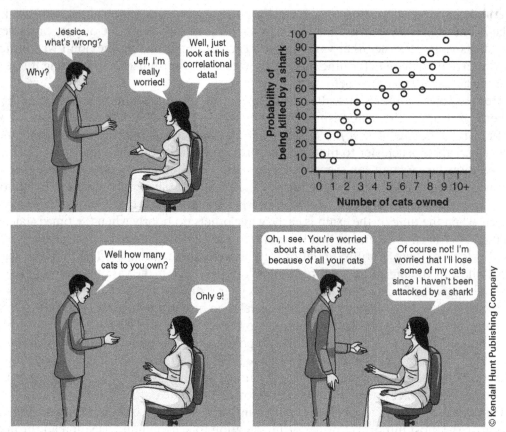

What mistake is Jeff and Jessica making in their discussion of this *fictional* correlational study?

other; maybe aggressive individuals are more prone to watch aggressive television and watching aggressive television makes them more prone to act in aggressive ways. The point is that with correlational research alone, we cannot determine anything beyond that a relationship between the variables is present. The second problem that we have previously discussed is that of the third variable. The **third-variable problem** argues that there is an alternative explanation that better explains the changes in one or both of your variables better than either of them can alone. Let's take a look at Figure 5.2 for an example that demonstrates this.

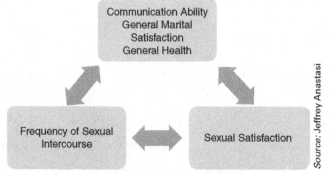

Figure 5.2 Is there are relationship between sexual satisfaction and the frequency of sexual intercourse?

It probably won't surprise you to find out that there is a positive correlation between sexual satisfaction and sexual intercourse. As we have already discussed, based on directionality, this could mean that the more sexual intercourse you have, the more sexually satisfied you are (makes sense), but it could also mean that the more sexually satisfied you are, the more sexual intercourse you will have (also makes sense). But, what might not be as obvious is that this relationship is actually better explained by several other variables—you and your partner's communication ability, your overall level of marital satisfaction (or dissatisfaction), and your overall health. It turns out, that those three variables better explain both sexual satisfaction and frequency of sexual intercourse better than those two variables alone do. And this turns out to be a big issue in correlational research; you can never be sure, based on correlational research alone, that you do not have some other variable that you haven't thought of yet that better explains the relationship.

Some other issues that can occur when conducting correlational research have to do with the measurements themselves. Three of these issues will be discussed: nonlinear relationships, restricted ranges (or truncated ranges), and different populations (outliers). (Each of these are discussed in detail in the statistics chapters of this book.)

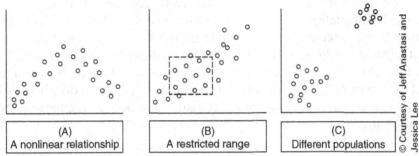

Figure 5.3   Special issues with correlations.

When you conduct a Pearson's *r*, what you are looking at is a linear relationship between two variables, but what happens when the relationship isn't linear? Does that mean that there isn't a relationship at all? Nonlinear relationships are easy to spot if you are using a scatterplot, but if you are relying solely on your correlation coefficient you might miss them. Imagine that you have a speech you have to give in your class that accounts for 30% of your grade. Are you nervous? Chances are, you should be, at least a little. If you aren't nervous, it could mean that you just don't care. That probably means that you won't make a very good grade on your speech. But what about the opposite; what if you are very nervous? Can being too anxious negatively affect your grade? Absolutely, anyone who dislikes public speaking can attest to the negative effects that nerves can have on performance—shaky voice, lots of "ums," stuttering, shaking from head-to-toe, etc. And not surprisingly, this fear tends to lower your performance and therefore your grade. So, who is likely to do the best? The person who is nervous, but not too nervous. This hypothetical situation would create a pattern similar to the one shown in Figure 5.3, example A. While the relationship is clearly not linear, there is certainly something going on here. All you need to do is look at the scatterplot and you can clearly see that there is a relationship between the performance and the nervousness. But if you had just relied on your correlation coefficient, you would fail to see that relationship since a line of best fit would not work here.

Now let's look at the situation depicted in Figure 5.3. example B. This is an example of what a restricted range might look like. A restricted range occurs when we are overly narrow on one or both variables. Restricted ranges lead to errors in claims of directions, strength, and whether the relationship is linear or nonlinear. Let's take a simple example for this illustration. Do you think there is a relationship between a child's age (2–15 years of age) and their shoe size? Sure. We would expect that there would be a positive correlation here; the older the child, the larger their shoe size. But let's say that I restrict the age range I'm looking at and only look at the children between the ages of 6 and 7. This might give us a scenario like the one depicted in our figure—while there is a relationship overall, the limited range that I am looking at (the dashed box) fails to capture it because it is too limited. If I based my results off of these two age groups I would likely conclude that there is no relationship between the age a child is and their shoe size, but clearly, based on our full data, there is a relationship there.

Finally, let's look at our last example in Figure 5.3. In this case, we are basing our correlation off of data that are looking at two different populations. This is the case where we have outliers in our data that are affecting our findings. Outliers can either increase the strength of the correlation (if it falls along the line of best fit) or decrease it (if it falls farther away from the line of best fit). In the case of our graph, the outliers in the upper right hand corner would increase the strength of our correlation, indicating that there is a relationship while just looking at the lower data (ignoring the outliers in the upper corner) suggests that there is likely no relationship or at the very best, a weak one. Clearly, the data points in the upper right hand corner represent a different sort of subject from those clustered down in the bottom left corner. As a hypothetical example, imagine that we were to compare the width of the brain of individuals of average and above average intelligence to see if there is a relationship. Some researchers have claimed that Einstein's brain was around 20% wider than the average brain. So let's make him our outlier. If we conducted this study and found the relationship similar to the one depicted in our figure, we would (based on the correlation coefficient) incorrectly conclude that there is a positive relationship between brain width and intelligence. Just because some people do have a wider brain, doesn't mean that they are the norm for our species. In fact, Neanderthals had wider brains than the average human does today, but most scientist would agree that we are more intelligent today than our ancestors from 200,000 years ago. But by looking at our scatterplot we can see that our data are being affected by outliers that don't represent the majority of individuals in the population. (What to do when outliers appear in your data is something you should cover in advanced statistic courses.) Clearly, the moral of these three issues is to always look at your scatterplot!

Final Thoughts on Correlational Research

At this point you might be wondering if correlational research is even worth all these issues. The simple and short answer is, Yes. Correlations are useful because they can tell us if variables are related and in what way they are related to each other. This is important if you plan on doing later research. As you will see in Chapters 6 and 7, when we conduct experiments and form our hypothesis, we have more statistical power if we can predict how the data will react. With a correlation we have an idea of how the relationship works. We also can determine if it is even worth our time and effort to conduct and experiment. If I find that two variables are only correlated at $r = 0.10$ (a very small correlation), then I might decide that it isn't worth my time to conduct an experiment. We sometimes conduct correlations first because they are easier and cheaper to do than a full blown experiment. As you will find in the next chapter, experimental research is not an easy process, and if I know going into the study that the two variables of interest aren't strongly related, I can save myself time and money.

And one very big benefit of a correlation (and really all nonexperimental research) is that I can look at variables that would be unethical to manipulate. You hear a lot in the media that smoking and lung cancer are related. Erroneously, people think that this is based on experimentation. But really, how could it be? We cannot randomly assign you to either smoke a pack of cigarettes a day or not. It just wouldn't be ethical. But I can conduct a correlational study to see if there is a relationship between smoking and lung cancer. While it won't allow me to say that smoking *causes* lung cancer, it will allow me to predict that it will with a degree of certainty. A lot of the theories that you hear about in psychology are based on correlational research because it would be either impossible or unethical for us to experimentally test them. For instance: Do children of divorce suffer from higher levels of psychological problems? Does the amount of time spent in active conflict increase the likelihood of developing posttraumatic stress disorder (PTSD)? I cannot imagine a situation where either of these questions could ethically be tested using experimentation. So for psychology, where we deal with issues of mental health and relationships (and many other topics), correlations may be the only option for some of these topics.

Quasi-Experiments

A **quasi-experiment** is going to be similar to a true experiment, but it will lack control groups and random assignment. In essence, a quasi-experiment is *like* an experiment, but not quite an experiment. While correlational research looks at how variables are related to each other, a quasi-experiment goes further. Where possible, it manipulates variables (such as the race of a photograph shown). But you are not able to manipulate at least one variable. These variables are known as **subject variables.** A subject variable is a variable related to the participants; such as their age, race, gender, mental health. As you can imagine these types of variables are of particular interest in psychology, a field that studies human behavior. But, no matter how much we want to, we cannot manipulate certain aspects of our participants. Sometimes it is due to ethical reasons (e.g., smoking vs. nonsmoking individuals) and sometimes it is because it just cannot be changed (e.g., male vs. female). Now, you may be thinking, "Well can't we just change their appearance, even if it is temporary?" Simply put, no. While you could add makeup to a person to make them look like a different race or to change their weight, or any other number of physical alterations, the fact is they do not have the same life experiences as someone who grew up that way.

Here is an example of a quasi-experiment. Let's say that I want to look at the effects of aging on your IQ. I decide to compare the IQ scores of two age groups: 75–80 year-olds and 20–25 year-olds. After administering my IQ tests, I find that the older adult group has an average IQ of 85, while the younger adult group has an average IQ of 110. After running my analyses, I find that this difference is statistically significant. So, can I conclude that advanced age leads to a decrease in IQ based on this study? NO! Just as we discussed with our correlational research, there could be a third variable here that we have not considered. Now, it is quite possible that advanced age leads to declines in intelligence, but it is also possible that the experience with standardized tests (including IQ tests) differs between my groups, that their educational background had an impact on their scores, or perhaps it just a matter of motivation. I don't know about you, but my grandmother really couldn't care less what an IQ test said about her. Nothing about that score is really going to change anything about her life. She isn't going to go out and find a new career with this information. She isn't going to redefine herself based on a high or low score. But a young adult probably would care. At 20 years of age, you don't want to be labeled as having a low IQ, so you are more motivated to do well on the test because it holds more meaning to you. You are just more motivated. This could explain the difference in the scores. I'm sure you can think of several other reasons that these groups might perform differently.

But why is this example a quasi-experiment and not a true experiment? Think back to our groups, older adults and younger adults. As you should recall from Chapter 2 and Chapter 4, a true experiment means that you can randomly assign your participants to the groups. Can you do this with our IQ study? If I were to randomly assign my participants to either group, then I would end up with individuals in each group that don't belong there (I would have 20 year-olds in my older group and 80 year-olds in my younger group). Since we clearly cannot randomly assign our participants, we are not able to make causal claims with our findings. In addition to not being able to randomly assign my participants, I will also not be able to randomly select my participants from the population (this may not happen in a true experiment, too). In this case, I cannot randomly select from the population because, again, I would end up with a lot of individuals in my study that I'm not interested in (such as a 50 year-old). Both assignment and selection issues will mean that we will have bias in our study. But it is due to our lack of random assignment that we will be unable to make a causal statement with regard to our findings.

A quasi-experiment is somewhat similar to correlational research, albeit with much more control. While correlational research looks at variables as they happen naturally, quasi-experiments allow us to have some control over the variables, although we still aren't able to manipulate these variables. And really, they are quite common in psychological research. So why don't you see researchers labeling their work as a quasi-experiment? It's nothing nefarious, instead, it is because they know that those individuals reading their research will recognize that their study is using a subject variable. If you read a study that says that they compared the scores of men versus women on some test, you shouldn't need the researchers to tell you that they didn't randomly assign their participants to be either male or female, you should just know that they didn't. And because they didn't use random assignment, you should also know that they cannot make a causal claim as to why they obtained their results.

Another consideration you must keep in mind as you read and conduct this type of research is that there are always alternative explanations for interpreting your results. For instance, when IQ tests were first introduced they were used to separate various groups. In fact, you may still hear people make outrageous claims such as "White people are just smarter than Blacks…just look at how they perform on an IQ test." This statement is based on faulty (and bigoted) interpretations of research. As you have already surmised, this has to be a quasi-experiment (and not just because it is in this section). We know that we cannot randomly assign someone to be either Black or White, so random assignment will be out of the question. But what this research failed to do was to look at other variables that might affect IQ scores, such as one's socioeconomic status (SES). The American Psychological Association (APA) published a report showing that Black children are three times more likely to be of a lower SES than White children (American Psychological Association, 2016). Living in poverty comes with its own issues, all of which can have an impact on IQ. For instance, in the same report, the APA found that minority children (particularly Black and Hispanic children) are much more likely to go to a school in a high-poverty area and that these two groups represent the highest dropout rates of all students. Even among high-achieving Black students, those living in poverty are less likely to receive a challenging curriculum, they have fewer resources available to them at school (such as computers), and their teachers expect much less out of them compared to their White counterparts. Further, living in poverty will also affect one's access to healthy foods, which can have an adverse effect on your IQ. All of these issues could explain the difference in IQ rates among groups. So what can you do? One solution is to use *matching*. **Matching subjects** (or a **matched-groups design**) is pretty much what it sounds like; you match a subject in one group (in this case Black student) to a subject in the other group (White student) on all factors other than the variable of interest. So for our example, we would ensure that they are of a similar SES, have similar educational resources, diet, etc. Then we can compare the scores to each other to see if there is a difference in IQ scores between Whites and Blacks (as a side note: there's not a difference). Matching is a great solution to this issue, but it is not without its faults. One major issue with matching is that you may lose participants; for example, if a participant decides that he or she no longer wants to participate in the study. When this happens in a matched-groups study, you must also drop his or her matched counterpart (because you have no score to compare his or her counterpart to). But even with the best matching, we will never be able to make a causal statement; there is always the chance there is some other variable we haven't controlled for.

So why then do we use quasi-experiments? Well, just like with correlational research, we may not actually be interested in causal claims. Instead, we are just wanting to know if there is a relationship there. Of course, it is very likely that you conduct this type of research because it is the only way you will be able to study a particular variable (such as race). Due to ethics or just feasibility, there are just some variables we cannot manipulate, leaving us with quasi-experiments as our only option.

Archival Research

You may decide that you want to examine behavior that has already occurred but that you did not directly observe. When you use information that comes from outside your research, such as government documents (e.g., census reports, crime reports, marriage licenses), the media (e.g., news reports, documentaries), personal documents (e.g., photographs, letters, emails), and any other form of preexisting records, you are using **archival data**. Archival data is useful to see changes in groups or trends over time. Maybe you are interested in understanding how the media has depicted minorities in films and whether there has been a change over the last 20 years; you can access this by viewing films during this time frame. But don't think this is going to be as easy as a binge session on Netflix. Just like with our observational research, you will need to develop a coding system, operationally define your terms, and train your observers. The benefit of archival research over observation is that you cannot influence the behavior of the group(s) you are observing since you have no contact with them as the behavior occurs.

Sounds good, right? I mean, the data have already been collected for you, you just have to access it. Well that is actually the biggest potential problem to archival research. While it is possible to access some information (and for relatively cheap), you have to worry about the completeness of the data. For instance, if we were interested in how minorities have been depicted in movies, we would need access to all the films that were made during that period, but if you are solely relying on those that are available through a streaming service like Netflix, you won't have access to all of the films. You also, regardless of how you access the movies, will find it difficult to find all of them, and if you are missing films, you are missing information and that information may be important for your interpretation of the data. Completeness of data is especially concerning when you are trying to access public records. While you can have access to marriage licenses, divorce decrees, etc. you are limited on the amount of information that they provide. Let's say that you are wanting to determine if the number of individuals going to the hospital emergency room has changed since the addition of new emergency clinics; you can gain access to the number of individuals going to each, but you will not be able to have access to the patient information due to HIPAA law. So it

Even personal photograph collections can be used for archival research. They can provide valuable information about a person's past, a time period, photographing techniques, etc.

is not just having an incomplete record that is the concern here, but also our ability to gain access to the information we are interested in. This means that our interpretation of the data should always be cautious and you should always remember that it is only descriptive in nature. Recently, research has shown that the divorce rate is decreasing slightly (just under 50%), but this seems to be the case only for those individuals who are more educated (the numbers have not changed for those with less education). Good news for you as you are reading this textbook, but when you hear information like that, remember that it is only describing the data. While knowing that an education may protect you from divorce, it doesn't tell us why that is or why it only seems to protect some individuals but not all. Of course, we can use this information as a starting point for future research, just as we were able to use our correlational studies as a starting point for a true experiment.

One final concern with archival research is that it can (and usually does) take a lot of time. Just think about some of the topics we have discussed already. A quick google search informed me that there were almost 500 films released in 2015. Now not all of those will be relevant to our topic, but even if only 10% of them are, that's 50 films you need to watch for just one year, and we want to examine the last 20 years?! So what's the take home message? Just because you aren't actively collecting data from participants, doesn't mean that you are going to have it easy. All research takes time and energy and it isn't done overnight.

Meta-Analysis

As a student, you will find that one particular form of archival research can be very helpful if you're interested in learning about a new research topic: a meta-analysis. A **meta-analysis** is a procedure in which we combine all of the previous research findings on a related topic to provide a summary of these previous findings. Just like with archival research, a meta-analysis' data has already been collected, so there is no direct contact with participants. The added benefit here is that you will have a summary of the relevant literature for a given topic. When you decide to conduct a meta-analysis, you will need to identify all of the variables of interest (e.g., age of participants, race of photographs, type of food provided, etc.). If you were interested in understanding the research around the own-age bias, you could read every study on the topic and try and make sense of an array of studies with varied research techniques, different statistical tests, different measures, and a multitude of various variables; or you could start by reading a meta-analysis on the own-age bias that would summarize the major findings of all those studies (see Rhodes & Anastasi, 2012, for a splendid meta-analytic review of the research on the own-age bias). A meta-analysis, therefore, serves as a great starting point on understanding a research topic and finding the relevant studies in that area. This is why it often becomes the best friend of a student who is assigned a topic by their professors on something they have no prior knowledge of.

Just as with archival research, meta-analyses can have issues with the completeness of the data. Of particular concern with this type of research is what is called the "**file drawer effect**." We need all studies that are relevant for our topic to avoid issues of bias in our data, but not all research gets published. But if a study doesn't get published, does that make it irrelevant to your meta-analysis? Not necessarily. There are many reasons that a study might not get published (see Chapter 13 for a more complete discussion on the potential reasons that research might not see the light of day), but the information in an unpublished study may include relevant variables that you are using in your meta-analysis. So, what is a budding researcher to do? You will need to reach out to the researchers in the field and see if they have any unpublished manuscripts that would be of help to your meta-analysis. This sounds like it should be an easy step, but, as one of the authors of this book can tell you, you could be waiting a long time to get the studies sent to you. At some point, you may just have to leave out anything that you haven't received so that you can get your meta-analysis completed. But missing research may hold important data that could affect the interpretation of your data, so always be cautious when drawing your conclusions.

Another issue you will undoubtedly encounter when conducting a meta-analysis is the difficulty involved with getting all the necessary data. When you are examining prior research within a given topic, you will be dealing with different terms, different methodologies, and different statistical analyses and you will need to find a way to take this chaos and make it work together. For instance, some facial recognition studies will use a simultaneous line-up procedure (where you have six faces shown to you at once), others may use a sequential line-up procedure (where you are presented with a single face at a time). Some may have you rate your confidence on a given answer ("I'm 75% sure I saw that face before), while others may have you say if you "remember" seeing the face or "know" you saw the face. These differences in methodological techniques can yield very different data. They also may be assessing different phenomena. As the researcher conducting the meta-analysis, you not only have to understand all of the techniques used, but also determine if they are relevant and related to one another.

Finally, as we have already mentioned, you will have to identify which variables you are interested in. For an own-age bias, you would likely be interested in the age of the participants and photographs, but what other variables may be important? How long the participants had to view the photographs, the type of presentation, encoding instructions, etc. may all hold important information in the understanding of the research, but if you leave something out, your interpretation will be flawed. Important missing variables will have huge implications on your research.

Meta-analyses are incredibly useful (for students and researchers alike), but they are not easy to conduct. It is a huge endeavor to take on. It will take time and patience, just like the more traditional form of archival research requires.

Nonexperimental Research Techniques: A Review

In both the prior chapter and the current chapter we have looked at the ways you can conduct research without experimentation. The types of research that were discussed are descriptive only, but can help us to understand behaviors better. The information obtained in these types of studies can set the stage for a later experiment or can serve as their own end.

Nonexperimental research techniques are usually easy to conduct and are relatively inexpensive (though, as we saw, there are some exceptions). While most people think of true experiments as the heart of scientific discovery, nonexperimental techniques can be just as useful and far more practical. For one thing, we are more easily able to generalize the findings from these techniques than we would be to some true experiments. In addition, nonexperimental methods may be the only option we have for topics that raise ethical concerns (such as the effects of brain damage on human memory).

But, as we have also seen, there are limitations to relying solely on nonexperimental methods. For one thing, and this is a big one, we cannot make causal statements. No matter how good my study is or how well I matched my participants, if I am not manipulating the variables and randomly assigning my participants to different groups, then I can never say that I know what "caused" the behavior. Now, this may not be an issue for you. Sometimes we really just want to describe the information or investigate a relationship, not explain its cause; but when a cause is your goal, you cannot rely on the nonexperimental approaches discussed in this chapter.

One of the other issues we discussed several times is that of reactivity of your participants. Whether they are reacting to our presence, our body language, or from the length of a questionnaire, we must always be aware that our results may be a reaction to what the participants are feeling about the study, about the researcher, or about themselves, and not about what you are actually investigating.

A concern that we may see with animal studies is what is known as **anthropomorphizing** —the process where we give human characteristics to the animals or objects we are researching. For instance, many of you probably have a pet. When you get home from class, is your pet happy to see you? How do you know? The reality is that you don't. It may be 100% accurate to say that your pet is happy to see you, but it's not scientific. With animal research, we must always be careful not to attribute human characteristics to our research subjects. Since I cannot ask my pet if they are happy to see me, I cannot know that they are actually happy to see me. It is just as likely that they are excited because the food dispenser is home or because they know that they get to go outside, and they really, really need to go to the bathroom. Sometimes animal researchers avoid giving their animal subjects names, instead referring to them as numbers, in order to keep the "relationship" more professional and to help them to avoid anthropomorphizing the animal's behavior.

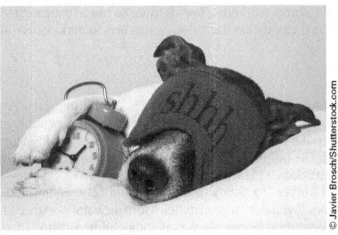

Do dogs dream? Is this a question we can answer?
Why do people think that dogs dream?

And finally, as we discussed with survey research, we must always be aware that our participants' responses may not be accurate. Whether it is due to faulty memories or purposively lying, the responses that have been provided may not reflect reality. This means that we must always be cautious when relying on self-reported data (like surveys). It is not unheard of for participants to lie in order to appear more socially desirable. In fact, *social desirability* tends to affect all of us. If I were to ask you "do you smoke marijuana daily," your answer can be influenced by what society deems as appropriate. While participants may not feel it necessary to lie if they are asked "have you ever smoked marijuana" since it is not seen as being socially undesirable (especially among college students), the former question asking about daily use may garner more lying since there is a more negative view of daily smokers in our society. Another example that is commonly seen in survey research with regard to social desirability is asking participants how many sexual partners they have had. Research studies find that typically men and women both lie when it comes to this question, but that they lie in different ways; men tend to increase the actual number and women tend to decrease their actual number. Again, this has to do with what is considered a socially desirable behavior. As a researcher, you must be aware that this may occur in your research, especially when asking socially relevant questions. One final issue you may find with your participants is that they may show specific response styles that can influence the outcome of your study. A response style is just the way that the someone answers questions. Some of your participants will show *response acquiescence* (they are "yea-sayers") in which they select the answers they think are desirable- such as giving an instructor teaching evaluations with all top marks, even on questions that don't apply to their class. Others may show *response deviation* (they are your "nay-sayers"), in which they respond in ways that are uncommon or unexpected, regardless of the questions. They appear to be trying to work against the questionnaire or researcher. Being vigilant in your testing and data collection can help you to detect inaccurate responses, but it is impossible to catch them all.

Concluding Remarks

Researchers have a number of nonexperimental methods that can be used to evaluate various research questions. As stated previously, each of these techniques provides different information and allows the researcher to make certain conclusions. Additionally, each of these approaches has specific advantages and weaknesses. As a competent and knowledgeable researcher, it's up to you to carefully weigh these advantages and disadvantages along with the ultimate goals that you have. While the methods discussed in Chapter 4 are descriptive in nature, the methods from this chapter are generally predictive as well. Thus, the techniques discussed in this chapter are generally stronger in that they allow researchers to make somewhat stronger conclusions than those discussed in Chapter 4. However, it's important to note again that none of the nonexperimental research methods allow us to make causal statements. Only the true experiments, which will be described in the next chapters, allow researchers to make causal statements and conclusions.

References

American Psychological Association (2016, January 15). Ethnic and racial minorities and socioeconomic status. Available from http://www.apa.org/pi/ses/resources/publications/factsheet-erm.aspx.

Anderson, C. A., Berkowitz, L., Donnerstein, E., Huesmann, L. R., Johnson, J. D., Linz, D., . . . Wartella, E. (2003). The influence of media violence on youth. *Psychological Science In The Public Interest*, *4*(3), 81–110. doi:10.1111/j.1529-1006.2003.pspi_1433.x

Associate Press (2011, October 26). Study finds correlation between amount of soda children drink and violent behaviors. Available from http://jacksonville.com/news/health-and-fitness/2011-10-26/story/study-finds-correlation-between-amount-soda-children-drink

Chavis, S. (2010, August 28). Study finds correlation between positive mood and yoga. Available from http://psychcentral.com/news/2010/08/28/study-finds-correlation-between-positive-mood-and-yoga/17395.html

Cohen, J. (1988). *Statistical power analysis for the behavioral sciences* (2nd ed.). Hillsdale, NJ: Lawrence Earlbaum Associates.

Howard, J. (2016, January 5). Late-night snacking may have a surprising effect on your memory. Available from http://www.huffingtonpost.com/entry/late-night-snacking-memory-learning_568a9f78e4b06fa68882e0f9?utm_hp_ref=science&ir=Science&section=science

Kounang, N. (2012, September 5). Football players more likely to develop neurodegenerative disease, study finds. Available from http://www.cnn.com/2012/09/05/health/nfl-neurodegenerative-disease/

Paulos, J. A. (2015, July 1). Do SAT scores really predict success? Available from http://abcnews.go.com/Technology/WhosCounting/story?id=98373&page=1

Rhodes, M. G., & Anastasi, J. S. (2012). The own-age bias in face recognition: A meta-analytic and theoretical review. *Psychological Bulletin*, *138*(1), 146–174. doi:10.1037/a0025750

End of Chapter Quiz

___1. Nonexperimental methods are often used when:
  a. an experiment would not be ethical or possible.
  b. the experimental hypothesis is not testable.
  c. external validity is less important than internal validity.
  d. we want to establish a causal relationship.

___2. _____ is a method of reviewing and summarizing literature in which you statistically combine or compare the results from different studies.
  a. A traditional literature review   c. Literature analysis
  b. Meta-analysis   d. Library research analysis

___3. Danielle feels like her professor has been really supportive of her this semester. Since she wants to make sure everyone knows how amazing her professor is, she gives the highest score on the course evaluation, even on things that don't apply to the course. This is an example of:
  a. nay-saying   c. willingness to answer
  b. position preference   d. yea-saying

___4. Cory conducted a survey study and found a correlation of $r = -0.02$ between income level and happiness, this would suggest that:
  a. higher income was associated with increased happiness.
  b. higher income was associated with reduced happiness.
  c. income and happiness affected each other.
  d. there was no appreciable relationship between income level and happiness.

___5. Jacob computed a Pearson Product-Moment Correlation Coefficient from some sample data and found that $r = +1.88$. What may be concluded from this data?
  a. there was a strong, positive relationship between the two variables.
  b. there was a weak, negative relationship between the two variables.
  c. there was no relationship between the two variables.
  d. Jacob should recheck his calculations.

___6. Sammy conducts a correlational study of the relationship between maternal age and attachment. He finds that the two variables are significantly related. Sammy can safely conclude that the two variables are:
  a. causally related.
  b. causally related but the direction of causality is not clear.
  c. related in some way, but no causal inference should be made.
  d. none of the above

___7. Which is a critical difference between quasi-experiments and true experiments?
  a. Experimental designs randomly assign subjects to different treatment conditions.
  b. Experimental designs use preexisting life events as treatments.
  c. Quasi-experiments are lower in external validity than experiments.
  d. Quasi-experiments are able to determine cause and effect relationships.

___8. Which of these is NOT an example of archival data?
    a. academic transcript   c. memories of your first date
    b. checkbook entries   d. wedding photo album

___9. Which of the following describes a negative correlation?
    a. Grades go down as individuals drink more alcohol.
    b. Height goes down as IQ goes down.
    c. Sexual drive of the average American goes up as the stock market goes up.
    d. When there is no relationship between the variables.

___10. The correlational method is especially good for:
    a. predicting one variable from another.
    b. understanding a complicated meta-analysis.
    c. determining cause-effect relationships among variables.
    d. comparing an independent variable to a dependent variable.

Homework Assignment #1

For each of the following studies, your task is to evaluate each and determine which of the nonexperimental techniques is being used for each of the described studies. While some of these could be conducted in different ways, try your best to evaluate the most likely nonexperimental approach and provide a brief explanation for why you've selected the option that you opted. Select from the following options for each study:

Correlational Research   Quasi-Experiment   Archival Research

1. Research indicated that the average American is sleeping less than the recommended 8 hours of sleep per night. Scientists believe that this might lead to a decrease in academic performance in high school students. In this study, students who get less than 7 hours of sleep per night and those who get more than 9 hours of sleep per night were evaluated on various cognitive functioning tests.

2. Researchers were interested in whether the jersey color of professional football teams had an impact on the number of penalties that were called against the teams. It was shown through data kept by the football league that teams wearing black jerseys were much more likely to be penalized than teams wearing nonblack jerseys.

3. A recent study found that the older we get, the quieter we are in social situations. Participants who were 50, 60, 70, and 80 years of age were invited to several social get-togethers at a local community outreach center. The number of times that they spoke as well as the number of words that they used was recorded. The study found that the oldest participants spoke the least amount and the 50-year olds spoke the most.

4. Researchers asked people how much of their income they spend on others or donate to charity, and then asked them how happy they are. The researchers found that the more money people spent on others, the happier they were.

5. Researchers divided individuals into a high, medium, and low income groups. These individuals were then given a questionnaire that evaluated their level of happiness in order to see if money can bring happiness. Their findings indicated that the medium income group had the highest level of happiness, whereas the low income group had the lowest levels of happiness.

6. Researchers conducted a study where they were interested in evaluating how news anchors have changed over the years. In order to do this they evaluated the published gender, race, and ethnicity of news anchors for the past 50 years. Their research found a general trend that the gender has decreased from 84% men to 61% men and 92% Caucasian to 66% Caucasian.

7. Researchers were interested in determining if there was a relationship between mathematical abilities and income levels for men and women. The researchers evaluated individuals who had strong quantitative SAT scores with those who had lower scores. The income levels of these groups was then compared. It was found that men with stronger mathematical abilities had higher income levels, but that there was no difference in income levels for women based on their quantitative SAT scores.

8. A study evaluated whether there was a relationship between taking vitamins and overall general health indicators such as body mass index, cholesterol levels, and bone density. The study found that individuals who take vitamins scored better on each of the general health indicators than individuals who do not take vitamins.

9. Researchers were interested in determining if keeping preelection promises had an effect on politicians later approval ratings. In order to answer this question, the preelection promises of the last 10 presidents was analyzed to determine if the president kept these promises three years into their presidency. The public approval ratings were then evaluated to see if there was a relationship between these variables.

10. Numerous studies have evaluated the face recognition abilities of witnesses. It has generally been shown that individuals remember faces from their own race better than faces of individuals from another race. In order to test this, White and Black participants were shown faces of both White and Black individuals.

Homework Assignment #2

Think about a research problem that you could investigate using a nonexperimental approach. First, describe the research question (hypothesis). Second, describe how you could answer this research question using each of the following nonexperimental research approaches. If you don't think this approach can be used to answer this question, explain in detail why the approach cannot be used.

1. Correlational Research

2. Quasi-Experiment

3. Archival Study

4. Meta-Analysis

Chapter 6

True Experiments: Between-Subject Designs

In this chapter, we need to discuss additional aspects of true experiments. Specifically, we'll discuss the specifics of between-subject designs: When to use them, when to not use them, advantages of using between-subject designs, and disadvantages of using between-subject designs.

As discussed in Chapter 2, when you have a **between-subjects variable** each participant will receive only one of the levels of the independent variable (IV). For example, if you were manipulating the level of a drug and had three different drug doses (e.g., low, medium, and high), you would have different groups of participants who would each receive only one of the different drug doses. One group would receive the low dose of the drug. Another group would receive the medium dose of the drug, and the third group would receive the high dose of the drug. When we speak of these different levels, we refer to these as different groups or different conditions. Either term, groups or conditions, is appropriate when using a between-subjects design. As we'll mention later in the within-subjects chapter, the term groups is only appropriate when you have a between-subjects variable. The term conditions is a more generic term and is appropriate for referring to the levels of either a between- or within-subjects manipulation.

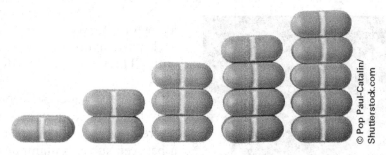

Most drug studies evaluate a drug by giving different doses to different groups of participants.

Advantages of Using a Between-Subjects Design

There are many advantages of using a between-subjects design. The first advantage is simply that between-subject designs are much simpler for people to understand; they just make more logical sense to people. For example, if you wanted to test the effectiveness of a drug, how would you design your study? Think about it for a moment. What would you do? If you ask this question to 100 undergraduate research methods students, about 95 of them would give you a between-subjects design. The remaining 5 individuals would probably give you a nice mixed-factor design, but we'll get to that later when we discuss mixed-factor designs. So, our 95 students are going to look at this problem and determine that it makes the most sense to divide our participants into two groups. One group will receive our drug and the other group will receive a placebo. These groups will be the same as each other and will be treated exactly the same, except that one group receives the actual drug while the other group receives the placebo. Thus, any difference that is found between these groups MUST be caused by the effects of the actual drug. The logic is very straightforward and valid, it makes intuitive sense, and it would be relatively easy to conduct. Between-subject designs are just easier for people to think about because the logic is very straightforward.

The other major advantage of between-subject designs is that they're generally easier to conduct than within-subject designs. There's really only one thing that you have to worry about and control when you conduct a between-subject design: making sure that your groups are equivalent before you administer any treatment or manipulation. Because of this, there's really much less to worry about when conducting a between-subjects experiment. The major issue in within-subject designs is carryover effects. A **carryover effect** is when the effects of one condition carry over to the other condition. For example, if we were to test our drug using a within-subjects manipulation then participants would receive one level of the drug (e.g., the actual drug) as well as the other level (e.g., the placebo). In a within-subjects design there would be many different issues to worry about. Using this example, let's say that our drug was supposed to reduce anxiety levels in participants. So, we start our experiment by giving our participants the placebo for a week and then measure their anxiety levels. The next week, we give them the drug and then measure their anxiety levels. Our findings indicate that anxiety levels were higher when participants were taking the placebo compared to when they received the drug. What does this mean? Well, it MAY indicate that the drug worked to lower anxiety levels. We'd love to make this conclusion, but we really can't. There are other alternative explanations that are possible, due to the effects of potential carryover effects. MIGHT the drug have worked? Yes, of course. However, it may also be that participants were more nervous at the beginning of the study because they didn't really know what to expect. They may have been unsure what the experimenter was going to do to them to test their anxiety levels. Thus, they may have been more anxious at the beginning of the study, at the same time that they received the placebo. When they returned to the study for the drug phase, they knew what to expect and were less anxious about their participation. Thus, it may not have been the drug having any effect on the participants at all.

In a between-subjects design, it's crucial that participants in your different conditions are equivalent to one another.

So why are these carryover effects not a problem with a between-subject design? Well, because each participant is only being tested one time, with EITHER the drug OR the placebo. Thus, the effects of the earlier testing can't have an impact on their later performance because they're only tested once in a between-subjects design. Therefore, carryover effects can't be a problem in a between-subjects manipulation. Thus, the only real concerns on the part of the researcher are to make sure that that different groups being tested are equal to one another and that they're treated the same, other than the manipulation. After we discuss the potential disadvantages of using between-subject designs, we'll come back to this idea of equal groups.

Disadvantages of Between-Subject Designs

When you conduct a study using a between-subjects variable, you must have at least two groups or conditions. We know this. As previously discussed, the purpose of this other group is so that you have a group or condition that doesn't receive the manipulation or treatment so that you can then compare the results that you obtained from your experimental group. The logic is simple in that the only difference between these groups is that one receives the treatment and the other does not. Otherwise they're treated exactly the same. Therefore, any difference found between these groups must be caused by the manipulation or treatment. While I realize that this is the case, and I completely understand the logic, it seems to be somewhat of a waste of resources. Consider this example: let's say that we're going to test our drug. In order to test our drug we're going to need a lot of participants in our study, let's say that we need 1000 participants, half of them will receive the drug and half will receive a placebo. Let's further assume that in order to test the drug, we need to evaluate each individual for about 6 months. They'll be required to come into our lab at the end of the 6 months for us to conduct a complete checkup that will require about 5 hours of their time. As is common in many drug studies, we're going to compensate each of our participants for their participation in our study. For 6 months of participation, let's say that we pay each participant $1000. For the participants who receive the drug, there is the possibility that the drug could have some potential side-effects or dangers. Thus, it seems reasonable that these individuals should receive the full compensation—$1000 for each of our 500 participants. This would be a total of $500,000 for the drug group!! Additionally, the checkup will take a total of 2,500 hours to complete!! This is just for the drug group. Because we have to have a comparison group, we're going to do the same thing with our placebo group. If we treat them equally (which we have to do), it's going to take an additional $500,000 and an additional 2,500 testing hours for the control condition. Now, what exactly do we expect to happen with the control condition? The answer: NOTHING!!! So, we're going to pay $500,000 and spend 2,500 hours of our time for a control group that we expect absolutely nothing to happen with!! Again, I do understand the logic behind a between-subjects design, and I do see why it's necessary to do this, but at some level this just seems to be such a waste of resources. You may ask, "OK, then since the placebo participants really aren't in any danger and there shouldn't be any side-effects from the drug since they're only receiving the placebo, why can't we just pay them less?" From the frugal part of my personality where I really don't like to spend money unnecessarily, I like the way you're thinking here! However, from the scientist aspect of my personality, this won't work. If we decided to save some money and just paid the placebo participants $100 for their participation, it would only cost us $50,000 instead of $500,000. However, now we've introduced a confound! Our two groups are not being treated the same. They differ in both whether they receive the drug/placebo AND the amount of money that they received in compensation ($100 vs. $1000). Now if we get a difference between our drug group and our placebo group, we don't know if the difference is being caused by the drug or the amount of money that we're paying our participants. So, while at some level, it just seems to be such a waste to spend all this time and money on individuals that you expect absolutely nothing to happen to, you still have to do it so that you can compare your experimental group with another group that has been treated exactly the same, other than the manipulation.

Participants in the experimental and control groups must be treated exactly the same, other than the experimental manipulation. This includes any kind of pay or credit that they receive.

Separate from this idea of having to test a completely separate control group, but seemingly related, is the second potential disadvantage of between-subject designs: the fact that you have to test more participants in a between-subjects design. Let's assume that you have an experiment where you'd like to test some variable. For consistency, let's say we're going to test our anti-anxiety drug. Further, let's say that we'd like to evaluate three levels of our drug: a placebo group, a low dose, and a high dose. In order to test the drug, we need to have 50 participants in each of these conditions. If we were to conduct this study as a between-subjects manipulation, we'll need 50 participants in each of our 3 groups for a total of 150 individuals in our study. If we conducted this same study as a within-subjects manipulation, we'd need 50 participants in each of the 3 conditions as well. However, since each individual receives each of the different levels of the IV in a within-subjects design, we'd need only 50 participants in total since each would receive each of the different drug dose levels. The more levels that you have, the more of a disadvantage the between-subjects design would become. With 5 drug levels, we'd need 250 participants for a between-subjects design (5 levels x 50 participants per level). For the within-subjects design it would still just be 50 participants since each participant would receive all 5 of the levels. With 10 levels, you'd need 500 participants in the between-subjects design, but still just 50 participants in the within-subjects design. The within-subjects design seems to have quite an advantage over a between-subjects design!

A third disadvantage of a between-subjects design is that the individual differences of your participants have a much larger impact on a between-subjects design compared to a within-subjects design. As a result, between-subject designs have lower statistical power than within-subject designs. **Statistical power** refers to the likelihood that a study will detect an effect of the IV when there is an effect to be detected. Individual differences have the effect of making it more difficult to see the effects of an IV in any study because they add statistical noise (or error variance) to your data. Individual differences occur in every study, but the impact of those individual differences is somewhat stronger in a between-subjects design. Think of it this way, in a within-subjects design you have individual differences between your various participants in your study. However, the individuals who are in the different conditions are the same people. Therefore, you do have individual differences *within* each of your conditions, but you don't have any individual difference *between* your conditions since it's the same people in each of your conditions. In a between-subjects design, you have those same individual differences within each of your groups, AND you also have individual differences between your groups as well, since there are different individuals in each of your groups. So there is a lot more statistical noise in a between-subjects design compared to a within-subjects design.

While there are definitely some advantages to between-subject designs, there are also some potential issues to be wary of. In the next chapter, we'll discuss the potential advantages and disadvantages of within-subject designs. Knowledge of these differences will help you to weigh the options that you have so that you can make an informed, intelligent decision on which design would be better for your own research.

Say hello to Statistical Power Man! Able to leap tall buildings AND detect small effects in experimental studies.

Importance of Variance

In the previous section, we mentioned error variance and how that error variance can lead to lower statistical power. In this section, we'd like to briefly discuss variance and how it affects statistical power. While this discussion would be perfectly appropriate in a discussion of statistics, we think that it's also very appropriate here as well in order to better explain statistical power. Furthermore, we think that any discussion of research methods would be incomplete without some mention of how those methods affect various statistical decisions that researchers make. Additionally, any discussion of statistics would equally be deficient without mentioning the appropriate methodology used to obtain those statistics.

In discussing variance, we need to mention that there are two general classes of variance: systematic group variance and nonsystematic group variance. **Systematic group variance** is variance that occurs in conjunction with your manipulation. There are two potential sources of systematic group variance. The first source of systematic group variance is **experimental variance**, or the differences between your groups that is caused by your manipulation. If you were manipulating the amount of a drug you administered to participants, the experimental variance would be caused by giving some participants the drug and other individuals the placebo or other doses of the drug. Experimental variance is obviously a good type of variance that you'd generally like to see since it's being caused by the experimental manipulation that you're using. Another source of systematic group variance would be any other difference between your groups that isn't your manipulation, or **extraneous variance**. For example, in the drug testing example that we discussed earlier in this chapter, we mentioned paying the experimental group $1000 for their participation and the placebo group only $100. As previously mentioned, this would cause a confound and would not be a good type of variance. **Nonsystematic group variance**, or **error variance**, is that part of your variance that is not due to differences between your conditions or groups. Nonsystematic group variance typically refers to the individual differences between your participants or the different ways your participants behave even when they're treated the same way. For example, the fact that some individuals are more intelligent than other individuals or have different weights or fat content or motivation or wakefulness. Any individual difference that makes individuals different from each other or behave differently from each other even when treated the same would be error variance. Further, this error variance (or individual differences) can occur both within a group, or **within-groups error variance**, as well as across groups, **between-groups error variance**.

Let's use these different types of variances to discuss an important concept in research methods. First, we'd like you to be aware of why these different types of variance are important and, secondly, how these different types of variance affect your statistics. The third concept is that you can't have a good understanding of research methods without understanding the accompanying statistics AND you can't have a good understanding of statistics without understanding the accompanying research methods. We'd like to use a simple theoretical formula for computing the F-ratio. This F-ratio is the inferential statistic that is computed when you conduct an Analysis of Variance (or an ANOVA). The specifics about inferential statistics are, of course, discussed in more detail in the inferential statistics chapter (i.e., Chapter 9). Regardless, take a look at the formula below:

$$F = \frac{\text{(systematic variance + between-groups error variance)}}{\text{(within-groups error variance)}}$$

As you can see, the F-ratio is a result of these three sources of variance: systematic variance, between-groups error variance, and within-groups error variance. One important note to keep in mind is that the individual differences between-groups (i.e., how different the people are between the different experimental groups) is about the same as the individual differences within each of the groups (i.e., how different the people are within each of the different groups). As a result, the between-groups error variance and the within-groups error variance are typically going to be fairly similar. Let's just insert some values for these two nonsystematic variances. We'll just use values of 2 for each, but they should be about the same.

$$F = \frac{\text{(systematic variance + 2)}}{\text{(2)}}$$

Now, let's assume that we have no systematic variance for the moment. So, insert the value of 0 for the systematic variance in the formula above. When you do this, what is the value of F?

$$F = \frac{(0 + 2)}{(2)} = \frac{2}{2} = 1$$

As you probably already figured, and from the equation above, the F-ratio will be 1. Thus, when you have no systematic variance, you'd expect to obtain an F-ratio of approximately 1. Now observe what happens when we have systematic variance. Assume that our error variances are the same with values of 2 and our systematic variance is now 4. What is the value of F now?

$$F = \frac{(4 + 2)}{(2)} = \frac{6}{2} = 3$$

As you can see from the above equation, the F-ratio is now a value of 3. When you have systematic variance, you get a larger F-ratio. Let's try one more. Assume again that our error variances are the same with values of 2 and our systematic variance is now 10. What is the value of F now?

$$F = \frac{(10 + 2)}{(2)} = \frac{12}{2} = 6$$

Now the F-ratio is 6. So, as you can see, the more systematic variance you have, the larger your F-ratio will become. The F-ratio is typically used to determine if the performance of your conditions was different. In order to determine if your drug made a difference, you would conduct an Analysis of Variance to determine if they were different enough from one another in order to conclude that the groups performed differently. For example, we might want to know if those individuals who received the drug had lower anxiety levels than those who were given the placebo. We'd like to find that there was some systematic variance that is being caused by our drug manipulation. If there is then we'd see an F-ratio that is larger than 1. If the drug had a really large effect, we'd expect to see an F-ratio much larger than 1. Thus, the more systematic variance, the larger our F-ratio will be.

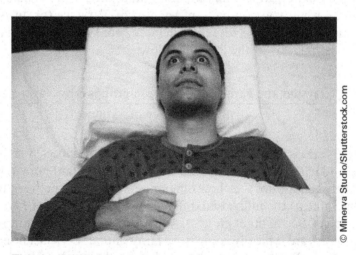

This individual is having trouble sleeping because of his anxiety. He must be in the placebo condition.

Now for the third concept: that you can't have a good understanding of research methods without understanding the accompanying statistics AND you can't have a good understanding of statistics without understanding the accompanying research methods. Let's assume that we conduct our drug study, analyze our data properly, and we obtain a large F-ratio (e.g., $F = 14.74$). This F-ratio indicates that we have a lot of systematic variance. Let's further assume that the drug group ended up with significantly lower anxiety scores than the placebo group. What can we then conclude based on these findings? I think the most obvious conclusion is that the drug worked! The drug caused our participants to have lower anxiety levels. Based upon the data, this would be a reasonable conclusion. However, what are the two sources of systematic variance? If you recall, systematic variance could be the result of our experimental manipulation AND it could also be the result of extraneous variance, or a confound. If we were to find out that the drug participants received $1000 for their participation and the placebo participants received only $100 for their participation, would you still conclude that the difference in anxiety levels was because of the drug? I would think not. While the differences between these conditions COULD be caused by the drug conditions, it COULD also be caused by the other ways that these groups were treated differently (i.e., the amount of payment they received). So you can't just look at the F-ratio, see that the groups are statistically different from one another, and conclude that the drug worked. You also need to evaluate the methodology of the study in order to ensure that the research was done well and is valid. Additionally, if you look at the methods and see that the study was done well, you have to look at the inferential statistics to determine if the performance of your conditions was statistically different from one another. In conclusion, knowledge of both research methods and statistics are necessary to come to a valid conclusion about your research. You can't come to any conclusions with just one of these sources of information.

$$F = \frac{(\text{systematic variance} + \text{between-groups error variance})}{(\text{within-groups error variance})}$$

Based on the formula and discussion above, obtaining large differences between your treatments (i.e., systematic variance) is good since it provides evidence for the effects of your treatment, IF there are no confounds. Obtaining large individual differences within your treatments (i.e., within-groups error variance) is bad since these may mask any true effects of your IV. As previously mentioned, these individuals differences provide a lot of statistical noise and make it difficult to see the effects of your treatment or obtain larger F-ratios.

Obviously it would then be very helpful to eliminate any confounding variables. With between-subject designs, making sure that the IV is the ONLY difference between your groups helps to ensure that any difference that you find is being caused by your manipulation. Confounding variables, or extraneous variance, make it impossible to determine if the differences that you obtain between your groups is caused by the manipulation (which would be good) or by the confounding variable (which would be bad). Moving on to the next section, we need to discuss the importance of having equal groups.

Importance of Equal Groups

As previously discussed with regard to between-subject designs, the primary concern is to make sure that your different groups are equivalent to one another at the beginning of your study. It's crucial that the only difference between your groups is your manipulation and that, other than your manipulation, these groups are treated exactly the same. Thus, the easiest way to ensure that they are treated identically is to standardize your procedures. By standardizing your procedures we mean that each individual that participates in your experiment is treated exactly the same way. An easy way to ensure that everyone is treated the same way and given the exact same instructions is to have researchers simply read the instructions to each of the participants. While it may seem a little silly to some people, this ensures that all the researchers are telling participants the same thing each time and that each researcher doesn't vary what they say to each participant. It can be difficult to make sure that you tell each participant the exact same thing each time if you ad lib your instructions, but it's quite simple if you just read the instructions each time.

Standardizing procedures is used in many other situations where providing the same instructions to everyone is crucial. For example, at my university we have a graduate course where our graduate students learn to administer standardized tests, such as IQ tests among others. A standardized test is a test that is given to many individuals but it MUST be administered in exactly the same way for each individual (and thus the name "standardized" test). The idea is that if each individual is given the exact same test, under the exact same conditions, then we can compare the results of the different individuals on this test no matter who they are, who administered the test to them, or where they were tested. While this class isn't a particularly difficult course, many of our graduate students have difficulty with the course because of the standardized procedures. Our graduate students are very intelligent, motivated individuals. When they administer the test, they are supposed to memorize the instructions that they give to each of the individuals that they test verbatim. They sometimes feel a little silly reading the instructions because they think it looks like they don't really know what they're doing. They think it's "beneath them" to read the instructions. Since they're pretty smart they change the instructions just a little bit and maybe even explain each of the tasks on the IQ tests just a little bit better. However, if they do this, they have broken the standardization of the procedures. If this happens, the test that they just administered becomes invalid. For the course, they are then not given credit for the three hour test that they just administered, scored, and wrote a report for. They have to start over again. This standardization of procedures is absolutely crucial not only for IQ testing but also for research studies. If you want to have the ability to compare the performance of your participants then they must have been treated exactly the same way, other than the actual manipulation, of course.

While we did mention that the participants in the different conditions/groups won't be treated exactly the same way due to them receiving different levels of the IV, this standardization is also very important *across* conditions. We do also want to make sure that the participants in each of the conditions/groups are treated exactly the same way other than the actual manipulation. This might be making sure that each individual is given the same instructions for all other parts of the experiment and even making the critical instructions the same, other than the specific manipulation part. You would like to make the instructions similar when they're presented, how they're given, and even how long they are. You wouldn't want to give 10-minute instructions to your experimental condition and strongly emphasize them doing their best, but then give 2-minute instructions to your control condition where you are unenthused about the study. This standardization of instructions is very similar to what we do in drug studies. If you were going to test a drug to see how effective it was, you would probably give your experimental group the drug and the control group a placebo. Another option would be to give the experimental group the drug and do nothing for the control group. Which of these options would be better?

Placebos can have a beneficial effect on participants, whereas a nocebo describes when the substance or drug has a negative effect.

I'm hoping at this point, there would be no question as to which would be better. Clearly including a placebo would be the better choice. As we've previously discussed, this placebo is critical because it makes the placebo participants *think* they might be receiving the drug. This potential placebo effect helps to make the placebo condition just like the drug condition with the only difference being that the experimental group receives the actual active ingredient in the drug. The purpose of the placebo is to make sure that the expectations that the participants have is the same for each condition. This placebo is even important when testing animals. While the animal may not have an expectation of what the drug will do to them, they still need to be treated exactly the same way. If you pick up the rats to inject them with the drug for the experimental condition, you'd need to pick up the rats to inject them with a saline solution for the control condition. If you don't pick up the control rats and don't give them an injection, any differences that you find could be because of the drug OR it could be because of how they were treated differently.

Factors Leading to Unequal Groups

As we've been discussing, there are many ways that your groups could become unequal in a between-subjects design. Thus, the researcher's job is to make sure that the groups are as equal as possible. We present below some additional ways that groups could become unequal.

Assignment Bias

Any type of bias where you have individuals put into the different groups in a nonrandom way could clearly lead to assignment bias. For example, if you wanted to test a new teaching technique and you wanted to use students who were enrolled in your two classes as participants, you could easily do this. The two separate classes would make things very simple since they're already divided into groups. Additionally, since you're the instructor for both classes, you would be controlling for the professor, so different personalities or teaching ability or other factors would be kept the same for the different classes. However, these are different classes and they may occur on different days or even at different times of day. Let's say that one of the classes meets each day at 8:00 am, while the other class meets at 1:00 pm. Is it possible that the students in these two classes are not the same? Of course it is! The 8:00 am students might be more motivated or more tired than the 1:00 pm students. Additionally, it may be that the 1:00 pm students are upperclassmen who were able to register for their classes earlier and the 8:00 am students are unfortunate underclassmen who couldn't get any better class times. Regardless of the specific nature of the classes, these groups may be very unequal, which would illustrate an **assignment bias** such that there is some sort of potential bias with how participants were put into, or assigned, to the different conditions.

Do the class on the left and the class on the right look the same to you? Of course not! So you wouldn't want one of these classes to serve as your control group and the other as your experimental group.

One of the easiest ways to have the same types of individuals in each of your groups would be to randomly assign participants to your different groups. **Random assignment** means that each of the participants has an equal chance of being assigned to the different conditions. If you have 100 people volunteer for your study (70 females and 30 males) and you have two groups of participants, you'll end up with 50 individuals in each of your groups. With random assignment, you would simply randomly assign these individuals to the different groups. How many females and males would you expect to be in each of your two groups? With random assignment, you'd expect something close to 35 females and 15 males in each of the groups. It may not be exactly this, maybe 33 females and 17 males in one group and 37 females and 13 males in the other group, but it would be expected to be pretty close when using random assignment. However, *could* it come out very differently? Is it possible? The answer is yes. While it's not very likely, it *could* occur where you ended up with 50 females and 0 males in one group and 20 females and all 30 males in the other group with random assignment. This would be extremely unlikely, especially with a larger number of participants, but it *could* happen. What are the chances of this occurring if you had 10 participants in your study—7 female and 3 males? What are the chances that you might have 5 females in one group and 2 females and 3 males in the other group? While this still wouldn't be highly likely, this would be much more likely than having unequal groups with larger numbers of participants. This random assignment tends to work pretty well with larger numbers of participants, but it may not work as well when you have smaller numbers of participants in your study.

Differential Attrition

Differential attrition is very important when looking at factors that could result in unequal groups. **Differential attrition** is when there are differences in the numbers of participants that drop out of the groups from your experiment. A great example of this is looking at commercials and the claims that are made. Let's take a hypothetical exercise program and let's call it P91X. The commercials for P91X are very fast moving, energetic, and exciting as the individual in the commercial tells you about how awesome the P91X exercise system is. Like many similar commercials they want you to know how effective their system is and they often make claims such as "Individuals who complete the P91X system show a 50% reduction in fat and a 73% increase in lean muscle." Why is this statement important? Well, let's take a look at the rest of our commercial. They also show that both groups of individuals who started their program had the same weight. They then show you that the individuals who completed the program lost approximately 80 lbs on average and 4 inches in their waist. However, individuals in the control condition who did nothing special lost 4 lbs and 0 inches in their waist. Are you convinced yet?? These differences are huge! So what's the catch?

This is one of the successful P91X participants – you can tell by the crazed look in his eyes!

If we started with 100 individuals in the P91X condition and 100 individuals in the control condition AND that an equal number of individuals completed the experiment from both conditions, say 97 people in each group, we might be pretty impressed. However, would you still be impressed if 97 people from the control condition completed the experiment but only 7 people completed the P91X program? Of course not! This is the problem with differential attrition. We have a lot more individuals dropping out of our P91X condition. The individuals who stay in the program to the end might be the only ones who are extremely motivated to get into shape and lose weight. There might be something special about these 7 individuals that made them stay in the program, whereas the other 93 individuals in this condition didn't or couldn't or wouldn't stay in the program. These 7 individuals are probably very different from the 97 people who were in the control condition. After all, what exactly was being asked of the control condition? The answer: nothing! They really didn't have to put forth any effort or do anything differently in their lives in order to stay in the experiment. The same wasn't true for our P91X participants. Thus, when many more individuals dropped out of the P91X condition (i.e., differential attrition), we probably ended up with very different types of individuals in the different groups.

Diffusion of Treatment

One potential problem with conducting research that involves some sort of deception or even when the researcher would like to withhold some information from the participants during the debriefing phase of the study is keeping this information from future participants. At the end of many of our studies, we debrief participants by telling them what the study was about and answer any questions that they may have about the study. Before discharging them from the experiment, we instruct them not to discuss the study with anyone else so that future participants will be unaware of the purpose of the study and what we'll be asking them to do. This is especially important when there's some sort of deception because future participants can't be deceived if someone has already told them about the deception in the study. When our participants get back to their dorm room or class and one of their friends who is signed up for our study asks them about the study, we're pretty sure that most of them tell their friend—"I'm sorry, but the researchers asked me to refrain from discussing the experiment with others so as to avoid ruining their study." I'm sure this is what you'd do, right? OK, OK, OK, I guess most participants are going to tell their friends everything, even though we specifically asked them not to discuss it. When participants in different conditions learn about the other treatments, it can affect the findings. For example, if you realize that you're in the control condition because you already know what the experimental condition is doing, you might not try as hard. I volunteered for an alcohol study in graduate school and found out that I was one of the control conditions (I received only a very small

As you can clearly see, the young lady is telling her friend about the research study that she just participated in.

amount of alcohol in my condition). Knowing that the drink that I was drinking wasn't really enough alcohol to affect me, even though it tasted like alcohol, surely affected my performance in the experiment. When the participants discuss the experiment and become aware of the other conditions, it can affect performance in those other conditions. This is referred to as **diffusion of treatment** and can affect the validity of your findings.

Compensatory Equalization

Imagine the following situation: You're a parent, and you have an elementary-aged child. Your child brings home a permission slip that is recruiting students for a new math study that is going to be carried out on your child's campus. The 8-week study will be administering a new math program that is believed to significantly improve students' understanding of math and their math grades. The control group will still get extra time to work on their math homework and will have access to a teacher who will help them using the current math approaches. Since your child is having some difficulty in math, you decide to sign your child up since it seems like a win-win situation. One day after school, you get into a conversation with another parent whose child is also in the math study. This parent is just effusive with praise about how wonderful the program is and how her child's math grades have increased from 60s to 90s. You mention that after being in the program for 4 weeks, you haven't noticed any changes in your child's grades. In further discussions with your children, you find out that the other student is getting the special math training. Your child reports that he is simply given time to work on math homework at school. There is a teacher there to answer questions, but your child just does his homework at school rather than at home. After hearing this, you get very angry that your child is just in the control condition. The next day, you go to your child's school, talk with the principal, and demand that your child be switched to the special math training condition. This is compensatory equalization. **Compensatory equalization** is when the untreated group learns about the treatment group and demands equal treatment.

This child is receiving additional math training as part of the study that he's participating in.

Compensatory Rivalry

Compensatory rivalry is when the untreated group learns about the treatment group and tries even harder. A nice example of this is in looking at studies that are evaluating the effectiveness of a smoking cessation program, a weight loss program, or any other type of program that is evaluating the effectiveness of some sort of intervention (e.g., SAT training program, math tutoring, etc.). In these types of studies, there has to be an experimental group and a control group. Individuals who volunteer for these types of programs would generally rather be in the experimental group. However, as we've discussed previously, you have to include a control group so that you have something to compare the experimental group to. If the individuals in the control condition realize that they're actually part of the control group, they may very well try even harder to "show the researchers" that they can do it on their own.

Resentful Demoralization

The opposite possibility to compensatory rivalry is resentful demoralization. **Resentful demoralization** is when the untreated group learns about the treatment group and gives up. A while back I was watching a documentary that followed several individuals who were part of an HIV study. The documentary followed eight individuals through the program. There were a lot more individuals who were part of this study, but they documented these eight individuals. They interviewed the individuals at the beginning of the study, followed their daily lives during the study, and checked in with them after the study was over. One of the individuals that I specifically remember was this one guy, we'll call him John. At the beginning of the study, John was very excited about the study and the possibility that he'd be getting the HIV cocktail that would aid his health and allow him to live a more normal life. Midway through the study, John became discouraged because his health hadn't really improved; it seemed to be just staying the same. He ended up dropping out of the study because he was upset that he was only in the control condition, and he had essentially given up. He wanted the researchers to give him the actual treatment, but the researchers couldn't disclose which group he was in. They also told him that even if he was in the control condition, they can't just switch someone in the middle of the study. As a result, John quit the study. The documentary crew continued to follow the remaining seven individuals and checked in on John periodically. Each time they checked in on John, they noticed that his health had gotten worse and deteriorated. It turns out that John was in the experimental condition all along. The drugs were what was keeping him healthy and stabilized his health. Unfortunately, John passed away shortly after the study was concluded.

When things get tough, some participants just give up, whereas others may try even harder. Their behavior can have repercussions on the study.

How to Make Groups Equal

As previously mentioned, one of the most important aspects of between-subject designs is to make sure that the different groups in your study are equivalent in every way other than your manipulation. One of the simplest ways to ensure that your groups are equal would be to randomly assign participants to your different groups. As discussed earlier, random assignment is particularly helpful when you have a larger number of participants in your study. While random assignment may be one of the simplest techniques that result in equal groups, there are a few other methods that can be utilized.

The primary purpose of trying to make the groups equal in a between-subjects design is to minimize the individual differences in the groups or to spread the individual differences equally across the different groups. Random assignment attempts to spread the individual differences equally across the different groups. Another technique attempts to minimize the individual differences altogether. This second technique utilizes participants with certain characteristics. We'll refer to this technique as **homogeneous sampling**. For example, many drug studies try to minimize the potential effects of various hormones by using only men or only women in their studies. One could test only individuals from a certain socio-economic status or a certain race or a certain body type or a certain religion. By only using individuals with certain characteristics, you can minimize many of the individual differences between the participants. For example, if you wanted to test a birth control pill, you might want to only test women if the birth control pill was being developed for women. This would help to control for differences in hormone levels and the types of hormones that women and men have, which would probably be very important to control for since birth control pills work by providing hormones. Having men take the birth control pill might not be a good test of the pill. However, if you did test men the pill would probably appear to be extremely effective since men rarely get pregnant. ☺

I guess the birth control pill being tested in this study didn't work very well for the women or the men.

There are various other characteristics that researchers might want to control for. Oftentimes this is done because, like the birth control pill example above, the treatment is designed for specific individuals in mind. For example, a treatment that should help increase children's math skills would be helpful for children who are struggling with math. Thus, testing only children who are having problems with math makes sense. A treatment that should help individuals lose weight would be great for overweight or obese individuals, but testing the treatment on individuals who are underweight or even of normal weight wouldn't make as much sense. These types of studies make a lot of sense, but there are times when using only certain individuals may seem more capricious. Say you have a study where you're evaluating drug use in high school students. Due to proximity and/or accessibility of certain school districts, you decide to test only high school students from suburban school districts. Your study would probably provide a good evaluation of suburban high school students, but how representative do you think these students are to inner-city high school students or students from rural areas? This is the primary issue when you have homogeneous sampling. While this may help to control individual differences, your ability to generalize your results, or your external validity, is potentially compromised. As the researcher, it's up to you to weigh the advantages and disadvantages of only testing individuals with certain characteristics. Under some situations it makes perfect sense; in other situations it really doesn't.

Another possibility that also minimizes the differences between the groups would be to use **matched-groups assignment** or a **matched-groups design**. With this technique, participants are assigned to each of the groups based upon a certain characteristic. However, unlike the homogeneous sampling, individuals can have various characteristics. The only stipulation is that each group would have a matching individual. For example, if you felt that having disproportionate numbers of different races in your different groups would have a significant impact on your findings then you might want to match individuals based on this characteristic. So, you wouldn't need to only test African-Americans in your study, you would just need to make sure that you have a match for each participant in each of your groups. So if you have three conditions and you wanted to match for race then you'd need three African-American participants. Once you've selected them to be in your study, you can then randomly assign them to the three different conditions. If you have a Caucasian participant, that's fine as long as you have two additional Caucasian participants so that you'll have matches for each of the three groups. You could even match individuals on various characteristics. Maybe you wish to match on race and socio-economic status (SES). If you have a wealthy Hispanic participant for your study, you'd need two other wealthy Hispanic participants so that you can randomly assign them to the different groups. If you match on several characteristics, you might run the risk of not having enough matches. You may not be able to find a match for the blond haired, blue eyed, high SES, Republican, female Native American in your study. If you don't have a match for this individual then you can't use this individual in your study. You must have one match for each of the different groups in your study.

Using a matched-groups design ensures that each of your participants has a match in the other groups. This method helps to keep your groups equivalent, at least on the variables that you match them on.

Using a matched-groups design is an excellent way to artificially make the different groups more similar. However, there are two primary issues to keep in mind. First, as we match individuals for our study and then assign them to the different groups, we'll be required to obtain certain information about these individuals in order to match them. In other words, we'd need to do some sort of pretesting of our potential participants prior to conducting the actual study. If we wanted to match them on sex, this might be relatively easy. We could simply ask them if they identify as male or female. If we would like to match them on race, we could similarly ask them to identify their race and use their answer to match them and then randomly assign them to the different groups. Other factors like SES would also be relatively easy to do. Matching individuals on these types of factors would be fairly easy and very simple to do. Thus, studies that involved this sort of matching wouldn't be burdensome. However, what if you wanted to match participants on some variable that was a little more difficult or took more time to determine. For example, perhaps you'd like to match participants on IQ (i.e., intelligence). We could simply ask them their IQ score, right? After all everyone knows their IQ? Right? Maybe not. Well that's OK if they don't know their IQ. We could just evaluate each of our potential participants for their IQ and then once we have the scores, we could randomly assign them to the different groups based on their score. So how difficult could this be? Well, it's pretty difficult. To take a standardized IQ test, you'll need to have researchers or evaluators who have been trained to administer this standardized assessment instrument. Standardized IQ tests can also be given to only one individual at a time and the test takes approximately three hours to administer. Imagine that you'd like to test 100 individuals in each of your three conditions in your study. Minimally, you'd have to test 300 individuals for 3 hours or spend 900 hours testing individuals just so you can match them for your study. This is just to match them!! This doesn't even include your actual study!! Thus, this pretesting could be extremely time consuming and burdensome. This would also be wishful thinking that after administering the IQ tests, you had matches for each of the individuals that you evaluated. You'd most likely need to test many more individuals so that you'd end up with your 300 individuals with matches. This isn't sounding nearly as much fun, is it?

A somewhat similar approach is to use stratified random sampling. In **stratified random sampling**, sub-groups of participants are selected for the study in the same proportions as they exist in the population. For example, if the population has 60% Caucasians, 25% Hispanics, and 15% African-Americans, then each group would be made up of individuals in this same percentage breakdown. As participants are selected to be in the study, they are randomly assigned to the specific group, but care is taken to keep these percentages the same. This technique would be replicated for each condition so that the groups are both equal to one another and so that they adequately represent the population from which they were selected.

A related issue concerns the situation where you've tested individuals but you don't have a match for that individual. If this occurs, what do you do with these matchless individuals? The answer: nothing. You can't use them in your study if you don't have a match for them.

Another big issue with using matched-assignment is dealing with subject attrition. As we defined previously, **subject attrition** is when participants drop out of your study. In a matched-groups design, if you lose a participant due to attrition, not only do you lose that individual, but you also lose his or her match(es). You can't use the data from an individual if they don't complete your study, and you can't use the data from individuals who don't have matches. If you just have two groups, you lose one additional individual when you lose a participant to attrition. If you have more groups, this problem gets exacerbated. If you have 5 groups and you lose one participant, you would then have to drop that individual's 4 matches!

Concluding Remarks

The logic for a between-subject design is that the groups are exactly the same as one another, except for the actual manipulation. Thus, if the groups differ from one another it must be the manipulation that caused that difference. As discussed in this chapter, the primary issue with using a between-subjects design or using between-subjects variables is making sure that the different groups are equivalent to one another and that the *only* difference between the groups is the manipulation. Otherwise, the study is useless, contains a confound, and no conclusions can really be determined from the study. If having perfectly equal groups is the main issue in your study, using the techniques discussed in this chapter would be an excellent start. If, even after using all of the suggestions from this chapter, you still can't get the different groups to be equivalent to one another, there's only one other option: use a within-subjects design. As discussed in the next chapter, a major advantage of the within-subjects design is that you have the same individuals in each of your different conditions. Thus, there's no better matching than having the same individuals in each condition.

End of Chapter Quiz

1. If you have a single-factor between-subjects study with 3 levels of the IV and you need 50 subjects per condition, how many subjects must you test?

2. True or False: Random selection with a larger number of participants is likely to lead to unequal groups?

3. What are the two sources of systematic group variance?

4. True or False: Carryover effects are often a problem associated with between-subject designs?

5. What is it called when a disproportionate number of individuals drop out of one of your conditions compared to another condition?

6. True or False: An F-ratio of about 1 is expected by chance if there was no effect of the manipulation.

7. List three ways that you can help to encourage equal groups in between-subjects studies.

8. True or False: The larger the F-ratio, the larger the effect of systematic group variance.

9. If the placebo group finds out that they are receiving the placebo and demands to receive the treatment, this is an example of what issue?

10. Which sampling technique selects participants into the study in the same proportions as they exist in the population?

Homework Assignment #1

Please answer each of the following questions to the best of your ability. Be sure to explain your answers where appropriate.

1. What are two advantages of using a between-subjects design?

2. What are two disadvantages of using a between-subjects design?

3. What is the primary issue to take care of when conducting a study using a between-subjects design?

4. Kelly wants to conduct a between-subjects study with four levels of a drug. If she would like to evaluate 20 participants for each drug condition, how many participants would she test?

5. If a researcher uses a 4 x 2 between-subjects design, how many <u>groups</u> of subjects will there be?

6. If a researcher uses a 4 x 2 between-subjects design, how many <u>conditions</u> will there be?

Chapter 7

True Experiments: Within-Subject Designs

A s discussed in Chapter 2, when you have a within-subjects variable each participant will receive all of the levels of the independent variable. When we speak of these different levels in a within-subjects design, we refer to these as different conditions, not different groups. Either term, groups or conditions, is appropriate when using a between-subjects design, but only the term condition is appropriate for a within-subjects variable since all of your participants will participate in each of the different conditions. The term conditions is a more generic term and is appropriate for referring to the levels of either a between- or within-subjects manipulation. Let's use the same example that we used in Chapter 6 here so that you can see how the way in which you manipulate the independent variable (i.e., between-subjects or within-subjects) impacts your experiment, even if you have the same manipulation, the same levels of the manipulation, and the same number of participants in each of your conditions. For example, if you were manipulating the level of a drug and had three different drug doses (e.g., low, medium, and high), you would have three different conditions in your study where participants would receive different amounts of the drug. In a between-subjects design, one group or condition would receive the low dose of the drug, another group would receive the medium dose of the drug, and the third group would receive the high dose of the drug. In a within-subjects design each participant would receive each of these different conditions. Perhaps our participants would receive the lowest dose of the drug for six weeks and then we'd evaluate the effect of the drug. They would then receive the medium dose of the drug for another six weeks and then we'd evaluate them again. Finally, they'd receive the highest drug dose for six weeks and we'd complete a final evaluation to see the effects of the drug. In this example, each participant would receive all three of the levels of our independent variable, drug dose.

Due to the nature of many within-subjects designs, where participants are measured several different times repeatedly, within-subject designs are often called **repeated-measures designs**. In fact, if you use SPSS to analyze your data from a within-subjects design, you might have difficulty determining the appropriate test to use to analyze your data because you won't find a within-subjects ANOVA in SPSS. You'll need to utilize the repeated-measures ANOVA to analyze data when you have a within-subjects variable. In fact, the most common type of within-subjects design is a **pretest/post-test design**, which uses a repeated measure. For example, if you wanted to determine if an SAT training preparatory class was effective, you might want to give the individuals a pretest, administer the 6 week class, and then give them another SAT test. This pretest/post-test design would involve giving a repeated SAT test and measuring their performance at two times (i.e., a repeated measure).

Advantages of Using a Within-Subjects Design

As discussed in the previous chapter with between-subject designs, there are also many advantages to using a within-subjects design. It's important to know the advantages and disadvantages of each type of design so that you can make a well-informed, educated decision concerning how you'd like to manipulate your independent variable(s). Probably the best reason to utilize a within-subjects design is that when you do so, each participant serves as his or her own control. As mentioned at the conclusion of the previous chapter, within-subject designs minimize the differences between the participants in each of the conditions since they're the same individuals. Thus, there aren't any differences between the individuals in the various conditions. No matching of subjects is required in a within-subjects designs since you can't do better matching than having the same individuals in each condition. Therefore, there would be no differences between the conditions due to any individual differences between your participants, eliminating any potential confounds that could occur due to having such differences between your conditions.

In a within-subjects design, each participant serves as his or her own control. This means that you'd need fewer participants in your study since you wouldn't need a separate control group. This makes within-subject designs quite a bit more efficient. Let's use the same example that we used in the previous chapter. Let's assume that you have an experiment where you'd like to test our anti-anxiety drug. In our study we'd like to evaluate three levels of our drug: a placebo group, a low dose, and a high dose. In order to test the drug, we need to have 50 participants in each of these conditions. If we were to conduct this study as a between-subjects design, we'd need 50 participants in each of our 3 conditions for a total of 150 individuals in our study. If we conducted this same study as a within-subjects manipulation, we'd need 50 participants in each of the 3 conditions as well. However, since each individual receives each of the different levels of the independent variable in a within-subjects design, we'd need only 50 participants in total since each participant would receive each of the different drug dose levels. The more levels that you have, the more of an advantage the within-subjects design would become. With 5 drug levels, we'd need 250 participants for a between-subjects design (5 levels × 50 participants per level). For the within-subjects design it would still just be 50 participants since each participant would receive all 5 of the levels. With 10 levels, you'd need 500 participants in the between-subjects design, but still just 50 participants in the within-subjects design. The within-subjects design seems to have quite the advantage over a between-subjects design!

In addition to simply requiring fewer participants since each individual serves in each of the different conditions in a within-subjects design, within-subjects designs require a fewer number of participants for another major reason. Within-subjects designs have greater statistical power than between-subject designs. As noted in the previous chapter, **statistical power** refers to the likelihood that a study will detect an effect of the independent variable when there is an effect to be detected. Since you have different individuals in each of your groups in a between-subjects design, you'll have more individual differences caused by having different participants in each of the groups. As noted in the previous chapter, individual differences have the effect of making it more difficult to see the effects of an independent variable in any study because they add statistical noise to your data. Individual differences occur in every study, but the impact of those individual differences is somewhat stronger in a between-subjects design. In a between-subjects design, you have

© Fon_nongkran/Shutterstock.com

The return of Statistical Power Man!!

individual differences within each of your groups since there are different individuals in each of the groups AND you also have individual differences between your groups as well, since there are different individuals in each of your groups. In a within-subjects design you have individual differences between your various participants in your study. However, the individuals who are in the different conditions are the same people. Therefore, you have individual differences *within* each of your conditions, but you don't have any individual difference *between* your conditions since it's the same people in each of your conditions. As a result, there is a lot more statistical noise (or error variance) in a between-subjects design compared to a within-subjects design resulting in higher statistical power for within-subject designs. Let's use the sample data below so that you can see what kind of a difference in statistical power we're talking about here.

Imagine that we have a study where we're evaluating anxiety scores for our participants such that higher anxiety scores depict more anxiety. We have three different treatments that are going to be used for our study. The data are provided below:

Between-Subjects Experiment with 3 separate Groups

Treatment 1		Treatment 2		Treatment 3	
Mary	20	Ricardo	24	Mary	28
Danielle	30	Ryan	35	Barry	39
Cory	40	Isabella	43	Oliver	47
Mark	50	Don	54	Kelly	58
Average =	*35*	*Average =*	*39*	*Average =*	*43*

Within-Subjects Experiment with 3 separate Conditions

Treatment 1		Treatment 2		Treatment 3	
Mary	20	Mary	24	Mark	28
Danielle	30	Danielle	35	Danielle	39
Cory	40	Cory	43	Cory	47
Mark	50	Mark	54	Mark	58
Average =	*35*	*Average =*	*39*	*Average =*	*43*

As you can see from the data, the averages for each of the treatments are exactly the same. Additionally, the scores for each individual in each treatment are also exactly the same for Treatment 1, Treatment 2, and Treatment 3 for both data sets. The only difference is that we have four different individuals in each of the between-subjects treatment groups on the top of the table, and the same four individuals received each of the three treatments in the within-subjects experiment on the bottom of the table. When we conduct the ANOVA using SPSS, we find that the data for the main effect of Treatments for the between-subjects experiment is the following: $F(2, 9) = 0.393$, $p = .686$, $\eta^2_p = .080$. If you recall from the statistics chapter, this indicates that there was no main effect of treatments. In other words, anxiety scores for the different treatments was statistically the same. An F-ratio of approximately 1 would be expected if there was nothing occurring, and our computed F-ratio is actually less than 1. When we analyze the data from the within-subjects experiment, which includes the exact same numbers, we get a different finding: $F(2, 6) = 288.00$, $p < .001$, $\eta^2_p = .990$. These findings indicate a strong main effect of treatment, indicating that the treatments were significantly different from one another. Thus, the treatments definitely made a difference and resulted in different anxiety scores. The differences between these two results is huge!! We're not saying that within-subject designs have a little bit more power than between-subject designs; we're arguing that the difference in statistical power is huge!!

You may be wondering why this statistical power is such a big deal. Well, there are a couple of situations that make this statistical power so important. First, if you don't have very many participants available to you to test, you need to use a design that provides a lot of statistical power so that you'll be able to see an effect of your treatment when there is one. Second, if you're evaluating a treatment or manipulation that has a very small effect size, you'll need to use a technique that has excellent statistical power so that you'll be able to detect a difference when there is one. If your drug or therapy or other manipulation has a gigantic effect then this power isn't as big of an issue, but if it has a relatively small effect size, you need all the power that you can get. Within-subject designs definitely provide this power to see effects of your treatment when your treatment is effective, even when you have access to only a small number of participants or a small effect size.

Potential Problems with Using Within-Subject Designs

Like we did with the between-subject designs in the last chapter, we can't just discuss all the advantages of using within-subject designs. While the advantages are fairly significant, we need to provide a balanced view of within-subject designs so that you understand both the pros and cons of using this design. One of the first potential issues with using within-subject designs is that since participants participate in each of the different conditions, participation will take a lot more time for participants. For example, if you had three conditions and each condition took 60 minutes to complete then participants would spend 180 minutes or 3 hours to complete your study. If this was a between-subjects design, since individuals only participate in one of the conditions, it would only require 60 minutes of their time. This makes the within-subjects participation quite a bit longer. At our university, we use a program that allows students to volunteer for the various experiments that are being conducted in our department. Students typically have quite a few studies to select from. Our students are given 1 research credit for every hour or part of an hour of participation. Imagine that you were one of our students. You have a choice between a 15 minute study and a 45 minute study. Both studies would give you 1 research credit toward your introductory psychology course. Which study do you participate in? The vast majority of our students are going to select the 15 minute study. The 15 minute study would be equivalent to a between-subjects study, whereas the 45 minute study would be equivalent to a within-subjects study with three conditions. This example provides a good illustration for this potential disadvantage of within-subjects designs. Since it takes more time for each participant, it may be more difficult to recruit participants to be in your study if participants know that the study will take longer. This is true of shorter 15 vs. 45 minutes studies. This problem gets exacerbated when you start looking at participation in cross-sectional vs. longitudinal studies. **Cross-sectional studies** are studies where different aged participants participate at one time. **Longitudinal studies** are studies where participants get tested over a long period of time when participants are of different ages and

This woman just completed a long within-subjects study that had several exercise conditions. Even though she appears very fit, the study has made her extremely fatigued.

typically involves multiple testing times. Cross-sectional studies are analogous to have a between-subjects manipulation of age, whereas longitudinal studies are like within-subject manipulations of age. Imagine that you wanted to test students during kindergarten, 2nd grade, 4th grade, 6th grade, and 8th grade. If you did this as a cross-sectional study, you'd test kindergarteners, 2nd graders, 4th graders, 6th graders, and 8th graders all around the same time. If you conducted this study as a longitudinal study, you'd test the same group of students five times in their lives: when they were in kindergarten, when they were in 2nd grade, 4th grade, 6th grade, and finally when they were in 8th grade. The cross-sectional study might take a few months to test everyone. The longitudinal study would be testing the same individuals over 8 years. Recruiting participants for your longitudinal study might be extremely difficult because participants would need to commit to your study for the next 8 years!!

Another potential issue that is related to this idea that within-subjects studies involve testing participants for a longer period of time is subject attrition. **Subject attrition** is a particular issue for within-subject designs because it takes more time from each participant. Due to this factor, participants are more likely to drop out of within-subjects designs. If an individual starts your study and participates in four of the five conditions but then drops out of your study before completing the fifth condition, you'll have to drop his data for all of the conditions. This individual's data won't be complete. This could occur in any study, and might make you very upset as a researcher because of all the time that you've already committed to testing this individual. Now consider what this attrition would mean for a longitudinal study. Imagine that you've tested this individual when he was in kindergarten and 2nd grade and 4th grade and 6th grade, but then the individual drops out of your study before he completes your study. You've invested 6 years in this participant only to lose his data since he never completed your study!!

Another potential issue is statistical regression or regression to the mean. **Regression to the mean** refers to the tendency of extreme scores to regress or return to the average over repeated tests. There are many examples of regression to the mean. One nice example of this is the "*Sports Illustrated* Jinx."

Each week or even after a season, the most impressive player adorns the cover of *Sports Illustrated*, a weekly sports magazine. According to this "jinx" a player who makes the cover of *Sports Illustrated* is now doomed and will have a terrible following week or subsequent season. However, the player made the cover because he or she had an extraordinary week or season, due simply to regression to the mean, we would expect him or her not to be able to replicate his or her amazing feat. You might experience something similar as you apply for graduate schools. If you plan on applying to graduate schools, you'll be required to take the Graduate Record Exam (or GRE). If you do amazingly poorly on this exam, let's say in the 3rd percentile (which means that you did better than 3% of the individuals who took this exam), would you retake the GRE? In case you aren't sure, this is an extremely low score. Just by chance alone or simply by randomly selecting answers on the test, you'd be expected to do better the next time. On the other hand, what if instead, you scored extremely well. Let's say that you scored in the 97th percentile. Would you take it again in hopes that you might improve your score? This is an extremely remarkable score and the chances of you replicating this type of score is extremely small. Just by chance alone, and regression to the mean, you'd be expected to do more poorly if you took the GRE again. I doubt

While this soccer player had an amazing season, he's now doomed to perform terribly in the upcoming season since he's on the cover of *Sporting Illustrated*.

you would regress to the 3rd percentile, but your score would be expected to move toward the mean (i.e., lower than the 97th percentile).

This regression to the mean is a potential issue in within-subject designs because of the fact that participants are being tested more than once. Imagine a participant who scores extremely poorly during the pretest. For the posttest after the treatment, we would expect this participant to do better simply due to regression to the mean. However, if our participant does perform better, it would be unclear if our treatment was effective in helping her to improve her score or if it was simply regression to the mean? The opposite could also occur with extremely high scores. The second time the participant is tested the score may go down because of the treatment or because of regression to the mean. Regardless of which it is, it makes it difficult to interpret the findings.

Another potential issue is history. No, we don't mean history such as the history of the United States or Texas history. By **history** we're referring to any outside event that occurs during the time of the study. It's possible that this outside event may be causing the changes that researchers are observing between the pretest and posttest. For example, let's say we have a high school student named Henry who is having difficulty with his math class. Because he's doing poorly in math, his mother decides to speak with his math teacher to see about getting a tutor to help him. In order to evaluate the effectiveness of the tutor, we may want to look at Henry's test and homework scores prior to hiring the tutor and then after he's received tutoring for a few weeks. If Henry's math grades have increased after the tutoring, we'd be inclined to determine that the tutoring has been very effective. Doesn't this sound reasonable? Of course it does, but it might not be correct. Due to Henry's poor math grades, his mother may have made him play less video games at home, grounded him from talking to his friends, took away his car, or not let him play on the school soccer team (because Henry really likes soccer). Perhaps it was the tutoring that led to Henry's higher grades or it could have been these other things that his mother did. Which is it? We really can't say for sure. This is the problem with history.

Here's Henry getting extra help from his math tutor.
Were his improved grades due to the tutor or history?

Another potential issue is a change in instrumentation. A **change in instrumentation** is any change in the measuring instrument over time. This could be a change in a physical measuring device such as a scale or a change in the observer. For example, if you used an analog scale to measure weight, the scale may not be broken in very well and so it has a bit of variability in its measurements. The scale could be worn out and just doesn't work very well. The problem is that if the scale has changed from when you did your pretest measurements to when you do your posttest measurements, it may be the scale that changed rather than any change caused by your manipulation. The same could occur if the observer has changed. For example, if you were going to a daycare or school and observing younger children on the playground for aggressive behaviors, your ability to pick up on the behaviors might change with time. During the pretest you might not be very good at picking up on the different types of aggressive behaviors exhibited by the children. However, by the time you do the posttest observations following your treatment, you might be very adept at picking up on their aggressive actions. You're now more practiced. Again, any change that you see from the pretest to the posttest may be because of a change in the instrumentation rather than a change that is being caused by your manipulation or treatment.

Will this scale give you the same weight each
time you use it or does it vary as it gets broken in?

Another potential issue with within-subject designs is that it may not always be a possible design. If you have uncontrollable carryover effects then a within-subjects design isn't a possible design option. This leads us to the next major topic which is *THE* major issue when using within-subject designs: carryover effects.

Carryover Effects

Carryover effects are when the effects of your treatment or manipulation carry over from one condition and affect another subsequent condition. Anytime an individual participates in more than one condition, as they do with within-subject variables, there is a danger of carryover effects. If a carryover effect is present, the researcher will be unsure if the changes that are being observed are being caused by the treatment or the carryover effect. There are several types of carryover effects. Let's take a look at some of the different types of carryover effects that could occur. We'll use the following example to illustrate these.

Let's say that you're the lead scientist for a drug manufacturing company that has developed a drug called Smartex that should help individuals to become smarter. In testing the drug, you've decided to recruit 100 participants into your study. You decide that you're going to give these 100 participants Smartex for 6 months and then measure their intelligence levels. After you've done this, you then give your participants a placebo pill without their knowledge for the next 6 months. After 6 months of taking the placebo you then administer an intelligence test and compare their intelligence score with when they were taking Smartex. This seems very reasonable since you've used a within-subjects design that will provide you with good statistical power and will help minimize the individual differences between conditions. See the results of your experiment below:

Smartex Testing Trial: Experiment 1

Intelligence Score w/Smartex	Intelligence Score w/Placebo
110	111

As you can see, the intelligence scores were pretty much the same after receiving the placebo compared to when participants received the drug. Based on these results, it appears that the drug didn't have any effect and didn't make participants more intelligent as you had hoped. As the lead scientist developing Smartex you decide to test Smartex again with a different group of 100 participants to see if these discouraging results can be replicated. This time your give the placebo for the first 6 months and then measure intelligence, and then provide Smartex for the next 6 months and then evaluate intelligence. This time you get the following results:

Smartex Testing Trial: Experiment 2

Intelligence Score w/Placebo	Intelligence Score w/Smartex
92	111

This time it appears that Smartex was very effective in increasing intelligence levels. What happened? Why did Smartex appear to work in your second experiment but not in your first experiment?

There are several potential explanations to help explain what may have occurred here, and the causes may have involved carryover effects. One simple type of carryover effect could occur if your treatment has an **enduring effect** or longer lasting effect than one expects. If your treatment permanently changes the participant this could cause a problem in your interpretation. In the first experiment, you gave participants Smartex for 6 months followed by the placebo phase. If Smartex caused permanent changes in your participants, perhaps causing changes in their brain structure or affecting their neurotransmitters, then we might expect participants to continue to do very well even after Smartex has been removed. Thus, in Experiment 1 participants continued to do very well even when receiving the placebo because the effects of Smartex carried over into the placebo condition. Any manipulation that could have a longer lasting or permanent change in the participant would also lead to a similar interpretation problem due to such a carryover effect.

Another type of carryover effect is a testing effect. A **testing effect** is where participants perform better (or worse) on a second test compared to the first test due to their previous experience with the test.

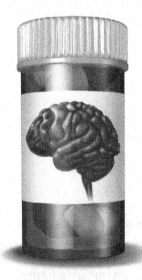

These testing effects could be due to **practice effects**, which would make performance better on the second test, or due to **fatigue effects**, which would make performance worse on the second test. In Experiment 2, we gave participants the placebo first and then Smartex during the second 6 months. When we saw the improvement in intelligence, we assume that the increase was because of the effects of Smartex. However, it could also be possible that participants did better on the second intelligence assessment because they were more practiced at taking intelligence tests. The experience that they had on the first intelligence test helped them or carried over to when they took the intelligence test the second time. So the increase may not have been due to Smartex at all; it could have just been due to the extra practice that they received. Obviously, a fatigue effect would be when the participant does worse on the second test simply because she's tired or fatigued following the first test. While this fatigue effect would be less likely in our current experiment since the tests are 6 months apart from each other, it would be more likely to occur in a repeated-measure design (or within-subject manipulation) that occurs closer in time, such as two long tests immediately following one another.

Informational effects are another potential carryover effect that could have occurred in our second experiment. Let's assume that you gave participants the same intelligence test on the second test (i.e., when participants received the Smartex) that you gave on the first test (i.e., when participants received the placebo). Why might participants do

© www.billionphotos.com/Shutterstock.com

When testing a drug like Smartex using a within-subjects design, be wary of any potential carryover effects as they're very common with this type of design.

better the second time? Well, it could be due to the effects of our drug, but it could also be because they've seen these questions before. Their experience with the test has helped them to do better the second time because they know some of the questions. Between the time that they took the first test and when they received the second test, they could have learned some of the answers to the questions. An **information carryover effect** is one where providing information in the first test carries over to the second test and allows the individual to perform better on subsequent tests due to this information. This type of carryover effect is fairly common in studies where participants are misled in the first condition (they become very resistant and distrusting in later testing if they realize they were misled) or if they receive special training or instructions in earlier conditions that could help them later. For example, when testing memory in younger children, we know that younger children don't always spontaneously use rehearsal (or repeating the items to themselves). If we test our children's memory first by telling them to use rehearsal and then tell them not to use rehearsal the second time we test them, they usually continue to do really well the second time. Is this because rehearsal doesn't help them to improve their memories or because they continued to use rehearsal the second time, even though we told them not to use it? It's because they realize that rehearsal was really helpful and they continue to use it.

The last carryover effect is subject maturation. **Subject maturation** is when participants do better on subsequent testing simply because they're getting older or maturing. In our second experiment, especially if we were testing children, it's possible that they did better on the second intelligence test not because of Smartex, but simply because their brains have developed further because they are getting older. A simple example of this phenomenon would be to imagine that you have some kind of treatment or training that you think will help children to acquire language better. In order to test this treatment, you take 100 2-year-olds and test their language capabilities. You then provide them with your treatment, whatever it happens to be, for the next 15 months. After 15 months you then evaluate their language skills again. Amazingly they show a huge increase in their language skills!! Is it because of your treatment? Maybe, but it's probably more likely that it's simply caused by the children maturing and improving their language skills as they would have done without your treatment.

Subject maturation is a very common reason for participants getting taller, weighing more, getting smarter, and having better language skills, regardless of any experimental manipulation that you may have administered.

Controlling Carryover Effects

So we've established that carryover effects are a major potential problem when using within-subject variables. They make it extremely difficult to determine if changes in behavior or scores are being caused by the treatment or manipulation as the researcher intends or if these changes are being caused by carryover effects. When left unchecked, carryover effects make it virtually impossible to come to a

134   Research Methods in Psychology

Table 7.1   Overview of Counterbalancing Options

Subject-by-Subject Counterbalancing	Across-Subjects Counterbalancing
Reverse counterbalancing	Complete counterbalancing
Block counterbalancing • Partial block counterbalancing • Complete block counterbalancing	Partial counterbalancing • Randomize partial counterbalancing • Latin-square counterbalancing • Balanced Latin-square counterbalancing

conclusion about the cause of the observed changes. This is a problem because determining the cause is exactly what experiments are supposed to allow researchers to do, compared to nonexperimental approaches. So what do we do to remedy this?

There is one tool that we have in our researcher "tool belt." That tool is counterbalancing. **Counterbalancing** is a method that is used to control order effects in within-subject (or repeated measures) designs by altering the orders that treatments are presented to participants. The purpose of counterbalancing is, in some way, to change the different orders of the treatments so that various orders are presented so that treatments are not always given in the same order. There are two major classes of counterbalancing techniques. These techniques differ in how the different orders are presented to participants. **Subject-by-subject counterbalancing** includes techniques that give the various treatment orders to each participant. **Across-subjects counterbalancing** includes techniques that give each participant only one of the various treatment orders. Thus, some participants receive one of the treatment orders and other participants receive other orders. For organization purposes, Table 7.1 provides the list of different counterbalancing techniques. In the next section we'll discuss the different types of subject-by-subject counterbalancing as well as the different types of across-subjects counterbalancing techniques.

Subject-by-Subject Counterbalancing

Reverse counterbalancing

As previously stated, subject-by-subject counterbalancing provides the various orders used to each participant. It's like a within-subjects manipulation of treatment orders. There are several different orders being used and each participant will receive all of the orders being used. The different subject-by-subject techniques are reverse counterbalancing and block randomization.

In **reverse counterbalancing** participants will receive the different treatments in order followed by the reverse order. Each participant will receive both the forward and reverse orders. For example, if we have three different treatments (Treatment A, B, and C) then each participant will receive the treatments in order:

Treatment A followed by Treatment B followed by Treatment C

They will then receive:

Treatment C followed by Treatment B followed by Treatment A

Thus, each participant will receive:

Treatment A → Treatment B → Treatment C → Treatment C → Treatment B → Treatment A

The reverse counterbalancing is nice because it's simple and it provides the different treatments in one order and then gives the same treatments in the opposite order in an attempt at changing the orders to combat carryover effects. So, if there's a carryover effect that occurs when Treatment C follows

Treatment B then this will only occur one time. Most of the time this carryover effect won't be a problem. If we had 5 treatments then the order would be:

$$A \rightarrow B \rightarrow C \rightarrow D \rightarrow E \rightarrow E \rightarrow D \rightarrow C \rightarrow B \rightarrow A$$

Block randomization

Similar to reverse counterbalancing, block randomization also involves presenting each participant with the various orders being used. However, in **block randomization** there are several more orders that will be presented to participants and each participant will receive several blocks of trials where participants receive a different order each time. As previously mentioned, there is both a complete block randomization and partial block randomization.

In a complete block randomization, you must first determine all of the potential orders that are possible. There's a simple way to do this; you just write down every possible sequence order. This seems simple enough. For example, if you have two treatments (Treatments A and B) then there would only be two possible orders: $A \rightarrow B$ and $B \rightarrow A$. This seems pretty simple. For complete block randomization, each of your participants would then receive Treatment A followed by Treatment B and then Treatment B followed by Treatment A. If there are three treatments (Treatments A, B, and C) then it becomes a little bit more difficult, but still very manageable. You would have six possible orders, as seen below:

$A \rightarrow B \rightarrow C$	$B \rightarrow A \rightarrow C$	$C \rightarrow A \rightarrow B$
$A \rightarrow C \rightarrow B$	$B \rightarrow C \rightarrow A$	$C \rightarrow B \rightarrow A$

In the case of three treatments, each of your participants would receive all six of the possible treatment orders given above for the complete block randomization. As a result, each participant would be tested with each treatment in each of the six different orders. Thus, each participant would be tested 18 times (3 treatments × 6 orders = 18 times tested).

So, how do we know how many possible sequence orders there are when using one of the complete counterbalancing techniques? We use a mathematical technique called K! (which is read "K factorial"). With K!, K refers to the number of treatments and the exclamation point (!) tells you to multiply that number by the next smallest number and continue to do this until you get to one. It actually sounds more complex than it really is. So, if you had three treatments it would look like this:

3 treatments: $3! = 3 \times 2 \times 1 = 6$ possible orders

If you have additional treatments, they would look like this:

4 treatments: $4! = 4 \times 3 \times 2 \times 1 = 24$ possible orders

5 treatments: $5! = 5 \times 4 \times 3 \times 2 \times 1 = 120$ possible orders

6 treatments: $6! = 6 \times 5 \times 4 \times 3 \times 2 \times 1 = 720$ possible orders

As you can see, with a smaller number of treatments, you have a reasonable number of treatment orders. The more treatments you add, the less reasonable and manageable the number of treatment orders seems. The main issue with a complete block randomization is that it may not be practical. It involves testing participants with each of the treatments in each of the different treatment orders. As we mentioned, with 3 orders this would result in each participant being tested 18 times. If we have 4 treatments with 24 possible orders, each participant would be tested 96 times (4 treatments × 24 orders = 96 times tested). It starts to really get crazy with 5 treatments, which would involve testing each participant

600 times (5 treatments × 120 orders = 600 times tested). Now, how unreasonable this is would be determined by how long it takes to test each participant during each treatment. Let's use the example of just 3 treatments, which is a fairly low number of treatments (which results in testing each individual 18 times). If it takes only 10 seconds to test each participant with a treatment (perhaps you're testing a simple decision task so that participants can be presented with each treatment or condition quickly, one after the other) then this may not seem unreasonable. With 3 treatments, it would only take us 3 minutes for each participant (18 times tested × 10 seconds each = 180 seconds or 3 minutes). With 5 treatments, it would only take us 20 minutes to test each participant (120 times tested × 10 seconds each = 1200 seconds or 20 minutes). If we had 100 participants then it would only take us 300 minutes (or 5 hours) to test all of our participants. With five treatments, we'd still only be looking at a total of 2000 minutes (or a little more than 33 hours of testing) for all of our participants. Does this seem reasonable to you? I think it sounds pretty reasonable, even with five treatments. However, if it takes 1 hour to evaluate each participant for each treatment then we're looking at 18 hours of testing for each of our 100 participants with only 3 treatments. If we have 100 participants then we're looking at 1800 hours of testing for the study. That's 75 complete 24 hour days of just testing for only 3 treatments. If we had 5 treatments (which resulted in testing each individual 600 times), we'd be looking at a total of 60,000 hours to test our 100 participants!!! 60,000 hours would be 2,500 complete 24 hour days or 6.94 years of doing nothing but testing participants!! Does this seem reasonable to you? We're hoping at this point that your response is "Absolutely not!!" So, what are your options?

If we'd like to minimize the number of times that we'd like to test our participants, instead of conducting a complete block randomization, we could instead use a partial block randomization. In a partial block randomization, we're going to use some of the orders that we've determined from the complete block randomization. By only using some of these orders, we can save ourselves a significant amount of time testing our participants since each participant will not receive every possible order. There are different ways to determine which specific orders that you give to each participant, but the number of orders that each participant receives in a partial block randomization will be the same. The rule is that the number of treatments determines the number of blocks. So if you have 3 different treatments then each participant would receive 3 of the different treatment orders out of our total of 6 possible orders. If we had 4 treatments then each participant would receive 4 of the different treatment orders out of our total of 24 possible orders. As you've probably already guessed, if we had 5 treatment orders, we'd select 5 of the different treatment orders out of our total of 120 possible orders. Typically, the different treatment orders are selected randomly, but it would be possible to select the different orders in the same way that we'll discuss later with the different across-subjects partial counterbalancing techniques. For our purposes now, we'll just assume that we'll determine these orders by randomly selecting the appropriate number of treatment orders. As we mentioned previously, if we had 3 treatments then there would be a possible 6 different treatment orders. Since there are 3 treatments, we'd need to select 3 different orders from the 6:

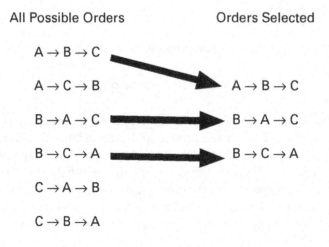

Table 7.2 Overview of Counterbalancing Options

	Complete Block Randomization	**Partial Block Randomization**
3 Treatments	1,800 hours	900 hours
4 Treatments	9,600 hours	1,600 hours
5 Treatments	60,000 hours	2,500 hours

Thus, each participant would be tested for each treatment using the following testing order: A, B, C, B, A, C, B, C, A. If you had 4 treatments, we'd do the same thing and randomly select 4 different orders from the 24 possible orders. As you can see, using the partial block randomization saves you a lot of testing time. See Table 7.2 to see how much time it would save us if it took us 1 hour to test each treatment for 100 participants:

As you can see from Table 7.2, the partial block randomization does save an extraordinary amount of time compared to the complete block randomization technique. This is especially true as we increase the number of treatments that we have. However, look at the table again. Even if we were to use the partial block randomization with 5 treatments, we're still looking at a lot of time to test each individual. Think about it. With 5 treatments, we'll end up with 5 different treatment orders. So, each participant will be tested 25 total times at an hour for each of these 25 assessments. Does that seem reasonable to have a participant in your study for 25 hours? Probably not. This is one of the main problems with the subject-by-subject counterbalancing techniques. They may not be very practical. Since we'll be testing each individual by giving them numerous trials with the treatments in different orders, they may become overly fatigued. They could become very bored or lose motivation. Subject-by-subject counterbalancing techniques can be extremely time consuming, which can be very costly in terms of time or money if you're paying your participants. This is obviously true of the complete subject-by-subject approaches, but can also be true for even the partial subject-by-subject approaches. So, if we don't want to test each participant nearly as many times, what can we do? Perhaps we need to come up with a way that we can evaluate each participant with only one of the treatment orders, but still use all of the treatment orders. This is why researchers may turn to across-subjects counterbalancing.

Across-Subjects Counterbalancing

In across-subjects counterbalancing, we're able to distribute any carryover effects (or progressive error) across participants. This progressive error will be equally distributed across participants and will cancel out when we pool our data. Take the example of the Pepsi Challenge, which was really big when I was growing up. Yes, it was a long time ago. Yes, I'm aware that I'm old. In the Pepsi Challenge, individuals were given Pepsi and Coke to taste. Since we'd like to have each individual taste both Pepsi and Coke, we'll be using a within-subjects manipulation for the type of soda. Let's say that we test each individual by first giving them Pepsi to taste and rate on a 10-point scale (where 10 is great tasting and 1 is terrible tasting) and then give them Coke to taste and rate. Let's imagine that when we do this, we get the following average ratings:

$$\text{Pepsi} = 9.3 \qquad \text{Coke} = 6.1$$

Based on these results, it appears that Pepsi received the higher ratings, and we can conclude that Pepsi was preferred to Coke, right? If you haven't been paying attention to anything in this chapter, you probably said "Yes." However, if you have been paying attention, you might have concluded: "Well, the results seem to point in that direction, but we could have a potential carryover effect where the first soda could just be preferred." I'm sure you were in this second group, right . . . ? Of course you were!! Because it's a within-subjects design, we need to use counterbalancing in order to take care of any potential carryover effects. Not unreasonably, let's imagine that it's a hot summer afternoon and there is a preference for the first soda that participants taste. When we provide the other order, Coke first followed by Pepsi, we get the following results:

$$Coke = 8.1 \qquad Pepsi = 7.6$$

This time it appears that Coke was preferred. If we tested half of our participants by giving them Pepsi first and the other half by giving them Coke first, when we pool our data we can see which soda was preferred AND this allows us to control or counterbalance the effects of the first soda preference. Pepsi has an advantage half of the time as the first soda and Coke also has an advantage half of the time as the first soda. It all equals out when we pool our data. Here are the findings when we pool the data:

	First Soda	Second Soda
Order 1:	Pepsi = 9.3	Coke = 6.1
Order 2:	Coke = 8.1	Pepsi = 7.6

Pepsi average: $\dfrac{(9.3 + 7.6)}{2} = 8.45$ Coke average: $\dfrac{(6.1 + 8.1)}{2} = 7.10$

According to our study, individuals have an overall preference for Pepsi even after we've counterbalanced for the potential order effect. This is the general idea behind using across-subjects counterbalancing. Each individual will only receive one of the different orders, which will save a considerable amount of time. However, we'll pool our data so that each treatment order is still given to an equal number of participants and is equally represented in our data. Let's take a look at each of our across-subject counterbalancing options.

Complete counterbalancing

Complete counterbalancing uses every possible sequence order of the treatments, but each participant receives only one of those orders when using an across-subjects counterbalancing technique. As discussed earlier, we'll use K! to determine the total number of orders and, like earlier, the number of orders would depend on the number of treatments:

3 treatments: $3! = 3 \times 2 \times 1 = 6$ possible orders

4 treatments: $4! = 4 \times 3 \times 2 \times 1 = 24$ possible orders

5 treatments: $5! = 5 \times 4 \times 3 \times 2 \times 1 = 120$ possible orders

6 treatments: $6! = 6 \times 5 \times 4 \times 3 \times 2 \times 1 = 720$ possible orders

Since this is an across-subjects counterbalancing approach, each participant would receive only one of these different orders. Keep in mind that when we utilize across-subjects counterbalancing, we must have an equal number of participants receiving each of the different orders to balance the orders. If we had differing numbers of participants receiving each order, it would completely defeat the purpose of the counterbalancing. So, we'd need a *minimum* of 1 participant to receive each of the different orders. If we had 3 treatments then, we'd need a minimum of 6 participants in our study; one to receive each of the 6 different treatments. If we wanted to test more individuals then we'd need to have an equal number of participants for each of the treatment orders. So if we wanted to test more we'd need to jump to 2 participants for each treatment order, giving us 12 participants. As you can see, when we increase the number of participants in our study, we'll need to increase it by 6 participants each time to make sure that we have an equal number of participants receiving each of the 6 different treatment orders. If we had 4 treatments, we'd have 24 possible orders. Thus, we'd need a minimum of 24 participants in our study. Any additional participants would require us to increase the number of participants by 24. With 5 treatments, we'd increase the number of participants by 120 each time. See below:

2 treatments require a minimum of 2 participants

- Additional participants necessitate 4, 6, 8, 10, etc. participants

3 treatments require a minimum of 6 participants

- Additional participants necessitate 12, 18, 24, 30, 36, etc. participants

4 treatments require a minimum of 24 participants

- Additional participants necessitate 48, 72, 96, 120, etc. participants

5 treatments require a minimum of 120 participants

- Additional participants necessitate 240, 360, 480, etc. participants

6 treatments require a minimum of 720 participants

- Additional participants necessitate 1440, 2160, 2880, etc. participants

Hopefully by looking at the information above, you can see that using a complete counterbalancing and needing to test additional individuals isn't a big issue with two or three treatments. It might even be fine with four treatments. However, beyond that, running any additional participants requires a pretty large jump in the number of participants that you'd need in order to equally represent each of the different treatment orders. Thus, one potential issue with complete counterbalancing with a larger number of treatments is that it may be very costly and inefficient. As a result, many researchers may turn to partial counterbalancing techniques.

Partial counterbalancing

Partial counterbalancing is a technique where we'll use some of the orders from the complete counterbalancing. If complete counterbalancing is a bit overwhelming or impractical, partial counterbalancing allows us to save ourselves a significant amount of time testing our participants since there will be far fewer orders that we'll be testing. There are several different partial counterbalancing techniques that we can use, and each will be discussed in this section, but the number of different orders that we'll take from the complete counterbalancing will be the same. As stated earlier in the block randomization section, the rule is that you will use the same number of orders as you have treatments. So if you have 3 different treatments then we would only use 3 of the different treatment orders out of our total of 6 possible orders. If we had 4 treatments then we would only use 4 of the different treatment orders out of our total of 24 possible orders. If we had 5 treatment orders, we'd select 5 of the different treatment orders out of our total of 120 possible orders. Each of the different partial counterbalancing methods below will be explained in order of effectiveness. Of the different partial counterbalancing methods, the simplest is randomized partial counterbalancing, but it's also the least effective. Latin square is a little more difficult, but really not much more difficult, and it's a more effective technique. The balanced Latin-square technique is a little trickier, but it's the best partial counterbalancing technique. Each of these techniques are fairly easy, but some take a little more practice than others before you feel completely comfortable using them.

Randomized partial counterbalancing

With randomized partial counterbalancing, we'll randomly select certain orders from the different complete counterbalancing orders. Like the random block counterbalancing technique mentioned previously, if we had 3 treatments then there would be a possible 6 different treatment orders. Since there are 3 treatments, we'd need to select 3 different orders from the 6. See below to see how this might look:

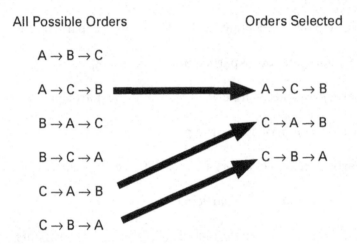

All Possible Orders

A → B → C

A → C → B

B → A → C

B → C → A

C → A → B

C → B → A

Orders Selected

A → C → B

C → A → B

C → B → A

Thus, each participant would be tested using one of the selected treatment orders. If you had 4 treatments, we'd do the same thing and randomly select 4 different orders from the 24 possible orders from the complete counterbalancing. With 5 treatments, we'd randomly select 5 different orders from the 120 possible orders. Keep in mind that the main difference between the randomized partial counterbalancing technique and the randomized block partial counterbalancing is that randomized partial counterbalancing is an across-subjects counterbalancing technique, while randomized block partial counterbalancing is a subject-by-subject counterbalancing technique. So, while the different orders may be selected in the same way, participants with randomized partial counterbalancing (i.e., across-subjects technique) would only receive one of the selected orders, whereas in the randomized block partial counterbalancing (i.e., subject-by-subject technique) participants would receive all of the selected orders.

While the randomly selected orders will most likely take care of the different carryover effects, since the orders are selected randomly, it's possible that it may not. After all, we're not using every single possible order. Clearly a complete counterbalancing approach would be a stronger form of counterbalancing, but we're trying to save some time and effort with the partial counterbalancing techniques. If you look at the three orders that were randomly selected in our example above, you'll notice that two of those orders start with our C treatment and there aren't any treatments that start with the B treatment. Additionally, two of our treatments end with the B treatment, but none of the selected orders end with the C treatment. Is this a problem? Maybe. If one of the treatments had a specific carryover effect then this could be a problem. So how can we still utilize a partial counterbalancing technique that makes it so that each treatment occurs equally often in each treatment position? I'm glad you asked! This is where the Latin-square counterbalancing comes in!

Latin-square counterbalancing

Latin-square counterbalancing is the most common partial counterbalancing design. Researchers really like it because it's pretty simple to use and it makes sure that each treatment or condition occurs equally often in each treatment position. In other words, if we had 3 treatments, the A treatment would occur equally often in the first, second, and third treatment positions. The B treatment would occur equally often in the first, second, and third treatment positions, and so on with the C treatment.

There are two Latin-square techniques that you can use. The first technique is the simplest and is the most commonly used. We refer to this technique as the "shift" technique. For the "shift" technique, you simply provide the first participant with the different treatments in order: A, B, and C. The second participant would get each of the same treatments, but we'd "shift" the treatments over one position: B, C, and A. In order to determine the order that the third participant would receive, we simply take the order that the second participant received, and "shift" the treatments one more time: C, A, and B. That's it! It's really that simple. Take a look at the different "shift" orders below to illustrate this technique:

3 Treatments	4 Treatments	5 Treatments
A B C	A B C D	A B C D E
B C A	B C D A	B C D E A
C A B	C D A B	C D E A B
	D A B C	D E A B C
		E A B C D

The other technique is more like Sudoku. If you enjoy playing Sudoku then you might like this Latin-square technique. In this technique, you really just plug the different treatment conditions into each space, making sure that each order contains each of the treatment conditions and that each treatment occurs in each of the treatment positions only once. Below are some examples to illustrate what these orders might look like:

3 Treatments	4 Treatments	5 Treatments
B C A	A B C D	A C E B D
C A B	B A D C	B D C E A
A B C	C D A B	C B A D E
	D C B A	D E B A C
		E A D C B

Regardless of which Latin-square technique you decide on using, you would use the different orders in the same way. Each participant would receive one of the different treatment orders, each of which is represented on each row. While the Latin-square counterbalancing technique is excellent, widely used, and better than the randomized partial counterbalancing technique, it's not the best partial counterbalancing technique. The best is the balanced Latin-square technique.

Balanced Latin-square counterbalancing

In the balanced Latin-square counterbalancing technique, each treatment appears only once in each order sequence, like in the Latin-square counterbalancing, and each treatment precedes and follows every other treatment an equal number of times. This is the balanced part of the technique. This technique is the best across-subjects partial counterbalancing technique that you can use. The only technique better than this would be to use the complete counterbalancing. Unfortunately, most researchers don't use this technique because they don't understand it or they weren't taught it because of its complexity. While it is more complex than any of the other partial counterbalancing techniques, we don't think that it's that difficult, and we think it's important for you to know how to use the best partial counterbalancing technique. It just takes a little practice, but we're sure you'll master it in a few minutes.

With balanced Latin-square you're going to set it up in columns rather than in rows as we did for each of the other techniques. However, once you've completed your counterbalancing grid, each participant will still be given one of the orders that are depicted by each row. Additionally, we're going to use the "shift" technique as we discussed with the Latin-square technique, but the shifting will be shifting columns up or down. The general rule is that the even columns will be shifted up and the odd columns will be shifted down. This will make more sense as we discuss how to get the different orders. Here are the steps to making your balanced Latin-square counterbalancing orders:

1. In the 1st column, write your treatments in order

2. In the 2nd column, "shift" your treatments <u>up</u> from 1st column

3. In the 3rd column, shift your treatments <u>down</u> from 1st column

4. For every additional even column (e.g., 4th, 6th, 8th, etc.), shift the previous even column up again.

5. For every additional odd column (e.g., 5th, 7th, 9th, etc.), shift the previous odd column down again.

These are the basic rules. Yes, it's definitely more complex than the other techniques, but it really isn't that difficult once you get some practice. So, let's take a look at how this works. The example below is for 4 treatments.

Step #1	Step #2	Step #3	Step #4
A	A B	A B D	A B D C
B	B C	B C A	B C A D
C	C D	C D B	C D B A
D	D A	D A C	D A C B

Let's follow along with each step, using the example above. In Step #1, we wrote the different treatments in order in the first column. In Step #2, we took the first column and shifted each of the treatments UP one position to make the second column. Treatment B was in the second position so we shifted it to the first position, Treatment C was in the third position so we shifted it to the second position, and Treatment D was in the fourth position so we shifted it to the third position. Treatment A was in the first position so we shifted it to the end of the line into the fourth position. In Step #3, we took our first column and shifted each treatment DOWN one position in order to make the third column. Treatment A was in the first position in the first column so we shifted it down to the second position, Treatment B was in the second position so we shifted it down to the third position, and Treatment C was in the third position so we shifted it down to the fourth position. Treatment D was in the fourth position so we shifted it to the front of the line into the first position. In Step #4, we simply took our previous even column (column 2) and shifted each treatment UP another position. If we had five treatments then we'd have a fifth column, which would be taking our previous odd column (column 3) and shifting each treatment DOWN another position. That's it! Is it more complex? Yes. Is it really difficult? No. If you'd like more practice, feel free to try the balanced Latin-square problems at the end of the chapter. With a little practice, you'll be very confident in your ability to use balanced Latin-square counterbalancing, as well as the other counterbalancing techniques discussed in this chapter.

Testing for Order Effects

Before we conclude this chapter, there's one final topic that we need to address. In this chapter, we've discussed the idea that these counterbalancing techniques should control for carryover effects. However, we've not mentioned how you'd know if they worked or not. Well, there's actually a fairly easy way to know for sure. All you need to do is conduct an analysis of variance (ANOVA) and include the different treatment orders as an independent variable in your analysis. So you'd conduct the normal ANOVA for your design, but you'd add another between-subjects variable for the different treatment orders. If you had 3 treatment orders then you'd add a treatment order independent variable with 3 levels. If you had 4 treatment orders then you'd add a treatment order independent variable with 4 levels. If you had 24 treatment orders then you'd add a treatment order independent variable with 24 levels.

If you find either a main effect of your treatment orders or an interaction of your treatment orders with any of your independent variables then you know that your counterbalancing didn't completely control for carryover effects. If this is the case, then you'd need to use a more complete counterbalancing technique. If you used a randomized partial counterbalancing technique then maybe you could use a Latin-square technique, which is a stronger counterbalancing technique. If you used Latin-square then maybe you could use a balanced Latin-square technique. If you used balanced Latin-square then maybe you could use a complete counterbalancing technique. What if you already used complete counterbalancing? This is the best counterbalancing technique you could have possibly used. Well, you only have one option. You've done everything that you can do to attempt to control for carryover effects and you were unsuccessful. You have what is called an uncontrollable carryover effect. An **uncontrolled carryover effect** is a carryover effect that despite your best efforts cannot be controlled using any counterbalancing techniques. Your only other option would be to not use a within-subjects design. When you have an uncontrollable carryover effect, your only option is to conduct your study using a between-subjects manipulation where carryover effects are no longer an issue. Now that you know each of your counterbalancing options, the choice on which to use is entirely up to you.

This man has several doors to select as options. As a researcher, you have many options as to what design to select and how to control for any potential issues that may arise.

Summary of When to Use Within-Subjects Design

We'll conclude this chapter with a short list of situations when you should consider using a within-subjects design. First, if you expect large individual differences between your participants, you should use a within-subjects design. Since each participant serves as his or her own control, you minimize individual differences between your different conditions. This leads to less statistical noise in your data and results in greater statistical power. Second, when the number of available participants is limited, you should consider using a within-subjects design since they require fewer individuals. Third, if the effect sizes of the phenomenon you're investigating are small, you should consider using a within-subjects design. As previously mentioned, within-subject designs provide for much greater statistical power. If the effect size is very small then you'll need this additional statistical power in order to observe an effect of your manipulation. Fourth, if carryover effects are absent or can be easily controlled then consider using a within-subjects design. The main reason to avoid using a within-subjects design would be the fear of having carryover effects. If they aren't a concern then within-subject designs are very powerful. Finally, if your overall goal is to assess changes in the performance of your participants due to some treatment then the only technique that allows you to do this would be a within-subject design. A between-subject design allows you to test different individuals after various delays or treatments, but only a within-subject design allows you to observe changes in the same individual after various delays or treatments. Overall, within-subject designs are extremely powerful, useful approaches to conducting research, with the one caveat: as long as carryover effects aren't a problem.

Mixed-Factor Designs

In the last chapter, we discussed between-subject designs. In this chapter, we discussed within-subjects designs. Before we complete this chapter, we should mention mixed-factor designs. A mixed-factor design is simply a design where there's a mix of between- and within-subject variables. This could include one variable that is manipulated between-subjects and one that's manipulated within-subjects or it could be two that are manipulated between-subjects and five that are manipulated within-subjects. So, it really could be ANY combination of variables. A fairly common type of mixed-factor design is one that involves two groups of participants (the between-subjects variable) that is evaluated prior to and following the treatment (the within-subjects variable). Many drugs are tested in this way since it really does have many advantages and comparisons that a solely between- or within-subjects design doesn't offer. Take a look at Table 7.3 to see what this design might look like.

Table 7.3   A simple mixed-factor design

Drug Group	PreTest	Receive the Drug	PostTest
Placebo Group	PreTest	Receives the Placebo	PostTest

This type of design is a mix of the advantages and disadvantages of both types of designs. For the between-subject variable(s), researchers must make absolutely sure that the groups are as similar as possible, just like it is necessary in a between-subjects design. For the within-subject variable(s), researchers must be extremely careful of any potential carryover effects. Any counterbalancing that must be done would be conducted with the within-subject variable.

Concluding Remarks

As discussed throughout this chapter, there are many advantages of using within-subjects designs. The primary issue with using a within-subjects design or when using within-subject variables is making sure that there are no carryover effects. With a good within-subjects or repeated measure design, the *only* difference between the conditions should be the manipulation. This can be done by making sure that there are no carryover effects or ensuring that these carryover effects are controlled by using an appropriate counterbalancing technique. A major advantage of the within-subjects design is that you have the same individuals in each of your different conditions; therefore, the groups are as equal as they could possibly be. As a result, a within-subjects design provides the best possible matching that one could have.

End of Chapter Quiz

1. If you have a single-factor within-subjects study with 3 levels of the IV and you need 50 subjects per condition, how many participants must you test?

2. True or False: Carryover effects are often a problem associated with within-subject designs?

3. Which is the best, across-subjects counterbalancing technique?

4. Which is the best, across-subjects partial counterbalancing technique?

5. True or False: When using an across-subjects counterbalancing technique, participants receive all of the different treatment orders.

6. What is the other name for a within-subjects design?

7. True or False: A between-subjects design has more statistical power than a within-subjects design.

8. What are the names of the two general types of subject-by-subject counterbalancing techniques?

9. True or False: One major problem with within-subject designs is to make sure that the two groups of participants are equal.

10. If you have 6 treatments, how many different orders would you have if you used one of the partial counterbalancing techniques?

Homework Assignment #1

Please answer each of the following questions to the best of your ability. Be sure to explain your answers where appropriate.

1. What are two advantages of using a within-subjects design?

2. What are two disadvantages of using a within-subjects design?

3. When should you NOT use a repeated-measures design? Explain your answer.

4. Ryan wants to conduct a study where she gives subjects a list of words to remember. After the list, she wants them to recall as many words as possible. Once they finish this task, she gives them special training instructions to help them remember more words. She then gives them the same list of words again and gives them a recall test once they've seen all the words. What are your thoughts concerning this study?

5. Mr. Loomis has been asked by Colgate to test market 4 new flavors of toothpaste: spearmint, chocolate mint, peppermint, and peanut butter. Mr. Loomis has decided to use a within-subjects design to test subjects.
   a. What is the primary advantage of using a within-subjects design for this study?
   b. What is the primary disadvantage of using a within-subjects design for this study?
   c. Is counterbalancing necessary in this study? Why?

6. Pete wants to conduct a within-subjects study with 4 treatment conditions. What is the minimum number of subjects he'll need if he uses a complete counterbalancing procedure? Explain your answer.

7. If an experimenter plans to use complete counterbalancing with five levels of an independent variable, this will take a minimum of _____ orders? Explain your answer.

8. An experiment in which each subject was asked to evaluate three kinds of kitchen appliances in both white and almond colors would most likely use a _____ design (e.g., 2×2 between-subjects, etc.). Explain why you would use this design.

9. An experiment comparing preferences of men and women for soft rock, hard rock, and alternative music would most likely use a _____ design (e.g., 2×2 between-subjects, etc.). Explain why you would use this design.

10. If you work for a company that has developed a new drug that should provide a permanent cure for baldness, what kind of a design would you use to test the drug (i.e., between- or within-subjects). Explain your answer.

11. If a researcher uses a 4×2 within-subjects design, how many groups of subjects will there be?

12. If a researcher uses a 3×5 between-subjects design, how many groups of subjects will there be?

13. If a researcher uses a 4×3 mixed-factor design, how many groups of subjects will there be?

Homework Assignment #2

Please read each of the following scenarios and answer each of the following questions to the best of your ability. Be sure to provide the counterbalancing grid if necessary.

1. Dr. Wenger has been asked by Mazda to test brake lights. They are specifically interested in which color is the most effective for drivers to detect (red, yellow, orange, and blue). Therefore, Dr. Wenger decides to use a within-subjects design where he presents each of the different brake light colors to each subject. Subjects are required to press a brake pedal as soon as they see the brake light turn on. Dr. Wenger has decided that some type of subject-by-subject counterbalancing would work best for this study.

    a. Provide the Reverse Counterbalancing for this study.

    b. Provide the Complete Block Randomization for this study.

    c. Provide the Partial Block Randomization for this study.

2. Dr. Blackwell is interested in testing three new computer programs. He'd like to conduct the studies using a within-subjects manipulation but needs to counterbalance the orders that he presents each computer program to each subject.

    a. What technique would you recommend Dr. Blackwell use?

    b. Please explain which counterbalancing you would use and explain why you'd use this technique.

    c. Provide the actual orders that you would use for the technique selected.

3. Dr. McDermott, who works in the marketing department for the GAP, would like to conduct a within-subjects study where he exposes subjects to 3 different marketing ideas to see which one is the most appealing to potential customers. Please provide the counterbalancing orders if he were to use:

    a. complete counterbalancing.

    b. randomized partial counterbalancing.

    c. Latin-square counterbalancing.

    d. balanced Latin-square counterbalancing.

4. Dr. Loomis has been asked by Colgate to test market 4 new flavors of toothpaste: spearmint, peppermint, chocolate mint, and peanut butter. Dr. Loomis has decided to use a within-subjects design to test subjects. In order to conduct this study, Dr. Loomis needs to make sure that he adequately controls for any carryover effects caused by the tastes of the toothpaste. Please provide the counterbalancing orders for:

    a. the complete counterbalancing.

    b. a randomized partial counterbalancing.

    c. a Latin-square counterbalancing.

    d. a balanced Latin-square counterbalancing.

Chapter 8

Descriptive Statistics

In this chapter, we'll introduce you to the basic statistics. Specifically, we'll discuss descriptive statistics in this chapter and then inferential statistics in the next chapter. We'll touch on what descriptive statistics are, what they tell us, and how to use them. We know what you're thinking: "I love statistics!! If I had to pick one topic that I look forward to more than any other, it would have to be statistics!" Said no one, EVER! OK, we get it. Most students aren't very excited to spend *any* class time learning about statistics, but it's really not that bad. We promise! Just keep a positive attitude, and it'll all be OK.

Let's start with the two main types of statistics: descriptive and inferential statistics. **Descriptive statistics** are the term given to statistics that simply summarize or describe the data. Descriptive statistics help us to organize and make sense out of the data or scores that we've measured. They do not allow us to come to any conclusions regarding these data or make any decisions regarding these data. These statistics are descriptive in that they simply describe the data. There are several types of descriptive statistics that we'll be discussing in this chapter. These include measures of central tendency, measures of dispersion, and correlations.

Inferential statistics are a little bit different. When we collect data for an experiment, we typically collect data from a sample of the population as a whole. Keep in mind that we don't collect data from the entire population, only our sample. Using the data that we've collected from this much smaller subset of our population, we'd like to infer that the population would be just like our sample. We use the data from our sample to make generalizations or decisions about the population. The primary way that inferential statistics are used is to determine if an observed difference between our conditions is a "real" difference or if a difference of the observed magnitude could have occurred by chance alone. Thus, we use inferential statistics to tell us if our manipulation made a difference or had an effect. As a result, **inferential statistics** are statistics that allow us to make decisions about our data using probabilities, and allow us to determine if our groups or conditions are the same or different. This "decision" that they help us to make is if the numbers we're comparing are the same or different. In essence, this is really all inferential statistics do; they simply tell us if our groups or conditions are different from one another.

Before we discuss the different types of descriptive statistics, we need to first identify the different scales of measurement. These scales of measurement are critical since this is what we'll be measuring in our studies. These scales are important because each scale provides you with certain information. All other things being equal, different scales provide you with more or less information. Additionally, some statistics can only be conducted with certain scales of measurement. So, before we discuss each of the different types of descriptive statistics, let's take a look at the four scales of measurement.

Scales of Measurement

There are four different types of scales of measurement. They are, in order from the least amount of information they provide to the most amount of information: nominal, ordinal, interval, and ratio scales. A nominal scale is the simplest scale. As the name implies, a **nominal scale** simply divides your data into groups or categories based on the name. For example, you could divide your data into males or females, or maybe you'd divide your data into nominal groups of college majors, to determine if there's a relationship between college Grade Point Average (GPA) and college major or gender. Nominal categories simply involve category assignment based on some nominal characteristic. As an aside, a nominal scale that only provides two categories, such as the sex category mentioned above, is referred to as a dichotomous scale. An **ordinal scale** provides a little more information than the nominal scale. Similar to the nominal scale, the ordinal scale also places data into distinct categories. However, with the ordinal scale these categories add the additional information of rank. A fairly common example of an ordinal scale is data that are measured using a Likert-type scale. You might be asked how satisfied you were with your meal at a particular restaurant: 1 = very satisfied, 2 = somewhat satisfied, 3 = neutral, 4 = somewhat dissatisfied, 5 = very dissatisfied. This information categorizes your data and ranks it. Another example of an ordinal scale would be how runners finish a marathon. Maybe we were interested in conducting a correlation between the runners' ordinal rank and their weight. We could place our individuals in the order of first, second, third, etc. such that their finishing rank would be measured using an ordinal scale. The main limitation of the ordinal scale is that it's unclear how much distance is between each of the scale units. With the example of runners' finishing rank, we don't know the distance between the first place and the second place runners or how far the fourth place runner finished ahead of the sixth place runner. The interval scale fixes this issue. An **interval scale** has all the characteristics of the ordinal scale, but then adds the aspect of equal spacing between the scale units. The typical example of an interval scale is temperature on a Celsius or Fahrenheit scale. The distance between 20 and 30 degrees is 10 degrees and is the same number of degrees as is between 80 and 90 degrees. Many of our statistical measures become available to us with the use of an interval scale. We can now compute means, medians, modes, variance, standard deviations, etc. The primary weakness of the interval scale is that there is no true zero point. We can have negative degrees on the Fahrenheit scale. With no absolute zero, we can't calculate ratios. While people sometimes make the following statement, it's incorrect to do so since we don't have an absolute zero. "Last night it was 40 degrees, but it's 80 degrees today; so it's twice as warm today than it was last night." It's easy to determine if there's an absolute zero with your scale. All you need to do is simply ask if when your scale reads zero if it indicates an absence of what you're measuring? In other words, when your temperature reads zero, does this indicate an absence of temperature? Of course not!! You still have a temperature. However, there are data measurements that do have a true zero. These scales are measured using a ratio scale. A **ratio scale** has all the characteristics of the interval scale and in addition has an absolute zero. Weight, length, height, etc. are all measured on a ratio scale. If something has a weight of zero then it has an absence of weight. Your scale doesn't have negative values because you can't have a negative weight. As with the interval scale, all of your statistics are now available to you with ratio scales, including inferential statistics.

Measures of Central Tendency

Most students are aware of and have extensive experience with the measures of central tendency. There are three measures of central tendency. These include the mean, median, and mode. The **mean** is the arithmetic mean or average of a set of scores. The main limitation of the mean is that you must have data that uses either an interval or ratio scale in order to calculate the mean; you can't calculate the mean with nominal or ordinal data. The mean is pretty simple to calculate, and we're fairly sure that you have a lot of experience using the mean. When you determine your grades in your classes, you probably use the mean to calculate your class average. The mean is calculated by adding up all of your scores and then dividing by the number of scores. For example, if you had the following scores: 5, 7, 8, 5, 10, you would calculate the mean by adding up all the scores (5 + 7 + 8 + 5 + 10 = 35) and then dividing by the number of scores (there were 5 scores here), which would give you a mean of 7.0.

$$Mean = \frac{(5 + 7 + 8 + 5 + 10)}{(5)} = \frac{35}{5} = 7.0$$

The median is one of the other measures of central tendency. The **median** is the middle score from a ranked distribution. If I were to give you the following scores: 5, 7, 8, 5, 10, what is the median? In looking at these scores, it appears that the middle score is 8, right? If you said "yes" then you're wrong. Keep in mind that the median is the middle score from a *ranked* distribution. You must first rank the scores. So, if we put the scores in order they are 5, 5, 7, 8, 10. It should now be easy to see that our middle score is 7; so our median is 7. What do you do when you have an even number of scores? So take a look at the following scores: 5, 5, 7, 8, 9, 10. What's the median now? There are actually two middle scores now, the 7 and 8. In order to compute the median, we take the average of these two scores. In this case, our median would be 7.5. In order to calculate the median, you must have at least ordinal data. The median and mean can't be calculated with nominal data. If you think about it, this make sense. If you wanted to see what the median college major is at your university, how would you calculate this? Since nominal data can't be ranked (since it doesn't provide order information), you can't rank your distribution to obtain the middle score.

The mode is a little bit different from the mean and the median. The **mode** is the most frequently occurring score. So again, let's take a look at our scores: 5, 7, 8, 5, 10. Which score occurs most often? Correct! It is 5; so our mode is 5. There are times when your distribution may have two or more scores that occur equally often. If you have two scores that occur equally often then you have a bimodal distribution. If you have a distribution that has more than two scores occurring equally often is referred to as multimodal. The mode can be used with any scale of measurement, which makes it quite useful, but it is the only measure of central tendency that can be used with nominal data. For example, if you wanted to determine the most common major at your university, you can't get a list of all the majors (e.g., psychology, business, biology, etc.) and divide by the total number of majors. However, you can determine the most frequently occurring major (i.e., the mode). There are some additional problems at the end of the chapter to give you a little more practice at determining the mean, median, and mode.

Now that you're able to calculate each of the measures of central tendency, which is the best measure of central tendency? This might seem like a pretty easy question. After all, you probably have calculated the mean more times in your life than either of the other measures. Additionally, it's probably the measure of central tendency that you've heard about or been given the most often when individuals are trying to give you a descriptive representation of a data set, but is it the best? Let's take a look at each by using a real example from back in the day. Back in "the day" after one of the energy crises that we've had in our country, the United States government passed the National Maximum Speed Law (NMSL) in 1974 that prohibited speed limits higher than 55 mph on U.S. highways. This law made the various states decrease the speed limit to 55 mph since it was thought to help conserve gasoline, which was seen as necessary in order to conserve gasoline and reduce gasoline consumption during a time of oil shortage. There was a side argument that it was also safer for Americans. Most Americans were not pleased with the 55 mph speed limit. In fact, Sammy Hagar, a rock musician released a protest song in 1984 called "I Can't Drive 55." After the gas crisis passed, most states returned their regular highway speed limits back to 65 mph or faster after the U.S. government passed a law allowing them to increase the speed limits in 1987. The then governor of New York, Mario Cuomo, steadfastly refused to raise the speed limit in New York State above 55 mph. He argued that the lower speed limits kept New Yorkers safer. He even provided data of the highway fatality rate per 100 million vehicle miles traveled to support his argument. Mario Cuomo provided the average fatality rate for the 5 years before 1987 and the five years after 1987 for New York State, which kept the speed limit at 55 mph, and Pennsylvania, which raised the speed limit to 65 mph. The data are below:

Table 8.1 Average Rate of Highway Fatalities per 100 Million Vehicle Miles Traveled

State	Pre-1987	Post-1987
New York	1.64	1.64
Pennsylvania	1.62	1.82

By looking at Table 8.1, it appears that the average highway fatalities remained the same in New York, but increased in Pennsylvania. Critics of Mario Cuomo provided alternative data to dispute Governor Cuomo's data. These data are provided in Table 8.2.

In looking at Table 8.2, it appears that the median highway fatalities remained the same for both states. If anything, Pennsylvania may have actually decreased the number of highway fatalities even though they raised the speed limit to 65 mph, while New York kept it at 55 mph. How could these two measures of central tendency utilize the same data, but come up with different conclusions? This issue occurs based on the way in which each of these measures of central tendency are calculated. In Table 8.3, let's take a look at the raw scores, the rate of highway fatalities, which went into our mean and median calculations. Each of the numbers (i.e., the means and medians) that we observed in the previous tables was based on 5 years of fatalities. Table 8.3 provides those scores for each of the 5 years.

In looking at Table 8.3, are there any years that seem to stand out to you? It looks to me that the 3.1 for Pennsylvania in the post-1987 years stands out quite a bit. While all of the other years seem to be fairly consistent between 1.4 and 1.8, this one year seems to be very different from the others. This is referred to as an outlier. An **outlier** is a score that is very different from the other scores. The relevant question here is how does this outlier affect our measures of central tendency? Let's start by asking a different question. How many of the scores go into the calculation on the mean? The correct answer would be all of them. Each score is added up and then we divide by the number of scores, so each score goes into the actual calculation. How many of the scores go into the calculation of the median? The correct answer would be one score (or possibly two scores when there's an even number of scores). We rank the scores and select the middle score. When we rank the scores where would the outlier be? If it's an extremely low score or an extremely high score (i.e., an outlier) then it would be at the extremes, not in the middle. The only scores that actually go into the calculation of the median is the middle score(s). Therefore, outliers have no real effect on the median, but they do have an effect on the mean. As a result, the mean may be overly sensitive to extreme scores since it uses all of the scores in its calculation. The median, since it uses only the middle score(s), is insensitive to outliers. If you don't have any outliers then your mean and median should be somewhat comparable to each other. If your mean is much lower than your median then this tells you that you have a low outlier, whereas if you have a high outlier then your mean would be much higher than your median.

As for the original question about which is the best measure of central tendency, the answer is that it really depends on your data set. Both are helpful and both provide you with excellent information. If the data are fairly normal without any outliers then both the mean and median work equally well. If the data do contain an outlier or outliers then the median is probably the better, less biased measure. Generally, if you can look at both the mean and the median, it provides you with a better understanding of the data and together they provide a better summary of the underlying data.

Table 8.2   Median Rate of Highway Fatalities per 100 Million Vehicle Miles Traveled

State	Pre-1987	Post-1987
New York	1.60	1.60
Pennsylvania	1.60	1.50

Table 8.3   Rate of Highway Fatalities per 100 Million Vehicle Miles Traveled for Each Year

State	Pre-1987	Post-1987
New York	1.8, 1.5, 1.6, 1.8, 1.5	1.7, 1.6, 1.7, 1.6, 1.6
Pennsylvania	1.7, 1.5, 1.6, 1.5, 1.8	1.6, 1.5, 1.4, 3.1, 1.5

Measures of Dispersion

Like the measures of central tendency, most students have been previously exposed to the measures of dispersion earlier in their education. **Measures of dispersion** inform us about how spread out the scores in a data set are. The three measures of dispersion are the range, variance, and standard deviation. Like the measures of central tendency, each of these measures of dispersion provide different information and each has some advantages and disadvantages.

The **range** is easily calculated by subtracting the smallest score from the highest score. For example, in the following set of scores: 1, 2, 3, 4, 5, the range would be 4 (or 5 – 1 = 4). The major advantage of the range is that it's a very quick, very easy calculation of dispersion. The idea behind the range is also fairly easy to grasp; to determine how spread out the scores are find the difference between the highest and lowest score. However, there is one major weakness to using the range. Knowing that you're only using the absolute highest and lowest scores in your calculation of range, you've probably already figured it out. The problem, like we've mentioned earlier with the mean, is extreme scores or outliers. If you have a very high score, how does this affect your range? It makes your range appear to be much larger than is representative when looking at all of the other scores. Similarly, if you have a very low score, this affects your range in the same way. For example, take a look at the two sets of scores below. These scores are very similar, but due to an outlier, the scores from Group B have a much larger range.

Group A: 1, 2, 3, 4, 5   Group A Range: 5−1 = 4

Group B: 1, 2, 3, 4, 28   Group B Range: 28−1 = 27

Our next two measures of dispersion don't just use the most extreme scores. They both use all of the scores. As a result, extreme scores will still have an impact on both of these measures, but they won't have an effect that is anywhere close to the same magnitude as how the range is affected by outliers. The second measure of dispersion is variance. **Variance** is defined as the average of the squared deviations from the mean. In essence, the variance provides a measure of how far each score in a data set is from the mean. One major disadvantage of the variance is that the calculation of the variance isn't nearly as easy as calculating the range. If you look at the definition of variance, you can easily determine how to calculate the variance. Here are the steps to calculating the variance:

1. Determine the mean of the set of scores
2. Determine each scores deviation from the mean
3. Square each of these deviations
4. Calculate the mean of the squared deviations

That's all there is to it! No, it's not as easy as calculating the mean, but the mathematics involved really aren't that difficult. Using Figure 8.1, let's take a look at calculating variance using the two sets of IQ scores from two hypothetical schools.

So the variance for School A is 8 and the variance for School B is 1,320. In looking at these two variance scores, which school has more variance or has scores that are more spread out? Clearly, 1,320 is larger than 8; therefore, School B has a greater amount of variance. I think this is pretty easy to understand. However, there is one potential issue with variance that confuses a lot of people. Clearly School B has more variance than School A, but what do these variance scores actually mean? We've already said that variance provides a measure of, on average, how spread out the scores are from the mean, but what's the unit of measurement here? When we look at our variance scores that we just calculated. What's the unit of measurement? Is it IQ? Most individuals would look at these scores and say "Yes, our unit of measurement is IQ since our scores were IQ units." So this would mean that School A scores are, on average, spread out about 8 IQ units from the mean and School B scores are, on average, spread out about 1,320 IQ units from the mean. Does this sound reasonable to you? I would hope that you'd notice that for School B that sounds ridiculous. The scores aren't spread out approximately 1,320 IQ units.

Figure 8.1 Example of variance calculation.

School A: 96, 98, 100, 102, 104

School A Mean = 100

School B: 60, 70, 90, 120, 160

School B Mean = 100

Scores	Deviation	Deviation^2
96	− 4	16
98	− 2	4
100	0	0
102	+ 2	4
104	+ 4	16

Sum = 40

Variance = 40/5 = 8

Scores	Deviation	Deviation^2
60	− 40	1600
70	− 30	900
90	−10	100
120	+ 20	400
160	+ 60	3600

Sum = 6600

Variance = 6600/5 = 1,320

If we compute the range for School B you'll notice that the range is only 100 (160 − 60 = 100), so clearly the scores aren't spread out 1,320 IQ points on average. For School A the range is 8 and our variance is 8. Again, each score isn't spread out from the mean 8 IQ points on average when the entire range, the difference between the smallest and largest scores, is 8. So what did we do to make these variance scores so big? If you look at the calculation steps that we discussed earlier, you'll notice that in the third step we squared the deviation scores. By squaring these deviation scores we just made our unit of measurement *squared* IQ points!! So variance isn't actually on the same scale as the original scores; variance is measured on a squared scale! This is the main issue with variance. While you can easily look at the scores from our two schools and see that School B clearly has more variance, interpreting these scores is more problematic with variance because it's on a squared scale. We have a difficult time interpreting these scores and what they mean because it's hard for us to think about squared scales. So what we'd really need to do is return these scores to our original scale. How could we return these squared scores back to our original scale? If you said take the square root of the variance scores then you'd be correct.

When you take the square root of the variance scores, you've just computed standard deviation. **Standard deviation** is the average distance that each score deviates from the mean. Since standard deviation is measured using the same scale as the original set of scores, it's much easier for people to understand. For our two schools, let's calculate the standard deviations. Since we've already calculated the variance, standard deviation is simply taking the square root of each variance score.

School A Variance = 8 squared IQ units

School A *SD* = 2.83 IQ units

School B Variance = 1,320 squared IQ units

School B *SD* = 36.33 IQ units

Thus, our standard deviation for School A is 2.83 IQ units and School B is 36.33 IQ units. On average, School A scores are dispersed from the mean by 2.83 IQ units on average, whereas School B scores are dispersed from the mean by 36.33 IQ units.

Correlations

Correlations are an interesting statistical concept. A **correlation** is defined as a statistical measure that indicates the extent that two or more variables fluctuate together. In order to measure this correlation between our variables, we must compute a correlation coefficient. A **correlation coefficient** describes both the direction of this relationship (positive or negative) and the strength of this relationship. The higher the correlation coefficient, the stronger the relationship; the lower the correlation coefficient, the weaker the relationship. We oftentimes use these correlation coefficients in order to make predictions. If we know the value of one variable and we know the strength of a correlation, we can then make a prediction about the other variable. The stronger the correlation, the more precise the prediction we can make. The weaker the correlation, the less precise prediction we can make. These correlations can also be depicted graphically, as can be seen in Figure 8.2. These graphical representations are called scatterplots and will be discussed below.

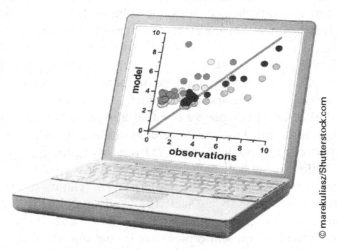

Figure 8.2   Correlation scatterplot sample.

So let's take a look at how to interpret correlational data. Let's assume we have the following correlation coefficients:

$$r = 0.36 \qquad r = 0.62$$

Which of these correlations is stronger? Clearly the 0.62 is the larger number so it must be the stronger correlation. If this is what you concluded then you're correct. What about these next two correlations?

$$r = 0.43 \qquad r = -0.61$$

If you said the 0.43 is the larger correlation because it's the larger number, you'd be incorrect. The strength of the correlation is determined by the absolute value of the correlation coefficient. The strongest correlation is +1.0 or −1.0; the weakest correlation is 0.0. The sign of the correlation doesn't make any difference with regard to the *strength* of the correlation. See Figure 8.3 to see how the correlation coefficient relates to the strength of the correlation. As you can see, the closer the correlation coefficient is to +1.0 or −1.0, the stronger the correlation. The closer the correlation coefficient is to 0.0, the weaker the correlation.

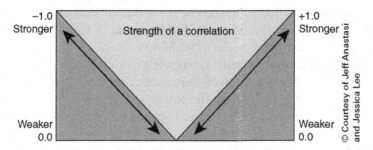

Figure 8.3   Graphical depiction of the strength of a correlation.

So what does the sign (+ or −) mean for a correlation coefficient. The sign refers to the direction of the relationship. When you have a **positive correlation** coefficient, this means that your variables vary together, in the same direction. As the value of one variable increases, the value of the other variable would also be predicted to increase. As the value of one variable decreases, the value of the other variable would also be predicted to decrease. In other words, the variables are predicted to move in the same direction. However, when you have a **negative correlation**, the variables are predicted to vary in opposite directions. As the value of one variable increases, the value of the other variable would be predicted to decrease. As the value of one variable decreases, the value of the other variable would be predicted to increase. In order to see these relationships (i.e., the strength and direction of correlations), take a look at the three scatterplots depicted in Figure 8.4. **Scatterplots** are graphical representations of the correlational data. Each point on the scatterplot represents one participant. The more points on the scatterplot, the more participants there are. Each participant on the scatterplot is graphed by using their scores on the two variables. On the first two scatterplots, we've inserted a line of best fit for each of the scatterplots. This line of best fit displays a line that minimizes the average distance between each of the participants on the scatterplot. This line is useful in looking at both the strength and direction of the correlation. There are two major points to observe from this figure. First, note the correlation coefficients below each scatterplot. You'll notice one is very strong ($r = +0.85$), one is moderate ($r = -0.50$), and one is extremely weak ($r = 0.00$). Look at the scatterplots in relation to the correlation coefficients. You should note that the points on the strong scatterplot fall very close to the line of best fit. On the moderate correlation, you can see that the points have a pattern, but that the points fall a little further from the line of best fit. In the weakest scatterplot, you'll note that there isn't a line of best fit. Since there is no relationship, there is no pattern to the data. The second point to note is the slope of the line of best fit. The first scatterplot depicts a positive correlation. As Scholastic Assessment Test (SAT) scores increase, college GPA also increases. As SAT scores decrease, college GPA also decreases. For the second scatterplot, we have a negative correlation. As hours watching TV increases, high school GPA decreases. As hours watching TV decreases, high school GPA increases. For the third scatterplot, again there is no appreciable relationship between the variables; therefore, there is no direction of the relationship.

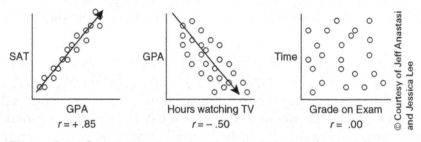

Figure 8.4 Correlational scatterplot depictions of strength and direction.

One additional aspect of the scatterplots and correlations in general, is that correlational data is oftentimes used to make predictions. If you know the value of one of your variables, you can make predictions about the value of the other variable. For example, if you know an individual's SAT score then you can, using correlational data, make a prediction about the individual's college GPA. If you know how many hours a high school student watches television, you can make a prediction about that individual's high school GPA. The accuracy of that prediction is very much related to the strength of the correlation. Since the points in the first scatterplot in Figure 8.4 lie very close to the line of best fit, we can make very accurate predictions. In the second scatterplot, since we have a moderately strong correlation, we make predictions, but these predictions won't be nearly as precise. For the third scatterplot where we have no correlation, we really can't make any predications concerning how long a student takes to complete her exam and her resulting grade on that exam.

Primary Limitations of Correlations

The primary limitation of correlational data is the fact that you cannot make causal statements based on correlational data. For example, do you think that smoking leads to lung cancer in humans? In other words, if someone smokes heavily for their entire life, will they get lung cancer at some point? The answer to this is probably yes, but they may die of something else before they die or acquire lung cancer. The issue, as discussed in Chapter 1, is that much of the research evaluating this question is correlational in nature (or quasi-experimental). The correlation between smoking and lung cancer in humans is about +.72. This means that there is a moderately strong relationship between smoking and lung cancer. There's also the Surgeon General's warning on cigarette packs that says that smoking causes lung cancer. There are also various experiments with all kinds of different animals that show that smoking does cause lung cancer in virtually every kind of animal tested. So, can we use our correlational data to conclude that smoking cause lung cancer in humans? Unfortunately, the answer is "no." Even if the correlational coefficient was a +1.0 (a perfect correlation), we still can't say that it's causal. Even though we really do think that smoking does cause lung cancer in humans, we can't make this conclusion until we've conducted true experiments with humans that show this causal relationship. The correlations show that there is absolutely a relationship, but there are some fairly major limitations to correlational data. So what are these limitations?

The first limitation is the directionality problem. The **directionality problem** states that we're unsure if variable A is causing variable B or if variable B is causing variable A. The American Psychological Association, in 2015 completed an 8-year study investigating the relationship between playing violent videogames and violent behavior. Their findings indicated that there was a relationship between the amount of violent videogames and the amount of violent behaviors that children engage in. Does this then indicate that playing violent videogames causes children to behave aggressively? Due to the directionality problem, we don't know. It's also likely that children who are already violent enjoy or are attracted to violent videogames. Which is the more likely explanation? Correlational data doesn't tell us this since correlational data can't assess directionality.

The second limitation is the third-variable problem. The **third-variable problem** refers to the situation where there appears to be a relationship between two variables, but the relationship isn't actually a direct relationship between the two variables being observed. Rather there is a third variable that is linking these two variables together. For example, one of my favorite third-variable examples is the correlation between ice cream sales and shark attacks. The chances are probably pretty low that sharks are eating people who have eaten ice cream because they taste sweeter. While that really would be an interesting causal relationship, it seems that there's a third variable at work here. That third variable is warm weather or the summer. People are more likely to eat ice cream in the summer when it's warm and people are more likely to swim in the ocean during this time as well. Obviously shark attacks would be much more likely when swimmers are actually in the ocean. So there isn't any type of causal or even direct relationship between ice cream and shark attacks. Another interesting third variable problem is one between toasters and birth control in Taiwan (Li, 1975). This study evaluated the number of electrical appliances individuals had and the number of children they had. The relationship was such that the more appliances they had, the fewer children they had. Fewer appliances were related to more children. You're probably somewhat skeptical that owning appliances has a causal relationship with birth control such that appliances are causing individuals to not be fertile. So what is the third-variable here? Any ideas? It seems to be education or money. The more educated individuals were, the more likely they were to use birth control of some sort. The more educated they were, the more money they had which allowed them to purchase more electrical appliances. Just so we're clear, purchasing many electrical appliances is not a reliable form of birth control.

In addition to the directionality problem and the third-variable problem, there are some other potential problems that may occur with correlations. It's important to keep these additional issues in mind when evaluating correlational data. The first of these is nonlinear relationships. An example of a nonlinear relationship is depicted in Figure 8.5A. If you take a look at the figure, you can see that there is definitely a pattern to the data depicted in the scatterplot. However, the relationship is not in a straight line. When you conduct a correlation or compute a correlational coefficient, you are typically looking at the line of best fit. This is the *straight* line of best fit. In the case of nonlinear relationships the straight line of best fit isn't going to provide an accurate representation of the data. However, a curved line would provide a very nice fit to this scatterplot. Some computer programs, such as SPSS, will provide both a linear and nonlinear correlation. In the case of Figure 8.5A, the linear correlation would be very weak, whereas the nonlinear correlation would be moderately strong.

Figure 8.5B shows a scatterplot where you have a restricted data range. In this scatterplot, you can see that if you were to look at all of the data, you would have moderate correlation. However, if you only looked at the data depicted in the dotted line box, there doesn't appear to be any relationship at all. For our purposes here, imagine that the x-axis is age. If we look to see if there's a relationship between our variables and we looked at individuals of all ages, we'd see a moderate relationship. However, if we only looked at children (i.e., the dotted box), it would appear that there was no relationship between our variables.

Figure 8.5C provides a similar issue. In this scatterplot, the line of best fit would simply connect these two groups or populations. For this example, imagine that the bottom left group is males and the top right group is females. There doesn't appear to be any correlation within each of these groups. The correlation exists only because males behave in one way and females behave in another way. So the predictive ability of the correlation is simply that the correlation is able to depict which population the individuals are in, but nothing more specific about individuals within these two groups.

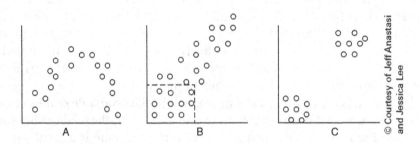

© Courtesy of Jeff Anastasi and Jessica Lee

Figure 8.5 Potential issues with correlations.

Types of Correlations

Now that we've discussed some of the various problems and issues with correlations, we need to now turn to issues related to conducting the actual statistical correlation. The first issue to consider is which type of correlation we should conduct. Yes, there are multiple kinds of correlations. The correlation that you conduct is dependent upon the type of data that you've collected. As discussed earlier in this chapter, there are four different types of data measurement scales: nominal, ordinal, interval, and ratio scales.

The different types of correlations might make a little more sense since the type of correlation that you conduct is determined by the scale of measurement that you've used. The most common correlation is the **Pearson product-moment (or Pearson's *r*) correlation**. If your data have been measured using either interval or ratio scales then the Pearson correlation would be the proper correlation to conduct. However, if one of your data sets was measured using an interval scale and the other was measured using a nominal scale then you'd need to use a **Point-biserial correlation**. If your data are measured using ordinal scales then you'd want to use a **Spearman rank-order correlation**. While this may seem odd, you could even conduct a correlation where your data are measured using only dichotomous scales. If this was the case then you'd need to use a **Phi coefficient**.

The primary issue with knowing this information is that we typically have some very powerful statistics software available at our fingertips. For example, most university students have access to SPSS. This allows virtually anyone to conduct some pretty impressive statistical analyses. Unfortunately, these analyses may be conducted incorrectly, and you may never know that you've messed up. SPSS may give you an output complete with probabilities to allow you to determine the significance. However, if you've conducted the incorrect statistical test, you may never know. SPSS doesn't always tell you if you've done things incorrectly. It's really up to you to know what the proper statistical analysis is.

The Normal Distribution

The **normal distribution** (or **Gaussian distribution** or **bell-shaped curve**) refers to a frequency graph that provides the raw score along the x-axis or abscissa and the frequency along the y-axis or ordinate. The raw score can be anything that you'd like to measure such as test scores, height, weight, rating scores, etc. Data that fall on a normal distribution are perfectly symmetrical such that half of the data points fall above the mean and half fall below the mean. Figure 8.6 and 8.7 provide examples of normal distributions. Interestingly, the percentage of scores that fall in each section of the normal distribution are always the same, regardless of the raw scores.

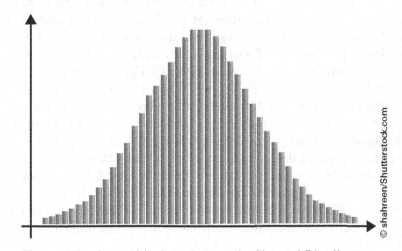

Figure 8.6   A graphical depiction of a Normal Distribution.

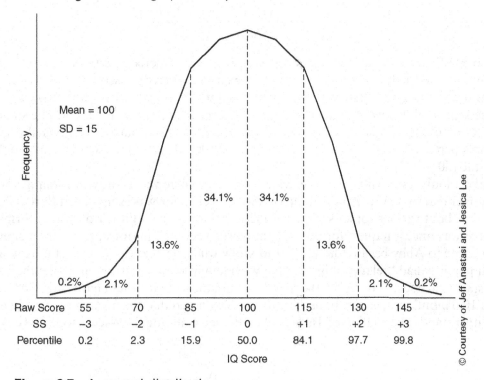

© Courtesy of Jeff Anastasi and Jessica Lee

Figure 8.7   A normal distribution.

As can be seen in Figure 8.7, a normal distribution provides a lot of information. The data in Figure 8.7 depict IQ scores, which have a mean of 100 and a standard deviation of 15. The mean IQ score is 100, as is the median (since the normal distribution is symmetrical) and the mode (since the most frequent score is in the middle of the curve). As previously mentioned, the percentage of scores that fall beneath different sections of the normal distribution will always be the same. For example, 68.26% of the scores will fall between −1 and +1 standard deviations from the mean, 95.44% of the scores fall between −2 and +2 standard deviations from the mean, and 97.74% of the scores fall between −3 and +3 standard deviations from the mean. As you can see from Figure 8.7, the percentage of scores between the mean and one standard deviation below the mean is exactly the same as the percentage of scores between the mean and one standard deviation above the mean (34.1% of the scores in both cases).

Another important aspect of the normal distribution is the standard score (SS). A standard score is a fairly simple concept. **A standard score** tells you how many standard deviations your score is from the mean. For example, a standard score of + 2 indicates that you are two standard deviations above the mean. A standard score of −3 indicates that you are three standard deviations below the mean. On our normal distribution in Figure 8.7, a raw score of 115 is one standard deviation above the mean. Thus, 115 would correspond to a standard score of + 1. You might be wondering why anyone would need to know a standard score. Let's use an example. Let's say that you have two children who have been assessed using intelligence tests. Unfortunately they were not assessed using the same intelligence tests, but we'd like to compare them. If Pierre's score was a 130 on a test that has a mean of 100 and a standard deviation of 15, and Monzor had a score of 15 on a test that has a mean of 10 and a standard deviation of 5, who did better? It's difficult to determine who did better because their scores are different, and the means and standard deviations are also different. This is where the standard score comes in. We compute the standard score by determining how many standard deviations our score falls from the mean. Once we've determined this, we can compare the standard scores. The most common standard score is the z-score. With our example, we can see that Pierre has scored two standard deviations above the mean. Thus, his standard score or z-score would be +2. Monzor has scored one standard deviation above the mean. Thus, his standard score or z-score would be +1. Thus, Pierre's performance on the test was better. We could also compute the z-score using a formula. The formula is fairly simple as well and can be seen below:

$$\text{z-score} \quad \frac{(Raw\ Score - Mean)}{Standard\ Deviation}$$

We can also use this z-score to determine a percentile rank. A percentile rank tells you what percent of individuals scored below a certain score. For example, Pierre's z-score was a +2. If we look at our normal distribution in Figure 8.7, we can see that 97.7% of the scores fall below a z-score of +2 (50% of the scores fall below the mean + 34.1% of scores between the mean and one standard deviation above the mean + 13.6% of scores between one and two standard deviations above the mean). Thus, Pierre's percentile rank would be the 97th percentile. Monzor's percentile rank would be at the 84th percentile (50 + 34.1).

Let's take a look at one final example. Many years ago there was an advice columnist who went by Dear Abby. Her real name was Pauline Phillips and her pen name was Abigail van Buren. People would write to Abby about various topics such as etiquette, family issues, and various other forms of general advice. There was once a request for advice that works very well in our current discussion. A man in San Diego wrote to Abby because he wanted to know what the chances were that a baby was his. The man had apparently had "relationships" with a woman and the woman claimed that the baby was his. Here's the statistical issue: in order for the baby to be his, the woman would have had a 308 day gestation period or a 10.3 month pregnancy. In her response, Abby noted that the normal or average pregnancy is 268 days with a standard deviation of 16 days. We can then compute the z-score for a 308 day pregnancy.

$$\text{z-score} \quad \frac{(308 - 268)}{16}$$

If you complete the math here, you'd find that the z-score would be 2.50. Using a standard z-score table (like that found in Figure 8.8), we could look up a z-score of 2.50 and find out what percentile rank this corresponds to. The way to look up the proportion of scores that fall under a certain area is done by looking up the basic score in the first column in Figure 8.8. Any additional decimal places are determined by using the first row on the table. For example, if we had a z-score of 1.33, we would find 1.3 on the first column and then go to the fourth column (the 0.03 column) to find our score of .4082. This score tells us the proportion of scores that fall below this specific z-score on the positive side of the normal distribution. We would then simply add the other half of the proportion of scores below the mean (or .5000). Thus, the proportion of scores that fall below a z-score of 1.33 is .9082 (or .5000 + .4082). Therefore, a z-score of 1.33 corresponds to the 90.82nd percentile (or the 91st percentile if we round our number to the nearest percentile).

Figure 8.8   Z-score Table to Indicate Proportion of Scores Under the Normal Distribution.

	0	0.01	0.02	0.03	0.04	0.05	0.06	0.07	0.08	0.09
0	0	0.0040	0.0080	0.0120	0.0160	0.0199	0.0239	0.0279	0.0319	0.0359
0.1	0.0398	0.0438	0.0478	0.0517	0.0557	0.0596	0.0636	0.0675	0.0714	0.0753
0.2	0.0793	0.0832	0.0871	0.0910	0.0948	0.0987	0.1026	0.1064	0.1103	0.1141
0.3	0.1179	0.1217	0.1255	0.1293	0.1331	0.1368	0.1406	0.1443	0.1480	0.1517
0.4	0.1554	0.1591	0.1628	0.1664	0.1700	0.1736	0.1772	0.1808	0.1844	0.1879
0.5	0.1915	0.1950	0.1985	0.2019	0.2054	0.2088	0.2123	0.2157	0.2190	0.2224
0.6	0.2257	0.2291	0.2324	0.2357	0.2389	0.2422	0.2454	0.2486	0.2517	0.2549
0.7	0.2580	0.2611	0.2642	0.2673	0.2704	0.2734	0.2764	0.2794	0.2823	0.2852
0.8	0.2881	0.2910	0.2939	0.2967	0.2995	0.3023	0.3051	0.3078	0.3106	0.3133
0.9	0.3159	0.3186	0.3212	0.3238	0.3264	0.3289	0.3315	0.3340	0.3365	0.3389
1	0.3413	0.3438	0.3461	0.3485	0.3508	0.3531	0.3554	0.3577	0.3599	0.3621
1.1	0.3643	0.3665	0.3686	0.3708	0.3729	0.3749	0.3770	0.3790	0.3810	0.3830
1.2	0.3849	0.3869	0.3888	0.3907	0.3925	0.3944	0.3962	0.3980	0.3997	0.4015
1.3	0.4032	0.4049	0.4066	0.4082	0.4099	0.4115	0.4131	0.4147	0.4162	0.4177
1.4	0.4192	0.4207	0.4222	0.4236	0.4251	0.4265	0.4279	0.4292	0.4306	0.4319
1.5	0.4332	0.4345	0.4357	0.4370	0.4382	0.4394	0.4406	0.4418	0.4429	0.4441
1.6	0.4452	0.4463	0.4474	0.4484	0.4495	0.4505	0.4515	0.4525	0.4535	0.4545
1.7	0.4554	0.4564	0.4573	0.4582	0.4591	0.4599	0.4608	0.4616	0.4625	0.4633
1.8	0.4641	0.4649	0.4656	0.4664	0.4671	0.4678	0.4686	0.4693	0.4699	0.4706
1.9	0.4713	0.4719	0.4726	0.4732	0.4738	0.4744	0.4750	0.4756	0.4761	0.4767
2	0.4772	0.4778	0.4783	0.4788	0.4793	0.4798	0.4803	0.4808	0.4812	0.4817
2.1	0.4821	0.4826	0.4830	0.4834	0.4838	0.4842	0.4846	0.4850	0.4854	0.4857
2.2	0.4861	0.4864	0.4868	0.4871	0.4875	0.4878	0.4881	0.4884	0.4887	0.4890
2.3	0.4893	0.4896	0.4898	0.4901	0.4904	0.4906	0.4909	0.4911	0.4913	0.4916
2.4	0.4918	0.4920	0.4922	0.4925	0.4927	0.4929	0.4931	0.4932	0.4934	0.4936
2.5	0.4938	0.4940	0.4941	0.4943	0.4945	0.4946	0.4948	0.4949	0.4951	0.4952
2.6	0.4953	0.4855	0.4956	0.4957	0.4959	0.4960	0.4961	0.4962	0.4963	0.4964
2.7	0.4965	0.4966	0.4967	0.4968	0.4969	0.4970	0.4971	0.4972	0.4973	0.4974
2.8	0.4974	0.4975	0.4976	0.4977	0.4977	0.4978	0.4979	0.4979	0.4980	0.4981
2.9	0.4981	0.4982	0.4982	0.4983	0.4984	0.4984	0.4985	0.4985	0.4986	0.4986
3	0.4987	0.4987	0.4987	0.4988	0.4988	0.4989	0.4989	0.4989	0.4990	0.4990

Back to our Dear Abby example, our z-score table indicates that a z-score of 2.50 would be .4938. We would then add the .50 from the other side of the normal distribution (.5000 + .4938 = .9938), which would tell us that a z-score of 2.50 would be at the 99.38[th] percentile. This means that only 0.62% of births (100 − 99.38 = 0.62) occur in 308 days or more. Is it *likely* that this is his baby? Of course not, but is it *possible* that the baby is his? The answer is that while it is very unlikely, it is possible. This idea of probability is the general idea behind inferential statistics, which will be covered in the next chapter.

Concluding Remarks

Descriptive statistics provide some very helpful information and typically provide one or two numbers that describe some aspect of the data that they represent. The main types of descriptive statistics provide measures of central tendency, measures of dispersion, and correlations. Each statistic has both advantages and disadvantages. While there are typically several descriptive statistics that one could use—such as the mean, median, or mode—it's ultimately up to the researcher to determine which of these statistics would be the most appropriate and which represent the data the most accurately. Descriptive statistics simply provide a description of the data, but they don't allow the researcher to make decisions or come to conclusions. In Chapter 9, we'll discuss inferential statistics that are used for this purpose: to make decisions.

End of Chapter Quiz

___1. A limitation of the median is that
   a. is difficult to calculate.
   b. does not take into account the magnitudes of the scores above and below it.
   c. it is not measured on the same scale as the original set of scores.
   d. cannot be used with interval data.
   e. all of the above

___2. Students surveyed about the number of MP3s they downloaded each week report widely diverse numbers. This pattern of results illustrates what we mean by:
   a. central tendency   c. regression to the mean
   b. probability   d. variability

___3. Which of the following sets of scores has the greatest variability?
   a. 3, 5, 6, 8, 10   c. 0, 1, 6, 16, 26   e. it is impossible to tell
   b. 1, 3, 5, 7, 9   d. 14, 16, 18, 21, 22

___4. Calculate the median of the following sets of scores: 3, 7, 2, 8, 2
   a. 2   b. 3   c. 4.4   d. 6   e. 22

___5. The variance is the
   a. average of the squared deviations about the mean
   b. difference between the highest and lowest scores
   c. sum of the deviations about the mean
   d. square root of the standard deviation

___6. The primary problem with using the mean is that
   a. it is difficult to compute.
   b. finding statistical significance is difficult.
   c. it is susceptible to issues related to statistical power.
   d. it is susceptible to the effects of extreme scores.

___7. Which of the following correlations indicates the strongest relationship?
   a. $r = +.89$ b. $r = -.68$ c. $r = +.34$ d. $r = -.12$ e. $r = +.01$

___8. In a normal distribution with a mean of 100 and a standard deviation of 10, a z-score (or standard score) of +4 would correspond to a raw score of
   a. 104   b. 140   c. 60   d. 100   e. cannot be determined

___9. A z-score of 0 corresponds to a percentile rank of
   a. 15.9   b. 50.0   c. 84.1   d. 97.7   e. cannot be determined

___10. What percentage of the scores in a normal distribution fall between −1 and +1 standard deviations?
   a. 13.4   b. 68.2   c. 97.7   d. 99.9   e. cannot be determined

Homework Assignment #1

1. Calculate the mean, median, and mode for the following sets of scores:
   (a) 5, 8, 12, 10, 5
   (b) 1, 5, 4, 2, 3
   (c) 10, 20, 50, 20, 30

2. Imagine that you're a professional soccer player and have just been drafted by your team. You're in negotiations with your team for your salary. The following are the salaries of six comparable players that were drafted the previous year. As the soccer player, which measure of central tendency would you use to argue for a fair salary? If you were the general manager of the team that drafted you, which measure of central tendency would you use to argue for a fair salary? Explain if you'd use the same measure of central tendency and why.

Player Name	Annual Salary
Leonardo	$120,000
Daniella	$180,000
Joseph	$190,000
Sargento	$200,000
Miguel	$300,000
Anastasi	$1,200,000

3 If you have a mean score of 100 and a standard deviation of 10, what raw score would correspond to a z-score of:
   (a) $+3$
   (b) -2
   (c) 0
   (d) -1
   (e) $+1$

4. What are the two "problems" that could occur with correlational studies and that indicate why we can't make causal statements with correlational studies?

5. If you obtained the following correlational coefficients, describe each correlation based on the correlation coefficient.
   (a) $r = +0.90$
   (b) $r = -0.94$
   (c) $r = +0.02$
   (d) $r = +1.21$

Chapter 9
Inferential Statistics

In the previous chapter, you were introduced to the basic descriptive statistics. In this chapter, we'll introduce you to inferential statistics. Specifically, we'll discuss what they are, what they tell us, and how to use them.

Inferential statistics are a little bit different from descriptive statistics, and they allow us to do some different things. When we collect data for an experiment, we typically collect data from a sample of the population as a whole. Keep in mind that we don't collect data from the entire population, only our sample. Using the data that we've collected from this much smaller subset of our population, we'd like to infer that the population would be just like our sample. In fact, the term "inferential" comes from this idea that we'd like to infer or make inferences about our population based upon the data that we observe from the sample. We use the data from our sample to make generalizations or decisions about the population. The primary way that inferential statistics are used is to determine if an observed difference between our conditions is a "real" difference or if a difference of the observed magnitude could have occurred by chance alone. Thus, we use inferential statistics to tell us if our manipulation made a difference or had an effect. As a result, **inferential statistics** are statistics that allow us to make decisions about our data using probabilities. This "decision" that they help us to make is simply if the numbers we're comparing are the same or different. In essence, this is really all inferential statistics do.

There are two general classes of inferential statistics: parametric and nonparametric inferential statistics. There are different statistics that are parametric (e.g., *t*-tests, ANOVA, etc.) and others that are nonparametric (e.g., chi-square tests, Mann-Whitney test, Wilcoxon signed-rank test, Kruskal-Wallis test, etc.). The way that these two types of statistics come to their decisions is somewhat different, but the decision is still the same; are the groups or conditions being compared the same or different? Parametric statistics utilize the normal distribution and the resulting probabilities described in Chapter 8 to come to decisions. Thus, in order to utilize parametric statistics, there is an underlying assumption that the data are normally distributed. If the data are not normally distributed then nonparametric statistics are recommended, as they do not make these assumptions about the underlying data distribution. Either type of statistic will generally lead to the same decision, although parametric statistics are typically thought to have greater statistical power than nonparametric statistics and are more common than nonparametric tests. Regardless, the appropriate assumptions should be met to utilize the specific inferential statistic and to ensure that the ultimate decision made is a correct one.

In using inferential statistics, there are two major limitations or factors that should be considered. First, as previously mentioned, you are obtaining your data from the sample of the population. You then use these data to conduct your inferential statistics. These statistics are only as good as the data that were collected from the population. If the data that you collect is not representative of the population, then your statistics may come to an incorrect conclusion. Since your statistics that you calculate are based on your sample, and not the entire population, there's always some uncertainty here. Second, the decision that is being made using these statistics is one based on probability. Any time that decisions are made based on probability, there is always the potential that an incorrect decision may be made. While it's fairly unlikely that an incorrect decision may be made, this is always a possibility when using probability.

For example, imagine that a friend of yours is flipping a coin, and you're making wagers about each flip. If you call "heads" each time and lose the first two flips, you probably aren't going to accuse your friend of cheating. If you lose five times in a row, how will you feel? What about if you lose ten times in a row? Is it possible that this could occur? The answer, of course, is yes. Is it likely to occur? Of course not. Probabilistically speaking, it *could* happen, although it's very unlikely. In the previous chapter we used the Dear Abby example where the man from San Diego wanted to know if a baby was his. We concluded that it was *possible* that the baby was his, but it was very unlikely based on the statistics. Using inferential statistics is very similar to these examples.

How to Utilize Inferential Statistics

To begin our discussion of inferential statistics, we need to first introduce the idea of the null hypothesis. The **null hypothesis** states that the independent variable had no effect. Any differences that are observed, according to this null hypothesis, are due to random variation rather than any real differences between the groups or conditions. The **alternative hypothesis** or the **experimental hypothesis** states that the independent variable did have an effect such that the different groups or conditions are different from one another. This difference is presumed to be due to the effects of the independent variable. When applying inferential statistics, there are several steps to be followed. The first step is to state the null hypothesis and assume that it's true. This first step seems somewhat odd to a lot of people. Why state the null hypothesis and assume that it's true. Think of the example where you work for a drug company, and you've spent millions of dollars developing a drug. Do you really think that the drug won't have an effect? Of course you're really praying that the drug works, otherwise it's a lot of wasted money. However, for our purposes we state the null hypothesis that the drug will have no effect and assume that it's true. A good analogy for this situation is our justice system. In America, our justice system assumes that the individual is innocent unless he or she can be proven guilty. Other countries (e.g., China) have a system where the individual is assumed guilty unless the individual can prove that he's innocent. Are these the same? Of course they're not! If you were to be arrested in one of these countries, I'm sure you'd agree that these aren't the same. The difference is that in America, we assume that the individual is innocent; the default is innocence. This means that all things being equal, the default is letting individuals go unless we can prove that they did it. The Federal Drug Administration has a similar bias in their testing. They utilize the null hypothesis as well. They assume that a drug doesn't work, unless it can be proven that it does. Would you rather use a drug that has been proven to work or a drug that no one has proven that it doesn't work? The use of the null hypothesis does bias the results some, but it biases them in a way that makes it so that we say that there's a difference only when we're sure that there really is.

The second step in using inferential statistics is to specify the level of statistical significance. This is essentially determining how sure we need to be in order to make our decision. Being 100% positive would be excellent, but as we've mentioned earlier, we're using probabilities here to make decisions. There's always a small chance that we could come to the wrong conclusion, but we want to minimize this chance. So 99% sure would be excellent. In fact, in some areas of psychology, we use 99% certainty. This would be the same as selecting an alpha level of .01. This means that 1% of the time we could say that there's a difference when there really wasn't one. When we say that there's a difference when there really wasn't one is referred to as making a **Type I error**. The Type I error is equal to our alpha level. A **Type II error** is when we say that there's no difference when there really was a difference. Obviously we'd like to avoid making either of these errors, but generally the Type I error is thought to have more serious consequences. In most areas of psychology an alpha level of .05 is the norm. This means that we could make a Type I error about 5% of the time, but 95% of the time we'll make the correct decision. Again, we'd love to be correct 100% of the time, but this might bias things so that it would be near impossible to ever reject the null hypothesis. To put this in perspective, let's take a look at a simple question that I ask my students in class. If you were to have sexual intercourse with another person, how sure would you like to be that the woman will not get pregnant? Of course 100% would be great, but this isn't realistic or possible. The only way to reach this 100% is to not have intercourse at all. According to Jones, Mosher, and Daniels (2012), birth control pills have evidence to suggest that they are 99% effective, as long as you take the pill every day at the same time each day. If you vary when you take it or miss a pill, the effectiveness goes down to about 90% effective. The condom, on the other hand, is about 82% effective with normal use. Withdrawal is about 78% effective. I mention these because unwanted pregnancies are a pretty big deal to most people, and many sexually active individuals appear to be generally pretty happy with the effectiveness of condoms and withdrawal, which make up about 20% of those using some sort of contraceptives (Daniels, Daugherty, & Jones, 2012). Those taking the pill make up 26% of contraceptive users (Daniels et al., 2012). Our point here is that the decisions made using inferential statistics in the less conservative areas of psychology utilize the .05 alpha level, which is still significantly more rigorous of a threshold than condoms and withdrawal methods of birth control as well as birth control pills not taken properly, each of which have fairly important repercussions.

The third step is to collect the data (i.e., test the sample of participants selected from the population). The fourth step is to then apply the appropriate inferential statistics. Finally, we then make a decision based on the probability of the null hypothesis. The inferential statistics provide the probability of the null hypothesis. In other words, the inferential statistics give you the probability that the groups or conditions are statistically the same. We compare this probability to our alpha level that we set in Step #2. If this probability is greater than our alpha level, in other words if the probability is greater than .05, then we conclude that there is no difference and accept our null hypothesis (i.e., the groups or conditions are statistically the same). If this computed probability is less than our alpha level then we reject the null hypothesis and conclude that there is a difference between our groups or conditions. In other words, these groups or conditions are found to be statistically different from one another.

Let's use a quick example to look at this decision-making process relative to the null hypothesis. As an example, let's revisit our drug that we've developed. Let's say that our drug, Smartex, is expected to have the effect of improving memory performance. We've evaluated our drug by having one group receive the drug and another group receive the placebo. Upon evaluation, we find the following results when participants are given a memory test:

$$\text{Drug Group} = 94\% \text{ accuracy}$$

$$\text{Placebo Group} = 82\% \text{ accuracy}$$

As you can see, the drug group may have had a higher accuracy than the placebo group, but we need to determine if this is a real difference. In order to determine this, we'll use an inferential statistic. One of the simplest parametric inferential statistics is the t-test. The result of our t-test is the following:

$$t(19) = 1.56, p = .34$$

If this was our result, we'd see that our p-value is .34. This p-value is higher than our alpha level of .05. In this case, our conclusion would be that we would accept the null hypothesis. In other words, the drug group and the placebo group would be statistically the same; our drug didn't work. On the other hand, what if our result was the following:

$$t(19) = 3.13, p = .02$$

Table 9.1   The Five Steps to Using Inferential Statistics

1. State the null hypothesis & assume it's true

2. Specify the level of statistical significance (usually .05 or .01)

3. Collect data

4. Apply the appropriate inferential statistics

5. Evaluate the probability of the null hypothesis

In this case, our p-value is .02, which is less than our alpha level. Our conclusion here would be to reject the null hypothesis. Therefore, our drug group performed statistically better than the placebo group; our drug did work. This is the simplicity of using inferential statistics. While there are several numbers that you can look at that tell you different things about your inferential statistics, the decision is made based on the p-value, and that decision is as simple as determining if the null hypothesis should be accepted or rejected.

Types of t-tests

A t-test is one of the simplest parametric inferential statistics as it allows you to compare two groups or conditions. However, it's important to know the design of your study (i.e., if your independent variable was manipulated between- or within-subjects). If your independent variable was manipulated between-subjects then you would have two groups of participants to compare. An **independent-samples t-test** would be appropriate when you're comparing groups from a between-subjects independent variable. On the other hand, if your independent variable was manipulated within-subjects then you would have one group of participants but you'd compare the different levels of the independent variable that these participants serve in. A **paired-samples t-test** (or a dependent means t-test) would be the appropriate t-test to conduct when comparing the levels of a within-subjects independent variable.

Another determination that must be made when analyzing data using t-tests is whether you'd like to conduct a directional or nondirectional t-test. A **directional t-test** or a **one-tailed t-test** can be used when you expect a difference between your groups or conditions in a particular direction. For example, if you expect your drug group to perform better than the placebo group, a directional t-test would be appropriate since your hypothesis involves a directional prediction. With a directional t-test, if the drug condition performs statistically better than the placebo condition, then the directional t-test will let you know that your results are statistically significant. However, if there was no difference or if the placebo condition actually outperformed your drug condition, then the t-test would indicate that there was no difference. If you'd like to know if there's a difference either way, whether the drug condition does better or if the placebo condition does better, then you'd want to conduct a nondirectional t-test. A **nondirectional t-test** or a **two-tailed t-test** is used if you don't have any particular expectations regarding the direction of your hypothesis or if you'd like to be aware of differences in either direction.

Your choice of whether you select a directional or nondirectional t-test can make a difference in your conclusions. Generally speaking, it's easier to obtain statistically significant findings with a directional t-test. Thus, the nondirectional t-test is a more conservative test of significance. For this reason, the default t-test for most statistical software programs is the nondirectional or two-tailed t-test. Another related issue to keep in mind is that some researchers will plan on using the nondirectional t-test. Once their study is over, they use this two-tailed t-test to determine if their groups were different. If there wasn't a lot of statistical power or if the effect size wasn't very large, this t-test will result in nonsignificant findings. If the results of this nondirectional t-test are close, sometimes researchers will then, after the fact, determine that they really had a directional hypothesis and rerun the t-test, this time using a directional t-test. The results now come out significant, showing that the groups were actually statistically different from one another. Of course doing this would be unethical, but it does sometimes occur in the literature. When we're reading a research article and the researchers evaluate their hypothesis using a one-tailed or directional t-test, my first thought is that they may have done this for the reasons stated above. If the directional t-test is highly significant then it wouldn't have mattered if they conducted a directional or nondirectional t-test; the results would have been significant regardless. However, if the results of the directional t-test are somewhat close then this unethical behavior might be a real possibility. However, keep in mind that *theoretically* a directional t-test may be warranted, but the default is typically to conduct the nondirectional t-test. Regardless of which t-test is conducted, the determination should be made *prior* to analyzing your results, not after.

Analysis of Variance

The Analysis of Variance (or ANOVA) is another parametric inferential statistic. Like the *t*-test, the ANOVA allows you to compare groups or conditions and tells you if those groups or conditions are statistically the same or different from one another. So in a sense, the ANOVA is very similar to the *t*-test. However, unlike the *t*-test, the ANOVA allows you to compare much more than just two groups or conditions. A simple one-way ANOVA allows you to compare several groups or conditions at the same time when you have a single independent variable with two or more levels. For example, if you had an independent variable, say a drug, with several drug dose levels, say a low, medium, and high dose, the ANOVA allows you to make an overall comparison between all three of these levels to let you know if your drug dose manipulation had an effect. This is referred to as a main effect. A **main effect** compares each of the levels of an independent variable and determines if that manipulation by itself made a difference. Therefore, if you have two independent variables, you'd need to evaluate two main effects; three independent variables would give you three main effects to evaluate, and so on. Additionally, with the ANOVA you can evaluate main effects of multiple independent variables at the same time as well as interactions. **Interactions** evaluate the effect one independent variable has on another independent variable. In the drug dose example above, we could add another independent variable of time of day (morning or night). We might find a main effect of drug dose such that the higher the dose, the more effective the drug is. Additionally, we might also find an interaction such that the increasing drug dose is only more effective when taken in the morning, while at night the different drug doses work equally well. In the section that follows, we'll take a look at several data sets so that you can get some practice at seeing and understanding main effects and interactions. We'll be using 2 × 2 tables of means in order to keep things simple at this point, but the same ideas hold true regardless of the design.

Evaluating Main Effects and Interactions

For each of the examples below, we'll take a look at some sample data sets. For each data set we'll need to determine if there's a main effect of the first independent variable, if there's a main effect of the second independent variable, and if there's an interaction. We'll also make the assumption that if the numbers are different from one another then they are significantly different from one another. Obviously we wouldn't do this with real data, but we'll make this assumption for now to make sure that you understand the concept before moving on to real data.

ANOVA example #1

For our first example, let's imagine that we've conducted an experiment where we were interested in the effects of violence on television using two types of television shows (cartoons and live actor shows). The data are below. The numbers represent the number of aggressive actions that children have on the playground after watching the specific shows.

	Violence		
Type of Show	**Nonviolent**	**Violent**	**Average**
Cartoon	0	5	2.5
Live Actor	0	10	5.0
Average	0.0	7.5	

The following three questions need to be answered:

1. Was there a main effect of Violence?
2. Was there a main effect of Type of Show?
3. Was there a Violence x Type of Show interaction?

Let's address the first question. The main effect of Violence is asking if we obtained different findings for the levels of Violence. In other words, did our manipulation of Violence have an effect. In order to determine this, we'd compare the overall average for those participants who received the nonviolent shows to the overall average for those participants who received the violent shows. This would compare the 0.0 and 7.5 averages at the bottom of the table. Since these numbers are different, we'd conclude that we have a main effect of Violence such that participants who received the violent shows had more aggressive actions than those receiving the nonviolent shows.

To determine if we have a main effect of Type of Show, we're asking if the levels of Type of Show (i.e., cartoon or live actor) were different from one another or if our manipulation of Type of Show had an effect. To determine this, we'd compare the overall average for those participants who received the cartoons to those participants who received the live actor. This would compare the 2.5 and 5.0 on the right side of the table. Since these numbers are different, we'd conclude that we have a main effect of Type of Show such that the participants who received the live shows had more aggressive actions than those receiving the cartoons.

Finally, we need to evaluate the presence of an interaction. The interaction is a little different. For the interaction we need to determine if the independent variables had an effect on each other. In other words, we need to determine if the participants who watched the cartoons were affected by the violence manipulation in the same way as the participants who watched the live actor shows. In order to determine this, we'll be looking at the four numbers inside the table. For the participants who received the cartoons, we can see that they had 0 violent actions with the nonviolent cartoons but increased to 5 violent actions when watching the violent cartoons. So we have an increase of +5 violent actions for the participants who watched the cartoons. For the participants who received the live actor shows, we can see that they had 0 violent actions with the nonviolent live actor shows but increased to 10 violent actions when watching the violent live actor shows. So these participants showed an increase of +10 violent actions. The question to determine if we have an interaction or not is if these two groups are doing the same thing or are they doing something different (i.e., are they behaving the same or differently). The participants watching the cartoons showed an increase of 5 violent actions, while those who watched the live actor shows displayed an increase of 10 violent actions. Since they're showing different increases, they're different, and we'd conclude that there was an interaction. Another way to think about the interaction would be to look at a graph of the data. If the lines are parallel to one another then there's no interaction. If the lines are not parallel then there is an interaction. The graph for these data would look something like this:

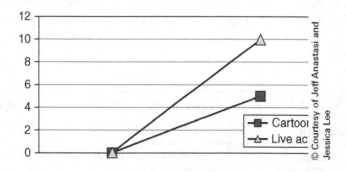

As you can see from the graph, these lines are clearly not parallel to one another and thus there is an interaction between Violence and the Type of Show.

ANOVA example #2

Let's take a look at another data set. For this study, let's imagine that we've conducted a study to evaluate the effectiveness of a Scholastic Assessment Test (SAT) preparation class. Our participants either received an SAT preparation class or didn't receive the class, and all participants were tested just prior to the class and were tested again after the 8 week class was completed. The data are below. The numbers represent their score on the SAT test.

| | Test | | |
Prep Class	Pre Test	Post Test	Average
SAT prep class	800	1200	1000
No prep class	700	1100	900
Average	750	1150	

Again, the following three questions need to be answered:

1. Was there a main effect of Test?
2. Was there a main effect of Prep Class?
3. Was there a Test x Prep Class interaction?

In order to determine if there was a main effect of Test, we'd look at the average scores for the Pretest and compare them to the average Posttest scores. We can see that the 750 is different from the 1150 so there was a main effect of Test. Participants scored higher on the posttest than the pretest. In order to determine if there was a main effect of Prep Class, we'd look at the average scores for those who received the prep class (i.e., 1000 on the right side of the table) and compare that to those who did not receive the prep class (i.e., 900 on the right side of the table). Since these numbers are different, we would conclude that there was a main effect of Prep Class. For our interaction, we'd look at the numbers on the interior of the table. For the individuals who received the prep class, they scored an 800 on the pretest and increased to 1200 for the posttest. So they showed an increase of 400 points. For the participants who did not receive the prep class, they scored an 700 on the pretest and increased to 1100 for the posttest. So they also showed an increase of 400 points. Since both groups showed the same amount of increase, we would conclude that there was no Test x Prep Class interaction. The graph for these data would look something like this:

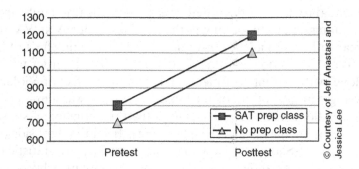

As you can see from the graph, these lines are parallel to one another and thus there is no interaction between Test and the Prep Class.

Hopefully these examples help you to better understand main effects and interactions. As previously mentioned, in these examples we used some fairly simple numbers and made the assumption that any number that was different we would treat as if it were *statistically* different. Unfortunately, we really can't do this with real data. In order to make these decisions if the numbers are the same or different, we'll need to conduct an ANOVA. The ANOVA will tell us quite easily if these numbers are the same or if they're different. So, let's take a look at our first ANOVA example where we manipulated Violence and Type of Show. We'll change the data a little, just to provide another example. The sample data are below.

| | Violence | | |
Type of Show	Nonviolent	Violent	Average
Cartoon	2.0	3.0	2.5
Live Actor	2.0	5.0	3.5
Average	2.0	4.0	

If we were going to make the same assumptions that any numbers that were different are significantly different, then we'd have a main effect of Violence (which compares the 2.0 and the 4.0 at the bottom of the table), a main effect of Type of Show (which compares the 2.5 and 3.5 on the right side of the table), and a Violence x Type of Show interaction (which looks at the changes between the numbers in the middle cells of the table). However, as we mentioned, we can't really do this with real studies. So in order to determine if we have main effects and/or interactions, we need to conduct an ANOVA and look at the ANOVA Summary Table. Our ANOVA Summary Table for these data is below:

ANOVA Summary Table

Source	SS	df	MSe	F	p
Violence	72.077	1	72.077	31.502	.001
Type of Show	12.127	1	12.127	5.301	.081
Violence x Type of Show	22.011	1	22.011	9.620	.004
Error	64.055	28	2.288		

So, let's take a look at what we have here. We could simply look at the ANOVA Summary Table to determine if we have main effects and interactions by just looking at the p-values in the far right column. If the p-value is greater than .05 then there was no difference and thus no main effect or interaction. If the p-value is less than or equal to .05 then the differences are statistically significant and thus there would be a main effect and/or interaction. In looking at the p-values in our ANOVA Summary Table, we can see that there was a main effect of Violence (p-value of .001), no main effect of Type of Show (p-value of .081), and there was an interaction (p-value of .004). However, in order to interpret these findings, we need to "follow along" with our table of means. For our main effect of Violence, we'd be comparing the 2.0 and the 4.0 averages at the bottom of the table. Since there was a main effect, we would say that there were more violent actions with the violent shows than the nonviolent shows. For our main effect of Type of Show, we'd compare the 2.5 and the 3.5 averages from the right side of the table. Since there was no main effect of Type of Show, we know that these numbers are statistically the same. Thus, we would say that overall there was no difference between the participants who saw the cartoons and those who watched the live actor shows. For the Violence x Type of Show interaction, we'd look at the scores inside the table of means. The participants who watched the cartoons had 2.0 aggressive actions when they watched nonviolent cartoons and 3.0 aggressive actions when they watched violent cartoons. For the participants who watched the live actor shows, they demonstrated 2.0 aggressive actions with the nonviolent live actor show and 5.0 aggressive actions with the violent live actor show. Since we have an interaction, we know that these two groups (i.e., those watching cartoons and those watching live actor shows) are doing something different. Keep in mind that the interaction simply tells us that these two conditions (cartoons vs. live actor shows) are behaving differently with the levels of violence, but it doesn't tell us if the 2.0 and 3.0 for the nonviolent cartoons and violent cartoons are different from one another or if the 2.0 and 5.0 for the nonviolent live actor show and the violent live actor show are different from one another. In order to determine this, we'd need follow-up t-tests to make these comparisons. Let's say that we conducted t-tests for both the participants who watched the cartoons and those who watched the live actor. For those who watched the cartoons, our t-test results might be something like this: $t(14) = 1.066$, $p = .617$. By looking at this p-value, we can clearly see that the 2.0 for nonviolent cartoons and the 3.0 for violent cartoons was equal. Thus, participants who received the cartoons showed no significant increase in aggression when they watched violent cartoons compared to when they watched nonviolent cartoons. For participants who watched the live actor shows, our t-test might look something like this: $t(14) = 6.417$, $p = .001$. This p-value clearly indicates that the 2.0 for the nonviolent live actor show and the 5.0 for the violent live actor show are different. So, participants showed more aggression when they were exposed to the violent live actor show compared to the nonviolent live actor show.

We hope that this explanation of how to evaluate your data makes sense. In this way, we must use our table of means, ANOVA summary table, and follow-up t-tests to completely evaluate our study. Each of these pieces of information provide you with certain information, but you really need all of these to properly interpret your findings. There are additional sample statistics at the end of this chapter to provide you with additional practice interpreting data.

Writing Statistics

Before we move on to our next topic, we thought we'd spend a brief amount of time here discussing how to express your statistical findings. As part of writing a Results section in an APA-style manuscript, you'll need to know how to interpret your findings but then also to express your findings in an intelligent and easy to follow way to your reader. The best way to express your findings to the reader is to simply guide the reader through the table of means, using your inferential statistics to support your statements. All you need to do is let the reader know which group had the higher or lower score (or say that they were the same) and then provide the inferential statistics to support each of your statements. For example, using the data that we just discussed with the aggressive television shows, we've written a brief part of a Results section below to illustrate how to guide your reader through your findings.

> Results indicated that overall there was no difference in the number of violent actions for participants who saw the cartoons compared to the live actor shows, $F(1, 28) = 5.301$, $p = .08$. However, there were more aggressive actions for participants who received the violent shows compared to the nonviolent shows, $F(1, 28) = 31.502$, $p < .01$. Additionally, results also demonstrated a Violence x Type of Show interaction, $F(1, 28) = 9.620$, $p < .01$. In order to better understand this interaction, two follow-up t-tests were conducted to evaluate participants who were exposed to the cartoons and live actor shows. The participants who watched the violent cartoons had the same number of aggressive actions as the participants who watched the nonviolent cartoons, $t(14) = 1.066$, $p = .62$. On the other hand, the participants who watched the live actor shows displayed more aggression when they were exposed to the violent live actor show compared to the nonviolent live actor show, $t(14) = 6.417$, $p < .01$.

This sample Results section, provides an example of how you can guide the reader through your findings. We'd strongly recommend guiding the reader through your results using normal, everyday language so that the reader understands your findings. Additionally, adding the inferential statistics at the end of each statement, provides the proof that what you're saying is true. Additionally, these statistics will satisfy anyone who is really interested in the statistics. As a result, you're making the novice reader happy by using normal language that's easy to understand and also satisfying the more advanced reader because you've included the proper statistics to support your statements.

Effect Size

The final topic that we need to mention in this chapter is this idea of effect size. **Effect size** is a measure that quantifies the strength or magnitude of an effect. Whereas our p-value tells us if the numbers are the same or different from one another, the effect size gives you an idea of how large an effect this difference represents. The American Psychological Association (APA) in their Publication Manual (see page 89 of the APA Publication Manual) strongly encourages that researchers always provide effect sizes when presenting inferential statistics. The effect size measures the proportion of the total variation that is attributable to the independent variable and excludes other nonerror variation. The size of the experimental effect is simply the difference between the two conditions means divided by the standard deviation. There are two main types of effect sizes: effect size estimates for ANOVAs and effect size estimates for t-tests. The effect size measure that is typically used for ANOVAs is partial eta squared, which is written as such η^2_p. The effect size measure that is typically used for t-tests is Cohen's d, which is written as such: d. So what do these effect sizes mean? Well, according to Cohen (1992) and Keppel and Wickens (2004), an effect size of .20 is a small effect size, .50 is a medium effect size, and anything greater than .80 is a large effect size. These, of course, are just estimates, but they give you an idea of when something is considered a small, medium, or large effect size. We'll briefly discuss each of these effect size measures below:

Partial Eta Squared (η^2_p)

Providing the partial eta squared measure is necessary after providing the results from main effect or interaction data. The nice thing about partial eta squared is that it's very easy to compute by hand, if necessary. The formula is below:

$$\eta^2_p = SS_{treatment} / (SS_{treatment} + SS_{error})$$

The formula shows that you simply divide the sum of squares from the treatment by the sum of squares from the treatment plus the sum of squares from the error term. Additionally, statistics programs such as SPSS also allow you to simply add the effect size measure when you conduct an ANOVA. In SPSS when you conduct an ANOVA, you simply select the options button and then select the "display effect size" option and it will give you the partial eta squared estimates for each main effect and interaction(s). When you provide your inferential statistics, you simply add the partial eta square measure to the end of the inferential statistics that we've already discussed. For example, you might have something like this:

> The results revealed a main effect of Immediate Task, as the participants recognized more items from the recall task ($M = 0.82$) than the opposition task ($M = 0.69$), $F(1, 66) = 7.54$, $p = .01$, $\eta^2_p = .21$.

Cohen's d

Cohen's d works the same general way as the partial eta squared. The primary limitation on the Cohen's d is that it can only be used to compare two groups or conditions. Thus, it was developed to provide effect size estimates for t-tests which, as you recall, can only be used to compare two groups or conditions. The formula for Cohen's d is:

$$\text{Cohen's } d = (M_1 - M_2) / SD_{pooled}$$

You simply subtract the second mean from the first mean and divide by the pooled standard deviation. It should be noted that while your partial eta squared cannot be greater than 1.0, a Cohen's d can be. Similar to the partial eta squared, the Cohen's d effect size measure is simply added to the end of your t-test results. So, you might have something like this:

> Older adults recognized fewer list items ($M = 0.54$) than younger adults ($M = 0.63$), $t(66) = 2.46$, $p = .02$, $d = .78$.

Oddly, SPSS doesn't allow you to easily compute Cohen's *d*. It seems odd to us that this powerful statistics program doesn't provide an option for a very important statistic that's really simple to compute. Regardless, there are some very helpful materials that allow you to easily compute Cohen's *d*. One of these is an article by Thalheimer and Cook (2002) where they provide formulas for calculating Cohen's *d* for *t*-tests and for *F*-tests (i.e., ANOVAs). On the other hand, if you'd rather not compute Cohen's *d* yourself, there is a very helpful website that you can use that provides a nice Effect Size Calculator: https://lbecker.uccs.edu/. This calculator allows you to compute Cohen's *d* regardless of what information you have. You can compute it using the means and standard deviations from your condition data or you can use the *t*-test results. Either way, Cohen's *d* is a very helpful statistic to use and is very easy to compute.

Concluding Remarks

Inferential statistics allow researchers to determine if two scores are different from one another. In other words, inferential statistics allow us to know if our manipulation made a difference or if the groups or conditions behaved similarly. As mentioned throughout this chapter, the decision made with the use of inferential statistics is determined based on probabilities. While an incorrect decision could be concluded based on these probabilities, the correct decision is typically made. Having a good understanding of inferential statistics, what they are, what they do, and what your choices are, is crucial to becoming a knowledgeable and competent researcher.

References

Daniels, K., Daugherty, J. & Jones, J. (2013). Current contraceptive status among women aged 15–44: United States, 2011–2013, *National Health Statistics Reports*, 173, http://www.cdc.gov/nchs/data/databriefs/db173.pdf.

Jones, J., Mosher, W. D., & Daniels, K. (2012). Current contraceptive use in the United States, 2006–2010, and changes in patterns of use since 1995, *National Health Statistics Reports*, 60, http://www.cdc.gov/nchs/data/nhsr/nhsr060.pdf.

Thalheimer, W., & Cook, S. (2002). How to calculate effect sizes from published research: A simplified methodology. *Work-Learning Research*, 1–9.

End of Chapter Quiz

1. When we say that there's a difference when there really wasn't one, we are referring to a
   _____ error.

2. True or False: Inferential statistics help to describe and organize the data.

3. The _____ states that the independent variable had no effect. Any differences that are observed, according to this hypothesis, are due to random variation rather than any real differences between the groups or conditions.

4. Which *t*-test would be appropriate when you're comparing groups from a between-subjects independent variable.

5. True or False: The best measure of central tendency is the standard deviation.

6. Which *t*-test has the most statistical power?

7. True or False: An ANOVA provides information regarding the effects of each independent variable by itself as well as any interaction between the variables.

8. When the lines on a graph are parallel to one another, this typically indicates that there is _____ present.

9. True or False: It is generally easier to obtain significant findings with a one-tailed *t*-test.

10. What does the following statistical symbol mean: η^2_p?

Homework Assignment

What follows is Homework Assignment #1. This is a statistics packet that includes many different ways to evaluate your knowledge of both descriptive and inferential statistics, your understanding and ability to apply your knowledge of the basic terms used, and interpreting these statistics. Please complete this packet to help you better understand your knowledge of inferential statistics and data interpretation. Alternatively, if you think you have a pretty strong grasp of these concepts, these assignments can help you to know how strong that grasp is.

Homework Assignment #1

1.   **IV1**

10	20
40	30

IV2

Main Effect IV1?
Main Effect IV2?
Interaction?

2.   **IV1**

40	20
20	40

IV2

Main Effect IV1?
Main Effect IV2?
Interaction?

3.   **IV1**

10	20
10	20

IV2

Main Effect IV1?
Main Effect IV2?
Interaction?

4.   **IV1**

20	10
30	20

IV2

Main Effect IV1?
Main Effect IV2?
Interaction?

5.   **IV1**

10	10
20	10

IV2

Main Effect IV1?
Main Effect IV2?
Interaction?

6.   **IV1**

10	0
0	10

IV2

Main Effect IV1?
Main Effect IV2?
Interaction?

7.   **IV1**

10	10
10	10

IV2

Main Effect IV1?
Main Effect IV2?
Interaction?

8.   **IV1**

20	10
20	30

IV2

Main Effect IV1?
Main Effect IV2?
Interaction?

9.   **IV1**

10	30
20	20

IV2

Main Effect IV1?
Main Effect IV2?
Interaction?

10.   **IV1**

10	10
20	20

IV2

Main Effect IV1?
Main Effect IV2?
Interaction?

11.   **IV1**

10	20
10	30

IV2

Main Effect IV1?
Main Effect IV2?
Interaction?

12.   **IV1**

10	0
20	10

IV2

Main Effect IV1?
Main Effect IV2?
Interaction?

For each of the following, please provide the descriptive statistics in the table provided that would give an example for each of the following. Also, please graph your data on the graph provided to the right. Provide an example of:

13. Two main effects & no interaction

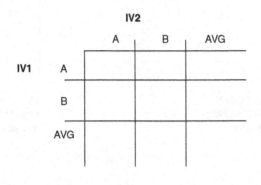
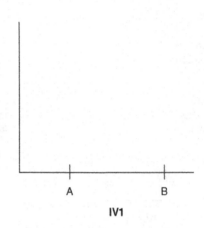

14. One main effects & no interaction

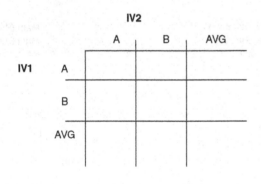
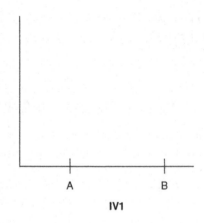

15. No main effects & no interaction

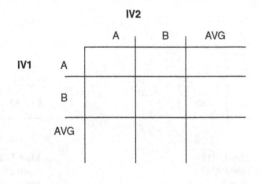
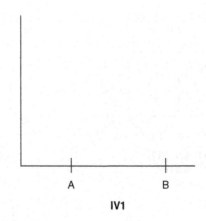

16. Two main effects & an interaction

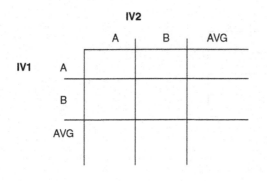

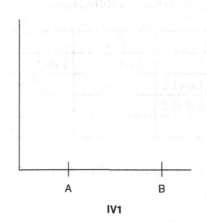

17. One main effects & an interaction

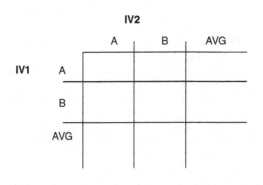

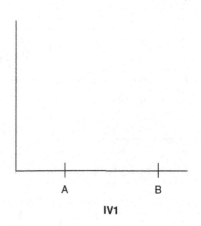

18. No main effects & an interaction

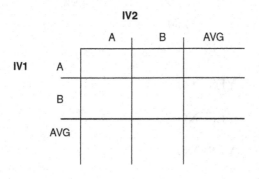

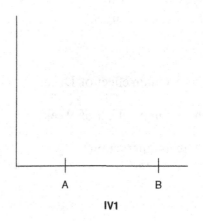

For each of the following two data sets please answer the appropriate questions and assume that any differences are significant differences.

		IV2		
		Level 1	Level 2	
IV1	Level 1	30	20	
	Level 2	10	20	

19. Is there a main effect of the IV1?   YES   NO

20. Is there a main effect of the IV2?   YES   NO

21. Is there an interaction?   YES   NO

Please answer the questions using the data provided below. Use the inferential statistics provided to answer the questions.

		(Week)			
		Week 1	Week 2		
(Drug Dose)	**Drug**	2.3	4.5		
	Placebo	8.5	8.1		

Source	SS	DF	MS	F	P
Drug	8.79	1	18.79	15.78	0.024
ERROR	21.44	18	1.19		
Week	15.21	1	5.21	1.85	0.144
ERROR	50.54	18	2.81		
Drug × Week	1.09	1	18.99	4.94	0.074
ERROR	69.15	18	3.84		

22. Is there a main effect of Drug?   YES NO

23. Is there a main effect of Week?   YES NO

24. Is there an interaction?   YES NO

Please answer the following questions using the data provided.
Dr. Williams has approached the Peoria School District and has informed them that he has a new training technique that will raise SAT scores. The supervisor is skeptical and asks Dr. Williams to prove that his methods work. Dr. Williams allows the school superintendent to train one group of students while he trains the other group. Dr. Williams randomly assigns 100 students to receive either his or the school superintendent's training method so that half of the students are trained with the superintendent's method and half are trained using Dr. Williams method. Dr. Williams tests each of the students before the training session and then after the training session. Here are the results:

SAT Training		Test	
		Pretest	Posttest
SAT Training	Superintendent Training	800	900
	Williams' Method	900	1200

Source	SS	DF	MS	F	P
Test	8.79	1	6.79	3.10	0.074
ERROR	7.44	18	2.19		
SAT Training	15.21	1	15.21	5.41	0.039
ERROR	50.54	18	2.81		
Test × SAT Training	1.09	1	17.09	6.02	0.024
ERROR	69.15	18	2.84		

_____25. Was there a main effect of Test?
   a. Yes   b. No   c. it can't be determined

_____26. Was there a main effect of SAT Training?
   a. Yes   b. No   c. it can't be determined

_____27. Was there a Test × SAT Training interaction?
   a. Yes   b. No   c. it can't be determined

_____28. Did students perform better on the Pretest or the Posttest?
   a. Pretest   b. Posttest   c. They were the same   d. it can't be determined

_____29. Did students perform better with the Superintendent's Training or with Dr. William's method?
   a. Superintendent's   b. Dr. William's   c. They were the same   d. it can't be determined

_____30. Did the students who received the Superintendent's Training method show an increase in SAT scores from the Pretest to the Posttest?
   a. Yes   b. No   c. They stayed the same   d. it can't be determined

_____31. Did the students who received the Dr. Williams' Training method show an increase in SAT scores from the Pretest to the Posttest?
   a. Yes   b. No   c. They stayed the same   d. it can't be determined

_____32. Were the SAT scores higher on the pretest with the Superintendent's Training or with Dr. William's method?
   a. Superintendent's   b. Dr. William's   c. They were the same   d. it can't be determined

_____33. Were the SAT scores higher on the posttest with the Superintendent's Training or with Dr. William's method?
   a. Superintendent's   b. Dr. William's   c. They were the same   d. it can't be determined

Experiment:

The current study tested men and women to determine if there are differences in their taste sensitivity for different types of tastes. Each male and female subject was tested using a sweet (chocolate syrup), bitter (quinine), salty (salt), and sour (lemon juice) taste. Scores reflect which trial subjects were able to detect the particular taste in a solution of distilled water. The maximum number of trials subjects were given was 10. Subjects could not use their sense of sight or smell.

Means (trial #):	Sweet	Bitter	Salty	Sour
Male	3.1	7.4	3.5	5.2
Female	2.5	6.9	3.1	4.9

ANOVA summary table

Source	SS	DF	MS	F	P
Gender	2746.4	1	1373.1	40.5	0.001
Error	555.2	49	15.55		
Taste	5858.5	3	522.5	3.2	0.092
Error	522.2	98	1558.5		
Gender × Taste	5285.5	3	5485.5	20.2	0.003
Error	555.6	98	5854.5		

Taste	Follow-up-*t*-tests:	t	df	p
Sweet	Male vs. Female	5.25	24	0.01
Bitter	Male vs. Female	1.12	24	0.12
Salty	Male vs. Female	1.69	24	0.21
Sour	Male vs. Female	4.22	24	0.02

_____34. Was there a main effect of Gender?   a. YES   b. NO

_____35. Overall, which gender identified the tastes in the fewest trials?
        a. Males   b. Females   c. They were the same   d. It's impossible to say

_____36. Was there a main effect of Taste?   a. YES   b. NO

_____37. Overall, which taste was identified in the fewest trials?
        a. Sweet   c. Salty   e. They were the same
        b. Bitter   d. Sour   f. It's impossible to say

_____38. Was there a Gender × Taste interaction?   a. YES   b. NO

_____39. Did males or females detect the sweet taste in the fewest number of trials?
        a. Males   b. Females   c. They were the same   d. It's impossible to say

_____40. Did males or females detect the bitter taste in the fewest number of trials?
        a. Males   b. Females   c. They were the same   d. It's impossible to say

_____41. Did males or females detect the salty taste in the fewest number of trials?
        a. Males   b. Females   c. They were the same   d. It's impossible to say

_____42. Did males or females detect the sour taste in the fewest number of trials?
        a. Males   b. Females   c. They were the same   d. It's impossible to say

_____43. For only the males, did they detect the sweet taste or the salty taste in the fewest number of trials?
        a. sweet   b. salty   c. They were the same   d. It's impossible to say

Please answer the following questions using the description and data provided below:

The following data were collected to test a new drug that should help individuals is control their anxiety levels. Half of the individuals were given the drug and half were given the placebo. Each individual was then given a job interview over the telephone and in person. The dependent variable was the interviewee's anxiety rating on a 1–5 scale (with 1 being totally calm and 5 being extremely anxious).

	Telephone	In Person	MEAN
Placebo	3.1	4.9	4.0
Drug	1.7	2.3	1.5
MEAN	2.4	3.1	

ANOVA summary table:

Source	SS	DF	MS	F	P
Drug	33.61	1	13.61	3.66	0.01
Error	104.04	24	3.72		
Interview Type	109.96	1	54.98	20.23	0.12
Interview Type × Drug	6.49	3	3.24	1.19	0.31
Error	152.22	49	2.72		

Independent-Samples t-test for TELEPHONE: $t(49) = 0.57, p = 0.576$
Independent-Samples t-test for IN PERSON: $t(49) = 6.00, p = 0.001$

Paired-Samples t-test for the DRUG group: $t(98) = 5.71, p = .012$
Paired-Samples t-test for the PLACEBO group: $t(98) = 2.13, p = .228$

_____44. What is the design of this study? (write your answer below)

_____45. Was there a main effect of Drug?
   a. Yes   b. No   c. it can't be determined

_____46. Were interviewees less anxious with the Drug or the Placebo?
   a. Drug   b. Placebo   c. They were the same   d. It can't be determined

_____47. Was there a main effect of Interview Type?
   a. Yes   b. No   c. it can't be determined

_____48. Were the interviewees less anxious with the Telephone or the In Person interview?
   a. Telephone   b. In Person   c. They were the same   d. it can't be determined

_____49. Was there an Interview Type × Drug interaction?
   a. Yes   b. No   c. it can't be determined

_____50. Did those who were interviewed over the telephone show less anxiety with the drug or with the placebo?
   a. Drug   b. Placebo   c. They were the same   d. It can't be determined

_____51. Did those who were interviewed in person show less anxiety with the drug or with the placebo?
   a. Drug   b. Placebo   c. They were the same   d. It can't be determined

_____52. Did the interviewees who received the drug, show less anxiety with the Telephone or the In Person interview?
   a. Telephone   b. Live Audience   c. They were the same   d. it can't be determined

_____53. Did the interviewees who received the placebo, show less anxiety with the Telephone or the In Person interview?
   a. Telephone   b. Live Audience   c. They were the same   d. it can't be determined

Homework Assignment #2

Experiment:

The current study tested men and women to determine if there are differences in their taste sensitivity for different types of tastes. Each male and female subject was tested using a sweet (chocolate syrup), bitter (quinine), salty (salt), and sour (lemon juice) taste. Scores reflect which trial subjects were able to detect the particular taste in a solution of distilled water. The maximum number of trials subjects given was 10. The subjects could not use their sense of sight or smell.

Means (trial #):	Sweet	Bitter	Salty	Sour
Male	3.1	7.4	3.5	5.2
Female	2.5	6.9	3.1	4.9

ANOVA Summary Table

Source	SS	df	MSe	F	p
Gender	2746.4	1	1373.1	40.5	0.001
Error	555.2	49	15.55		
Taste	5858.5	3	522.5	3.2	0.092
Error	522.2	98	1558.5		
Gender x Taste	5285.5	3	5485.5	20.2	0.003
Error	555.6	98	5854.5		

Taste	Follow-up t-tests:	t	df	p
Sweet	Male vs. Female	5.25	24	0.01
Bitter	Male vs. Female	1.12	24	0.12
Salty	Male vs. Female	1.69	24	0.21
Sour	Male vs. Female	4.22	24	0.02

Be sure to:	specify the ANOVA, DV, & IV	_____ (out of 10 points)
	provide descriptive statistics	_____ (out of 10 points)
	provide inferential statistics	_____ (out of 10 points)
	guide the reader through the results	_____ (out of 20 points)

Chapter 10

An Introduction to Statistical Packages

The purpose of this chapter is to provide you with the information that you'll need to analyze your data with a statistical software package (i.e., SPSS). We'll first introduce you to the proper way to set up your data files and then introduce you to a statistical database as well as an overview of statistical programs in general. In order for the information in this chapter to make sense, you'll need to be comfortable with the terminology that was used in previous chapters (i.e., independent variables, levels of an independent variable, dependent variables, between-subject variables, within-subject variables, etc.), as you'll be applying that information here.

Data Files

As soon as you start to collect your data you will find that you have a need to organize all the data coming in. It is crucial that you keep on top of your data entry as well as stay organized. One of the main ways to organize your data is to use a spreadsheet program, such as Microsoft Excel. Data files should be clearly labeled and include all of your collected information. While it is likely that in your classes you discuss less complex research designs, when it comes to actual studies, it is likely that you will have multiple variables, measures, and demographic information that you will need to keep track of. For this section, we will be discussing setting up your data file in the most efficient way using Microsoft Excel. You may find that in your academic career that you or your research advisor may choose to use a different program; regardless, the overall guidelines provided here are useful no matter what program you use and are important nonetheless.

Setting Up Your Data File—A General Overview

One of the best pieces of advice that I ever received in statistics was to label *everything*. As most studies will actually take quite a bit of time to conduct, it is likely that you will be working on more than one study at a time. Labeling your data files and your data will help you to remember exactly what the data means as well as ensure that you put your raw data in the right place. On top of that, with proper labels, if you decide to take a vacation or stop working on your research for a while or have another person help you later with the study, you will be able to pick up where you left off. Additionally, with proper labels others can more easily understand your data. As you can see in Figure 10.1, everything from the columns and rows down to the different page tabs is clearly labeled. Again, this is essential for you to do. Now, you may decide to use codes for ease and to save time, there isn't a problem with this, just make sure that you save the coding that you use somewhere so you can later interpret it. One trick I use is to insert a comment to anything I use a code on so that I can read my notes right there. This has saved me a lot of stress and has made it easy for someone else to go in and read my data without me there.

Now, as far as actually setting up your data file goes, it's pretty straightforward, even if it does look intimidating. There are some general rules that you should always use when setting up your data file.

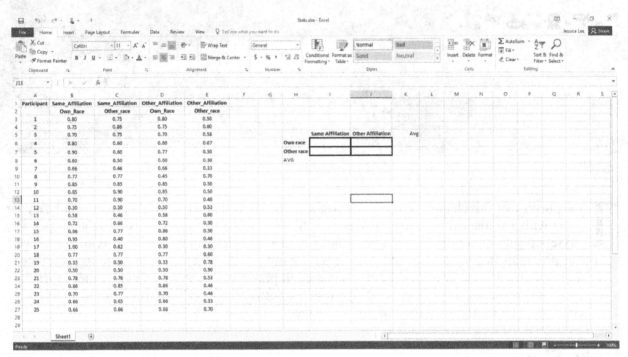

Figure 10.1-A   Example of a simple data set.

- Each row will represent the data for one of your participants in the study
- Each column represents the data points or dependent variables (these include scores, demographic information), but a column can also include the dummy-coding used for group membership when using a between-subjects variable.

As we look at specific data sets, we will further discuss the specifics of setting up your data files for each type of research design. As we do so, these general rules will make a lot more sense to you.

Let's take a look at our simple data set from Figure 10.1-A. As you can see we have labeled the participants using numbers. As you recall from Chapter 3, one of the responsibilities of the researchers is to ensure that a participant's information remains confidential. Within your data file you should not have the participants' personal information, such as name. This doesn't mean that you shouldn't have this somewhere, in fact, you should. A separate file (often referred to as a subject log) should be created to store all of the information related to your participants' identity. This way, one file alone will not reveal any confidential information about the participants' responses or performance and allow anyone to link that data with a particular individual. But, should the need arise, you would be able to link the data backup to the participant. Ok, so back to Figure 10.1-A. The next four columns represent the raw data in this hypothetical study. Each of the columns is clearly labeled, so that even though you are not sure what the study was about, you know what the information in the columns is related to. Now, if you look at Figure 10.1-B you will see that there is a lot more information (and much more off the screen that we couldn't capture). For instance, we have also listed the age of the participants in the second column as well as which presentation group they were in. Again, this information is clearly labeled and coded so that after being away from the data for some time we would still be able to read it if needed. You will also note that at the bottom of the Excel sheet on Figure 10.1-B there are multiple tabs, again, keeping your data files all together (with the exception of the subject log) is wise and will save you from conducting an extensive search to locate each of your data files later.

The type of design you are using in your research (between-, within-, or mixed-factor designs) will alter how you set up your data. The general rules are still the same, but the data files will look different. We'll discuss each of these designs in this chapter. Our discussion will include setting up the data file properly as well as how to conduct the analysis and the follow-up analyses for each of these three designs.

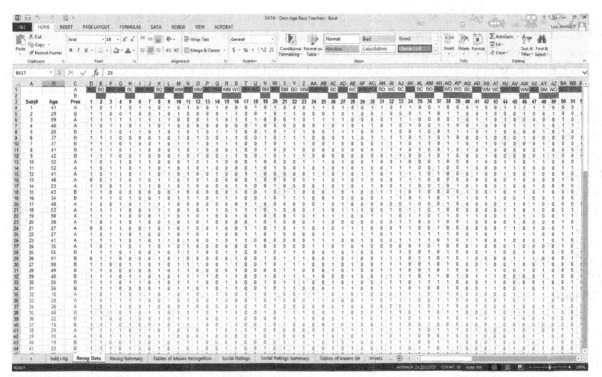

Figure 10.1-B   Example of a more complex data set.

Final Thoughts on Data Files

Assuming that you have multiple researchers using the same data file to input data from the same study, it may be wise to have periodic meetings to ensure that everyone is inputting the data correctly. Having to go back to fix data input is a waste of time. It can also be extremely helpful for individuals to go back and "spot check" the data that others are inputting. Again, finding mistakes at this point is much simpler than finding these mistakes after the study has been completed or even published.

One thing you can, and should, do before you run your data through a statistics program, is to create a table of means. In Figure 10.1-A, you can see that we have set up a blank table of means. This is useful so that you can quickly take a look at the means from each of your groups or conditions to see if it looks like there are any differences or if your manipulations made any difference. Your table of means just allows you to take a quick look at your data to see what might be occurring, it is NOT all you have to do to interpret your data. You will still need to conduct the inferential statistics to determine if any of the differences that you see are significant from one another or not. The other use of your table is to help guide you in which comparisons make the most sense or to give you an idea of where you may find differences. Additionally, this table of means can be very helpful as you make various comparisons using your inferential statistics. Typically, when you conduct various comparisons, SPSS or whatever other statistical package you use will provide you with the means as you compare different groups or conditions. By looking at your table of means, you can follow along and make sure that you're comparing the groups or conditions that you think you're comparing.

Using Statistical Packages

It is possible to run your statistics in your Microsoft Excel file, but most researchers and universities use a statistical program for this. In this section, we will be guiding you through the basics of IBM® SPSS® Statistics software-22 (SPSS)*, but there are many other statistical programs out there such as SAS and

*SPSS Inc. was acquired by IBM in October, 2009.

MatLAb. Typically, the head of your research lab and/or your statistics professor(s) will inform you which program you will be using while working with them, but SPSS is the most popular statistical program used in psychology today; therefore, we'll focus on it. If you understand how to use SPSS, you can typically easily transfer these skills to other statistical software programs, as they are often quite similar.

In this section, we'll include a step-by-step guide for ANOVAs and *t*-tests for between-subject, within-subject, and mixed-factor data sets. First things first, you have to get your raw data (the data from your Excel file) into SPSS. Thankfully, this isn't difficult—a simple copy and paste function will work perfectly for this. When copying your data over, you need to only select the columns that are needed for your data analysis, not any of the labels that you may have made. Be sure that you are pasting your data into the SPSS "data view" tab and not the "variable view" tab. You do have the option to manually type in your data from your Excel sheet, but I would advise against this as you are more likely to make a mistake during input, which could alter your results. There is also an option to import your data into SPSS as well. Many people import the data without any troubles, but you do need to make sure that your excel data file only has the data that you're using and no labels or tables of means or any other extra information. If you are choosing to just copy and paste your data into SPSS, then just highlight all of the data that you'd like to copy in your excel file, copy it, and then paste it into the SPSS spreadsheet.

Once you have pasted your raw data into your SPSS spreadsheet, you want to click on the "variable view" tab and start labeling your variables. The variable names are the first column on this sheet. We label here for the same reasons we labeled in our Excel spreadsheet—ease and clarity. These labels will also appear on your output making it easier for you to read your results. Changing the name of the variable is easy, just click in the box (the default label will be something like "VAR00001") and start typing. Figure 10.2 shows what this will look like once you've changed your label names. Be aware that SPSS doesn't like spaces or dashes or really anything, so when you create your variable name it might look weird—SATTraining. One trick that you can use (if you hate the way the long combined words look) is to use an underscore (SAT_Training). Don't ask me why SPSS won't allow dashes but is OK with an underscore, it just is.

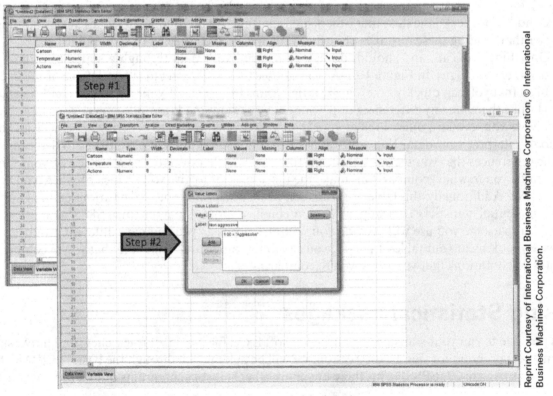

Figure 10.2   SPSS screenshot for changing variable labels.

When you have a variable that is based on nominal data, such as a group membership, you can also create labels for them based on the numbers you have been using as group identifiers in your data. Looking at Table 10.1, you can see that we have labeled our groups of Cartoons and Temperature as either being 1 or 2 (above the data you can see our coding system). These numbers are used for coding but by themselves have no meaning in SPSS, so we can create a label by selecting the "value" box on our variable view on the row of the variable that needs labels. In order to do this, you will need to click on the three little dots in the corner of the "value" box where it says "none." This is depicted in Step #1 of Figure 10.2. When you click to add values, an edit box will pop up. You then provide your code in the value box (such as 1) and what the code means in the label box ("aggressive"), then click "add." This is depicted in Step #2 of Figure 10.2. Once you have labeled each of your values you can now begin to run your various analyses.

Between-Subjects Data Sets

Let's start our discussion of data sets and data analyses with a study utilizing a between-subjects design. Table 10.1 provides a sample data set that we'll be referencing as we go through the steps for conducting an ANOVA and follow-up *t*-tests.

If you are conducting an analysis of a between-subjects design, you will need to run a univariate ANOVA. Looking at our data set in Table 10.1, you can see that we are measuring the effects of aggressive cartoons as well as the temperature of the room on a child's aggression level. You can see that we have two independent variables: cartoons (aggressive, nonaggressive) and temperature (hot room, cool room) and that our dependent variable is the number of aggressive actions. As always, each row represents the data from one participant, and you can see that each subject (the subject number is in the far left column) is in one of the groups and has one score. As you recall from Chapter 2, when you have factorial designs, you will create multiple groups or conditions. When we create our columns in our between-subjects data

Table 10.1 Sample Between-Subjects Data Set

Effects of Aggressive Cartoons and Room Temperature on Children's Aggression

| | 1 = Aggressive | 1 = Hot Room | |
| | 2 = Nonaggressive | 2 = Cool Room | |
Subj #	Cartoons	Temperature	# Actions
1	1	1	1
2	1	1	11
3	1	1	10
4	1	2	7
5	1	2	6
6	1	2	6
7	2	1	5
8	2	1	8
9	2	1	7
10	2	2	2
11	2	2	1
12	2	2	2

set, we form different groups. As can be seen in Table 10.1, when we have a 2 x 2 between-subjects design for this example, we end up having four different groups. The table below depicts these four groups:

Aggressive Cartoon Hot Room	Nonaggressive Cartoon Hot Room
Aggressive Cartoon Cool Room	Nonaggressive Cartoon Cool Room

Since this is a between-subjects design, each participant will then serve in only one of these four different groups. Also, since this is a between-subjects design, each participant will only have one data score (the number of aggressive actions). So a participant will receive either level 1 or 2 for the cartoon and receive either level 1 or 2 for the room temperature. For example, you can see that Subject #1 saw the aggressive cartoon (level 1 of Cartoons) and was in the hot room (level 1 of Temperature). On the other hand, Subject #7 saw the nonaggressive cartoon (level 2 of Cartoons) and was in the hot room (level 1 of Temperature). Thus, each participant served in one of the four groups seen in the table above. So to review, the first column in Table 10.1 gives the subject number for each participant. The second and third columns provide what's called the "dummy coding" for each of our two independent variables. This dummy coding allows the statistics program to separate the groups in a way that it can understand. For the Cartoons column, it uses the dummy code of "1" for the aggressive cartoons and "2" for nonaggressive cartoons. For the Temperature column, it uses the dummy code of "1" for the hot room and "2" for the cool room. The fourth column contains the dependent variable or our measure for each participant (i.e., the number of aggressive actions).

Now we can conduct our univariate ANOVA. Once that we have our data file imported into SPSS and are confident that it's in the proper format, we can start our univariate analysis. Figure 10.3 provides the step-by-step screenshots to help you visually see what we're describing in the text here.

First you will need to select the Analyze tab from the menu options at the top. Next you need to select General Linear Model and then select Univariate. This can be seen as Step #1 in Figure 10.3.

This will bring up your Univariate box, which is depicted as Step #2 in Figure 10.3. All of your variables should be listed in the left most box. You will now need to transfer them over to the appropriate boxes on the right side of the screen. Let's start at the top box on the right side of the screen. The first variable it is asking for is your dependent variable. As you recall, our dependent variable is Actions. Select this variable from the left box and use the arrow beside Dependent Variable to move it over to the Dependent Variable box.

Next we need to move our independent variables (Cartoon and Temperature) to our Fixed Factors box. The fixed factors is another name for your between-subject variable. You can select these individually and move them over one at a time, or you can use the Ctrl button on your keyboard to select multiple variables at once and move them over at the same time. Either way is perfectly acceptable. You will notice that there are other options available for you on this screen, we won't be using them in this course, so you can ignore them for now. Step #3 in Figure 10.3 shows what this will look like once you've selected the appropriate variables and placed them where they belong.

Once you have your variables in the appropriate locations, you can just click OK to run your analysis. This should provide you with your ANOVA results. You can see an example of your ANOVA findings in Table 10.2.

Reading a univariate table is pretty easy. Just look for your factor names —in this case Cartoon and Temperature. As you recall from Chapter 9, an ANOVA can tell us if there are any main effects and if there is an interaction between your variables. To determine if your results are significant, look for your variable names within the table and then look at your "Sig." value in the right column. In this case, our significance value for Cartoons is $p = .148$, Temperature is $p = .110$, and our interaction, shown with an asterisk (Cartoon*Temperature) is $p = .264$. This means that our results overall are not significant (sad day in the research lab). To use your output to write your inferential statistics in your papers, you would just need to "plug-and-chug" using the following formula: F(df, df error) = F-value, p = sig. So, if you were to write out our inferential statistic for Cartoon, it would be: $F(1, 8) = 2.560$, $p = .148$. For Temperature is would be: $F(1, 8) = 3.240$, $p = .110$. For the Cartoon x Temperature interaction it would be: $F(1, 8) = 1.440$, $p = .264$.

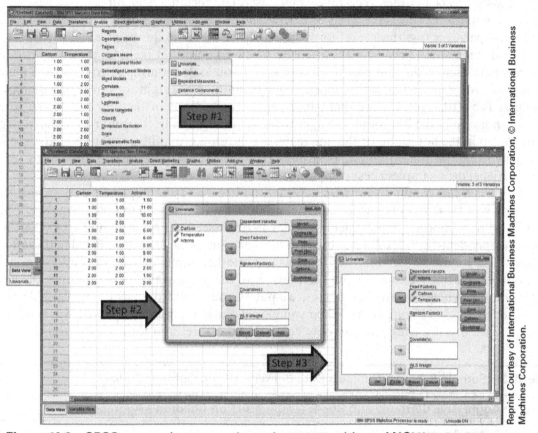

Figure 10.3 SPSS screenshot to conduct a between-subjects ANOVA.

Table 10.2 Sample ANOVA Output for a Between-Subjects Design

Tests of Between-Subjects Effects

Dependent Variable: Actions

Source	Type III Sum of Squares	df	Mean Square	F	Sig.
Corrected Model	60.333[a]	3	20.111	2.413	.142
Intercept	363.000	1	363.000	43.560	.000
Cartoon	21.333	1	21.333	2.560	.148
Temperature	27.000	1	27.000	3.240	.110
Cartoon * Temperature	12.000	1	12.000	1.440	.264
Error	66.667	8	8.333		
Total	490.000	12			
Corrected Total	127.000	11			

a. R Squared = .475 (Adjusted R Squared = .278)

Follow Up t-tests

While the interaction wasn't significant for our data set, oftentimes you'll want to better understand the interaction to see exactly what's going on with the data. In order to do this, you could easily conduct some follow-up *t*-tests. In order to do this, you'll simply conduct independent-samples *t*-tests since we'll be making comparisons across the levels of a between-subjects variable (See chapter 9 for a review). For example, comparing across the levels (hot vs. cool) of our temperature variable.

The first thing you'll need to do is to create a new column that includes a dummy code to allow you to compare each of the four groups more easily. If you look at our updated data, which is depicted in Table 10.3, you can see that we've added a new column on the right for our group dummy coding. Looking at Table 10.3, you can see that participants can be in one of the four groups (i.e., the aggressive cartoon group in the hot room, the aggressive cartoon group in the cool room, the nonaggressive cartoon group in the hot room, or the nonaggressive cartoon group in a cool room). By labeling these four groups using the dummy coding of groups 1, 2, 3, or 4, this will simplify the process of running multiple independent-samples *t*-test comparisons in SPSS.

Now you can just conduct your *t*-tests. We'll explain each of the steps here and provide the screen shots for each of these steps below. To conduct our first *t*-test, you need to select "Analyze," "Compare Means," and then choose "Independent-samples *T*-Test" (see Step #1 in Figure 10.4). This will bring up the "Independent-Samples *T*-Test" box where all of your variables will be listed in the left hand box (see Step #2 in Figure 10.4). "Test Variables" is just another name for your dependent variable. Since we are only measuring Actions, we put "Actions" into the test variable box, and since we created our dummy coding to help us with our groups, we put "Group" into the Grouping Variable box on the bottom (see Step #3 in Figure 10.4). When you place your grouping variable, you will need to "Define Groups." Since this is a *t*-test, we can only compare two scores at a time, so you can only select two

Table 10.3   Sample Between-Subjects Data Set With Group Dummy Coding

Effects of Aggressive Cartoons and Room Temperature on Children's Aggression

	1 = Aggressive	1 = Hot Room		
	2 = Nonaggressive	2 = Cool Room		
Subj #	**Cartoons**	**Temp**	**# Actions**	***Dummy Code***
1	1	1	1	1
2	1	1	11	1
3	1	1	10	1
4	1	2	7	2
5	1	2	6	2
6	1	2	6	2
7	2	1	5	3
8	2	1	8	3
9	2	1	7	3
10	2	2	2	4
11	2	2	1	4
12	2	2	2	4

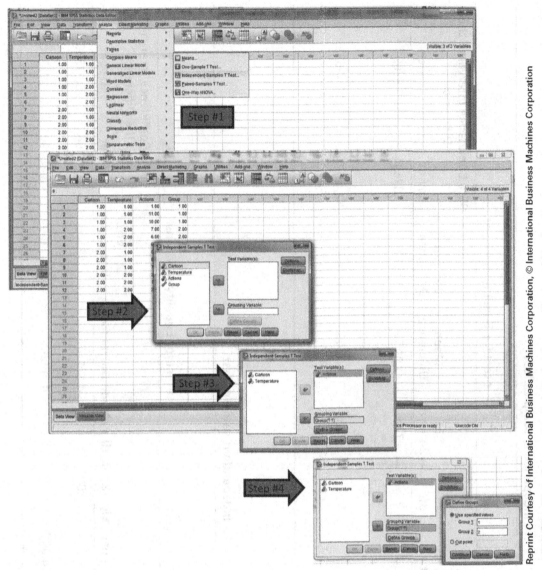

Figure 10.4   SPSS screenshot to demonstrate how to conduct independent-samples *t*-tests.

groups to compare (remember, you have 4!). Click on the "Define Groups" button to label which two groups you'd like to compare (see Step #4 in Figure 10.4). In Step #4 of Figure 10.4, you can see that we've opted to first compare group 1 with group 2. Once you select which groups you wish to compare, you just click "OK." This completes the first independent samples *t*-test. Remember, you will need to run one independent-samples *t*-test comparing group 1 to group 2, run a second to compare group 1 to group 3, a third to compare group 1 to group 4, and so on until you have conducted all of your comparisons (for our example this means you would conduct six *t*-tests). To do this you would simply go through these same steps, but simply change which groups you'd like to compare by clicking on the "Define Groups" button and comparing the other groups by putting in the group numbers to be compared.

We have provided examples of the output for two of the potential *t*-tests for this example in Table 10.4.

When looking at an independent-samples *t*-test, you are only interested in the information in the third, fourth, and fifth columns. In particular, we want to know if our "Sig (2-tailed)" is less than .05. In the case of our first *t*-test, it isn't, $p = .770$. This means that for those groups, the scores were not significantly

Table 10.4   Sample Independent-Samples *t*-test Data

Independent-samples Test

	Levene's Test for Equality of Variances		t-test for Equality of Means					95% Confidence Interval of the Difference	
	F	Sig.	t	df	Sig. (2-tailed)	Mean Difference	Std. Error Difference	Lower	Upper
Actions Equal variances assumed	11.796	.026	.313	4	.770	1.00000	3.19722	−7.87691	9.87691
Equal variances not assumed			.313	2.044	.783	1.00000	3.19722	−12.47692	14.47692

Independent-samples Test

	Levene's Test for Equality of Variances		t-test for Equality of Means					95% Confidence Interval of the Difference	
	F	Sig.	t	df	Sig. (2-tailed)	Mean Difference	Std. Error Difference	Lower	Upper
Actions Equal variances assumed	.000	1.000	9.899	4	.001	4.66667	.47140	3.35784	5.97550
Equal variances not assumed			9.899	4.000	.001	4.66667	.47140	3.35784	5.97550

different from each other. For the second *t*-test, the "Sig (2-tailed)" value is significant, $p = .001$, this means that the two scores were different from each other. To write this in the correct formula, you would again just plug in the correct numbers to this formula: $t(df) = $ t-value, $p = $ sig(2-tailed). So, for our first *t*-test result, we'd write: $t(4) = 0.313$, $p = .770$. For the second *t*-test, our result would be: $t(4) = 9.899$, $p = .001$.

Within-Subjects Data Sets

Now that we've discussed how to conduct analyses for a between-subjects data set, let's take a look at the steps for analyzing a within-subjects data set. The steps are very similar, but you'll be setting up your data a little differently and selecting different options for the analysis in SPSS.

If you are conducting an analysis for within-subjects data, such as the one displayed in Table 10.5, you will need to run a repeated measures ANOVA. This table represents a hypothetical study that looks at changes in plant growth over time (in this case, we're looking at growth over Time 1, 2, and 3). This is a single-factor design study, with only one independent variable—Time. Our dependent variable will be the growth of the plant measured in centimeters.

As you can see, the data for each subject (or each plant) is given in a single row. In this case, each subject has three data points: a score for Time 1, Time 2, and Time 3. If a score appears in the same row, then that score belongs to that subject or participant and indicates that you have a within-subjects variable. No other information should be placed in a row except what belongs to that participant.

So let's see how we analyze this data set. First you will need to select the Analyze tab from the menu options at the top. From there, you will need to select General Linear Model and then Repeated Measures. This can be seen as Step #1 in Figure 10.5.

From there, you will be prompted to provide your Within-Subject Factor Name as well as the number of levels for that factor (as depicted in Step #2 in Figure 10.5). For our example, our within-subject factor is "Time," which has 3 levels (Time 1, Time 2, and Time 3). This is depicted as Step #2 in Figure 10.5. Once you've typed this information in, you click on the "Add" button (shown as Step #3 in Figure 10.5). Once you "Add" this information into the box, the define box will be available to click (see Step #4 in Figure 10.5).

This will bring up your Repeated Measures box, which is shown as Step #5 in Figure 10.5. Your next step will be to move your variables to the appropriate box. Since this is a within-subjects design, we will

Table 10.5   Sample Within-Subjects Data Set

Plant Growth Over Time

Subj #	Time 1	Time 2	Time 3
1	2	4	9
2	3	7	10
3	3	5	11
4	4	8	11
5	2	6	10
6	4	5	7
7	2	7	10
8	3	6	8
9	1	4	8
10	4	5	9

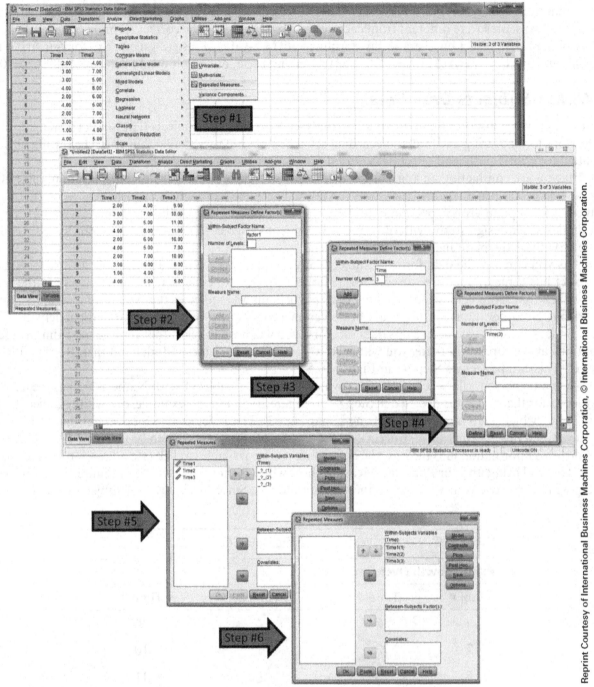

Figure 10.5   SPSS screenshot to demonstrate how to conduct a repeated measures ANOVA.

move over all of our variables to our Within-Subjects Variables box, as seen in Step #6 in Figure 10.5. You can select them and then send them over using the top middle arrow. Once you have your variables in the correct spot, you can just click OK.

This should provide you with your ANOVA results. You can see a version of your ANOVA findings in Table 10.6. SPSS provides you with a lot more information than this, but for simplicity, we're just going to focus on the "Tests of Within-Subjects Effects" table.

Table 10.6   Sample Repeated Measures ANOVA Data

Tests of Within-Subjects Effects

Measure: MEASURE_1

Source		Type III Sum of Squares	df	Mean Square	F	Sig.
Time	Sphericity Assumed	212.067	2	106.033	102.613	.000
	Greenhouse-Geisser	212.067	1.807	117.341	102.613	.000
	Huynh-Feldt	212.067	2.000	106.033	102.613	.000
	Lower-bound	212.067	1.000	212.067	102.613	.000
Error(Time)	Sphericity Assumed	18.600	18	1.033		
	Greenhouse-Geisser	18.600	16.265	1.144		
	Huynh-Feldt	18.600	18.000	1.033		
	Lower-bound	18.600	9.000	2.067		

Follow up t-tests

Your follow-up *t*-tests for your within-subjects design studies will require that you conduct a paired-samples *t*-test. These are actually very easy to conduct. First you will need to go to your Analyze tab, select the Compare Means option, and the select the Paired-Samples *t*-tests option. This is shown as Step #1 in Figure 10.6. This will bring up your Paired-Samples TTest box, which is Step #2 in Figure 10.6.

You will now have to select which comparisons you wish to make. Remember that your *t*-tests will only compare two means at a time. In order to make all of the comparisons that you'd like, you may need to make several comparisons, but you can do each of these at the same time here. So for our single-factor within-subjects data set from Table 10.5, you would need to compare the scores at Time 1 to Time 2, Time 1 to Time 3, and Time 2 to Time 3; this will ensure that you have all comparisons available to you.

To do the comparisons, you will need to select your variables on the left side of the Paired-Samples T Test box and move them over to the right side. You can do this two different ways—you can select each variable one at a time (so click on Time 1) and use the arrow between the boxes to move it over, then just select the second variable (Time 2) and move it over or you can hold down your Ctrl key to select the two variables that make up your pair at the same time (Time 1 and Time 2) and move them over together. Regardless, you're setting up the two levels that you'd like to compare. As you can see in Step #3 of Figure 10.6, pair 1 will compare Time 1 with Time 2, pair 2 will compare Time 1 with Time 3, and pair 3 will compare Time 2 with Time 3. If you make a mistake, you can just send the variable back over to the left box or hit the Reset button on the bottom of the box.

The nice thing about the paired-samples *t*-tests (as compared to our independent-samples discussed earlier) is that you can set up all your pairs to run at the same time (versus having to do them individually). Once you have your pairs set up, you can just hit "OK." You can see an example of your output in Table 10.7.

But what happens if you aren't conducting a single-factor design like the one in Tables 10.1 and 10.5? As we have discussed throughout the book, research studies are hardly ever simple, so here is a data set that is made a little more complicated by adding a second independent variable. Most of our steps will stay the same, but as you will see, an important step is added.

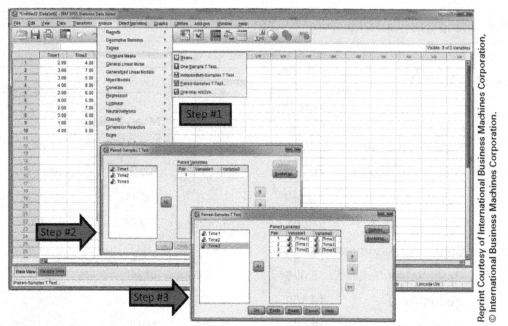

Figure 10.6 SPSS screenshot to demonstrate how to conduct paired-samples *t*-tests.

Table 10.7 Paired-Samples *t*-tests Data Output

		Paired Samples Test							
		Paired Differences							
					95% Confidence Interval of the Difference				
		Mean	**Std. Deviation**	**Std. Error Mean**	**Lower**	**Upper**	**t**	**df**	**Sig. (2-tailed)**
Pair 1	Time 1–Time 2	−2.90000	1.37032	.43333	−3.88027	−1.91973	−6.692	9	.000
Pair 2	Time 1–Time 3	−6.50000	1.64992	.52175	−7.68028	−5.31972	−12.458	9	.000
Pair 3	Time 2–Time 3	−3.60000	1.26491	.40000	−4.50486	−2.69514	−9.000	9	.000

In this case we are looking at recognition scores of each participant as it pertains to affiliation and race. Looking at this table may be a little more confusing than the single-factor table, but it still reads the same way. One thing that might make this seem a little confusing is that labels are repeated in our table (Same Affiliation and Other Affiliation as well as Own Race and Other Race). As you recall from Chapter 2, when you have factorial designs, you will create multiple groups or conditions. When we create our columns in our within-subjects data set, we are just using the conditions formed by having two or more variables. Just like this table shows:

Same Affiliation Own Race	Same Affiliation Other Race
Other Affiliation Own Race	Other Affiliation Other Race

Table 10.8   Sample Data Set for a Two-Factor Within-Subjects Design

Own-Race Bias Data with Same- and Other-Groupw Affiliation

Participant	Same Affiliation Own Race	Same Affiliation Other race	Other Affiliation Own Race	Other Affiliation Other race
1	0.80	0.75	0.80	0.50
2	0.75	0.86	0.75	0.60
3	0.70	0.75	0.70	0.58
4	0.80	0.60	0.80	0.67
5	0.90	0.60	0.77	0.50
6	0.60	0.50	0.60	0.30
7	0.66	0.46	0.66	0.33
8	0.77	0.77	0.45	0.70
9	0.85	0.85	0.85	0.50
10	0.85	0.90	0.85	0.50

Since this is all within-subjects, each of our participants will serve in each of these four conditions. So, how do we analyze this type of data set? Again we will need to run a repeated measures ANOVA.

Remember that you can access this ANOVA by selecting the analyze tab from the menu options at the top of your SPSS screen. From there, you will need to select General Linear Model and then Repeated Measures. This is the same as what you did in Step #1 of Figure 10.5. As we saw with a single-factor design, you are prompted at this stage to provide the name(s) of your within-subjects variable(s). In this case we have two within-subject variables—Affiliation and Race (see Step #2 of Figure 10.5). This is actually where it becomes a bit trickier than before. You will want to add the "slowest moving variable" first. I know what you're thinking…what the heck does that mean? In this case, if you look at our data set in Table 10.8, you'll notice that "race" is moving *faster* than affiliation. Basically this just means that it is changing across the columns faster. Whichever variable moves slower across your columns should be the variable you input **first** into your Within-Subject Factor Name. So, take a look at our data file in Table 10.8. Same Affiliation, Own-Race is in the first column and Same Affiliation, Other Race is in the next column. When we move from the first column to the second column Affiliation stays the same, but the levels of our Race variable change. Thus, Affiliation is moving slower than Race which is changing.

Once you "Add" your within-subject variables and their levels into the box (as you did in Steps #3 and #4 in Figure 10.5 previously), the define box will be available to click. This will bring up your Repeated Measures box (similar to Step #5 in Figure 10.5). As explained before with the single factor example, your next step will be to move your variables over to the appropriate box. Since this is a within-subjects design, we will move over all of our variables to our Within-Subjects Variables box, as was previously shown in Step #6 of Figure 10.5. Only, this time, you need to do so in a specific order to make reading your output easier. If you put your slowest moving variable first in the prior screen, then you would be able to select them in the order they appear in the left box and just move them over to the Within-Subjects Variables box. If you didn't put your slowest moving variable first, you may need to look at the coding provided for you at the top of the Within-Subjects Variables box and match up your columns appropriately.

Once you have everything set up correctly you can just click OK. You can see our ANOVA findings in Table 10.9.

Just like with the univariate ANOVA, a repeated measures ANOVA will provide us with the results of your main effects and your interactions. For this example, we had two main effects- Affiliation and Race. The interaction for this example can be found on the Affiliation*Race row.

Table 10.9   Sample Repeated Measures ANOVA Data

Tests of Within-Subjects Effects

Measure: MEASURE_1

Source		Type III Sum of Squares	df	Mean Square	F	Sig.
Affiliation	Sphericity Assumed	.010	1	.010	.077	.787
	Greenhouse-Geisser	.010	1.000	.010	.077	.787
	Huynh-Feldt	.010	1.000	.010	.077	.787
	Lower-bound	.010	1.000	.010	.077	.787
Error(Affiliation)	Sphericity Assumed	1.417	11	.129		
	Greenhouse-Geisser	1.417	11.000	.129		
	Huynh-Feldt	1.417	11.000	.129		
	Lower-bound	1.417	11.000	.129		
Race	Sphericity Assumed	.111	1	.111	.354	.564
	Greenhouse-Geisser	.111	1.000	.111	.354	.564
	Huynh-Feldt	.111	1.000	.111	.354	.564
	Lower-bound	.111	1.000	.111	.354	.564
Error(Race)	Sphericity Assumed	3.459	11	.314		
	Greenhouse-Geisser	3.459	11.000	.314		
	Huynh-Feldt	3.459	11.000	.314		
	Lower-bound	3.459	11.000	.314		
Affiliation * Race	Sphericity Assumed	.269	1	.269	.946	.352
	Greenhouse-Geisser	.269	1.000	.269	.946	.352
	Huynh-Feldt	.269	1.000	.269	.946	.352
	Lower-bound	.269	1.000	.269	.946	.352
Error(Affiliation*Race)	Sphericity Assumed	3.123	11	.284		
	Greenhouse-Geisser	3.123	11.000	.284		
	Huynh-Feldt	3.123	11.000	.284		
	Lower-bound	3.123	11.000	.284		

For our data in Table 10.8, you would run your paired-samples t-tests in the same way as we did previously, but you will have many more comparisons that you will need to run since there are more combinations (refer to Figure 10.6 for a review). For the data from Table 10.8, the t-tests are provided for you below (Table 10.10).

Table 10.10 Paired-Samples *t*-tests Data Output for a Factorial Design

				95% Confidence Interval of the Difference				
	Mean	Std. Deviation	Std. Error Mean	Lower	Upper	t	df	Sig. (2-tailed)
Pair 1 SA_OwnR - SA_OtherR	.05333	.12265	.03541	−.02459	.13126	1.506	11	.160
Pair 2 SA_OwnR - OA_OwnR	.12083	.29296	.08457	−.06531	.30697	1.429	11	.181
Pair 3 SA_OwnR - OA_OtherR	−.12500	.88241	.25473	−.68566	.43566	−.491	11	.633
Pair 4 SA_OtherR - OA_OwnR	.06750	.32839	.09480	−.14115	.27615	.712	11	.491
Pair 5 SA_OtherR - OA_OtherR	−.17833	.86005	.24828	−.72478	.36812	−.718	11	.488
Pair 6 OA_OwnR - OA_OtherR	−.24583	1.08703	.31380	−.93650	.44483	−.783	11	.450

Paired-samples Test / Paired Differences

Table 10.11 Sample Data Set for a Mixed-Factor Design

Effectiveness of an SAT Training Course
1- Training
2- No Training

Subj #	Training	Week 1	Week 2
1	1	800	850
2	1	1120	1140
3	1	980	1020
4	1	990	1050
5	1	1280	1290
6	2	1180	1170
7	2	1200	1220
8	2	890	940
9	2	980	1000
10	2	980	950

Mixed-Factor Data Sets

Now that we've described between-subject data sets and within-subject data sets, we need to discuss mixed-factor data sets. The general steps for mixed-factor data sets is nearly the same as within-subject data sets, with one small addition. So, let's take a look at a mixed-factor data set. The data set in Table 10.11 represents a hypothetical study looking at the effects of SAT training courses and Time (Week) on SAT scores. The participants are either given no training or they receive the SAT training course (so Training is a between-subjects manipulation). The test scores are measured at the start of the study (Week 1) and at the end (Week 2) for all participants (so Week is a within-subjects manipulation).

If you are conducting an analysis of a mixed-factor design, such as the one displayed in Table 10.11, you will need to run a repeated measures ANOVA. As before, you will first need to select the Analyze tab from the menu options at the top. From there, you will need to select General Linear Model and then Repeated Measures. This screenshot is shown as Step #1 in Figure 10.7. Any time that you have a within-subjects variable, you select the Repeated Measures option to conduct the ANOVA.

From there, you will be prompted to provide your Within-Subject Factor Name as well as the number of levels for that factor. So for our example in Figure 10.7, our within-subject factor is "Time," which has 2 levels (week 1 and week 2), can be seen in Step #3 in Figure 10.7. Once you "Add" this information into the box (see Step #4 of Figure 10.7), the define box will be available to click.

This will bring up your Repeated Measures box, which is shown in Step #5. As discussed previously, your next step will be to move over your variables to the appropriate boxes. We have already said that Week is our within-subjects variable and Week 1 and Week 2 are our levels, therefore, we will move this over to our Within-Subjects Variables box using the top middle arrow as can be seen in Step #6 of Figure 10.7.

Next, you need to move over your Between-Subjects Factor(s). For our example, we only have one between-subjects variable - the SAT Training Course, however, in your own studies you may have several

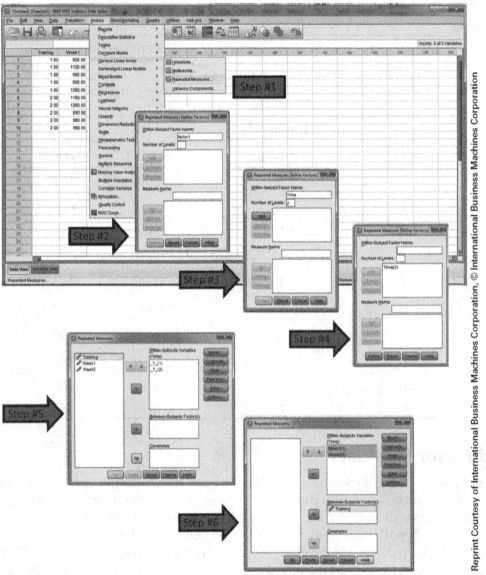

Figure 10.7 SPSS screenshot to demonstrate how to conduct a mixed-factor ANOVA.

more. So you select the "Training" item in the left box and move it to the Between-Subjects Factor(s) box (see Step #6 of Figure 10.7).

Once you have your within-subjects variables and between-subjects variables in the correct spots, you can just click "OK." This will provide you with your ANOVA results. You can see an example of your ANOVA findings in Table 10.12.

Since a mixed-factor design is a combination of both between- and within-subject factors, it should not be surprising that you will have data in the "Test of Within Subjects Effects" as well as the "Test of Between-Subjects Effects" boxes to look at. These are read just like in our prior discussions, only in this case, you will have one main effect for your within-subjects variable (in this case "Time"), which is located in the Tests of Within Subjects Effects box and one main effect for your between-subjects variable (in this case "Training") in your Tests of Between-Subjects Effects box. Additionally, you'll also have the Time x Training interaction in the Tests of Within-Subjects Effects box. Be sure you don't forget about

Table 10.12   Sample ANOVA Output for a Mixed-Factor Data Set

Tests of Within-Subjects Effects

Measure: MEASURE_1

Source		Type III Sum of Squares	df	Mean Square	F	Sig.
Time	Sphericity Assumed	2645.000	1	2645.000	7.667	.024
	Greenhouse-Geisser	2645.000	1.000	2645.000	7.667	.024
	Huynh-Feldt	2645.000	1.000	2645.000	7.667	.024
	Lower-bound	2645.000	1.000	2645.000	7.667	.024
Time * Training	Sphericity Assumed	845.000	1	845.000	2.449	.156
	Greenhouse-Geisser	845.000	1.000	845.000	2.449	.156
	Huynh-Feldt	845.000	1.000	845.000	2.449	.156
	Lower-bound	845.000	1.000	845.000	2.449	.156
Error(Time)	Sphericity Assumed	2760.000	8	345.000		
	Greenhouse-Geisser	2760.000	8.000	345.000		
	Huynh-Feldt	2760.000	8.000	345.000		
	Lower-bound	2760.000	8.000	345.000		

Tests of Between-Subjects Effects

Measure: MEASURE_1

Transformed Variable: Average

Source	Type III Sum of Squares	df	Mean Square	F	Sig.
Intercept	22113045.000	1	22113045.000	475.805	.000
Training	5.000	1	5.000	.000	.992
Error	371800.000	8	46475.000		

your between-subjects main effect since, depending on your printer, it may print these results on a page of their own. You will read, interpret, and write the ANOVA findings in the same way that we discussed in our previous discussions for within-subjects and between-subjects data sets.

Follow up t-tests

For your follow up *t*-tests in a mixed-factor design, you will be conducting both independent and paired-samples *t*-tests. Your independent-samples *t*-tests will be conducted the same as they were in the between-subjects only design. However, you will need to do some additional steps in order to complete your paired-samples *t*-tests. See Figure 10.8 for the steps in conducting the independent-samples *t*-tests with the mixed-factor data.

As previously mentioned, there are some additional steps for conducting paired-samples *t*-tests when using mixed-factor data. If you were to run your paired-samples *t*-tests from just the data set provided (without any changes), you would be lumping together both of your between-subject groups—meaning that you would be looking at the differences between Week 1 and Week 2 overall (something that our ANOVA already told us with the main effect of Time), but not how *each* training group did on Week 1 compared to Week 2. In other words, you need to see if the Training group performed better on Week 1 or Week 2 and if the No Training group did better on Week 1 or Week 2.

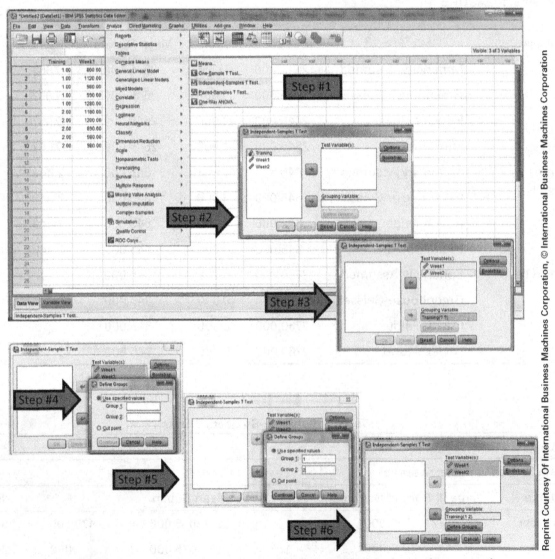

Figure 10.8 SPSS screenshot to demonstrate how to conduct independent-samples *t*-tests.

In order to just analyze the data from one group, we will need to make sure that SPSS only looks at the data associated with each training group alone. To do this, we will need to do what is called a "Select Case." First, you will need to go to your Data tab on the menu tab. Second, from the bottom is an option called "Select Cases," click on this option. This is shown as Step #1 on Figure 10.9.

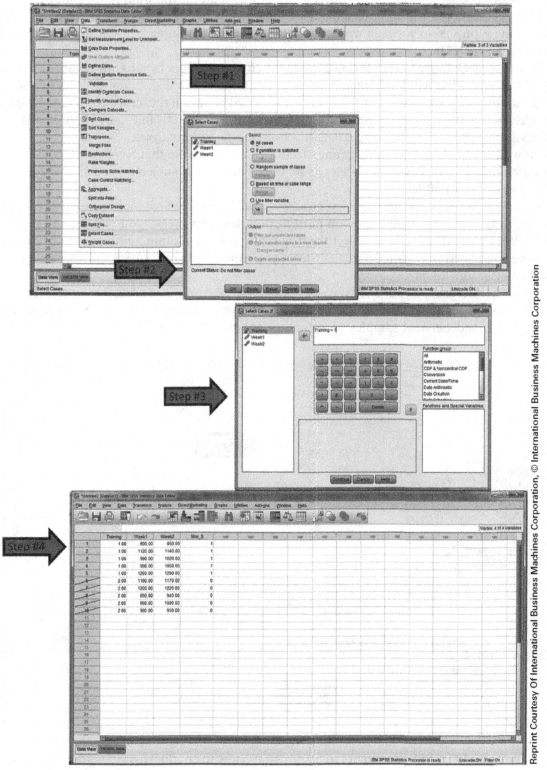

Figure 10.9   SPSS screenshot to show how to select cases.

This will bring up a box that will allow you to set up which data you want SPSS to examine. For our purposes, you will need to select the "If condition is satisfied" option by clicking the "If" button. This is shown as Step #2 in Figure 10.9.

This brings up the Select Cases: If box, which is shown as Step #3 in Figure 10.9. Since we want to only look at one of the groups in our study, we will send over to the top right box our between-subjects variable (SAT Training Course). Once you have sent that over, select the "=" option or you can just type it from your keyboard. Now you just need to select which group you want to look at. So it is likely that for your first test, you will want to look at the first group: Training. So we would select 1 since this is the training group. Your formula would look like this: SAT_Training = 1. Once you have created your formula, just click OK.

You can check to see if your formula made the correct changes by looking at your raw data on your Data View tab. SPSS will have created a new column for you called "filter_$" (see Step #4 in Figure 10.9). Additionally, by looking at the Data View tab, SPSS will indicate which data will be ignored or not selected because it will have lines through those rows (see Step #4 in Figure 10.9). It is always a good idea to double check that the correct data has been selected for analyses.

Now that you are only looking at one of the groups (the group that received the SAT Training) you can now run your paired-samples t-tests as we did in our within-subjects discussion above. These steps are shown in Figure 10.10.

Once you run your test for your first group, you will need to follow these same steps for any remaining groups (i.e., the No Training group in our example). This means you will need to go in and alter your Select Cases: If formula to reflect the new group you are examining (in our study, group 2). Once you have completed your paired-samples t-tests, you can go back to your Select Cases and just click "All cases" to clear any filters.

As far as interpreting your t-tests, you will examine, interpret, and write these t-test results the same way as we discussed previously with the within and between-subjects data sets. You just now have both kinds of tests, independent-samples t-tests and paired-samples t-tests, to evaluate.

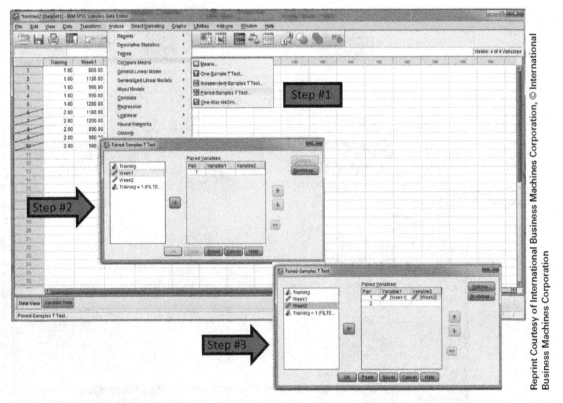

Reprint Courtesy of International Business Machines Corporation, © International Business Machines Corporation

Figure 10.10   SPSS screenshot to demonstrate how to conduct paired-samples t-tests.

Concluding Remarks

So there you have it, something that seems rather daunting (running data analyses) is actually not so bad. Your statistics are the most important part of your study, without them you wouldn't be able to infer anything about your results. From the chaos that is a raw data set (Figure 10.1 B), we can obtain order through our easy to read output (For example, Table 10.12). The important thing to be cognizant of prior to analyzing your data is to know your research design (i.e., the design from your raw data). The answer to this question will tell you which type of tests and follow-up tests you'll need to conduct. Always create your table of means from your initial data set to help you keep track of all the analyses you will need to conduct and to follow along as you analyze and interpret your data. That table will allow you to quickly map out each of your comparisons and follow along making sure that you're making the comparisons that you think you're making. They also give you an idea about where you can expect to see significant differences and to interpret your results more easily.

End of Chapter Quiz

___1. Which type of ANOVA will you conduct if you have two IVs that are both manipulated within-subjects?
a. paired-samples
b. univariate
c. repeated measures
d. one-way

___2. If you are conducting a univariate ANOVA, what type of design do you have?
a. mixed factor design
b. between-subjects design
c. within-subjects design
d. any of these could be analyzed a univariate ANOVA

___3. In a 2 x 2 mixed factor design study, how many *t*-tests will you run?
a. 3   b. 1   c. 6   d. 4

4. Based on question 3, what type of *t*-tests will you need to run? Please explain each.

___5. What does each row represent in your raw data file?
a. A single participant's data.
b. A single factor's data point (such as age, photograph race, and time).
c. The dummy-coding for the levels of a between-subjects variable.
d. The dummy-coding for the levels of a within-subjects variable.

___6. What does each column represent in your raw data file?
a. A single participant's data.
b. A single factor's data point (such as age, photograph race, and time).
c. The dummy-coding for the levels of a between-subjects variable.
d. The dummy-coding for the levels of a within-subjects variable.

___7. What option under the Analyze tab will give you access to your ANOVAs?
a. compare means
b. general linear model
c. ANOVA
d. data select

___8. Why do you need to run a "Select Cases" for your paired-samples *t*-tests in a mixed factor design?
a. So you only look at one group's scores.
b. So you only look at one variable.
c. So you only have to run one *t*-test.
d. So you can analyze the data from only one participant.

___9. What is a subject log used for?
a. to report the raw data for each participant
b. to keep track of participants while keeping their names separate from their raw data
c. so you can decide which group to place them in
d. to allow you to analyze their raw data at a later point

10. Why should you always create a table of means in your data set? Please explain.

Homework Assignment #1

1. In this hypothetical data set we are looking at facial recognition of both Marvel Superheroes and DC Superheroes to determine if they show an in-group bias in facial recognition. Please provide your table of means, conduct the appropriate ANOVA and follow-up *t*-tests, and finally, briefly describe what the data found, including your inferential statistics.

	1= Marvel Superheroes		
	2 = DC Superheroes		
	Participant	Face Type	
Participant #	Group	Marvel Superheroes	DC Superheroes
1	1	97	60
2	1	77	68
3	1	98	65
4	1	94	76
5	1	94	60
6	1	90	75
7	1	87	68
8	1	84	71
9	1	97	71
10	1	77	61
11	2	80	92
12	2	76	77
13	2	76	91
14	2	81	83
15	2	69	75
16	2	79	95
17	2	66	95
18	2	67	80
19	2	78	78
20	2	68	89

***Please note that superhero names have been removed to ensure confidentiality.

2. In this hypothetical data set we are looking at how both the smell of the individual and their gender influence the likelihood of being attacked by a zombie. Please provide your table of means, conduct the appropriate ANOVA and follow-up *t*-tests, and finally, briefly describe what the data found, including your inferential statistics.

The Effects of Scent and Gender on Zombie attack Likelihood

Subj #	1 = Pizza scent 2 = Vegetable scent Scent of Participant	1=Female 2=Male Gender	# Zombie Attacks
1	1	1	8
2	1	1	11
3	1	1	10
4	1	2	7
5	1	2	4
6	1	2	5
7	2	1	1
8	2	1	2
9	2	1	0
10	2	2	2
11	2	2	1
12	2	2	2

3. In this hypothetical data set we are looking at participants' likely use of the Ghostbusters. We are looking at their ratings before being possessed by a ghost, after one day of possession, and finally after two weeks of being possessed. Please provide your table of means, conduct the appropriate ANOVA and follow-up *t*-tests, and finally, briefly describe what the data found, including your inferential statistics.

The Effects of being possessed by a Ghost on the likelihood of using the Ghostbusters

Participant	Not Possessed by Ghost	Possessed by Ghost 1 Day	Possessed by Ghost 2 Weeks
1	3	3	8
2	1	2	8
3	2	2	6
4	4	3	10
5	1	3	8
6	1	2	10
7	3	2	7
8	2	2	7
9	4	4	9
10	1	1	9
11	2	2	6
12	3	2	6
13	1	2	5
14	1	1	3
15	2	3	8
16	1	2	7
17	3	2	7
18	1	2	9
19	2	1	5
20	2	3	6

Chapter 11

Starting Psychological Research

As we have seen throughout the book, there are numerous ways in which you can get started with conducting psychological research. In this chapter, we will look more closely at finding a topic to research, determining the research approach needed, obtaining the approval of the Institutional Review Board (IRB), and how to actually start writing and keep writing.

What Should I Research?

As a student, you are probably being forced to write about a topic that your professor finds interesting and there is a good chance that you find the topic boring, tedious, confusing, or just annoying (some of you may actually like the research, but from our experience, many of our students don't enjoy the same topics that we enjoy). Students often ask us "why do we have to research your topic and not something that we finding interesting?" Well, in part, it's self-serving—we like the topic and know the research area, so if we are going to read a paper, we want to enjoy it and know something about it. We also recognize that it is difficult to choose a topic to research that is feasible and ethical, particularly within the confines of a classroom project. At some point in your academic career you will have to do this. In graduate school, for instance, you will likely have to write a thesis and dissertation, which will be based on your research interests. At that point, you'll be wishing that your professor would just tell you what to write your paper on because coming up with a feasible research question isn't as easy as most students think it is.

So, how do we begin? By this point you should have a good idea of what a hypothesis is and know that it is far more than just a guess as to what will happen in your study. But, contrary to what some people think, you don't start with a hypothesis in your research; instead, you start with ideas that you must go out and research before you can decide what your predictions should be. Where can you start? The easiest start would be to research topics that you are interested in. As a student, you will find that there are some topics that just appeal to you more than others. It may be a very broad topic, such as memory, or more specific, such as false memory production. Either way, this is a good place to start. Of course, if you are interested in the topic, it is likely that you have read some of the research on it, but get ready to read more. In order to develop a study, you need to first determine what has already been investigated in the field. There is no point in you reinventing the wheel and wasting yours and everyone else's time if the topic has already been researched to death. In the Cognitive Research lab at our university, we have everyone read a relevant journal article (preferably published within in the last 10 years or so) every week. This is to help students learn to read research, but it also helps all of us to develop future research questions. As we read the articles, we look for ways to improve on the study or look for questions that they have left unanswered (in fact, they will sometimes even tell you what future research should study or tell you about the unanswered questions). This is another great way to come up with research studies—expand on what has already been done.

Of course, everything we just discussed probably seems like it is easier for the head of your research lab or your professor, as they are likely studying in their area of interest and may even be considered an expert in that field. But don't worry, just because they have more years of experience than you doesn't mean that you can't develop an awesome research idea and find new areas of investigation. If you have a good research idea, share it. Your professors can be excellent guides by helping you to develop your own experiment. Also, don't be afraid to ask your professors to collaborate with you. Maybe the idea you have is a little outside their normal research interests, but collaboration allows for a better understanding of the topic. By working with individuals from other subdisciplines, or even entirely different disciplines, you can gain important insights into the topic and to the interpretation of the findings. A more complete picture of your research can form with this collaboration.

One final way to find topics in which to study is to look at what others are actually studying within the field. As a student, this will also help you to expand your research interests. As of the writing of this book, the APA recognizes 54 areas of interest in psychology; don't limit yourself to just what your professors have talked about. By reading a variety of research, you will familiarize yourself with other subdisciplines, but you will also see what topics are the "hot items" in research at that time. The benefit here (and something we further discuss in Chapter 13) is that you will be more likely to see your research published if it is actually on a topic that your fellow researchers want to read about.

Specific Steps When Conducting Research

Once you finally have your topic nailed down, you will need to start researching it. As we have already alluded to, you need to be reading research. This should really become part of your routine. It may not be as exciting as the latest Stephen King novel, but it is important for your development as a productive member in the field of psychology. In addition to helping you stay on top of the new research in the field, it will also help you save some time. When you decide on a topic of research, you need to be sure to find *and read* all of the past relevant research on that topic and its related issues. By understanding what has been done in the past and what theories have been used (or discarded) to explain it, you will finally be able to develop your hypothesis. This is why people say a hypothesis is an "educated guess." It is because you have become a temporary expert on the topic through your recent readings. You know what has been found in the past, how the theories have explained the behaviors or responses, and therefore, you can come up with a reasonable prediction concerning how your study will turn out. In other words, you are educated enough on the topic that you can make a prediction that is supported by the existing literature.

Of course, your prediction may be wrong. And that's ok. As you develop your research question, remember that it must be a testable theory. What this really means is that your research question is falsifiable. Anything you choose to study must be capable of being proven false. This may seem counterintuitive; after all, why would a researcher want to prove that his or her theory is wrong? But really, the question of falsifiability and testability are at the heart of science. Only by proving when a theory doesn't work can we actually advance the field. Let's say that you want to test if babies dream. It seems like a legitimate question, right? But could you really test this? The answer is no, at least not with our current technology. To determine if a person is dreaming, we have to wake them up and ask them if they were dreaming (we can't "see" their dreams). Now, in older children and adults we have done this enough to determine that during the REM stages of sleep we dream. We aren't always dreaming during REM sleep, but dreams are much more likely during REM. But can we say the same for infants? We can certainly determine that babies do enter into REM sleep. In fact, they spend around 50% of their time asleep in REM sleep while you only spend around 20–25% of your sleeping hours in REM sleep. So, can we conclude then that babies are dreaming? Since we can't wake the newborns up and ask them if they were just dreaming, we can't conclude that they were. This would not be a testable question. As you start to determine your hypothesis, you must always keep in mind if the question is testable. Both technology and ethics may limit your research topic.

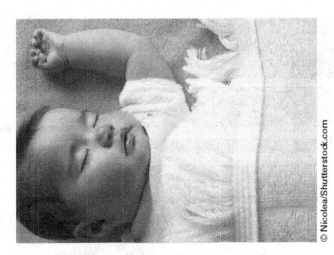

Is this baby dreaming? How can you tell?

The next steps in your research process you have already studied throughout this book. Once you have determined your research question, you now have to determine which approach you are going to take: experimental or nonexperimental? If you decide you want or need to conduct your study using the nonexperimental approach, you will also need to decide which type of design you want. As discussed in Chapter 4 and 5, you have many nonexperimental approaches to choose from such as a case study, a survey, observational approaches, a correlational study, or a quasi-experiment. To determine this, you have to decide what type of question you are actually asking. For instance, if you are wanting to determine the relationship between naturally occurring variables; such as SAT scores and college GPA, then a correlational approach might be the way to go. On the other hand, if you are dealing with a rare psychological disorder, such as dissociative identity disorder (DID), then a case study might be a good option. Then again, you may decide that you'd like to make a causal statement concerning your findings. If that's the case, then you might opt to utilize a true experiment. If you decide that you are wanting to take an experimental approach to your question, you will have to determine what your variables will be. Your independent variables will be the things that you are manipulating in the study; such as the age and race of the photographs. Your dependent variable, on the other hand, will be the behavior that you are trying to measure; such as facial recognition accuracy. Depending on your experiment, you will likely have multiple variables that you are measuring and manipulating, so it is always best to clearly define and label this at the start of your study. If you fail to notice a variable that impacts your study, you could end up with a confound and be limited in your interpretation of your results. For a more complete description of all of your options, see the earlier chapters that explain nonexperimental and experimental approaches, if you haven't already done so.

Now that you have nailed down what you are looking at and how you are manipulating it, you need to decide what materials you will need for your study. Depending on your study, you could be looking at various issues with regard to materials. For instance, in our research lab, we often run into issues with collecting photographs that we can use for our research. For obvious reasons, we cannot just photograph our students and then test them on their own faces. Depending on the variables we are interested in, it can take months to collect enough faces that fit our criteria. If your research requires expensive equipment, you may need to fill out grant proposals or departmental forms to acquire the funds needed to obtain the equipment.

Before you can go further and test participants, you need to be sure to obtain IRB (i.e., the institutional review board) approval. As you recall from Chapter 3, the IRB is responsible for ensuring the safety of our research participants and to ensure that all research is conducted in an ethical manner. Depending on your research topic and the current number of studies that the IRB is looking over, your approval can take a week or two to several months. The more ethical concerns there are (such as the use of deception), the longer it will usually take. Of course, as the researcher, you should be considering all ethical issues with your research throughout the entire process, from the initial question development all the way to presenting your research findings. Ultimately, conducting ethical research that protects the rights of your participants, whether animals or humans, is up to you.

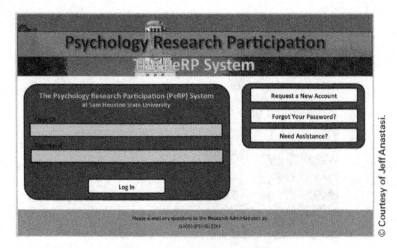

Our university uses an online platform (PeRP) to publicize research opportunities to our students.

It is important that once you have all of your materials gathered and have obtained approval from the IRB that you do what is known as a pilot study. Before testing your research on actual participants, you can have research assistants run through it to look for issues. They can help you spot problems, such as timing issues, mistakes in spelling, work out any kinks in the equipment or measurement tools, and so on. Once you have done that, gather a small group of participants and run them through your study. This pilot study can serve as a practice run to further check for issues. It can also help to test out new materials, such as a new scale that you have created. Finally, you can move on to the real data collection. You will need to recruit your participants, and this can be done through campus servers, postings, ads, etc. At our university we post most of our study opportunities for psychology on the Sona System (although we've ingeniously named it the PeRP [Psychology Research Participation] system since our university is known for its forensic-based programs). Most universities have a similar system, if not the same one. This system allows you as a researcher to share your study with all the individuals registered in the system for your school. In addition, it can allow you to contact potential participants that meet your specific requirements. Of course, this only works if the individuals you are interested in studying are on the system. If you are wanting to study groups outside of the university system, then recruitment becomes much more difficult.

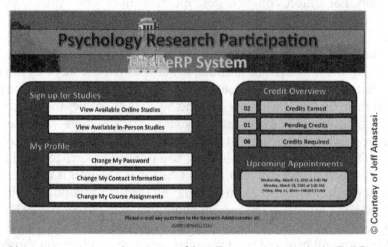

Here you can see how user friendly our university's PeRP system is.

When recruiting non-university students, you will have to offer them something other than research credits. If you have attained some sort of funding to conduct your research, such as a grant of some sort, you can certainly offer them financial compensation for their time and participation. Keep in mind, though, that whatever you offer them cannot be so great as to be coercive. For instance, I cannot offer someone $10,000 to let me inject him or her with a drug. The amount is so great that the participants might not truly evaluate the risks the drug may pose to them. If your research isn't being funded, there are other things you can do to obtain participants; such as asking for volunteers, running a raffle, providing food or candy, or some other type of compensation.

After you have recruited your participants, you can finally run your study. This process is one that you have studied throughout this course, so we won't say much about it here. But remember that your data must be collected in a systematic way in order to be useful to you. This is where those practice runs of your study can really come in handy. It is also advisable to have a handout for every researcher on the study explaining step-by-step what they need to do during the data collection process. Provide a script for what they should say to participants and when they should say it. Even if it is your study, always have a written script to follow. It will help to eliminate bias in your study by making sure that each participant is being treated exactly the same way and may help to control for extraneous variables.

Once you've tested all of your participants, and this may take a while, you'll have your data so that you can finally analyze it. Most students think this is the dreadful part of research; it's not, we promise! Writing the research up is the most difficult part! Analyzing our data is actually pretty exciting since this is when you get to see if your predictions and all your hard work paid off. Of course, you are also aware that it might not have, but you'll never know until you analyze your data.

In either case, once your data have been analyzed and you've made sense out of your findings, you have to decide what to do next. If your results are worthy of a write up or a presentation, you should do that immediately. Don't hesitate. It is hard to go back to a project you finished months or years ago and start writing it up then. If your results don't merit a publication or presentation, then you need to go back to the drawing board. This is where you need to decide what went wrong and if you can make your study better. Listen to your colleagues, fellow researchers, and professors here. At this point you may be so immersed in your research that you might be missing the obvious. Bring in an outsider to help you look for any issues within the study and if possible, fix them and test again. As a researcher, you must always be willing to pick yourself up after a failure and start again. It's just what we do and failure is part of the process.

Exploring the Literature

The How and Why of the Literature Review

Your introduction of your paper serves as a *complete* review of the research in a particular field. Yes, you read that right, we said *complete*! This probably feels a little daunting to you; after all, aren't there hundreds if not thousands of articles on your topic? Probably not. The key to a literature review is that it is a complete review of the *relevant* research. While numerous studies may be somewhat or loosely connected to your own research topic, they really don't add anything to what you are studying. So, as you start to explore the research in the field, you should be asking yourself "does this study help to explain my own research." If the answer is "No," then move on. No one wants to read a review that is all over the place and you don't want to write it.

A literature review is an important part of the publication process. For you, the writer, it serves as a way to make you more familiar with the literature in the area. Keep in mind that even the best researchers haven't read everything there is. In addition to that, it helps you get up-to-date on the newer studies in your area of interest. The newer studies can help you to fine tune your research and ensure that you are not "reinventing the wheel" so to speak. Further, a literature review can help you to understand how research was conducted in the past. Don't think that just because a study is 25 years old or older that it is useless. This research can explain why the topic was examined in the first place, the initial theories, and the rationale to explain these previous findings. Sometimes when we are expanding on research, we lose track of where it started; your literature review can help you remember. It is important to note here that just because you read a research article, and even if you found it interesting, doesn't mean that you are going to include it in your own paper. Remember that as you write your paper, you always want to ask yourself if the study helps to explain your own study. Don't waste time writing something that doesn't.

Reviewing the literature also can help you to develop the methods you are going to use in your study. By reviewing other studies, you may find that one method works better and this can save you time and frustration. In one of our studies, we reviewed the literature to see if there was an ideal time period to show photographs to the participants. Doing this not only helped us to set our time limit, but it also helped us to explain our reasoning in our presentation of the research. Beyond just helping you with your methodology, it can also help you develop your predictions and point out variables that you may have overlooked or confounds that you need to control for.

Finally, a thorough review of the literature will help you to organize your write-up. The information you obtain from your review can help you to understand the topic (which will help you in your writing of the introduction), it will provide you the background information on the topic(s) you are discussing (again, extremely useful for your introduction), and finally, by reviewing other research, you can gain insight into the interpretation of your results and explanations (such as theories) with regard to your predictions (helping your introduction, results, and discussion sections). Basically, your literature review can help you at every step of the research project, from understanding the topic, to developing the study, and finally in the interpretation and explanation of the results.

On occasion, hopefully rarely, you may find that the topic you were interested in studying has already been conducted by other researchers. This is of course frustrating. We become attached to our ideas, thinking we are geniuses for coming up with it. So when someone else not only had the same idea, but had it well before you did and has already published the findings, you might just be a little disheartened. But don't fret, you have some options here. Potentially, you could conduct your study and use it as a replication study if they haven't already included one. You could also expand on their research, look for ways to improve on it—did they leave something out? Can you add another variable or level to one of their variables? Maybe there was a potential alternative explanation for their findings that they didn't consider; you could test this alternative explanation. You really have a lot of options on how you could proceed.

At other times though, you may find that the topic you are interested in studying has no related research. This can be just as frustrating since you do not have a clear precedence for why you are con- ducting the study, why you are expecting the outcome you have predicted, or which theories can be applied to your study. When this happens, you will have to be very thorough in your literature review. When writing your introduction, you will have to include more information and make the links between what was done in the past and your study. For instance, in one of our studies, we decided to look at the impact of videogames on the creation of false memories (super cool, we know). While there was a lot of research available on the creation of false memories and lots of information on the impact of videogames on memory for events that have actually occurred, there really wasn't anything that clearly predicted our hypothesis. So we had to spend a little more time with our literature review so that we could support our predictions. In this case, rather than just a clear sequence of prior studies to review, we had to look for studies that didn't necessarily connect to our study directly, but did create the link between our research and the current knowledge in the field. It takes more time to do this, and you may have to make logical connections between the available research studies, but in the end we were able to justify our study.

Where to Find Research?

At this point we have told you several times that you need to go and read the relevant literature. But you may not know where to find that literature, but not to worry, you have several options available to you.

The oldest method is the classic—go to your university's library and read the actual journals. Both of the authors of this text had to do this at some point and we would like to remind you that we had it harder back in our day! Finding research the old fashioned way was a pain and required you to review Psychological Abstracts; a publication by the APA that listed the abstract for all of the journal articles, reports, book chapters and books within the field. It was produced monthly for 80 years (it was stopped in 2006 as newer methods saved both time and money). If you remember the card catalog system from elementary school, it was similar. You first had to look up the topic you were interested in studying in the Subject Index (e.g., memory), then read the brief entry provided and write down the abstract number provided for those entries that looked promising. You would then need to take that abstract number to look up the abstract for the article in the appropriate volume of Psychology Abstracts. Once you found the right abstract you then had to go find the full article in the appropriate journal. Do you feel our pain!? Today, the process is much simpler and involves just a series of clicks on the computer.

While you can still access the old Psychology Abstracts and look up articles prior to 2006 this way, most students and researchers use their library's search engine. Your university likely still carries older journals and subscribes to recent publications as well. But if you are like most of our students, you will likely use online search engines and resources. The computerized version for Psychology Abstracts today is PsycINFO. As with Psychology Abstracts, PsycINFO contains the abstracts of the research articles and books written in the field of psychology. Updated weekly, it contains nearly 4 million records with an estimated 3,000–4,000 added each week. It contains research articles, dissertations, and other relevant scholarly literature. Importantly for your research, around 99% of their 1,800+ journals are peer-reviewed. Peer-reviewed articles are really the only ones you should be using in your research if possible. These are higher quality journals and each article has been evaluated by other researchers to be credible and well done. Nonrefereed journals may contain faulty research, pseudo-psychology, or just dribble since they don't use this peer-reviewed process. Some nonreferred journals, but not all, are similar to what are called "vanity press." They charge you a certain amount of money to publish your article and, as long as you pay their fee, they'll publish it even if it isn't good. When possible, avoid using research that has not been peer-reviewed.

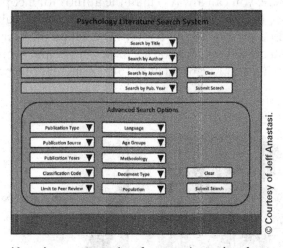

© Courtesy of Jeff Anastasi.

Here is an example of a search engine for finding your research articles. As you can see, there are many ways to search for research using keywords, titles, authors, years, etc.

One really useful option that you have at your disposal for finding research is to use the citations from the articles you already have found. If you are trying to find research related to false memories, for instance, and you really like the research in the article you just read, why not use the relevant articles they mention. This can really save you time and the frustration of searching through all the articles on PsycINFO or through the journals your university subscribes to.

One problem you may run into as you search for research is the inability to find an article or journal because your school doesn't carry it. You can typically request an interlibrary loan from another university. These are provided through your school's library and can take anywhere from 3 days to 3 weeks to arrive. Obviously this will not be an option to you if you are in a hurry, but for papers where you have more time it can be a useful tool. When you make a request through interlibrary loan, you may be able to get a copy of the article or even have an electronic version of the article e-mailed to you. To find out more about this option, feel free to ask your librarian. They're usually very happy to explain the process to interested individuals.

There are other options to you besides your school's library and search engines as, well, the internet! While Google will offer you some articles, they are likely not scholastic in nature; however, Google offers another tool for you—Google Scholar (https://scholar.google.com). This search engine offers you access to numerous journals, links to full text manuscripts, as well as abstracts. Often it will direct you to a page that will ask you to pay for the full article, in these cases I would suggest that you use one of your school's computers or their network. Just like they pay to have rights to journals in PsycINFO, they also can access the journals on Google Scholar as well. These may not always be peer-reviewed, so be cautious with your selections.

Additionally, you can use books such as your Introduction to Psychology textbook. Still another possibility is to use information you have obtained from conventions you have attended (such as from a talk or poster session). Believe it or not, you can even include information from personal communications (i.e., a talk you had with someone). While writing my thesis, for instance, I had to cite a conversation that I had with my mentor in defining a concept he had created. And yes, you do need to cite all personal communications, but since they are not something that someone else can look up and review for themselves, these communications do not appear in your reference section. And of course, you can always check your APA manual for more information on how to cite these and any of the other sources we have discussed. Finally, in the case of an unpublished manuscript, or just one you cannot gain access to or find anywhere, you can always email the author for a copy. Many students don't wish to bother experts in the field, but we can assure you that they will probably be thrilled that someone is actually interested in reading their research. If they have acopy of their article, they will often send you a copy via email. But you are at the mercy of his or her inbox and schedule. It may be a quick turn around on their reply or they may not respond at all. Just remember to be respectful in your email to them and be patient.

 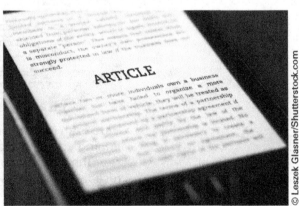

The old way vs. the new way to find your literature.

How Do I Actually Write This Paper?!

A recurring question that we hear from our students is "how do I actually write this thing?" If you are currently writing your paper and have this feeling, know that you are not alone. APA style papers are daunting in just their formatting and style, add in a literature review and it can be really stressful. So in this section, we are just going to offer some helpful tips that we suggest to our students and use ourselves.

First things first, read the literature: Your review of the literature is vital for your success on these papers. Whether you are writing a paper for your class, writing your thesis or dissertation, or writing to have your research published in a journal; you need to read the literature. Now, if it is your research, you have probably already done this (as we discussed earlier, it helps you to develop your study), but even if you have read everything out there, review it again. Understanding the prior research will greatly help you to not only start your paper, but organize it. And, there's new research being published weekly.

Once you have read some of the relevant literature, create an outline. We know a lot of students who think they can just "wing it" on these papers . . . you can't. This is not a paper you can write the night before; we promise! You need to carefully plan it out and devote time to it. Your outline, based on your literature review, will help you to plan that time better and help you not to get sidetracked and devote time and energy to unnecessary topics. Your outline can also help you to ensure that you don't leave anything out. As you create your outline, don't forget that your introduction should form a funnel, starting from the general information to the more specific information (see Chapter 12 for more information on structuring your introduction).

Once you have the articles you want to use as well as your outline completed, you need to just start writing. This seems like it should be easy, but a lot of students (and at least one of your authors) sit in front of that blank screen and just end up staring at it. I believe this is a holdover from your English writing classes in high school and college. There we are told that we need to "hook" our reader within the first few sentences. And, as we stare at our computers trying to come up with a catchy hook for our technical paper, we find that we can't seem to make it all that interesting. I mean, what can you say to hook your reader when your introduction isn't about your research, but about prior research? But that's the thing, you don't need to hook your reader, it is absolutely acceptable to just get right in to it. This doesn't necessarily make it easier to start; so one suggestion that we give to our students who feel stuck is to just write the topics from their outlines and/or write up the summary of the specific studies that they intend to include in their introduction. Once you have this general write-up completed, you can now turn your attention to connecting the topics to one another to ensure that there is a nice flow in your paper and that you are guiding your reader through the paper effectively.

One thing that we find students don't do often enough is to ask for help. There is nothing shameful about asking for help if you need it. You may even find that your professor is willing to review your paper for you as well. This review is likely to be less extensive than their grading process, but if they are willing to do it (and you make the changes they suggest) then it will help you to improve your grade or just end up with a stronger, more organized manuscript. You may not get an A by making only their changes, but you will certainly score higher than you would have without their changes. And if your professors are willing to make edits for you, use them. By not using the edits and suggestions that they have provided to you, you will essentially be showing them that you wasted their time . . . not a good idea. In addition to your professor, your university likely has a writing center where they will review your papers for flow, grammar, spelling, and in some cases, APA formatting.

And one last suggestion that I found in a book by Paul Silvia, *How to Write a Lot: A Practical Guide to Productive Academic Writing*, was to schedule time to write. You are never going to feel inspired to write a research paper, it's just not going to happen, so don't lie to yourself. These aren't particularly fun papers in general, so you have to force yourself to do it. A lot of people believe that they will only be able to write if they are feeling the inspiration, but that is a lie. Even fiction writers will tell you, you just have to write, you won't always feel like doing it, but you have to just do it. So schedule a time to write, put it on your calendar as if it were a meeting or a class. Since you wouldn't decide to just skip the class or a meeting, you shouldn't skip your writing time either. If you are planning your time properly, you won't need to schedule hours every day to devote to your writing, an hour will likely do just fine. During this time you are to do stuff related to your paper and nothing else. This means that you could be working on your literature review, creating your outline, etc.; you don't have to just use this time to be writing but you definitely shouldn't be on TikTok. Time management and perseverance is what will get you through these papers. Just stick with it, ask for help when you need it, and always be willing to accept the constructive criticism of those who review it.

Concluding Remarks

I don't know that you will ever get to a point where you look forward to writing a research paper, but you can definitely become skilled at doing so. And, honestly, the only way to get better at writing research papers is by practicing. Following the steps we have outlined in this chapter (as well as some that you may come up with on your own) you can make it a less painful process. Additionally, if you plan on attending graduate school, if you are currently attending graduate school, or if you plan on being involved with research in some way, the skills that you develop in writing research manuscripts is immeasurable. It's not an easy process, but with a lot of experience and practice, you can become very capable. Good Luck!

End of Chapter Quiz

1. Briefly explain why you need to conduct a literature review?

2. What are two options you have if the topic you were hoping to conduct your research on has already been examined by another researcher?

___3. What is the name of the primary search engine used to find psychology abstracts and articles?
   a. Psychology Abstracts
   b. PsycINFO
   c. Psychology Articles
   d. Psychology & Behavioral Sciences Collection

4. Why is it a good idea to schedule a time to write?

___5. What do we mean when we say a theory must be "testable?"
   a. that it has already been tested previously
   b. that you can form it as a question
   c. that you can potentially show that the theory is false
   d. you cannot test theories

6. List two ways that a review of the literature help you design your study?

___7. What is a pilot-study?
   a. A study just looking at pilots.
   b. A study that is expected to "take off."
   c. A pre-study that allows you to test your ideas before they become full blown experiments.
   d. A post-study that lets you evaluate the reliability of your results.

___8. Why can we not provide our participants with large sums of money to participate in our research?
   a. Because we are scientists and therefore poor.
   b. There is no funding for the social scientists.
   c. It could be seen as coercive.
   d. It would dissuade people from participating because they would assume that the study must be really boring if you are paying them that much.

9. Name one of the ways that you can obtain participants for your study.

___10. What is the purpose of a "script" for your study?
     a. To plan for all possible issues that arise.
     b. To ensure that all of your research assistants are saying and doing the same things.
     c. To ensure that you don't forget anything.
     d. all of the above

Homework Assignment #1

Create a research proposal using the following guidelines. Remember that this should be based on some prior research as well:

1. Choose a topic that you wish to study:

2. Write out your testable hypothesis:

3. Which experimental approach would you use to examine this topic (i.e., case study, correlation, experiment, quasi, etc.)?

4. What would be the methodology of your study? (Be sure to briefly explain what you would need, who your participants would be, how you would test them, etc.)

5. Based on prior research in this area, what would your expected outcome be?

Homework Assignment #2

Choose a topic that you are interested in studying (it does not need to be related to the class). Find three research articles related to that topic. Using the information from these three articles, provide a hypothesis for your topic, making sure to include your rationale for why you expect these findings.

Chapter 12
Writing Using APA Style

Once you've completed conducting your research study, you have numerous choices on how you'd like to disseminate your findings. While there are many possibilities, such as television talk shows, radio shows, newspapers, magazines, websites, and others, there are really two primary, professional outlets. These are presenting your research at conferences or publishing your results in a scientific journal. Chapter 13 will go into depth about the process of presenting your research at conferences and will outline the publication process. In this chapter, we'll focus on writing your research manuscript in the professional style that is used by virtually every psychological journal – the style that was developed by the American Psychological Association. In fact, this writing style is the required style that is used by most scientific journals in virtually every area of science.

Let me first start by saying that learning APA style isn't easy. There are no shortcuts to learning APA style. The only way to truly learn APA style is to practice it. When I was an undergraduate student, we were required to take a research methods course, probably just like you. However, our research methods course was a one year course such that the fall semester included animal studies and the spring semester involved human studies. Each semester we were required to write three complete APA-style research reports. The good news is that after this class, I was very confident in my ability to write APA-style research reports. The bad news is that it was extremely difficult, time consuming, and made me want to pull my hair out. Writing APA style and writing a research manuscript is a difficult process, but with practice, you'll be able to master it and be confident in your abilities. We hope that this chapter helps you to gain the knowledge so that you can start writing APA-style research manuscripts. However, getting a lot of practice at writing APA-style is really the only way to master it.

APA-Style Manuscripts vs. Published Articles

When we discuss APA style, we're talking about the style that is used for SUBMITTING a scientific manuscript for publication. We're NOT discussing the style that is used when the journal actually publishes a manuscript. Many students will look at articles that have been published in journals, even APA journals, and mimic the style from those published documents. It does make sense that an APA journal would use APA style when it publishes articles, but APA style isn't a style for publishing a manuscript in a journal. Each journal can take an APA-style manuscript and then publish it using whatever presentation style that they think is the most appealing. Some journals will publish articles with two columns, some prefer a single column. Most use both left and right justification of paragraphs, although this isn't APA style. Many use bold font for all headers or italicize some headers, which also may not be APA style. Thus, manuscripts are submitted to a journal in APA style, and then the journal will publish the final article in whatever style they feel is appropriate. To be clear, in this chapter we'll be discussing APA style, which is used when you submit a research manuscript for publication in a scientific journal (i.e., a professional paper). If you get a chance, compare the sample APA-style manuscript that is provided in Appendix 1 with one of the published articles that you find when you conduct a literature search.

I'm sure that you'll find them to be quite different, and it will allow you to see how very different the published manuscript is from the APA style that is used when you submit a manuscript for publication.

Student Papers vs. Professional Papers

In the history of APA writing style, the writing style has really only applied to professional, research manuscripts that, as mentioned in the previous section, were being submitted for publication. However, as APA style has become more popular over the years and one of the primary writing styles, professors in various areas started requiring their students to use APA style in writing papers for their courses. Since APA style had really only been used for professional manuscripts, a request for using APA style by professors was somewhat vague. Some professors may have been wanting their students to use the basic heading formatting. Others may have wanted the margins, fonts, etc. to be used. Most probably wanted their students to use the APA formatting for citations and reference sections. Regardless, it was very unclear. As a response to this somewhat vague request, the *Publication Manual of the American Psychological Association* (7th edition), which was released in 2020, now addresses information regarding student papers. This information starts on page 30 of the *Publication Manual*. As a result, the writing style, citation formats, reference formats, grammatical rules, heading levels, fonts, margins, etc. now can all be applied to both **student papers** (those submitted as a paper for a course) as well as **professional papers** (those submitted for publication in a professional journal). The largest difference between these types of manuscripts is clearly the content of the manuscript and the various sections within the manuscript will be markedly different for a research manuscript and the various types of student papers (e.g., essays, reaction papers, research topics, literature reviews, etc.). Additionally, the *Publication Manual* lists the minimum sections of a student paper should include a title page, the body of the manuscript, and references. There are also some other smaller differences between student papers and professional papers. For example, student papers do not have a running head, an author note, or an abstract, unless these a specifically requested by the instructor. Additionally, the title page for a student paper and a professional paper are drastically different. On page 32 of the *Publication Manual* and later in this chapter, you can find a sample title page for a student paper. Feel free to compare that title page format with the title page format for a professional paper, which can be found on page 31 of the *Publication Manual* and later in this chapter. The purpose of this chapter is to teach you how to write a professional paper (i.e., a paper that would be submitted to a professional journal for publication) so that you can learn the professional skills necessary to be successful in psychology. The vast majority of the information in this chapter can also be utilized to write student papers, but this isn't our primary focus. As previously mentioned, interested students can find more information about student papers in the *Publication Manual*, but we will address some of the issues in this chapter as well.

The History of APA Style

Probably one of the first questions that students have about APA style is WHY do we have to learn APA style? What's the purpose of even having APA style? Well, the answer is that it reduces the time, cost, and effort of conducting reviews of manuscripts. APA style allows individuals from different backgrounds a common style to writing and formatting a research manuscript. This common style makes it very easy for a journal reviewer to find information in a manuscript. For example, the title page will always be the first page. The Abstract can always be found on the second page. The Introduction will always start on the third page. The order of the sections will always be in a particular order, which makes finding the information significantly easier, and allows the reader to know where the information will be. Certain sections contain specific types of information. If you want to know how the study was conducted, you'll find that information in the Procedure section. If you want to know who was tested in the study that information can be found in the Participant section. Want to know what was found when the study was conducted? Go to the Results section. APA style also includes a specific way of writing, which helps one to communicate their ideas in a consistent manner that can be understood by individuals from different backgrounds. In essence, APA style helps provide a means to clearly communicate all of the necessary information to the reader.

In addition to providing specific formatting for writing research manuscripts, APA style also provides information to guide writers on the style of writing. For example, great emphasis is placed on economy of expression. In addition to using proper grammar and spelling, APA style also emphasizes an orderly expression of ideas as well as encouraging precision and clarity of language. Writers should avoid wordiness and redundancy as well as bias in language (i.e., sexist, racist, labels, etc.). While it may not always seem this way, it also encourages writers to avoid the use of jargon in order to help make the writing and dissemination of ideas accessible to anyone interested in reading about the topic being presented.

APA style unofficially began following a meeting of many journal editors and managers in 1928. Following this meeting, these individuals collectively published a 7-page writing style recommendation in the February, 1929 issue of the *Psychological Bulletin*, an APA journal. This recommendation called for a "standard of procedure, to which exceptions would doubtless be necessary, but to which reference might be made in cases of doubt." In 1944, the American Psychological Association's board of editors authorized a new 32-page writing guide. The purpose of this new guide was to provide more details about the preferred method and guidelines for writing, particularly for younger writers who were early in their careers and who were just starting to publish scholarly manuscripts. This guide was also published in the *Psychological Bulletin*. In a 1952 publication in the *Psychological Bulletin*, an updated 60-page guide was published. This publication marked the "official" beginning of APA style. As you'd expect, there have been many additional revisions to this guide since 1952. The guide was further updated in 1957 and again in 1967. In 1974, the APA published the 2nd edition of the *Publication Manual*. The 3rd edition was published in 1983 and was now a 208-page book. In 1994, the 4th edition had ballooned to a 368-page book. Not to be outdone, the 5th edition, which was published in 2001, was a 439-page mammoth. The 6th edition was published in 2009. Fortunately, or perhaps unfortunately, the 6th edition was shrunk down to a 272-page book. The obvious fortunate aspect of this edition was that it was back down to a reasonable length. The potentially unfortunate aspect of this edition was that it was much less detailed about certain issues than some of the previous editions, and there were numerous issues when it was published, as there were many mistakes in it where the samples didn't match the style described in the text of the manual. In 2020, the current edition, the 7th edition, was published. The 7th edition is 427 pages, but seems to be an improvement on the 6th edition. While it does provide the basic information on formatting a manuscript and helpful information covering appropriate writing style issues, it also discusses many other important topics such as explaining the publication process, which may be very helpful especially for early career researchers. Overall, we think the general rules are more straightforward in this edition as well. Past editions had many exceptions to the various rules that made it difficult to know exactly what the rule was.

To give you an idea of the topics covered in the current edition of the *Publication Manual of the American Psychological Association*, here is the Table of Contents with page numbers. You'll see that there is information on writing style as well as specific formatting issues and much more information. Even if it isn't required for your research methods course, we'd strongly advise you to purchase a copy of the *Publication Manual* for yourself. We'll probably be using this edition for the next 10 years or so.

Major Parts to an APA-Style Research Manuscript

For the majority of this chapter, we'll be discussing how to write each of the major sections of an APA-style research manuscript or professional paper. For each section, we'll discuss what information belongs in each of these sections as well as basic formatting of information for each section. Here are the major parts to an APA-style research manuscript that we'll be describing:

- Title Page
- Abstract
- Introduction
- Method
- Results
- Discussion
- References
- Tables, Figures
- Appendices

General Rules of APA Style

While all of the specific information regarding APA style is listed in the *Publication Manual of the APA* (7th edition), there are numerous general rules to APA style that are helpful to keep in mind. For example, the margins for an APA style manuscript should be set at 1" (see p. 45 of the *Publication Manual*). This includes the top, bottom, left, and right margins. Left justification is also appropriate, but don't use right justification (p. 45). Left justification simply refers to the margin on the left side of each page of your manuscript. You should have a nice, neat, straight left margin. The right margin, however, should be a regular jagged or ragged margin. The only exceptions to using only left justification are the title block and some headings, which would be centered. Therefore, do not use right justification as this would depart from APA style. Additionally, the entire manuscript should be double spaced (p. 45). The only exceptions to the double spacing are in the body of tables and figures (which *could* be single-spaced or one-and-a-half spaced, although double spacing would always be appropriate), footnotes (which should be single spaced), or equations (which could vary in spacing). While it may seem that this is a lot of room to provide and may waste space, double spacing is very helpful for individuals who are reviewing these manuscripts since it provides them with room to write comments or make notes concerning the manuscript. As an added bonus for students, double spacing makes it at least appear that your manuscript is even longer. I like to tell my students that the longer their manuscript is for my research methods class, the more sympathy they can get from their friends and family as they complain how cruel I am as an instructor. Double spacing really allows their manuscript to be twice as long as it would normally be. The preferred font for APA-style manuscripts is still the 12-point, Times New Roman font (p. 44); however, authors are now given more freedom in selecting a font in the 7th edition of the *Publication Manual*. Authors may now use 11-point Calibri, 11-point Arial, 10-point Lucinda Sans Unicode, 11-point Georgia, normal (10-point) Computer Modern, or 12-point Times New Roman. This is typical default font in most word processing programs such as Microsoft Word are generally one of these fonts so you may not need to change anything. Regardless of which font you ultimately select, you must use that same font throughout the manuscript and be consistent in its use.

Another general rule that is used throughout the manuscript is to insert one space after commas, colons, semicolons, periods that separate parts of a reference citation, and periods used in the initials in personal names (e.g., M. G. Rhodes). One change from the 6th edition is the number of spaces after end-of-sentence punctuation. The 6th edition and all prior editions required two spaces after end-of-sentence punctuation. However, the 7th edition requires one space after end-of-sentence punctuation marks, including periods, question marks, exclamation points, etc. For certain abbreviations, you do not insert any spaces after internal periods (e.g., i.e., U.S.). The general rule for using bold or italics is to not use them unless it's appropriate to do so. There are specific times, according to APA format, when you should use bold font or italics. For example, another major departure from the 6th edition is that in the 7th edition nearly all headings should be typed in boldface font. I believe that this is a positive change as authors were oftentimes unsure which headings should be bold and which should not be bold. Authors will still have to pay attention to which headings should be in italics, but the use of italics may be never needed in most manuscripts. However, if you're interested, Table 2.3 in the *Publication Manual* (page 48 of the *Publication Manual*) provides the formatting requirements for the different heading levels. This table can also be found on the inside front cover of the *Publication Manual* for easy access. Separate from headings, there are some general rules on when italics are appropriate. Italics are used to indicate most statistical symbols (e.g., F, p, t, Cohen's d, SEM, etc.), but not if the statistical symbol is a Greek letter. Greek letters would not be italicized (e.g., Σ or μ). The other main location for using italics would be in your Reference section. The names of journals and the volume number as well as the title of books in your reference section would be italicized. The names of species or genera would also be italicized (e.g., *geochelone sulcata*). While this may sound like a lot of words or symbols in your manuscript should be typed in bold or italics, the vast majority of your manuscript would be in your regular type font.

We provide sample manuscript pages in this chapter as well as a sample manuscript in Appendix 1. Similar sample manuscripts can be found in the *Publication Manual* of the APA. On pages 50–60 the *Publication Manual* provides a sample research manuscript or professional paper. On pages 61–67, you can find a sample student manuscript written for a course assignment. Each of these is very helpful if you'd like to take a quick look to see the general formatting of an APA-style manuscript. While the required style for submitting a manuscript to a journal is very clear, if you're writing a manuscript for a class that you're taking, it might be a good idea to verify with your instructor if they want you to write a professional research manuscript or if they want a student paper in APA style. As mentioned previously, the style is fairly consistent in most of the manuscript; however, the title page formatting is very different for the two styles.

The Title Page: Professional Paper/Research Manuscript

While the title page seems like it would be really simple, easy, and fast, there is a lot of specific information that goes on the title page. Obviously a very important part of the title page is the title. The title is typically going to be the first thing that a reader or potential reader will see from your manuscript. The title provides the reader with an idea of the contents of the manuscript. Thus, the title should be very descriptive, but according to the *Publication Manual*, should be focused and succinct (p. 31). Typically this includes some mention of the independent variable as well as the dependent variable. For example, here is a title from one of my manuscripts:

The Effects of a Levels-of-Processing Manipulation on False Recall

I know what you're thinking . . . awesome title. I hear you and completely understand your excitement. Alright, I admit that it isn't a catchy or sexy title, but it does include the independent variable (i.e., the levels-of-processing manipulation) as well as the dependent variable (i.e., false recall). It's also very professional, but I'll admit it may sound somewhat boring if you're not excited by false memory research. Another option would be to make your title catchy and exciting. This is an option, but I'd implore you to still keep in professional and descriptive. For example, here's an example title to a study that I came across:

Are You Still Talking?

Yep, that was it. What do you think? Do you know what the manuscript was about? Do you think it's descriptive and professional? While I do think the title is somewhat catchy and potentially interesting, I don't think this is a very descriptive title. I don't think a potential reader would have any idea what this research was about. If you're interested, it was about the nonverbal cues and changes in intonation that people use during discourse. When humans take turns when they talk they have to indicate to the other speaker when they are done talking and when it's the other individuals turn to speak. This article was evaluating the nonverbal cues that people use in indicating when they are done speaking and when it is the other person's turn to speak. I don't think most people would know this from this title. So perhaps the title could be changed to something like this:

Are You Still Talking?: The Influence of Nonverbal Cues in Discourse

Can you come up with a catchy title that is also professional and descriptive? While I think it may require a little more effort, I think it's possible. Here's a title that I think is somewhat catchy as well as descriptive and professional:

The Smell of Emotion: Olfactory Communication of Emotion in Humans

I think that the first part of this title is catchy and interesting and the second part keeps it professional and descriptive. This research was investigating how pheromones communicate our emotional state to others.

Now that we have our title, we can write the title block. The **title block** consists of the title of the manuscript, the names of the author(s), and the author(s) affiliation(s). If you envision an imaginary line that splits the upper and lower half of the title page, the title block should be at the bottom of the top half of the page, generally about 3 or 4 lines from the top of the page. The title block should be centered and will consist of upper and lowercase letters (This is referred to as **Title Case** in the *Publication Manual*). The first line of the title block will include the manuscript title in bold font. Insert an extra line after the title and then provide the author(s) in regular font (i.e., not bold). On the next line, you'd provide the departmental affiliation and the institution name separated by a comma. If there is more than one affiliation/institution then you should use superscript numbers to indicate the affiliation for each author. Refer to the sample title page to see what the title block should look like.

A second part of the title page is the Author Note. The title of the author note is Author Note, which should be bold, centered, and is located at the bottom of the title page. Each of the author notes will be indented like a paragraph (which is ½" for APA style) and each will begin on a new line. There are four potential author notes and each is given in separate paragraphs. The first author note paragraph should be the **ORCID iD** for each of the authors. An **ORCID iD** is an id number that authors can register in their name so that if they ever change their name for any reason (e.g., get married) or if they have the same name as another author, it will be easy to determine who the author really is and make sure that they receive credit for their publications. Obtaining an ORCID iD will probably become much more common than it is now, but anyone can register for an ORCID iD by going to the ORCID website (https://orcid .org). Each of the authors who have an ORCID iD should be listed here with the author's name, the ORCID iD symbol, and the full URL for the ORCIS iD. Each of these ORCID iDs will be indented and on a separate line. If any of the authors do not have an ORCID iD then don't list them here or if none of the authors have an ORCID iD then omit this paragraph. Each individual and his/her information is separated from each other author by using semicolons.

The second author note paragraph is to indicate any change in affiliation for each of the authors who have changed their affiliation from the time the study was completed. For example, I conducted a study while I was at Arizona State University, but I had moved to Sam Houston State University at the time that I was trying to publish my manuscript. Therefore, in the first author note, I listed my department at Arizona State University and, in the second author note paragraph, I mentioned my change of affiliation to Sam Houston State University. Thus, this paragraph should read - Jeffrey S. Anastasi is now at the Department of Psychology, Sam Houston State University. This change in affiliation could also be used to indicate the death of an author, which I guess would be somewhat of a change in affiliation. Obviously, if there was no change in affiliation then this paragraph would not be necessary.

The third author note includes disclosures and acknowledgments. If you received grant support or funding so that your research could be conducted, you'd want to mention that here. If there were any individuals who helped you to collect or analyze your data, you could thank them here. Others may have helped you with revisions by reading the manuscript. It would be appropriate to thank these individuals in this author note. I've even seen individuals provide thanks to their pets or loved ones. This paragraph would also be appropriate to provide any disclosures. For example, if the study was pre-registered or if the data or materials are being shared openly at some site, or if there are any conflicts of interest or to state that there are no conflicts of interest, they may be stated here. Again, if there are no disclosures or acknowledgments then you wouldn't need this author note.

The final author note is the contact information for the corresponding author. This author note is required for all manuscripts. Minimally you should include the name, mailing address, and e-mail address of the corresponding author. This is the author who individuals should contact if they have any questions about the research or if they would like to discuss the research. For example, an author note for one of my manuscripts would have the following text: Correspondence concerning this article should be addressed to Jeffrey S. Anastasi, Department of Psychology, Sam Houston State University, Huntsville, TX 77341, United States. Email: jeff.anastasi@shsu.edu

The final part to the title page is the running head. The **running head** is an abbreviated title that goes in the header of the title page. This running head should be against the left margin and can be a maximum of 50 characters (including letters and spaces). The running head should consist of the general topic being investigated and does not have to be the exact first few words of the title. For example, if your title was "The Effects of a Levels-of-Processing Manipulation on False Recall," your running head might be "Levels-of-Processing and False Recall." This running head would be in all capital letters and against the left margin in the header of each page in the entire manuscript. In addition to the running head, you should also include the page number against the right hand margin on the same line as the running head. This same running head will appear on this page and every subsequent page in your manuscript against the left margin and the page number will also appear on every page in the manuscript against the right margin. Please refer to the sample title page to get a quick look at what the title page should look like.

Evaluating Retrieval-Based Activation of False Memories Using the Deese-Roediger-McDermott Paradigm

Duncan MacLeod

Department of Psychology, University of the Highlands

Author Note

Duncan MacLeod https://orcid.org/0000-0002-1902-6045

Duncan MacLeod is now at the Department of Psychology, Sam Houston State University.

The authors would like to thank Gwen MacLeod, John Stone, and Caleb Smithy for their assistance with data collection. We have no known conflicts of interest to disclose.

Correspondence concerning this article should be addressed to Duncan MacLeod, Department of Psychology, University of the Highlands, Dunkirk, TX 77311. E-mail: DMacLeod1902@highlands.edu

The Title Page: Student Paper

As discussed previously, the title page for a student paper is very different than the title page you would use for a professional paper. While this chapter primarily deals with the information that would be included in a professional research manuscript, we did want to briefly discuss the information that would go on the title page for a student paper and provide you with a sample title page.

Much like the professional paper, you will need a title and title block for the student paper. The title of the paper should be approximately 3 or 4 lines down from the top of the page, placing it in the upper half of the title page. The title will be typed using Title Case, centered, and will be typed in bold font. Two spaces below the title, will be the author line. The author will be centered, but not be bold. Immediately after the author on the next line, will be the affiliation. This should include both the department and the school separated by a comma. The affiliation information will also be centered and not bold. On the next line, you provide the course for which the paper is being written. You should include both the university abbreviation and number for the course as well as the course name. Again, this will be centered and not bold. One the next line, you provide the name of the instructor for the course, which is again centered and not bold. One the next and final line, provide the date for when the paper was due or when it was submitted. While a running head shouldn't appear on the student paper, the page number should be inserted in the header against the right margin for every page. We provide a sample title page here so that you can see what the student paper title page should look like. You can also find this information in the *Publication Manual* on page 30 and there is a sample title page for the student paper on page 32 of the *Publication Manual*.

For the remainder of this chapter, we'll focus on the profession paper, rather than the student paper. The formatting for the student paper beyond the title page will vary considerably depending upon the type of paper that you're writing. However, the general style for a professional paper, while it may vary depending upon the approach, is much more consistent in style.

1

Evaluating the Limitations of the Own-Species Bias in Cats and Tortoises

Ruth J. Leigh

Department of Psychology, Sam Houston State University

PSYC 3336: Sensation and Perception

Dr. Daniela K. Cash

February 22, 2020

The Abstract

The abstract is a short paragraph that summarizes the key points of the *entire* manuscript. The purpose of the abstract is to allow readers the opportunity to quickly understand the content of the manuscript. This abstract is the reader's first contact with the manuscript (other than perhaps seeing the title), so having a strong abstract is crucial to the success of the manuscript. This abstract will end up being presented on most scientific search engines such that the potential reader will read this abstract to understand if the article is important or relevant to them. Thus, this abstract needs to be, as the name implies, very short, precise, complete, and to the point. According to the *Publication Manual*, the maximum length for the abstract is 250 words. While the *Publication Manual* provides a 250 maximum words length for the abstract, it defers the reader to the specific journal that the author is trying to publish the research with. The word limit for the vast majority of journals is 150 words; thus, it seems that authors should attempt to keep their abstract length to this limit. For a master's thesis or a dissertation, the 250 word abstract length seems reasonable. While 150 words may seem like plenty of space to describe your entire manuscript, it is somewhat difficult to do a good job in such a small amount of space. Be patient, as it does take some practice in writing a concise yet detailed abstract. When writing an abstract, I typically tell my students to think of the abstract as what you'd tell someone who asked about your research. For example, imagine that you were at a family dinner and your grandmother says, "Honey, I hear you're working on some research at school. Tell me about it." What would you say? Would you start explaining your topic and have your grandmother listen to you spew information about your research for the next 45 minutes? I would hope not! Instead, you'd probably give your grandmother a quick summary of each of the sections of your manuscript. This would be the abstract. For the abstract, you'll want to spend 1-2 sentences on each of the following items:

- Introduce the topic that you're investigating
- Give the general procedure that you used to evaluate this topic
- Provide the take-home findings or results
- Describe your primary conclusions
- Provide the implications or applications of your findings

Assuming that you're ready to write your abstract, which would normally be written once you've completed the remainder of the manuscript, you'll want to start the Abstract on a new page. The Abstract can always be found on the second page of an APA-style manuscript. The title of the Abstract is "Abstract" and should be in boldface font. One special characteristic of the Abstract is that it is the only paragraph in your manuscript that is not indented; the first line of your Abstract should begin against the left margin. At the bottom of your Abstract, on the next immediate line, you should provide 4-5 keywords or phrases. These **keywords** are potential search term suggestions that one could use if they wanted to locate your manuscript in a search engine. You will indent the term "Keywords" in italics followed by a colon, one space, and then your 4-5 keywords in lowercase separated by commas. Note, the 4-5 keywords you provide are not in italics.

Abstract

The majority of false memory research using the Deese-Roediger-McDermott (DRM) paradigm has demonstrated a clear role of activation in the creation of false memories at encoding, but far less is known about the role of retrieval-based activation. Expanding on previous work, the current study used several manipulations in order to investigate the role of false memory activation that occurs during retrieval. Results indicate that there may be a specific set of conditions under which activation at retrieval plays a significant role in the creation of false memories. More specifically, the placement of critical lures at the end of the recognition test seems to create a greater number of false memories than when critical lures are mixed with target words on the recognition test. Thus, the current study indicates the existence of retrieval-based activation in the DRM paradigm. Results are explained using the mechanisms proposed by the activation-monitoring framework.

Keywords: false memory, DRM paradigm, activation-monitoring, retrieval

The Introduction Section

Of all of the sections in the APA-style research report, the Introduction section has to be the most difficult section to write and the one section that will take the most preparation. First of all, in order to write the Introduction, you must first conduct a *complete* review of the literature (i.e., a **literature review**), identifying all of the research that has evaluated the specific topic that you're investigating. You'll need to provide a general understanding of the topic to your reader so that they understand the topic, and you'll need to explain what research has been conducted on this topic in the past so that your reader will better understand why your study is important and what it adds to the literature and our scientific understanding of the topic. The first part of your Introduction is to provide a complete background of the topic that you're investigating so that your reader knows everything that they need to know in order understand your study. Your manuscript should serve as a stand-alone manuscript and shouldn't require the reader to go and search other sources in order to understand your research. You'll also be using this section to convince the reader that the topic that you're investigating is worthwhile and important. So, in essence, you'll be "selling" the reader on the importance and relevance of your study. During this process, you'll want to show the reader the continuity between your study and the previous literature. The initial part of your Introduction should be fairly broad, making sure that you adequately introduce the general topic that you're investigating. You'll also want to introduce some of the research on this topic so that the reader can get a taste of this research and how this topic is typically investigated. The tricky part to writing the Introduction, and the part that requires an extensive amount of planning by the author, is that your ultimate goal is to tell the reader everything that they need to know about your topic while gradually getting more and more specific while leading them to your study. Thus, the next part of your Introduction should be introducing the reader to more specific issues that are more closely related to your study. Again, you'll want to provide some research that has investigated these more specific issues, being sure to say what they did in their study, why it was important, and what they found. Eventually, you'll want to discuss the issue that you're going to investigate and convince the reader that it's important, but you shouldn't mention your study until you've provided the complete review of the literature and led the reader to the issue that you want to investigate. Once you've led the reader to your study, you can mention your study and what you propose to do. You'll need to demonstrate to the reader why your study is necessary and explain how it adds to the literature and our understanding of your topic that hasn't been addressed by previous studies.

As previously mentioned, each paragraph in your Introduction section should get slightly more and more specific with the goal of leading the reader to your study. Part of this section of your Introduction is demonstrating the continuity of your study with the previous literature. You can do this by discussing what has been done previously by other researchers and then discussing why the current study is necessary. Just before you introduce your study, the reader should be thinking "I have an excellent idea for a study!" When they get to your paragraph where you introduce your study, your study should be the idea that they just generated. If this is the case, you did an excellent job writing your Introduction and leading the reader to your study. Thus, this next part to the Introduction is describing your study and how you're going to evaluate the specific topic or issue that you've convinced the reader is critical. After you've provided the general methods of how you're going to investigate this topic, you need to provide your

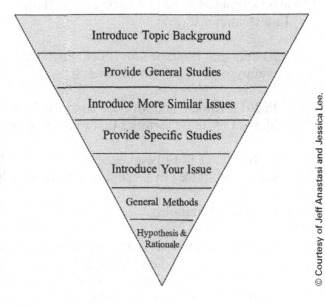

Introduce Topic Background

Provide General Studies

Introduce More Similar Issues

Provide Specific Studies

Introduce Your Issue

General Methods

Hypothesis & Rationale

hypotheses and the rationale for why you expect these findings. Be sure that your hypotheses are specific and try to include your independent variables and levels into your predictions.

In writing your Introduction section, you'll start your Introduction by typing the title on the first line of the third page of your manuscript. Thus, the Introduction starts on a new page. The title of the Introduction section is the EXACT title of the manuscript that you had in your title block on the title page. This title, like it is typed on the title page, will be boldface and centered. You'll then indent each paragraph using a ½" indent. There's really no specific length requirement to the Introduction. It really depends on the "story" that you tell and how much research exists on the topic of investigation, but you'll want to guide the reader to your study by getting more and more specific. The majority of your Introduction will be providing the background research and the last paragraph or two will be specifically about your study, what you're going to do, what you expect to find, and the rationale for why you expect this. That rationale will typically utilize some of the research or theories that you've provided in your literature review rather than your own personal opinions.

The Introduction section will probably be the first part of your manuscript where you'll include citations. Thus, this seems to be an appropriate time to discuss citations. A **citation** is used to reference a published or unpublished source of information and is a way to give credit to someone else's work or idea. If you discuss someone else's work or idea without giving them proper credit then you are committing **plagiarism**, which is when someone takes another person's work or idea and passes it on as their own work or idea. Plagiarism can take place whether you use someone's work or idea and purposely fail to cite them or whether it was inadvertent. Don't be afraid to cite other researcher's studies, as this shows a thoroughness in your review of the literature and is an indicator of your knowledge on the topic. As you discuss the literature and previous studies, your Introduction section should contain many citations. There is a very helpful table in the *Publication Manual of the APA* that provides examples of the basic citation styles. This information can be found in the inside cover or in Table 8.1 which is on page 266 of the *Publication Manual*. If you were to cite a research study that was conducted by a single author, you would cite the author and year of the publication each time throughout the manuscript. If you were to cite a study by two authors, you would cite the last name of both authors and the publication year each time throughout the manuscript. Additionally, when you are citing two authors as an in-text citation, you would use the word "and" between the two authors' last names; however, for parenthetical citations, you would use the "&" (this is called an ampersand). If you were to cite a study by three or more authors, you would cite the first author's last name followed by "et al." (which just means "and others" in Latin) and the publication year every time you cite the study. You can also decide whether you'd like to provide an in-text citation or a parenthetical citation. Generally, in-text citations are preferred when you are discussing a single study or source, while parenthetical citations are preferred if you're discussing the work of several individuals or you're making a statement that involves several research studies. See the examples below:

In-text citations:

Rhodes and McCabe (2017) demonstrated a reliable decrease in the lifespan of native tortoises that were given carnivorous diets.

In 2017, Rhodes and McCabe conducted a study that demonstrated a reliable decrease in the lifespan of native tortoises that were given carnivorous diets.

DiRossi et al. (2020) evaluated the impact of de-forestation on tortoise longevity and found that loss of habitat led to a significant decrease in lifespan.

Parenthetical citations:

Previous research demonstrated a significant decrease in the lifespan of captive tortoises that were given carnivorous diets (Allen, 2008; DiRossi et al., 2020; Rhodes & McCabe, 2017), whereas an increase in lifespan was observed when captive tortoises had herbaceous diets (DiRossi et al., 2020; Joseph & Daniella, 2006).

One final topic that should be addressed for the Introduction section is the use of quotations. Generally speaking, when you discuss the work of someone else, you should paraphrase what they said or did using your own words and then cite them to give them credit for this idea. You should NOT use their exact words and then simply cite them. To do so would be plagiarism, as would putting their thoughts or ideas into your own words and not citing them. If you do want to use their exact words you must use the proper quotation format. The general rule on quotations is to not use them. It's typically much better to use your own words and then cite the source. However, if it's absolutely necessary to use a quote then you may. The *Publication Manual* discusses quotes and paraphrasing on pages 269–278, and defines both short and long quotes. Generally speaking, direct quotations require the author(s) name, year of publication, and the page number where the quote can be found in the original source in order to be properly cited. Short quotes are less than 40 words in length and will be placed in the text but indicated as quotes with the use of quotation marks. See below for an example of short quotes with both parenthetical and in-text citations:

> Based upon the results, "memory enhancement strategies have proven ineffective" (Rhodes, 2015, p. 124), although retrieval strategies did help.

> Rhodes (2015) argued that "memory enhancement strategies have proven ineffective" (p. 124).

Long quotes on the other hand are used for quotes that are 40 or more words. These longer quotes or block quotes are presented in a block format and you don't use quotation marks, but the entire quote is indented 0.5 inches. If you're quote has more than one paragraph then you'd indent the entire quote and then also indent each paragraph another 0.5 inches.

> Rhodes (2015) found the following:

> While memory enhancement strategies have proven ineffective in both younger and older adults, they may aide the memory of children under the age of 8 years of age. Although these strategies do not appear to provide any added benefit for encoding, there are strategies that are beneficial at retrieval. (p. 124)

Here's a sample first page of the Introduction section so that you can see the general layout of this section:

Evaluating Retrieval-Based Activation of False Memories Using the Deese-Roediger-

McDermott Paradigm

Individuals often have the experience that an event occurred only to find out that it really

never actually occurred or that it occurred differently than what they remembered. From a

research standpoint both of these types of memory errors are labeled false memories (Roediger &

McDermott, 1995). Over the last two decades, research in the area of false memories has become

increasingly popular, and various approaches have been utilized to produce false memories.

Although numerous techniques have been used to produce false memories, the Deese-

Roediger-McDermott (DRM) paradigm (Deese, 1959; Roediger & McDermott, 1995) has been

the most commonly used approach for creating false memories in the laboratory. In the DRM

paradigm, participants study associates (e.g., *bed, rest, awake, tired, dream*, etc.) of a central

theme word, also known as the critical lure (e.g., *sleep*), that was never presented but was

semantically related to the presented words. The typical finding for studies employing this

paradigm is that participants recall or recognize the nonpresented critical lures at a rate that is

comparable to the studied words (e.g., Anastasi et al., 2000; Coane & McBride, 2006; Coane et

al., 2007; Lee & Anastasi, 2018; Marsh et al., 2004; Roediger et al., 1996; Roediger &

McDermott, 1995).

Since the seminal work of Roediger and McDermott (1995), numerous researchers have

focused on the specific factors that are responsible for the creation of false memories. For

example, Roediger et al. (2001) conducted a multiple regression analysis in order to assess the

contribution of seven factors that may play an important role in the creation of false memories.

Of these factors, the strength of the level of association between the list items and the critical

The Method Section

Now that you have presented the relevant background literature, convinced the reader of the importance of your study, and provided the hypotheses concerning what you expect to find in your study, it's time to let the reader know how you conducted your study. The Method section informs the reader of everything that they need to know in order to replicate your study. This section is fairly detailed and is divided into 4-5 subsections. The typical subsections are (in order):

1. Participants
2. Design
3. Apparatus
4. Materials
5. Procedure

It should be noted that the 7th edition of the *Publication Manual* is somewhat vague as to the specific subsections that are required in the Method section. What is included above are the typical subsections in an empirical, quantitative research manuscript. The general information and sections that should be included in a method section for a quantitative study can be found in section 3.6 of the *Publication Manual* (p. 82–86). However, other types of manuscripts may have other subsections, such as an Instrument section to describe a survey or questionnaire that was developed or used in the study. A Sample section could be used in place of a Participants section, particularly for survey research. The *Publication Manual* refers the author to the specific journal instructions to authors to determine the appropriate method subsections. For our purposes, we'll describe the subsections above as they generally consist of and contain the general information that would be appropriate for most research studies.

The Participants Section

The Participants subsection appropriately identifies the research participants or subjects who were evaluated in the study. Minimally, the Participants section will tell how many participants were in the study as well as describing who these individuals were and why they participated. If there are any other relevant pieces of information that would be helpful and would allow the reader to replicate your study then that information should also be presented here. One important note to keep in mind is that if you have a between-subjects variable, this typically means that you will be evaluating two or more groups of individuals. As discussed in Chapter 6, the primary issue with between-subject designs is making sure that your groups are equivalent, other than your actual manipulation. Due to this emphasis on making sure your groups are equivalent, it is extremely helpful to provide as much information as possible about these groups in the Participants' section in order to show that these groups are similar. Here is a sample Participants section:

> Thirty Sam Houston State University introductory psychology students participated as partial fulfillment of a class requirement for research participation. Half of the participants were given cognitive enhancement instructions, while the other half was given no such instructions (i.e., the control condition). Participants in the cognitive enhancement condition included 11 female and four male students with an average age of 21.4 years ($SD = 1.7$). This group consisted of eight Caucasian, four African-American, and three Hispanic individuals. Participants in the control condition included nine female and six male students with an average age of 21.7 years ($SD = 1.5$). These individuals included seven Caucasian, four African-American, and four Hispanic participants. Participants were tested in groups ranging from two to five individuals.

As this will probably be the first section where you will be using numbers, other than the dates for your citations, it seems as if a short discussion on proper use of numbers would be appropriate here. The *Publication Manual* provides information on numbers and how to report them on pages 178–182. Here are the general rules for numbers:

- Use words for numbers below 10 (e.g., eight)
- Use numerals for numbers 10 and above (e.g., 18)
- Use words when starting a sentence with a number
- Use numerals when referring to a specific item (e.g., Table 1, Figure 3), units of measurement (e.g., 5-mg dose, 33% correct, 9.5 cm, score of 3.5 on a 7-point scale), or numbers that represent time (e.g., 3 days), ages (e.g., 51 years old), or sums of money (e.g., $5).
- For decimals, put a zero before the decimal point in numbers that can exceed 1 (e.g., *t*-tests where $t(39) = 0.891$, $p = .855$ or ANOVAs where $F(1, 27) = 0.772$, $p = .756$), but do not put a zero before the decimal point in numbers that cannot exceed 1 (e.g., the *p*-values in the examples above or correlations like $r = +.78$, $p = .012$).

There are, of course, additional rules with regard to numbers, but these cover most of the issues that you'll encounter. For the complete list of rules, please see the *Publication Manual of the APA*.

The Design Section

The Design section is a very simple section to complete, as long as you know the design and dependent variable for your study. This section provides the overall design of the experiment and must include each of your independent variables, the levels of each independent variable, how each independent variable was manipulated, and the dependent variable. While this may sound like a lot of information, all of this information can be included by using approximately two sentences. If you use the format below, you can include all of this information clearly and succinctly:

> The current study utilized a 2 (Cartoon: violent, nonviolent) x 2 (Test: pretest, posttest) mixed-factor design with cartoon manipulated between-subjects and test manipulated within-subjects. The dependent variable was the number of aggressive actions performed by subjects.

Keep in mind that when you put the design information in this format, you'll want to capitalize the names of your independent variables (e.g., Cartoon, Test), but not the names of the levels of the independent variables (e.g., violent/nonviolent, pretest/posttest). Also, be sure that the dependent variable name is consistent with what you have in other parts of the manuscript, such as the name of your dependent variable in your Results section.

The Apparatus Section

The Apparatus section is an optional section that will most likely be absent in most research manuscripts. If the materials that you use in your study are relatively normal, non-specific items then an Apparatus section will be unnecessary. However, if you have a very specialized piece of equipment to test participants then you must provide enough detail about that apparatus so that anyone would be able to replicate your study with this item. If possible, provide the name and model number of the apparatus. Additionally, provide a description of the apparatus so that someone would be able to replicate the apparatus if, for some reason, they weren't able to purchase the apparatus. This could happen, for example, if the company that produced the apparatus went out of business or the apparatus was somehow no longer available. Here is a sample Apparatus section:

> The open-field apparatus used in the current experiment was an Open-Field "Prime" system, Model 80093, purchased from Lafayette Instrument Co., Lafayette, IN. The Plexiglas floor measured 40 x 44 cm with photobeams positioned 0.5 cm above the floor surface. Photobeam sensors were distributed every 8 cm along the walls of the open-field system.

Other examples of an apparatus might be if you were using an eyetracking machine or something very specific. A computer or an overhead projector or some other type of machine or equipment that you might use to conduct your study wouldn't really be appropriate in an apparatus section unless it was highly specialized equipment.

The Materials Section

The Materials section of the manuscript describes all materials that were used to test the participants in your study. The main rule for this section is that you must provide enough detail so that someone would be able to replicate each of the materials that you used in your study. To get an idea of the level of detail, see the Materials section excerpt below:

> The 18 lists used in the current experiment were taken from Stadler et al. (1999) and included the *window, cold, soft, anger, trash, chair, doctor, thief, slow, smell, rough, cup, sleep, sweet, smoke, high, mountain,* and *music* lists. The lists were divided into two groups of nine lists that were matched for their overall likelihood of recognizing the critical lure based on the Stadler et al. (1999) norms. Mean critical lure recognition for both groups of lists was 76.7%. These two groups of lists were counterbalanced such that each group served equally often as the studied and unstudied lists. For the encoding task, participants were presented with 135 items (nine 15-item lists) at a 2 s rate centered on a computer screen. The words were presented in a 72-point, Calibri font on a white background. The recognition test consisted of 54 items, with 18 list items (three items from six of the studied lists), nine critical lures from the studied lists, 18 unstudied "list" items (three items from six of the unstudied lists), and nine critical lures from the unstudied lists.

Keep in mind that any materials that you use for your study should be described in detail so that the reader would be able to replicate your study. Obviously you'd only need to describe the specific parts of your materials that are relevant. If participants used a blank sheet of paper to write their answers, it wouldn't be necessary to explain the weight of the paper or provide other nonsignificant descriptors, but you should mention the blank sheet of paper and what it was used for. Another material that you should include in this section would be any survey or questionnaire that you used. Surveys and questionnaires are used fairly often in psychology studies. If this is something that you've developed yourself or even if it's an established survey, you need to describe it in detail so that the reader is aware of what it is, what it is designed to assess, how long it is, how it is scored, what the scores mean, and any other information that might be important to assess the quality of the measure (i.e., validity or reliability measures).

The Procedure Section

The Procedure section of the manuscript describes the specific steps and instructions that were used to test the participants in your study. The Procedure section should provide paraphrased instructions that were given to the participants. These instructions should give a step-by-step description of how participants were treated and what they were told. This section is written from a third person perspective as if you were watching the researcher interact with the participants (i.e., participants were then instructed....). One additional note is that it is easiest to write and for the reader to understand if you provide the procedure information in chronological order. Again, the primary rule for this section is that you must provide enough detail so that someone would be able to replicate what you did in your study and the instructions that were given to each of your participants when you tested them. A short excerpt from a Procedure section is presented below:

> Upon arriving to the experiment, participants were given an informed consent document. They were instructed to read it and then sign it if they were willing to participant. Upon collecting the informed consent document, participants were instructed that they would be presented with 135 list items at a 2-second rate centered on a computer screen. They were told to pay attention to each of the words as

they were presented in anticipation of a memory test. Following an unrelated filler task, participants were given a yes/no recognition test for the presented lists. They were informed that each test word would be presented on the computer screen for four seconds and that they should indicate their memory for each item by circling their answer on the recognition test sheet that was given to them. Following the recognition test presentation, participants' recognition test sheets were collected. Participants were then informed of the purpose of the experiment and thanked for their participation.

Writing the Method Section

The Method section begins immediately following the Introduction section. This section does not begin on a separate page, but starts on the next line of your manuscript following the last sentence of the Introduction section. The title of the Method section is "Method" and this should be centered, typed in bold, and the first letter should be capitalized, as this is a level 1 heading. Each of the subsection titles should be against the left margin, capitalized, and bold, as these are level 2 headings. The text for each of the subsections should then begin on the next line and the paragraph should be indented. Keep in mind that these heading formats are appropriate for a single experiment manuscript. If you have a multi-experiment manuscript then each of these headings would be formatted using one heading level lower because Experiment 1 or Experiment 2 would be the level 1 heading. A table that illustrates the different heading levels is provided below, but can also be found inside the front cover and in Table 2.3 in the *Publication Manual of the APA* (p. 48).

Level of Heading	Format
1	Centered, Bold, Title Case Heading
2	Flush left, Bold, Title Case Heading
3	*Flush Left, Bold, Italics, Title Case Heading*
4	Indented, Bold, Title Case, Ending With a Period.
5	*Indented, Bold, Italicized, Title Case Heading, Ending With a Period.*

Below is an example of a Method section to show how these sections and headings should appear when the Method section is completed. Keep in mind that some of these sections were shortened and don't have the proper level of detail so that you can see the general formatting of the headings on a single page.

which were thought to provide more favorable conditions to detect retrieval-based activation

(Coane & McBride, 2006).

Method

Participants

Fifty-four Sam Houston State University students (42 females and 12 males) participated

for partial course credit and were tested individually or in groups of up to five participants. The

average age of the participants was 21.4 years (SD = 3.1) and consisted of 32 Caucasian, 12

Hispanic, and 10 African-American students.

Design

A 2 (Item Type: list, critical lure) x 3 (Prime Strength: zero strength, weak, strong) x 2

(List Presentation: studied items, unstudied items) within-subjects design was used. The

dependent variable was the proportion of words recognized.

Materials

The 18 lists used in the current experiment were taken from Stadler et al. (1999) and

included the *window, cold, soft, anger, trash, chair, doctor, thief, slow, smell, rough, cup, sleep,*

sweet, smoke, high, mountain, and *music* lists. The lists were divided into two groups of nine lists

that were matched for their overall likelihood of recognizing the critical lure based on the Stadler

et al. (1999) norms. Mean critical lure recognition for both groups of lists was 76.7%. These two

groups of lists were counterbalanced such that each group served equally often as the studied and

unstudied lists.

Procedure

Participants were presented with 135 list items (nine 15-item lists) using Microsoft

The Results Section

At this point in your manuscript, you've given the background literature and informed the reader of all of the materials and procedure so that they can replicate your study. It's now time to let the reader know what you found when the experiment was conducted. While the Results section is typically one of the sections that students are very hesitant to write, it's actually a fairly simple section to complete. With a little practice, the Results section becomes one of the easier sections to write. Certain information must be included in the Results section and this information generally follows a similar outline, regardless of the data that you're presenting. Once you've written a couple of Results sections, the rest will be very simple as they all essentially follow this same outline. Here's a basic checklist of information that belongs in your Results section:

- Identify the design of the ANOVA used to analyze data
  - Be sure to indicate the Independent variables, levels of the independent levels, and the dependent variable(s)
- Refer the reader to any Tables or Figures that provide summary information
- Give the Main Effect(s) Data for each independent variable
  - Include any planned-comparisons for each main effect, if necessary
- Give the Interaction Data
  - Include any planned-comparisons for the interaction, if necessary

Each of these outlined items are fairly self-explanatory, but here are a few points of clarification. First, when identifying the design of the analysis of variance, use the same format that you used in writing the design of your experiment in the Design section. This will allow you to very clearly and concisely identify each independent variable, the levels of each independent variable, and the dependent variable. Second, when referring the reader to the Table or Figure, be sure to be very specific in saying what the table or figure show. This can typically be easily accomplished by making sure that you mention the dependent variable as well as the independent variable in this referential statement. Finally, make sure that you understand the basic concepts of main effects, interactions, and any follow-up comparisons. If you don't understand how to interpret these kinds of data, it will be very difficult for you to effectively tell the reader what these mean. If you need a better understanding of your data, be sure to review Chapter 9 which explains data interpretation.

Before you begin writing your Results section, keep in mind a few basic pointers. First, when you write a Results section, your goal should be to present the data from your research in a way that both you and your reader will understand. The reader could be an expert on your research topic, someone who isn't an expert on this topic, a graduate student, an undergraduate student, or even a high school student. Because of the potentially huge amount of variability in who your reader may be, you should approach the Results section so that it's accessible to the majority of individuals. This means that you should really present your findings in normal, everyday language. Many students try to make the Results section overly difficult and fancy because it's something that they aren't as comfortable with and think it should sound complex. This shouldn't be the case. So just use normal language. If your data indicate that your drug group had lower anxiety scores than your placebo group then just say that. Part of your job in this section is to guide your reader through the results. Because of this, it's much more descriptive to say that the score of one group was higher than the score of the other group, rather than just saying that they were different. Second, any statement that you make when you're comparing something should always be supported with the proper inferential statistics. This could be statistics from your ANOVA summary table, a t-test, or some other test. Regardless, when you make statements about which group did better or if the groups performed similarly, provide the appropriate inferential statistics to prove that your statement is accurate. By providing the appropriate statistics, you're providing the information that the experts in the field will require. The typical inferential statistics will indicate the test used (F-ratio, t-test, etc.) with the degrees of freedom, the F- or t-value, the p value, and the measure of the effect size (partial eta squared or Cohen's d). By keeping these two pointers in mind, you're making your Results section accessible to everyone by using simple language to describe the comparisons and guide the reader, and at the same time, providing everything that's necessary for it to be very professional and to make the experts happy as well. Here's a sample sentence that illustrates the points above:

> Results indicated that individuals from the deep-processing condition remembered a greater proportion of words than participants from the shallow-processing condition, $F(1, 44) = 4.55$, $p = .02$, $\eta^2_p = .94$.

Even if you have no idea what the deep and shallow processing conditions are, you can read this simple sentence and see that the deep processing condition remembered more words than the shallow processing condition. You also have the appropriate inferential statistics to support this statement and show that the deep processing group did in fact perform significantly better than the shallow processing condition.

When writing the Results section, the title of the Results section is "Results." The Results section begins immediately after the last sentence of the Procedure section (not on a separate page). The Results title is centered, bold, and the first letter is capitalized. If you have more than one dependent variable or analysis, you can separate these by putting each analysis in a new paragraph. Alternatively, if your analyses are particularly complex then you could even add subsections in your Results section for the data for each dependent variable. An additional note here is that, according to APA style, all statistical symbols are to be typed in italics in order to indicate that they are statistical symbols. One exception to this is that Greek letters, which are oftentimes used in statistics, should not be italicized. Below is a sample Results section so that you can see the general format of this section as well as providing an illustration of how you can present the data using normal, everyday language and supporting each statement with the proper inferential statistics.

been made. This procedure was then repeated for the remaining six lists. List strength was

counterbalanced such that the strong and weak lists served equally often as the first set of lists

tested.

Results

The proportion of words correctly recognized for each condition are presented in Table 1.

These data were subjected to a 2 (Item Type: list, critical lure) x 2 (List Strength: weak, strong)

mixed-factor Analysis of Variance (ANOVA). Overall, participants recognized significantly

more list items than critical lures, $F(1, 46) = 49.55$, $p < .001$ $\eta^2_p = .52$. However, participants

recognized words from the weak and strong lists equally well, $F(1, 46) = 1.55$, $p = .221$ $\eta^2_p = .12$.

These findings were qualified by an Item Type x List Strength interaction, $F(1, 46) = 21.41$, $p <$

$.001$, $\eta^2_p = .32$. Planned comparisons revealed that participants remembered more list items from

weak lists ($M = 0.74$) than from strong lists ($M = 0.67$), $t(46) = 3.08$, $p = .003$, $d = 0.90$, but

recognized more critical lures from strong lists ($M = 0.57$) than from weak lists ($M = 0.44$), $t(46)$

$= 2.94$, $p = .005$, $d = 0.86$.

The proportion of critical lures falsely recognized are presented in Table 2 and were

analyzed using a 3 (Number of Prior List Items: 0, 4, or 8) x 2 (List Strength: weak, strong)

mixed-factor ANOVA. Results revealed a main effect of list strength, $F(1, 46) = 8.48$, $p = .006$,

$\eta^2_p = .16$, as participants recognized significantly more critical lures for strong lists than for weak

lists. Results also indicated a main effect of number of prior list items, $F(2, 46) = 10.48$, $p =$

$.003$, $\eta^2_p = .36$. Planned comparisons indicated that participants remembered more critical lures

when they were preceded by 8 list items than when they were preceded by 0 list items, $t(46) =$

The Discussion Section

The Discussion section is, in our opinion, the second most difficult section in the manuscript to write. This is partially due to the complexity of this section, but also since this is the most creative part of the manuscript where the author has a lot of freedom to "examine, interpret, and qualify the results of your research and draw inferences and conclusions from them." (APA, 2020, p. 89). In other words, the author has a lot of freedom in this section to say what they want to say about the results and what they mean. Sometimes authors will exaggerate their findings or even discuss findings as being statistically significant when they really weren't. Of course, this is not recommended as you should always interpret and present your conclusions in your Discussion section based on exactly what you found in your study without bias. In fact, the Publication Manual states that "there should be a tight relationship between the results that are reported and their discussion." (APA, 2020, p. 89)

The Discussion section can be thought of as almost a mirror image of the Introduction section. When writing the Introduction section, you were to think of an inverted triangle or funnel; starting very broadly and getting more and more specific. When writing the Discussion section, you'll do exactly the opposite. Think of a triangle or pyramid shape so that you'll begin by being very specific and discuss the take-home findings from your study and then get more and more general as you progress through the Discussion section. See the figure below for a general outline of sequence of topics that should be covered in your Discussion section:

Start your Discussion section by presenting your most important findings and interpret what they mean and why they're significant. Focus on your take-home findings and how they relate to your hypotheses that you stated at the end of your Introduction section. As you progress through your Discussion section, you should get more and more general. You'll then want to compare or relate your findings to the findings from other similar studies. You'll want to compare your findings with those studies that you presented towards the end of your Introduction that you used to lead the reader to your study. Try to place your study findings in the literature and discuss how they're similar or different from these other studies and be sure to provide an explanation of what they mean and why they were similar or different. You can then get more and more general by discussing the implications of your findings to the broader picture. Towards the end of your Discussion section, you'll want to discuss the general implications or applications of your findings and make sure that the reader is aware of the importance of your findings. Providing some sort of an idea about how your findings are relevant either to some theory that you've discussed or even discussing practical applications for your findings can be very helpful here. Feel free to return to the discussion that you may have had in the Introduction where you explained to the reader why the problem that you're investigating is important and worth investigating and what your findings have to say about this problem or issue. Another potential topic that you may want to address in your Discussion section might be any limitations of your study. For example, if you only tested college students or you only tested Caucasian participants in your study, it's possible that other populations may not show these same findings. Of course other studies could evaluate this in the future, but a limitation of your study would be that your results may not apply to these other populations. If you do address any limitations, don't just mention the limitation and move on. Discuss and explain why this is an issue and how this limitation could have affected the findings. Providing this explanation is extremely helpful for other researchers who may want to conduct additional investigations on this topic or it may be something that you might want to do.

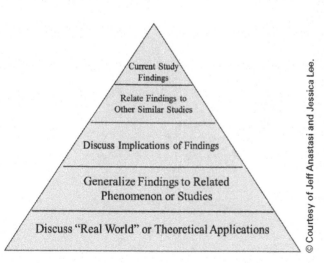

© Courtesy of Jeff Anastasi and Jessica Lee.

The Discussion section begins immediately following the last sentence of the Results section (not on a separate page), and the title of the Discussion section is "Discussion." The Discussion title should be centered, bold, and the first letter should be capitalized. See the sample Discussion section below to see the general layout of a Discussion section.

that critical lures were more likely to be recognized when 4 primes ($M = 0.62$) preceded the critical lure than when 0 primes ($M = 0.47$) preceded the critical lure, $t(31) = 2.18$, $p = .04$, $d = 0.44$. Additional priming occurred when 8 primes ($M = .76$) preceded the critical lure compared to 4 primes, $t(31) = 2.13$, $p = .04$, $d = 0.47$. Planned comparisons for the unstudied lists showed significant priming for 4 primes ($M = 0.38$) compared to 0 primes ($M = 0.27$), $t(31) = 2.86$, $p = .01$, $d = 0.63$, but no additional priming for 8 primes ($M = 0.46$), $t(31) = 0.97$, $p = .34$, $d = 0.22$. Thus, the current experiment indicated retrieval-based critical lure activation for both studied and unstudied lists.

Discussion

The primary purposes of the current study were to further examine any role that retrieval-based activation may contribute to the production of false memories in the DRM paradigm and to evaluate the discrepant findings in the literature regarding this matter. The principal conclusion from the current study is that retrieval-based activation does appear to have an influence on the production of false memories beyond that caused by activation that occurs at encoding. These data are thus inconsistent with those of Anastasi et al. (2003), Dodd et al. (2006), and Marsh et al. (2004), who demonstrated that increasing the probability that critical lures were activated during retrieval had little impact on the production of false memories. The findings of the current study indicate that retrieval-based activation does occur in the DRM paradigm and that this activation does contribute to the creation of false memories beyond that caused by activation at encoding. Thus, these results are consistent with those of Coane and McBride (2006).

Coane and McBride (2006) evaluated retrieval-induced activation by providing

The Reference Section

The reference section provides the reference information for every article or source that is cited in the text. Thus, if an article is cited somewhere in the text then it MUST be listed here. There are numerous types of potential citations depending upon the source of the information, but the primary sources are typically journal articles, books, and websites. Examples of each of these are provided below for your reference, but keep in mind that the *Publication Manual* covers virtually any kind of citation/reference that you could think of. Citation formats are covered in Chapter 8 (pp. 252–278), and references are covered in Chapter 9 (pp. 280–309) in the *Publication Manual*. So while articles and books may be the main types of citations you'll use, you could cite a conference presentation, a movie, a song, or even a personal communication you had with someone. The most common citation will probably be a journal article. You'll see two main types of journal articles below, those with a doi number and those without. A **doi number** is a digital object identifier number. The APA felt that providing this number would be very helpful for researchers to use to identify a specific article and to be able to access those articles by using the doi link. Most articles, primarily more recent articles published since 2000, will have this doi number, whereas many older articles (i.e., those published prior to 2000) may not have this doi number, although many articles that were published prior to 2000 are retroactively being given doi numbers. The idea behind the doi number is that each article will have a specific doi number that will never change, whereas using a URL (a uniform resource locator or web address) could change. So here's what journal references look like:

Journal article with a doi number:

> DiRossi, I., Trahan, S. C., & Jacoby, H. C. (2019). Hemispheric differences in the effects of cueing in visual recognition tasks. *Journal of Experimental Psychology: General, 33*, 367–373. https://doi.org/10.1037/02733.24.2.225

Journal article without a doi number:

> Rhodes, M. G., & McCabe, D. (2008). Evidence for the own-age bias with older adults. *Memory & Cognition, 18*, 125–142.

As you can see from the above examples, the doi information is written using the http format that is typically used for website address such as: http://dx.doi.org/10.1037/02733.24.225. This new style ensures that the doi information will be given as a working link to the article. Since the doi information is meant to be a working link to the journal article, which may be extremely helpful to the reader if they would like to access this cited article, you leave the doi information (as well as website links) as active links with the blue text and underlining.

Referencing books is done in much the same way as referencing articles, and like articles, books may or may not have a doi number. Here's an example of how to reference a book:

Book reference with a doi:

> Reese, T. J. (2018). *The biological basis of personality*. Erlbaum Publishers. https://doi.org/10.1037/0000092-000

Book reference without a doi:

> Joseph, C. A. (2019). *Tortoises of the world in captivity*. Random Publishers.

When providing a reference for an internet source, you should try to provide all of the relevant information that someone would need in order to find this website or information as you did. The format would be somewhat similar to what you'd cite for a journal article or book, but may include some additional information. The general format is as below:

> Author, A. (Year, Month Day). Title of document [Format description]. http://URL

However, this general format will depend upon what information is available at the website. Thus, providing references from websites can be a little trickier. Here are some common examples of references for websites:

Reference for an online journal article:

Loomis, B. T. (2013). The effect of pansexuality on traditional gender roles. *British Journal of Psychology, 44*(6), 889–915. https://www.BJOP.org/2013/47/pansex-genderroles.html

Reference for a website with an individual author:

Lee, J. R., & Anderson, J. H. (2017, June 16). *How kittens are able to overcome an own-age face recognition bias with adult cats.* https://www.rodentbeh.com/own-age.html

Reference for a website with a group author:

World Cat Organization. (2019, June 16). *How cats overcome the other-species face recognition bias with unfamiliar mice.* https://www.wco.org/feline-leukemia.html

Reference for a website with no author:

Wild tortoises escape from local zoo in mass stampede. (2015, January 16). http://www.nbcmiami.com/news/local/Wild-Tortoise-Stampede-288810831.html

An additional issue with the references is how to cite articles based on the number of authors. The general rule is to cite all of the authors in the reference section. The exception to this rule is if there are 21 or more authors. Thus, if there are three authors for an article that was cited in the text, then you make sure that all three authors are included in the reference like below:

DiRossi, I., Trahan, S. C., & Jacoby, H. C. (2014). Effects of superhero television program viewing on academic performance in science courses. *Applied Cognitive Psychology, 41,* 117–128. https://doi.org/10.1002/acp.3102

However, if there are 21 or more authors then you should cite the first 19 authors, followed by ellipses (which are three dots) and then the final author. Imagine that the following reference actually had 32 authors. The reference would look like this:

Anastasi, J. S., Lee, J. R., DiRossi, I., Anastasi, D. E., Trujillo, S. C., Joseph, C., Anderson, J. H., Lester, G. R., Reese, T. J., Panioto, M. E., White, S. J., Varela, J., Venta, A. D., Rhodes, M. J., Blau, C. D., Fox, M. M., Thompson, J., Crouch, A., Trahan, I. D., . . . Jacoby, H. C. (2015). Effects of superhero television program viewing on academic performance in science courses. *Applied Cognitive Psychology, 41,* 117–128. https://doi.org/10.1002/acp.3102

So now that we're clear on how to format each of the types of references, how should the Reference section itself be formatted? The title of the Reference section is "References," and the Reference section should begin on the next page following the end of your Discussion section. The Reference title should be centered, typed in bold font, and the first letter should be capitalized. The Reference section also uses hanging indents. With a **hanging indent**, the first line of each reference will be flush against the left margin and each subsequent line of each reference will be indented ½". The easiest way to do this is to use the Ruler function with the tab stops in your word processing software. If your ruler isn't already showing, click on the View tab in Microsoft Word menu at the top of the page and then click on the Ruler box to show the ruler. Once you've done this, you'll see the ruler at the top of the page. On the left side of the ruler you'll see two triangles (one on top of the other). You can use your mouse to click and hold the bottom triangle and slide it to the right until it's located at the ½" location on the ruler. Then select the top triangle and slide it back to the left margin. This will make it so that the text after a hard return will start against the left margin, but each additional line will indent ½" after a soft return. In Microsoft Word, there is also another way to get the hanging indent. If you go to the Paragraph settings menu and click on Special, a hanging indent is one of the options to select there as well. We *strongly* suggest not trying to tab each line to make the hanging indents because it will become a mess as you switch computers or printers or if you have to edit anything in your Reference section.

The order of references is based upon the first author's last name, and each reference should be listed in alphabetical order. If there are two articles that have the same first author but different second authors then you should place them in alphabetical order based on the second author. If there are two articles that have the same authors then you would put them in order based on the publication year, where the older publication would go first (age before beauty . . .).

One final note with regard to references/citations concerns the use of secondary citations. **A secondary citation** is where you find an article in another article, but you don't actually read this article yourself. For example, say that you were reading and article by Jacob and Smith (2020) and in that article they discuss a study by DiRossi that was conducted in 2016. As you read about this DiRossi (2016) article that Jacob and Smith discuss, you think it would be perfect for your manuscript. Obviously the best thing to do in such a situation would be to get this article, read it yourself, and cite it as you normally would. However, there are times when you're unable to get the article. Perhaps your library doesn't subscribe to that journal or you've tried interlibrary loan that was unsuccessful or you've even e-mailed the author to get a copy of the article with no response. If there's no other way, then you can still discuss the article, but you must do so based on the interpretation of the authors who have cited it in their own manuscript. You would cite this in your text as a secondary citation as below depending upon where it was an in-text or parenthetical citation:

DiRossi (2016, as cited in Jacob & Smith, 2020) conducted as study . . .

. . . . demonstrated a moderate effect of relationship status (DiRossi, 2016, as cited in Jacob & Smith, 2020)

In your Reference section, you would still need to cite Jacob and Smith (2020) as normal, but you wouldn't cite DiRossi (2016) since it was a secondary source that you didn't actually read yourself. When citing a secondary citation in this manner, it does two things for you. First, it's honest. It tells the reader that you didn't actually read this article yourself. Second, it removes any blame from you if your interpretation of this article is incorrect. If Jacob and Smith (2020) misrepresented the DiRossi (2016) article then you aren't to blame for this since you've been honest and said that you didn't read the DiRossi (2016) article. Jacob and Smith (2020) would be liable for this misrepresentation. Clearly, you'd like to avoid using secondary citations as much as possible, but if the need arises, a secondary citation is a possible remedy. See below for a sample Reference page to see the general format of the references as well as viewing how each reference would be listed.

References

Anastasi, J. S., Rhodes, M. G., & Burns, M. C. (2000). Distinguishing between memory illusions and actual memories utilizing phenomenological measurements and explicit warnings. *American Journal of Psychology, 113*, 1-26.

Brainerd, C. J., Forrest, T. J., Karibian, D., & Reyna, V. F. (2006). Development of the false-memory illusion. *Developmental Psychology, 42*(5), 962-979. https://doi.org/10.1080/09658210600648456

Brainerd, C. J., & Reyna, V. F. (2002). Fuzzy-trace theory and false memory. *Current Directions in Psychological Science, 11*(5), 164-169. https://doi.org/10.1111/1467-8721.00192

Brainerd, C. J., & Reyna, V. F. (2007). Explaining developmental reversals in false memory. *Psychological Science, 18*(5), 442-448. https://doi.org/10.3431/27658210602645451

Coane, J. H., & McBride, D. M. (2006). The role of test structure in creating false memories. *Memory & Cognition, 34*(5), 1026-1036. https://doi.org/10.2317/17958210600855453

Hutchison, K. A., & Balota, D. A. (2005). Decoupling semantic and associative information in false memories: Explorations with semantically ambiguous and unambiguous critical lures. *Journal of Memory and Language, 52*, 1-28. https://doi.org/10.1016/j.jml.2004.08

Lee, J. R., & Anderson, J. H. (2017, June 16). *How kittens are able to overcome an own-age face recognition bias with adult cats.* https://www.felinebeh.com/own-age.html

Reese, T. J. (2018). *The biological bases of illusory memory.* Erlbaum Publishers. https://doi.org/10.1037/0000092-000

Roediger, H. L., & McDermott, K. B. (1999). False alarms about false memories. *Psychological Review, 106*(2), 406-410. https://doi.org/10.1037/0278-7393.214.803

Tables and Figures

Tables and Figures are extremely helpful when presenting data to the reader. Tables allow the researcher to present a large amount of information to the reader in a fairly small amount of space. The researcher, as discussed in the Results section, will refer the reader to the table and let the reader know what the table shows. Tables then allow the reader to see specific numbers, such as the average performance of participants in each of the conditions as well as the marginal means. Figures also allow the researcher to present relatively complex data in a small amount of space and, and the researcher will refer the reader to the figure much like they do for a table. Figures are particularly helpful in showing the pattern of data, rather than specific numbers. Both can be extremely helpful, depending on the goal of the researcher.

According to the 7th edition of the *Publication Manual*, researchers can either place the table in the Results section, usually immediately following the paragraph where the table is referenced in the text, or following the Reference section. Placing the tables after the Reference section is generally preferable. If you decide to place the table after the Reference section then each Table will be given on a separate page. The first Table would start on the next page after the end of your Reference section. The first line of text would be the Table number against the left margin (e.g., Table 1, Table 2) and typed in boldface font. On the next line, you should give a very descriptive title of what the table shows. This title should be in italics, but not bold, and should use title case (i.e., capitalize the first letter of each of the important words; words like "of" or "a" are not capitalized). In order to be descriptive, the table should typically include the dependent variable so that the reader knows what the numbers or averages in the table depict. For example, here's a sample table title that is descriptive and that allows the reader to know what the numbers in the table refer to:

Mean Percentage of Words Correctly Recognized for Each List Type

When making the table, you can again use the Ruler to provide the tab stops in Microsoft Word. Once you've made the Ruler visible (by clicking on the View tab), you can place the tab stops wherever you'd like on the Ruler. The tab stops are to the left of the two triangles on the ruler that were described earlier in the Reference section. The first tab stop is a left tab stop, but if you click on it, it will change to a centered tab stop. Then click and hold the tab stop and drag it to where you'd like for it to stop on the Ruler. You can then move these around later to adjust them. Some individuals will manually align the columns in their table using the tab or spacebar keys, but this will lead to many more alignment issues. We strongly recommend not taking this approach. Another option for the table would be to use the "insert a table" function in Microsoft Word. However, there are a lot of formatting changes that you'd need to make to this inserted table to make sure that it's formatted according to APA style. For example, vertical lines are not permissible in an APA-style table. You should have horizontal lines to separate the information in your table, but not vertical lines. A sample table is provided below so that you can see the general layout of APA-style tables, but there are many examples of tables provide in the *Publication Manual* on pages 210–224.

Table 1

Mean Proportion of Items Called "Old" for Each List Strength Condition

List Strength	List Items	Critical Lures	Nonlist Items	Average
Strong	.69 (0.18)	.58 (0.29)	.25 (0.21)	.51 (0.23)
Weak	.79 (0.12)	.42 (0.32)	.12 (0.13)	.44 (0.17)
Average	.74 (0.14)	.50 (0.30)	.19 (0.16)	

Note. Standard deviations are in parentheses.

When making a Figure, each Figure will be given on a separate page; however, the Publication Manual does allow you to place the figures in the text following the paragraph where the figure is referenced. However, like tables, it is generally preferable to place figures after any tables that have been placed after the Reference section. Therefore, the first Figure should be placed on the next page after your final Table. The APA style for figures is nearly identical to the style used for tables. For example, the title of the Figure (i.e., Figure 1, Figure 2) is placed above the Figure against the left margin, is typed in bold, and is not italicized. On the next line, you should type the Figure title. Like the Table, the Figure title should be a very descriptive title that tells the reader what the Figure shows. Like the table, each of the important words in the figure title should be capitalized and the figure title should be italicized. Immediately under the descriptive title would be the body of the figure. A sample Figure is provided below so that you can see the general layout of APA-style Figures, but many more examples of figures are provided in the *Publication Manual* on pages 234–250.

RETRIEVAL-BASED ACTIVATION OF FALSE MEMORIES 38

Figure 2

Mean Proportion of Critical Lures Recognized Based on the Number of Primes Preceding the

Critical Lure

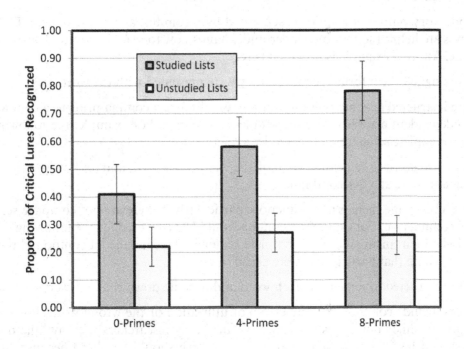

Note. Bars in graph indicate standard error.

Common Writing Errors

In addition to basic APA-style errors, there are many other errors that authors may make when writing a professional manuscript. Chapter 6 of the *Publication Manual* (pp. 152–191) is devoted to the mechanics of style and provides extensive information to help the writer to avoid many of these errors. Some of these errors are common writing errors regardless of discipline, but some are more specific to APA style and scientific writing. For example, we've seen many students misuse or simply not understand how to use commas. Commas can be used to separate elements in a series of three or more items, offset an introductory phrase in a sentence, or separate two independent clauses joined by a conjunction. When you have a list of items, such as in the following sentence, APA requires use of the Oxford or serial comma before the "and" that precedes the final item.

Participants were asked to write down their height, weight, and eye color.

If you use an introductory phrase, it should be separated by a comma (as we just did for THIS sentence). These commas are helpful so that the reader understands how to read the sentence and where to place the short pause. Another example is provided here:

After participants signed the informed consent, they were presented with the word lists.

As most of us where instructed at some point in our life, we also use a comma prior to a conjunctions that separate two independent clauses (i.e., two complete sentences). For example, the following sentence consists of two complete sentences separated by a conjunction.

Participants were instructed to remember each of the words presented, and each word was presented one-at-a-time at a 2-second rate.

A comma is not used every time there is a conjunction, particularly if there are not complete sentences on both sides of the conjunction. For example, a comma would NOT be used for the following sentence because "to write down their answers" isn't a complete sentence. This is called a compound predicate and indicates a second thing that participants were asked to do.

Participants were instructed to remember each word and to write down their answers.

Other common errors include common spelling errors or utilization of the wrong word. For example, "data" is a plural noun, while "datum" is a singular noun. Many researchers will say "the data was analyzed" when it should be "the data were analyzed." The verb should be plural because "data" is plural (i.e., we want to have good subject-verb agreement). Other common mistakes include the use of the wrong word:

1. then vs. than ("then" is used to say the next thing that occurred, while "than" is used to compare things.)
   Participants were debriefed about the experiment and were then excused.
   Participants in the drug group had lower anxiety than those who received the placebo.

2. affect vs. effect (generally, "affect" is a verb and "effect" is a noun)
   The drug did not affect the juvenile cats. (verb)
   The drug had a positive effect on juvenile cats. (noun)

3. e.g. vs. i.e. ("e.g." is a Latin abbreviation that means "for example" and "i.e." is a Latin abbreviation that means "that is").

4. it's vs. its ("it's" is a contraction that substitutes for "it is" and "its" is a possessive pronoun)
   It's not clear why we tested 30 participants. (contraction)
   The rat was hording its food. (possessive pronoun)

5. their vs. there vs. they're ("their" is a possessive pronoun; "there" is a location; "they're" is a contraction for "they are")

   Their scores were evenly skewed. (possessive pronoun)

   All of the participants placed their consent forms there. (location)

   The participants were very tired; however, they're strong swimmers. (contraction)

6. your vs you're ("your" is possessive while "you're" is a contraction for "you are")

   She picked up your informed consent. (possessive pronoun)

   I'm not clear why you're upset. (contraction)

Generally, do not use contractions in APA style anyway, so you should never have "it's"; instead you should be using "it is." This is true also for "they're" and "you're" as well.

As we previously stated, the *Publication Manual* provides extensive help on the mechanics of style in order to help readers better express themselves clearly and concisely. Using proper APA style as well as using proper grammar and avoiding these basic mistakes helps to make you and your writing appear much more professional and polished.

Concluding Remarks

There are some additional items that could be included in an APA-style manuscript, such as footnotes, appendices, etc., but the items discussed in this chapter are the primary sections and content that most research manuscripts will require. Since we can't include every piece of information from the 427 page *Publication Manual* in this chapter, we'll simply refer you to the *Publication Manual* for any additional information about the sections described here or the other potential sections that you could include in your manuscript. Regardless, most of the information that you'll need to write a complete APA-style research manuscript has been provided here. Once you master this information you'll be able to publish research in virtually any scientific journal. Additionally, you'll have some exceptional skills that psychology graduate programs will be looking for.

End of Chapter Quiz

1. What is the only section in the manuscript that you do not indent?

2. When you cite a source in your manuscript you provide the author(s) and the date, name 3 additional pieces of information that you should provide for that same source in the reference that you have put in your Reference section.

3. Name any four possible subsections of the method section that were discussed in the chapter?

4. True or False: The hypothesis is stated near the beginning of the Introduction.

5. True or False: The Discussion section can be described as a "funnel".

6. What type of indent is used in the References section?

7. When writing the Introduction section, when should you mention your study and what you did?

8. What are the specified margins used for an APA-style manuscript?

9. True or False: The abstract should be one of the last paper sections written.

10. True or False: All major sections in the manuscript should have boldface titles.

Bad APA-style Manuscript

For the following APA-style manuscript, please identify every mistake in the manuscript. There are numerous mistakes in this manuscript, some are APA-style mistakes, some are content mistakes. Please indicate your mistakes on the manuscript itself, being careful to identify each mistake. For example, if there is more than one mistake for a certain item, be sure to indicate each of those mistakes separately.

An own-age bias in face recognition for children and older adults

Jeffrey S. Anastasi & Matthew G. Rhodes

Footnotes

Correspondence for this article should be addressed to Elizabeth Loftus, University of California – Irvine.

Jeffrey S. Anastasi, College of Humanities and Social Sciences, Sam Houston State University; Matthew G. Rhodes, Department of Psychology, Colorado State University.

The authors would like to thank Mittens, Gambit, and Logan for their faith and support during the data collection and write-up phases of this study.

An own-age bias in face recognition

    The current study examined whether children and older adults exhibit an own-age face recognition bias. Participants studied photographs of children, younger adults, middle-aged adults, and older adults and were administered a recognition test evaluating their memory for these faces. Results showed that both children and older adults more accurately recognized own-age faces than other-age faces. These data suggest that individuals may acquire expertise for identifying faces from their own age group and are discussed in terms of Sporer's (2005) in-group/out-group model of face recognition.

INTRODUCTION

    A number of studies have demonstrated that older adults and children exhibit poorer memory for faces than younger adults (Chance and Goldstein, 1984; List, 1986; Adams-Price, 1992; Fulton and Bartlett, 1991). However, this difference may in part result from the stimuli typically used in face recognition studies. Specifically, the majority of studies have asked college-aged participants to remember the faces of similar-aged targets. Thus, much of the prior work on age differences in face recognition has ignored whether participants may demonstrate superior recognition of faces from their own age group (i.e., an own-age bias) (Wright and Stroud, 2002).

    Several investigators have examined this issue by manipulating the age of photographed individuals studied by participants (e.g., Bäckman, 1991; Bartlett and Leslie, 1986; List, 1986; Wright and Stroud, 2002). For example, Wright & Stroud (2002) presented younger (18-25 year olds) and middle-aged (35-55 year olds) adults with videos depicting a theft by a younger or middle-aged perpetrator. Results showed that younger participants were more likely to correctly identify the perpetrator in a line-up when the culprit was also young. Middle-aged participants, in contrast, did not exhibit a significant own-age bias. Fulton & Bartlett (1991, p. 47) reported a similar pattern, as younger adults in their study exhibited better recognition of younger than older adult faces, while older adults demonstrated equivalent levels of accuracy for younger and older faces. Based on these data, Fulton & Bartlett (1991, p. 51) suggested that an own-age bias exists for younger adults but is less reliable for older adults.

    Contrary to Fulton & Bartlett (1991), an own-age bias has been demonstrated in several cases for older adults (Perfect and Harris, 2003; Bäckman, 1991). For example, Bäckman (1991) found that face recognition accuracy was enhanced when older adults were presented with older faces. In addition, Perfect & Harris (2003) reported that older adults were nearly three times more likely to correctly identify an older adult compared to a younger adult from a lineup.

    Far fewer studies have examined whether children exhibit a similar own-age bias (List, 1986; Chung, 1997). Chung (1997; manuscript title: *Children fail to show an own-age recognition bias*) conducted the only face recognition study that, to our knowledge, has investigated the own-age bias in children. Specifically, Chung presented children (ages 7-12) and adults with photographs from those same two age groups. Results showed that, in addition to demonstrating superior recognition of faces compared to children, adults also exhibited an own-age bias. No such bias was reported for children.

Thus, it appears that an own-age bias is not consistently evident for older adults and is nonexistent for children. However, none of the previous studies have tested both children and older adults in the same study. This is important as the specific manipulations used in previous studies vary considerably, making comparisons across studies difficult (Felder, Walter, Reed, Scott, Rhodes, McCabe, and Perkins, 2011). Given the paucity of studies for both groups, particularly those with children, further research is needed. Thus, the primary purpose of the current study was to investigate the own-age bias in children and older adults using a single experiment with the same procedures for both groups. Specifically, both groups of participants attempted to recognize photographs of children, young adults, middle-aged adults, and older adults. If an own-age bias exists, participants should be most accurate when identifying individuals from their own age group and less accurate when identifying individuals from different age groups. Results showed that participants demonstrated an own-age bias such that children remembered the faces of children better than they remembered the faces of other-aged individuals. Similarly, older adults remembered faces of older adults better than they remembered the faces of children, young adults, and middle-aged adults.

METHODOLOGY

Participants. 70 individuals from two age groups participated in the current study. 40 children, aged 5-8 years (M = 6.9; SD = .91) and 40 older adults, aged 55-89 years (M = 71.6; SD = 10.4) participated. Children were tested at local elementary schools and after-school programs in the Phoenix area and received small toys or stickers for their participation. Older adults were recruited from retirement communities and activity centers in the Phoenix area and received $5 for their participation. All participants were active, healthy, and reported no physical or mental health problems. Participants were tested in groups of 2 to 4 individuals.

Procedure. Materials consisted of 128 digital photographs of sixty-four individuals taken in the Phoenix metropolitan area. Photographs were taken of each individual in two poses (smiling, not smiling) with the same white background and consisted of only their head and shoulders. The photographs were split into four groups of thirty-two photographs. Each group consisted of 8 photographs from each age range (5-8, 18-25, 35-45, and 55-75 years) divided equally among males and females. Half of the photographs from each age range were of individuals smiling and half were of individuals not smiling. The approximate size of the photographic image on the computer monitor for both the study and test phases was 7 x 6 inches. The recognition test consisted of sixty-four photographs. 32 of the photographs (8 from each age range with an equal number of males and females) were the alternate-pose photographs of individuals viewed during the encoding phase while the remaining 32 photographs (8 from each age range with an equal number of males and females) had not been studied.

Materials. In the first phase of the experiment, participants were presented with 32 photographs of both males and females of various ages at a 10-sec rate using Microsoft PowerPoint. Participants were instructed to categorize the individual in each photograph into one of four age ranges (5-8, 18-25, 35-45, or 55-75 year-olds) by circling the appropriate age range on a form provided. They were not informed about an upcoming memory test.

After completing the photograph ratings, participants were informed that they would be presented with 64 photographs at a 10-sec rate. Participants were instructed to indicate whether each individual was presented earlier by circling either "yes" or "no" on a form provided. They were told that some individuals had been presented earlier while others had not been seen previously.

STATISTICAL RESULTS

Data from the current study was analyzed using a 4 (Participant Age: children, older adults) x 4 (Photograph Age: children, young adults, middle-aged adults, older adults) mixed-factor analysis of variance on recognition accuracy. The recognition accuracy for each age group is presented in Table One. Given our a priori predictions, these data was then analyzed separately for each age group. The alpha level for all statistical tests was set to .05.

Recognition data are presented in Table One. These data indicate that an own-age bias was present as participants demonstrated superior recognition of photographs from their own age group. Analyses of recognition accuracy revealed a significant main effect of Photograph Age, $f(3, 198) = 3.81$, $p = .25$, but no main effect of Participant Age, as recognition did not differ between the two age groups, $f(1, 66) = 2.03$, $p = .16$. More importantly, a significant Photograph Age x Participant Age interaction was present, $f(3, 198) = 7.47$, $p = .016$, indicative of an own-age bias. Planned comparisons on children's corrected recognition scores showed that recognition of photographs of children (M = .46) was significantly higher than photographs of younger (M = .76), $t(38) = 1.99$, $p = .05$, and middle-aged adults (M = .44), $t(38) = 2.56$. Children were marginally more accurate for photographs of children compared to photographs of older adults (M = .57), $t(38) = 1.78$, $p = .08$. Older adults' corrected recognition scores were significantly higher for photographs of older adults (M = .56) compared to photographs of children (M = .72), $t(38) = 5.33$, younger adults (M = .59), $t(38) = 2.65$, and middle-aged adults (M = .59), $t(38) = 3.79$.

DISCUSSION

Overall, data from the current study are consistent with an own-age bias for older adults and children. Specifically, both age groups exhibited higher levels of recognition accuracy for individuals from their own age group compared to individuals from other age groups. Thus, the current study adds to a limited body of work demonstrating an own-age bias for older adults (Perfect and Harris, 2003; Bäckman, 1991;) and, to our knowledge, is the only study that has demonstrated an own-age bias in face recognition for children. Such data also suggests that age-related deficits in face recognition may be exaggerated when participants study faces of individuals from other age groups (Wright and Stroud, 2002).

Knowledge of the own-race bias has been crucial in the legal system (Sporer, 2001; Brigham and Malpass, 1985; Meissner and Brigham, 2001) where identification errors have serious consequences. The current study supports a similar memory bias and suggests that accuracy may be diminished when children or older adults must identify individuals of a different age. Thus, both the age of the witness and the age of the perpetrator are crucial factors when evaluating an individual's ability to remember previously seen faces.

BIBLIOGRAPHY

Anastasi, Jeffrey. S. & Rhodes, Matthew. G., (2006). Evidence for an own-age bias in face recognition. **North American Journal of Psychology, 8(2)**, 237-252.

Rodin, Margaret J. (2004). **Social Cognition, 5.** Who is memorable to whom: A study of cognitive disregard. 144-165.

Bäckman, Leon (1991). Recognition memory across the adult life span: The role of prior knowledge. **Memory & Cognition, 19**, 63-71.

Brigham, John C. & Malpass, Roy S. (1985). The role of experience and contact in the recognition of faces of own- and other-race persons. **Journal of Social Issues, 41**, 139-155.

List, Judith (1986). Age and schematic differences in the reliability of eyewitness testimony. **Developmental Psychology, 22**, 50-57.

Brigham, John C. & Meissner, Christopher A. (2006). Thirty years of investigating the own-race bias in memory for faces: A meta-analytic review. **Psychology, Public Policy, and Law, 7**, 3-35.

Sporer, Sigfried L. (2001). The cross-race effect: Beyond recognition of faces in the laboratory. **Psychology, Public Policy and Law, 7**, 170-200.

Stroud, John S. & Wright, Donald B. (2002). Age differences in lineup identification accuracy: People are better with their own age. **Law and Human Behavior, 26**, 641-654.

Table 1. TABLE OF MEANS.

Participant Age	Children Photo	Young Adult Photo	Middle Adult Photo	Older Adult Photo
Children	.56 (.24)	.46 (.30)	.44 (.25)	.47 (.26)
Older Adults	.46 (.30)	.57 (.28)	.49 (.35)	.71 (.28)

Note: Standard deviations are in parentheses.

Figure 1. TABLE OF MEANS.

Participant Age	Children Photo	Young Adult Photo	Middle Adult Photo	Older Adult Photo
Children	207 (25)	356 (30)	442 (25)	407 (26)
Older Adults	378 (31)	378 (28)	449 (35)	218 (28)

Note: Means represent reaction time in milliseconds.

Chapter 13

Presenting and Publishing Research

O ften after you finally finish your manuscript, all you want to do is never look at it again. But this would be a mistake. Think about it, you have already put in so much work conducting your research, then writing it up, so why would you stop now? One of the most important things you can do as a researcher in any field is to disseminate your research. It does no one any good for you to horde it away and let it collect dust. The whole point of research is to advance the field. In this chapter, we're going to discuss the different options that you have to disseminate or get your research out to those who might be interested in it. We'll also be discussing the process of how you disseminate your research for each of the different options discussed. You do have a lot of options. Some of these options are easier than others and some require quite a bit more effort and time. So, let's discuss your options.

How to Disseminate Your Research

To begin, let's talk about what options you have in getting your research out there. There are two main ways of sharing your research; **conferences** and **publication**. Both of these options have benefits, and of course, both have their own difficulties too. Let's begin with conferences.

Conferences

Conferences are a great way to get your work out there, even if you are still working on the research project. Conferences also allow you to meet a variety of researchers from various fields and to share ideas and theories. Psychology conferences occur all over the country and the world. There are your local conferences that may even occur at your own school (such as an undergraduate or graduate student research symposium), regional conferences (such as the Southwestern Psychological Association), national conferences (such as the annual meeting of the American Psychological Association), and international conferences (such as the Association for Psychological Science).

If you are not currently conducting research or if your research just isn't ready for public viewing, you should still consider going to conferences. The networking you can do there may help your own research. And as a student, you may find that you are able to better understand the schools you are looking into for your graduate work. You can talk to professors that are attending the conference and their students, look at the research they are conducting, and get an overall sense of what their research programs look like. Additionally, you can meet with other students who share your own interests as well as experts within the field. Conferences can expand your thinking and prompt you to look at your own studies in a whole new way. Keep in mind that the purpose of conferences is to bring together individuals with similar interests. You may have been working on a project for some time and attending or presenting research at conferences affords you the opportunity to discuss that research with others who are also interested in your research. You can also talk to individuals who you've been reading about and realize that most of them are just regular people just like you. It should be an exciting opportunity for you!

The Power of Social Affiliation: Eliminating the Own-Race Bias

Jessica R. Lee, Alissa N. Fleahman, Courtney T. Spiegel & Jeffrey S. Anastasi

Sam Houston State University

INTRODUCTION

The own-race bias occurs when one demonstrates better recognition for faces from one's own race than faces from another race (Meissner & Brigham, 2001). While researchers have yet to come to a consensus regarding an explanation of the own-race bias (Meissner & Brigham, 2001; Sporer, 2001), one of the most popular explanations for the own-race bias is predicated on social categorization (Sporer, 2001).

The own-race bias can best be explained by Sporer's (2001) In-group/Out-Group Model (IOM). IOM postulates that one's memory for faces is dependent upon the amount of processing that a face receives. IOM suggests that each individual we encounter is automatically categorized into an in-group or out-group based on various observable characteristics, such as age and race. In-group faces are then processed for additional individuating features which, in turn, facilitates better memory for such faces. On the other hand, out-group faces are categorized upon generic category features resulting in relatively shallow, non-individuating processing, resulting in poorer face recognition.

IOM has been very successful in explaining the own-race bias in studies where only a single social dimension has been manipulated. However, predictions from IOM are somewhat less clear when more than one social category is manipulated. For example, Ray, Way and Hamilton (2010) manipulated multiple social dimensions by crossing political party (i.e. Republican or Democrat) with abortion stance (i.e. pro-life or pro-choice). They evaluated face memory of White, pro-choice and pro-life Republicans. Results indicated that discriminability was significantly better for faces sharing two in-group dimensions than for faces sharing no in-group dimensions. Additionally, recognition for faces sharing one in-group dimension was equivalent to those sharing no in-group dimension.

While Ray et al. (2010) manipulated more than one in-group category dimension, only a single study has evaluated the impact of multiple category membership on the own-race bias. Shriver, Young, Hugenberg, Bernstein and Lanter (2008; Experiment 2) evaluated White, Miami University students' ability to remember Black and White students depicted as either Miami University students or as students from a rival university (i.e. Marshall University). Results indicated that discriminability was well predicted by the number of dimensions the faces shared with the participants. Specifically, participants showed superior discriminability for faces sharing two dimensions, followed by faces sharing a single dimension. These results indicate an additive effect of dimensions such that the more shared dimensions, the better face recognition.

While the findings in both studies are interesting, it is still unclear if manipulation of in-group dimensions would lead to an additive or non-additive effect. The goal of the present study was to evaluate what happens when more than one in-group affiliation is manipulated, and whether these manipulations lead to an additive or non-additive effect

EXPERIMENT 1

Method

Participants

- 120 Sam Houston State University students (60 Black, 60 White) participated for partial course credit.

Design

- A 2 (Participant Race: Black, White) x 2 (Photograph Race: Black, White) x 2 (Affiliation: student, police) mixed-factor design. Participant Race was treated as a between-subjects manipulation and Photograph Race and Affiliation were manipulated within-subjects. The dependent variable was discriminability (d') scores.

Materials and Procedures

- Digital photographs of 48 individuals were used. Each individual was photographed in two poses (smiling, not smiling). Some photographs were taken from Minear and Park (2004).
- Participants were presented with 24 photographs for the encoding task at an 8-sec rate and were instructed to rate the photographs on how similar the individuals were to their current social group (1-5 scale). Police officers were presented with their uniform visible, whereas students were presented in regular clothing.
- Following an unrelated 5-minute filler task, participants were then given a yes/no recognition test which consisted of 48 photographs at a 5-sec rate.
- The recognition test consisted of 48 photographs in a smiling expression. 24 photographs were of the same individuals presented in the encoding phase and 24 photographs were of other individuals not seen previously.

Results

Average Discriminability for White and Black Participants

EXPERIMENT 2

Method

Participants

- 22 Police Officers from various cities volunteered to complete the current study.

Design

- A 2 (Participant Race: Black, White) x 2 (Photograph Race: Black, White) x 2 (Affiliation: student, police) mixed-factor design. Participant Race was treated as a between-subjects manipulation and Photograph Race and Affiliation were manipulated within subjects. The dependent variable was discriminability (d') scores.

Materials and Procedures

- Digital photographs of 48 individuals were used. Each individual was photographed in two poses (smiling, not smiling). Some photographs were taken from Minear and Park (2004).
- Using an online survey format, participants were presented with 24 photographs for the encoding task at an 8-sec rate and were instructed to rate the photographs on how similar the individuals were to their current social group (1-5 scale). Each of the faces depicted a "student" or a "police officer" in a non-smiling (neutral) expression. Police officers were presented with their uniform visible, whereas students were presented in regular clothing.
- Following an unrelated 5-minute filler task, participants were then given a yes/no recognition test which consisted of 48 photographs at a 5-sec rate.
- The recognition test consisted of 48 photographs in a smiling expression. 24 photographs were of the same individuals presented in the encoding phase and 24 photographs were of other individuals not seen previously.

Results

Average Discriminability for White Participants

CONCLUSIONS

- Results from Experiment 1 provide evidence for an additive effect.
- Participants showed the highest discriminability when they shared two category dimensions with the face, moderate discriminability when they shared a single category dimension with the face, and the poorest discriminability when they shared no category dimension with the face. These findings can be explained by Sporer's IOM of facial processing (Sporer, 2001).
- Results from Experiment 2 do not provide evidence for an additive effect. There was no significant difference in White police officers' discriminability scores for White or Black students, and, overall, they remembered student faces better than police officer faces. However, the findings showed that White police officers had higher discriminability scores for White police officers than Black police officers thus supporting an own-race effect.

Once you decide to present your research at a conference, there are a few things you should keep in mind. For any conference you will be offered two ways to present your research. The first of these is known as a **poster presentation**. A poster presentation is, obviously, when you present your research in the form of a poster. The poster will typically be 5 × 8 feet, though you should always check with each conference on the correct size. We've attended conferences with posters up to 5 × 8 feet or as small as 3 × 4 feet. Now this may seem like a lot of space, but in reality this is a fairly limited amount of space. You can create your poster using Microsoft Publisher. It will allow you to set the size of the poster needed and allows you to add in both figures and tables. It also will allow you to make your poster using a variety of colors and backgrounds. You can even use a photograph or something very interesting and attention-grabbing as your background. When creating your poster, you should present it as if it was a brief APA style write-up. This means that you should have sections on the poster dedicated to the various sections of your paper (i.e., abstract, introduction, method, results, and discussion sections). Since this is in poster form, you should use a large font so that a person can read it easily from a few feet away. And the truth is, the other conference attendees will just be walking around looking for various topics that interest them. This is where you need to be creative. Using a large, easy-to-read font, along with eye catching colors can help draw people to your poster. When creating your poster, rather than using statistics to explain your results, consider tables and/or graphs. These give your poster some style, provide some variety to your poster presentation (rather than just paragraph after paragraph of text), provide nicer summaries of your data, and are easier for people to process at a further distance. To also make it easier for your viewers, you should provide a handout of your study for them. This can be done by just reducing the size of your poster down to an 8 × 11 sheet of paper. This handout allows other individuals to remember you and your research and provides them with a copy of your poster, in case they'd like to cite your research or get into contact with you later.

© Courtesy of Jeff Anastasi, Christina Stanford, and Darline Garrett.

Your poster can draw your audience in with images, figures, and bright colors; but don't forget that your sparkling personality can bring them to you as well!

The second option that you are presented with at a conference is a **paper presentation**. This is actually an oral presentation. A paper presentation, just like a poster presentation, is an abbreviated version of your APA-style paper. Just like with your poster, you will be talking about all of the different sections of your paper. This presentation will typically last between 10 and 15 minutes with five minutes given for questions. Since this is a fairly brief time to discuss your research, you want to be sure to focus on the highlights. At this point you probably are already aware that a literature review will cover many studies and topics. But only a handful of those are the "main" ones you are using for your research. These are the ones you will want to focus on when you cover your literature review. Your method section should focus on the primary tools used, such as scales, stimuli, and instructions. Your results will again be best if you present them using either a table or a graph, though you need to discuss what they mean and why you decided to run the type of statistical tests that you did. When you explain your findings, you'll really just want to guide the audience through your table or figure so that they can follow along. Finally, your discussion should wrap up what you found, discuss any limitations, and end with the implications and future directions of your research.

Paper presentations are setup a lot like a classroom. And just like a classroom, you need to know your audience.

Now, if you are anything like either of the authors of this book, you don't really relish the idea of speaking in public (in fact, the idea terrifies both of us). These talks are more likely to contain experts in the given field than a poster presentation. They are also likely to have only those individuals who are interested in that line of research sitting in on your presentation. With poster presentations, individuals will walk around the poster session and may stop and take a look at some research that catches their eye or that they're interested in. With paper presentations, the presentations are typically held in auditoriums or smaller presentation rooms at a certain time. Therefore, the individuals attending the paper presentations will be there because they're interested in the topic or they're also involved in this type of research. Your audience has planned and scheduled to be there for your talk. Thus, it is very important to really know your audience. Smaller conferences that cater to undergraduate and graduate student research will be more forgiving and patient when it comes to your paper presentation and the type of questions they will ask. However, a national or international conference that is attended by the top researchers in the field will have higher standards and expectations. It is incredibly important not to panic when it comes to your presentation and answering the questions at the end of your presentation, but it is understandable to be nervous. Just keep in mind that this is YOUR research! You know your research better than anyone else and it's typically a project that you've been working on for some time now. To help you with your paper presentation, we've compiled a list of helpful hints that should assist you when it comes time for your talk (and these will really help with *any* oral presentation that you do, even just for your class):

1. Practice your talk!

   It becomes painfully obvious when a presenter hasn't practiced his or her talk. He or she stumbles over his or her words, seems lost, and loses the interest of the audience quickly. When we say that you should practice your talk, we mean more than once. Start with your friends and/ or family. They are likely to be the easiest on you. They will critique you more than your talk (as it is unlikely that they know your research all that well). Also, since these individuals may not know the research very well, they provide the perfect audience. They can tell you if you've explained some of your ideas or concepts well enough. If they don't understand it then maybe you aren't explaining it well. From there you should practice with your colleagues and other individuals from your research lab. These are the individuals who will be able to ask you more complicated questions such as those related to the research topic and questions surrounding the type of testing and statistics you used. Since they are more familiar with the area of research, it is very important that you take their advice. Again, if they don't understand the way that you've explained something, be sure to use the feedback provided to you and make it better. If you present to five different people and they all say the same thing, you should probably listen to them. And remember, if you are using some type of visual display (such as a PowerPoint

   presentation) be sure to practice with it. Nothing is worse than finding out as you are about to present that your presentation is a mess or has a mistake in it. One final aspect of practicing your talk is to know your time limit. As previously mentioned, you typically will be given 10 or 15 minutes for your paper presentation. This time limit is typically very strict at conferences. Therefore, it's extremely important for you to know exactly how long your talk is so that you don't go over this time limit and/ or make sure that you adequately use all of the time allotted to you. The best way to know how long your talk is would be to practice it.

   Practicing and reviewing your presentation with your professor, colleagues, and fellow researchers is paramount to a good presentation.

2. Utilize visual displays!

   Using presentation software such as PowerPoint has now become a standard at conferences. Visual displays are a great way to guide the talk and keep the audience on track. They also provide a great safety net for you. If for some reason you get lost in your talk or forget your next topic, you have the presentation display to help keep you on track. So what makes a good presentation display? One of the greatest *faux pas* you can do is to put all of your information in the presentation. If you do this you are left with nothing to do but to read what is on the screen. Guess what, your audience knows how to read and they don't need you there to do that. You should use your presentation strictly as a guide to keep you and your audience on track. Use bullets to highlight the main topics, such as the authors of a study you are discussing or the name of a scale that you used. You want your audience to be listening to what you are saying, and if you put too much information on the screen, they won't be. Too much information will distract your audience as they'll be reading what you have on the screen while missing what you're saying. One really great hidden benefit of utilizing a visual display is that it will take the audiences' eyes off of you. Every time you advance your presentation, your audiences' eyes will move to the screen. You will feel less scrutinized this way.

3. Do not read your talk!

    Nothing is more frustrating than watching someone give a talk with his or her head down as he or she reads note cards. You should know your research, you should practice your research, and if you've done this enough, you shouldn't need any notecards. Now, I'm not saying you can't have something to make sure you stay on track, that's a good thing to have, but that is what your visual presentation is for. You should maintain adequate eye contact with your audience while you're talking. You should be reading your audience. If they look lost or confused, you should address it then. If you keep your eyes on your notes and don't establish good eye contact with your audience, you'll be unaware of how your presentation is going and if your audience is understanding your presentation. If we still haven't convinced you, one thing that we've noticed over the years is that when students rely on notecards for their presentation, they tend to stumble and trip over their words more. They show less confidence than when they just talk about their research. After all, like the poster presentation, this talk provides you with the opportunity to just talk about your research with a room full of individuals who are also interested in your research. So have some fun with it! Think about it, what other time are you going to have the opportunity to actually speak with a bunch of people who are actually interested in the research that you're conducting!?

4. Dress accordingly!

    This should be pretty self-explanatory, but in case it isn't, you should be dressed like a professional. Depending on the conference, you might be able to get away with a more casual look, but when in doubt, always dress to impress. Remember, you have some of the top researchers in the field listening to you; you want them to take you seriously. As a student, you might have a future instructor or colleague in that room, so be sure to put your best face forward. If you plan on attending graduate school or looking for a job after graduate school, these may be the individuals who will be making the decisions about you and your future. You don't want them to remember you as "that woman who was inappropriately dressed in her bikini" or "that guy who wore ripped jeans and a black concert t-shirt." In case you're wondering, yes, we have seen these individuals at conferences.

"No, I'm not familiar with the dress code ...
but I'm pretty darn sure that jammies aren't on it!"

© Cartoonresource/Shutterstock.com

5. Give them a handout.

    Just like with the poster presentation, you should provide those in the audience a handout. This can be the exact same thing that you handed out with the poster. Like with the poster presentation, this contact information provides them with the information from your talk and gives them a way to reach you if they have further questions.

If you follow these steps you will not only sound and look more professional, but you will also *feel* more professional. And after all, it's not just what you say, but how you say it. If you seem unsure, unprofessional, or just plain scared, your audience may just discredit you before you even get halfway through your talk.

Getting Your Research Published

At this point in the course you are probably acutely aware of just how much written research is out there for your viewing pleasure. What you may not fully realize is just how hard it is as a researcher to have your research actually get published. In this section we will address the steps involved in publishing your research, a typical timeline of the entire publication process and, finally, why one article is chosen to be published, while others are not.

Writing Up Your Research

At this point in the book you should already have a pretty good idea about how to write an APA-style manuscript (see Chapter 12). As you learned earlier, your research in psychology will mainly be written using the writing style and format as denoted by the APA. This is also likely the style you will use when you are writing up your thesis and dissertations in graduate school (though it is always best to check with your program for any specifics). Since we spent all of Chapter 12 discussing the nitty gritty of APA style, I see no reason to repeat all of that information again here, but here are some helpful hints to get your paper published in a reputable journal.

Now that you have collected all of your data and finalized your research, it is time to send your hard work off for publication. But there are steps that you will need to follow. First, it is extremely important that you determine which journal you want to send your manuscript to. This should be decided *prior* to you writing up your research. Each journal has their own unique perspective and writing style, and it is important that you write your paper with that in mind. Let's say that you have conducted research on the effects of age on the memory of faces. A paper on the own-age bias can be interpreted in multiple ways. You could discuss it as a strict memory phenomenon, making it more suited to *Memory & Cognition*, which is a very theoretically-based journal. You could also write up your research with the intention of discussing ways to apply your research to real world issues. In this case, *Applied Cognitive Psychology* might offer you a better fit for your research. Different journals focus on different topics, but also on the types of research they publish. If you're unsure, most journals have a website that tells potential researchers exactly what topics they publish as well as the focus of the journal. By deciding your journal *before* your write up, you will save yourself a great deal of revision time and a lot of headaches.

Hard choices are involved in picking which journal you are going to submit your manuscript to.

Speaking of revisions, as with the papers that you have probably already been working on for this course, one thing to remember is that you will need to revise your manuscript repeatedly. There will never be a time that your writing will not have to go through this revision process. Revising can be tedious; we know, but it is an essential part of the writing process. When your paper is ready for edits and revisions, don't just rely on yourself to see where changes need to happen. Talk to your friends, professors, and colleagues and ask if they would be willing to review your paper and suggest edits. Your university is likely to have a writing center, and they will gladly help you with the revision process. Keep in mind that the most useful revisions will come a individuals that have some background in the topic you are writing about. If you decide you want to research the effects of age biases in facial recognition, asking your mom or your best friend to look over it will likely yield you only a small benefit (unless of course this is also what they study). Don't get me wrong, their input can still benefit you; they are likely to point out spelling and grammatical errors, and their questions for clarification might enhance your paper as well. But the revision process is really about making your research shine, not just your ability to write a captivating paper. This is when the notes and feedback from your fellow researchers and professors will be of the most use. Not only will they be able to help you with the structure and formatting of your paper, but they are also going to help you with your presentation of your research; which studies are going to be of most help to you, what issues they see in your description of your methodology, what other theories would be beneficial to discuss, and what you should probably leave out. The revision process takes time, so be patient. Making multiple revisions to your paper will only enhance it, even if it means delaying your ability to send it out for publication.

What writers imagine as the revision process . . .   reality of the revision process.

The Review Process

After you have revised your paper numerous times, and you are happy with the final product (which is written to appeal to a specific journal), it's time to submit your manuscript to the journal editor. When you do this, you will want to include a cover letter that gives a brief summary of your paper along with some specifics, such as word length (particularly important if you are submitting to a *brief* journal where they limit the amount of space you can use). See Appendix 2 for an example cover letter. Many journals now have a manuscript portal on their website that allows you to submit your manuscript electronically. While the specific format may be slightly different than a cover letter, you'll still need to present this same information to the editor.

Once the journal editor receives your manuscript, he or she will identify experts within the field to review your paper. Typically, your paper will be reviewed by three individuals who have some background in your topic area. These experts will be asked to read your manuscript and comment on it. This is called the peer-review process, and it is very important to the scientific process. The idea behind **peer review** is that your research will be evaluated by individuals who are experts on this topic (i.e., they are your peers) in order to make sure that the research should be published. The experts assigned to your paper are looking to make sure that your research is up to the scientific standards as well as the standards set by the journal. Their comments will be broken down into two types: general and specific. In their general comments they make a broad assessment of the research. In this, they will make their recommendation to the journal editor as to whether they believe the research merits publication at that time and if the research adds something to the literature. They will also include specific comments, which will note any flaws in the design, statistics, and/or interpretation of the study. This is where the real critiques can be found. The specific comments can range from rather simple changes (e.g., cite a specific study or add in an additional theory) to rather detailed and sometimes manuscript altering comments (e.g., conduct a replication study to ensure the validity of your findings). These reviews can take some time, and the journal editor will ensure that the reviewers are given enough time to complete a full assessment of your manuscript. Typically, a reviewer will have anywhere from 2–16 weeks to complete their review and return their comments to the editor. During this time, you will just have to be patient as you wait for a response from the editor, and it can be very difficult waiting for the response.

Once all the reviewers have submitted their suggestions to the editor, the editor will then create an action letter that will be sent out to you. This letter can take anywhere from 2–16 weeks to be sent out after the reviews have been received. If you are keeping track, we are potentially up to 8 months from the time you submitted your paper to the journal. In the action letter, the editor will typically provide an overall assessment of the different things that the reviewers said. It will also include all of the general and the specific comments made by each of the reviewers. In addition to the suggested edits, the editor will include a decision about your paper. There are four possible decisions:

1. "Accepted without revisions"
2. "Provisionally accepted with minor revisions"
3. "Reject but revise and resubmit" (which can include minor or major revisions)
4. "Reject"

While we would all love to have our papers immediately accepted without revisions, it's extremely unlikely. While the standards vary depending on the different journals, the most likely decision is "reject." Quite honestly, the best decision that you can realistically hope for is "reject, but revise and resubmit." A revise resubmit decision may not sound like a good decision, but it's a very good decision. It says that your research topic is important and worthy of publication if you make the changes suggested. They're *inviting* you to resubmit your paper back to them after you make the revisions because they think it's good. It took us a long time to realize that "revise resubmit" is actually a positive response. By the way, we don't know anyone who has received an "accepted without revisions" decision for a manuscript on their first attempt to publish a manuscript. Ask your instructor about his or her publication experiences, and I'm sure they'll tell you the same thing.

As you can see, this researcher is carefully reading the action letter he received from the editor and is carefully evaluating each of the reviewer's comments.

Now once you receive your action letter (and possibly had a fit over what a reviewer said about your research- we haven't forgotten you reviewer 2!), you must make a decision. Would you rather make your revisions and resubmit to the same journal or take your research somewhere else and submit to a new journal. You might be tempted to submit someplace else (after all, how could they reject your amazing research?), but this may be more hassle than the changes that are being suggested in your action letter. Don't let your emotions guide you on this one. Be practical. After all, you have already spent a great deal of time getting your paper ready for this journal, and if you decide to submit your research to another journal, the entire process will begin again (including rewriting your paper to fit into the theme of the new journal). But, there will be times that you look at the amount of changes that are being suggested and decide that it isn't worth it to submit to the same journal again. The key is to determine what chance you actually have at getting your paper accepted in this journal, even if you make the revisions. So pay *very* close attention to what the action letter says and what each reviewer has said. If you do decide to resubmit your paper with the changes suggested in your action letter, you will need to include a detailed description of each of the revisions you made for each of the comments from all three reviewers (and possibly also the editor). Once you submit your revisions, the journal editor will decide if your paper will be sent back out for review or if he or she will make the decision unilaterally. If the editor decides that the paper will need to be reviewed by experts again, you may or may not get the same experts, but typically it is the same reviewers. This could mean another round of revisions for you. It also means another 2–16 weeks of waiting. After this, the editor will send out a final acceptance (or rejection) letter Hopefully, you've been very attentive to all of the revisions that were requested and that you documented your changes well. If you did this well, the initial reviewers and the editor should see that you've done everything that they've asked and will now accept your manuscript.

Clearly this researcher has just received her acceptance letter. Too bad her joy will be short lived; there is still a lot of work to be done.

Assuming your manuscript was accepted, you *still* aren't finished. You now have to deal with the publication office and proofs. This is where they will format your manuscript in the specific layout that the journal will use to ultimately publish your manuscript in. As we're sure you realized as you conducted your literature reviews for your manuscript, the specific format that journals use to publish articles may be somewhat different from each other and differ from the APA style that you used to write your manuscript. For instance, in your papers for this class, your tables and figures are most likely at the end of the paper, after your references, yet as you read an article published in a journal, you don't have to keep flipping to the back of the paper to see what they are referencing; the tables and figures are provided near the paragraph that references them. This is because the journal decides where in the layout these will appear. But you do have a little say in the layout of how your published article will be laid out.

At this point, the publications office for the journal will send you a set of proofs. This is a copy of exactly what your manuscript is going to look like when they publish it. It is important to really pay attention to what the publications office sends you. This is your last chance to make minor formatting or wording changes in your manuscript. If they mislabel your table, flip something in your graph, or list your affiliation wrong in the paper, it is up to you to catch these mistakes before they go to printing. If there are typos in the manuscript or you've made a mistake on a reference, this is your last chance to fix it. Keep in mind that once your paper is published, it's published forever. Make sure that you fix anything that needs fixing. Once you are satisfied with the final product, you will now have your article placed in line for publication. This publication line varies quite a bit for different journals, but it could take as little as a couple of months to more than a year. It really depends on many factors such as how many researchers submit their research to the journal, how good or bad the journal is, and how efficient the journal editor is, how efficient the publications office is, and how many issues the journal publishes per year.

How Long Is the Complete Publication Process?

You probably noticed that at several points we talked about the amount of time it takes to have your research published. Let's look at this issue a little more closely. When you conduct your research, this will take a decent amount of time. You have to wait for your research to be approved by your institutional review board (IRB; see Chapter 3), a process that varies based on your school, topic of interest, and the number of research proposals ahead of yours in their cue. From there you have to design and conduct your research, and at the very least this will take a few months. After that, you have to analyze your data and then write up your research using APA style. This can easily take over a year from start to finish. Now we need to add on the time it takes for the review process. The review process can easily take over a year but typically averages between 3–9 months. If you have to revise the manuscript extensively or if you must conduct additional studies, this could take quite a bit longer. Once your manuscript is finally accepted, you still have to wait anywhere from 2 months to over a year before your article goes to print. In fact, in each article that is published, you can see when the manuscript was received and when it was finally published (this is usually at the end by the references or just prior to the references). All in all, publishing research in scientific journals is a very time-consuming (and soul sucking) process that leads to a great deal of frustration among researchers. But it is important to remember that without this process we wouldn't be able to disseminate our research and advance the field. The steps added for the peer-review process, which can sometimes feel frustrating, are there to ensure that good science is not being placed next to pseudoscience. While we may complain about this process, and some changes to it may need to be made, we are better because of it.

Other Aspects of the Review Process

Even though the idea of a peer-reviewed paper is to eliminate bias, some bias still remains. We are now going to discuss the criteria for the acceptance of your manuscript. One of the biggest pieces of the acceptance puzzle will be the significance of your findings. A journal won't waste its time or limited space on research that does not add to the knowledge in the field. The articles that are considered to be the most influential and that add the most to the field of study will typically be a lead article. A lead journal is the first article in each issue of the journal when it's published. In fact, this is a good way to see what type of research appeals to a specific journal, just look for what articles and topics they publish first in each issue.

Another criteria for publication is the statistical findings of your research. It's *extremely* rare to have a null finding published. In fact, when a null finding is published, it is because its presence is exceptionally significant. If a study's null finding is contrary to a major theory for example or it shows that a drug believed to be effective isn't, then you *might* find the results published. However, results are more likely to be published if they are statistically significant and consistent with prior findings and/or theories within the field. Having said this, it is very unlikely that you will have the same findings published again, without some change to the study (such as adding levels to the IVs or changing the population group of interest). As previously stated, the research must add something to the literature and help the literature to advance. You probably also noticed that a lot of the research articles you have read contain more than just a single experiment. Multiple experiments within the same manuscript allows for replication to occur in that single publication. Remember from Chapter 2, replication is an important step in ensuring that our findings are not due to chance or error.

Another major factor in the decision process is the editor's personal preferences or decisions. Each journal's editor has quite a bit of power when it comes to deciding what research will appear in the journal. For instance, an editor may find that your topic is out-of-date or determine that there has already been a lot of research published on that topic. The editor of a journal is similar to the editor of a newspaper where he or she must determine if your research will be of interest to their readers. And, as we already mentioned, space is limited and there are lots of research studies vying for a position within the journal. Part of the editor's job is to make sure that he or she publishes only the best articles that add to the field and are of interest to the journal's readers so that the limited amount of journal space is not wasted. On occasion we end up with trendy research within the field. This research might be on a trendy, hot topic (for instance, right now mindfulness research is invading all areas of psychological research). However, the editor may feel that by the time this research would be published, it may no longer be of interest to anyone. On the other hand, in the case of a hot topic that the editor believes is of high importance and would be of interest to most, if not all, of their readers, he or she may set aside a special edition of the journal for just that topic. Now at first this sounds like a great idea, but it may be a long wait for the researchers who submitted their manuscripts first, as they have to now wait for the next issue for their article to get published. If their research is consistent with this hot topic, they may need to wait a bit longer for there to be a sufficient number of manuscripts to fill the special issue. No one can tell how long this could delay the publication of your manuscript.

One last caveat when it comes to publications. Earlier in this chapter we mentioned that the journals are reviewed by your peers, a step that is necessary to ensure publication of only high quality research. This process is designed to be blind, but isn't always. The idea of a blind review is that neither you nor the reviewer will know the other's identity. However, this process can be flawed. For one, it is often easy to tell who wrote an article, even if they remove their name(s). Just flip to their references and see who they cite a lot. It's probably themselves. Now, this doesn't mean that researchers are narcissistic (though some most certainly are); instead, they may be just very familiar with their own research, and it's easier for them to talk about their own past work. After all they are writing about a topic that they're interested in which means they probably have a lot of related research that they've previously published. In addition, it's very likely that their past research influenced their current study, therefore it only makes sense that they would want to reference back to a prior publications that led to the current research. Think about your own work—you have probably spent a great deal of time working on your own research papers in this course (or you will). Would you really want to start from scratch every time? Probably not. Researchers are no different. Writing these manuscripts is a tedious and arduous task for all of us. Anything that can make this process easier is greatly appreciated.

For the final potential flaw in the peer-review process, imagine that you're working on your research, and in the process you have found that a very popular theory in the field is actually not supported. In other words, you are going against this popular theory. How do you think the creator of the theory will feel about your research? Now imagine that he or she is one of your reviewers. I'm sure you can see where this is going. If your research goes against a reviewer's own theory, they may be overly harsh and critical, making it nearly impossible for your manuscript to be accepted by that journal. This shouldn't happen, of course. We *should* want the research to advance in spite of our own egos, but the reality is that we can all have a bit of an ego from time to time. Research that disputes our theory would certainly provide a blow to our ego. What about the reverse of this situation? Your research supports my theory; you mention my theory a lot, telling everyone that it is far superior to the other theories available. How do you think the creator of that theory will feel? Do you think they may be more supportive of your manuscript being published? If you said yes, you are probably right. Again, our ego may have an influence on our decision on whether the manuscript should be published, and sometimes we like to have our ego stroked. A related idea is that reviews are actually pretty subjective. You might have a bias against a particular researcher. Maybe you have met him, and he rubbed you the wrong way. Maybe she insulted your own research in the past. Maybe you just don't like his haircut. Whatever the reason, these can lead to a potential situation where, no matter what, you just won't like what they have to say, and you will therefore become overly critical and harsh. In addition to not liking a particular person, you may also not like certain research topics. Some journals are very specific in the type of research they publish (e.g., *Memory*). But other journals are meant to cast a wide net when it comes to topics (e.g., *Journal of General Psychology*). In these broad topic journals, the expert reviewer may not be quite the expert you were expecting. You may be assigned someone who works within a cognitive field, but has no interest in your research topic of face recognition. And as a student, we know you are aware of how difficult it is to read something that is not of interest to you. It feels like a chore and can even alter your mood. In the case of a manuscript, you may inadvertently be overly critical when the topic is one you aren't familiar with or if you aren't particularly fond of the topic. For example, in a manuscript that one of your authors tried to have published a few years back, one of the reviewers was adamant that the research be explained with regard to a social psychological theory. This would be fine if the research had anything to do with social psychology, but instead it was basic memory study. This reviewer, uninterested in the basic (as opposed to applied) research on facial recognition decided it could be improved upon if only it was related to the topic that they were interested in.

Concluding Remarks

So as you can tell, you have options when it comes to disseminating your research. While conferences (either poster or paper presentations) allow you to present your research to a large audience in which you can get immediate feedback, they do not carry the same weight as a publication will on your **Curriculum Vita (CV)**. This is not to say you shouldn't participate in conferences, because you absolutely should. They are a fantastic way to network, explore, and learn; something you will need to do for your entire career. As we've discussed the lengthy publication process, it should also be noted that conferences allow you to be exposed to some of the most up-to-date research, whereas most of the published research was conducted one or more years prior. So definitely present your research at conferences, but don't just present your research at conferences. You will reach a larger audience by having your research published. And remember, the goal of research is to keep moving forward, and in order to do that, we have to show where we have been. So we encourage you to always strive to do both. The more people who hear about your research, the more you can do to better the field.

End of Chapter Quiz

1. What are the two primary ways to disseminate one's research findings?

2. When attending conferences, what are the two options to present one's research?

3. True or False: When giving a presentation at a conference, it is usually best not to use visual displays since they can distract your audience.

4. What is the name of the process where your paper is reviewed by three individuals who have some background in your topic area and they are asked to evaluate the manuscript?

5. True or False: From the time that you submit a research manuscript to a journal, the typical amount of time for it to get published is about 3 months.

6. What is the most common decision made on manuscripts that have been submitted for publication?

7. True or False: It's typically easier to get research published if it has obtained null findings.

8. When is the best time to determine which journal you'd like to submit your manuscript to for publication?

9. True or False: The typical paper presentation is typically 30 minutes in length.

10. Which is the more informal method for presenting research at a conference?

Homework Assignment #1

1. Find five psychology journals of your choice. For each of the journals, determine the impact factor of the journal. Based on this impact factor, provide an explanation of the quality of that journal compared to the other journals that you've identified. Second, provide an estimate of how long manuscripts take to be published in each of these journals. Provide an explanation for how you determined how long the review process is for each of the selected journals. Finally, provide an estimate for the "publication line" for each of the selected journals. In other words, determine how long articles typically wait before being published after they've been accepted for publication.

2. Identify five psychology conferences. First, provide the approximate date that submissions are due for each of the conferences. Second, provide the approximate date that each of the conferences are held. Finally, for each conference, list the last three cities that hosted each conference.

Chapter 14

Graduate Study in Psychology

If you've enrolled in a psychology research methods class, you've probably decided to major in psychology. After all, few students would put themselves through such a challenging course if they didn't have to. Many students decide to major in psychology because they "want to help people." I also hear many students discuss that they want to get into psychology because they aren't really very good at science. By this point in this textbook, I hope that you've determined that psychology is a scientific discipline and that you need to be good at science and the scientific method in order to be good at psychology. Unfortunately, it's important to note that an undergraduate degree (B.A. or B.S.) does not provide you with adequate training to be a psychologist. If you'd like to pursue some career in psychology, you can all but guarantee that you're going to need some sort of graduate training. You could potentially earn a master's degree, which typically requires 2 years of additional study beyond the bachelor's degree, or a doctoral degree, which typically requires 4–5 years of additional study beyond the bachelor's degree. Many students are unaware that they can go directly from a bachelor's degree into a doctoral program if they are highly competitive. We'll discuss this issue a little later in this chapter.

In this chapter, we'll discuss what it means to major in psychology and what types of jobs you can look forward to if you plan on pursuing psychology as a career. We'll also discuss the types of experiences you should have during your undergraduate career if you'd like to be competitive for post-baccalaureate programs. Finally, we'll cover the process of how to apply to the various types of psychology graduate programs and what to expect if you're accepted into these programs.

Majoring in Psychology

Whether you're wanting to find a job in psychology after your bachelor's degree or if you plan on pursuing graduate school, an important question to ask yourself is what kind of job do you eventually want? By asking yourself this fairly simple question, you can work backward to see what kind of degree you'll need and what area you might be interested in studying. For example, if you know that you'd like to work as a therapist helping individuals, then clinical psychology would be the most obvious choice. If you'd like to work with children, you might be interested in clinical psychology with a focus on children, school psychology, or maybe even developmental psychology. If you're interested in how the brain works, then physiological psychology or neuropsychology might be the areas you'd consider. Many students don't know the answer to this question, and that's alright too. As you learn more about psychology, the different areas of study within psychology, and what topics excite you, this question may become a little easier.

As a psychology major, there are specific courses that you'll be required to take. This course is probably one of those courses. The point behind your training in psychology is to teach you and allow you to develop the skills that you'll need as you enter the workforce or continue your training in graduate school. The training that psychology majors receive is very good at helping them to understand and gain insight into human behavior. Psychology training does more than simply train individuals for a specific job, but rather, helps students to gain skills that are adaptable to virtually any employment setting. Psychology programs also emphasize writing, speaking, and problem-solving skills. In addition to the coursework that you'll be required to take, you may also want to focus on those elective courses that can help you to obtain your ultimate job or graduate school goals.

As will be discussed later in this chapter, you'll want to also focus on those skills that will be necessary for these later goals. For example, if you plan on pursuing graduate studies, obtaining research experience while you're an undergraduate student is extremely helpful. At most universities psychology faculty members engage in various research activities. Oftentimes they are looking for undergraduate or graduate students to assist them with their research. These research assistants may help with data entry, running participants through the studies, preparing manuscripts, designing studies, etc. The type of work that research assistants are allowed to engage in varies greatly with their abilities and training as well as the needs of the particular faculty member. Once you've completed this course successfully, you'd most likely be qualified to serve as a research assistant. As discussed in the "Applying for Graduate Study in Psychology" section below, serving as a research assistant serves a number of purposes for you, particularly if you plan on attending graduate school. Most importantly, serving as a research assistant allows you to gain some experience and skills that virtually every graduate program in psychology will value. Graduate programs, particularly Ph.D. programs, emphasize the scientific or research aspects of psychology. By gaining research experience, you are demonstrating to graduate programs that you are going beyond the regular in-class instruction and gaining skills that they're looking for. The things that you do as a research assistant are the same things that you will be required to do in graduate school. If two equally qualified applicants (based on their GPA and GRE scores) are attempting to gain entrance into a graduate program, the one with research experience will gain the advantage.

Like most doctoral students, this graduate student is actively involved in research . . . and loving it!

As you serve as a research assistant, you'll not only gain experience and skills, but you may also be given the opportunity to present your research at local, regional, national, and even international conferences. You may even be able to get some of this research published with you as an author on the published manuscript. Showing that you have research experience AND that you are demonstrating research productivity, really puts you in a completely different category of applicants as you will be highly valued by various graduate programs. While not the norm, I had two model undergraduates who served as my research assistants starting in their sophomore year of college. Both individuals had very good GPAs (around the 3.5–3.7 range) and had good, but not great GRE scores. One of them applied to 13 graduate programs in cognitive psychology, the other applied to 14 graduate programs in clinical psychology. The cognitive psychology student had seven conference presentations and two publications by the time he completed his bachelor's degree. He was accepted into 12 of the 13 programs that he applied to. The clinical psychology student had 14 conference presentations and three publications by the time she graduated and was accepted into 13 of the 14 clinical psychology programs that she applied to. The point is to get involved with research early in your undergraduate career. Doing so can allow you to not only get experience as a research assistant, but to also show research productivity that is highly valued by graduate programs. As you can see in Chapter 13, the publication process is a very lengthy process. Getting started early allows you the time to demonstrate this productivity. If you start pursuing research experience as a junior, you might have some time to get some conference presentations, but getting publications would be more difficult, but not entirely impossible. Starting your research experience as a senior really doesn't allow you time to get any research published, but still might allow you to get a conference presentation or two.

Courtesy of Jeff Anastasi, Christina Stanford, and Darline Garrett.

These amazing researchers are presenting their study at a professional psychology conference. They are presenting their poster, which is in the background.

© Monkey Business Images/Shutterstock.com

Another option for presenting research at professional psychology conferences is an oral presentation, which is called a paper presentation.

Job's with a Bachelor's Degree in Psychology

Psychology isn't a major like accounting or teaching or physical therapy that specifically trains students for a specific job. This can be a good thing as it allows you to develop skills that would be applicable to all kinds of different jobs or it could be a negative as there won't be a specific job waiting for you upon graduation in the field. Many employers are looking for the types of skills that are part of a major in psychology. For example, several skills are emphasized in psychology programs such as writing, speaking, problem solving, computer skills, statistics, as well as a general understanding of human behavior and different personalities. These are skills that are valued by virtually any employer. Many psychology majors pursue jobs in law, medicine, computer science, advertising and marketing, sales, human resources, social work, business, and various research areas. Many more psychology majors pursue graduate study in various topics in and out of psychology.

Applying for Graduate Study in Psychology

When I discuss graduate school with my undergraduate students, I ask them in class to raise their hand if they plan on attending graduate school. Typically about 85%–90% of my students raise their hands. This is probably very unrealistic and speaks volumes of either their overconfidence in their abilities or their lack of knowledge as to how competitive graduate study in psychology can be. As someone who has gone through this process, served on admissions committees, and served as the director of graduate programs, I have some insight into what graduate programs would like to see in potential students. When I discuss what programs are looking for and what would make applicants competitive for these programs, many of my students who raised their hands aren't very happy with me. Some of them either don't believe me or are upset because they feel that I'm telling them that they can't get into graduate school. For some of them, they won't get into any reputable graduate program. For others, they might be able to get into a marginally good graduate program. For the rest, they could be competitive in virtually any program that they apply for. So, what differentiates these individuals from one another? Well, the first two things that virtually every graduate program is going to look at will be your GPA (i.e., grade point average) and your GRE scores (i.e., Graduate Record Exam).

Most programs have a minimum GPA requirement. The minimum acceptable GPA at my university is a 3.0. Individuals who have a GPA below this minimum won't be considered for our program. If you get accepted into a graduate program, you MUST maintain at least a 3.0 GPA in the program. If you don't, you're kicked out of the program. Thus, if you couldn't maintain this minimum 3.0 GPA at the undergraduate level, what makes you think you would be able to actually do better at the graduate level? Graduate school in psychology is much more difficult than the work that you do at the undergraduate level and there's a lot more of it. As a result, most graduate programs have the 3.0 as a minimum GPA level for entrance into their program. Keep in mind that having this minimum does not mean that you'd be accepted. This is a minimum. For most programs, the average GPA of the students who are accepted into the program are much higher than this minimum. For example, the average GPA for our clinical psychology master's program is a 3.71. This average will vary depending on the program, but you should expect that it will be competitive.

The general GRE test is analogous to the SAT or ACT tests that you may have taken to get into college. There is also a subject GRE test for psychology (as well as numerous other areas of study). Most programs require the general GRE test and some require or recommend the psychology subject GRE as well. Most programs don't have a minimum GRE score, but they do evaluate your GRE scores and will look at them. Obviously the higher your GRE score, the stronger you'll look. Unlike your GPA, the GRE scores are one objective test score that graduate programs receive that allows them to compare individuals from very different

This student is studying and working hard in order to maximize his GPA since he plans on attending graduate school.

schools and training. In order to be competitive, you'll want to have higher GRE scores. When you take the GRE, you'll receive a score for the verbal and the quantitative sections, as well as a writing score. The scores for each section range from a 130–170. Most programs focus primarily on the verbal and quantitative sections. With the new scoring, a score of 151 in either section would place you at about the 50th percentile, meaning that you performed better than roughly half of the individuals who took the GRE. A score of 160 would place you closer to the 80th percentile, which indicates that you did better than roughly 80% of the individuals who took the GRE. Clearly the better you do on this test, the better you look as an applicant. Scoring at the 80th percentile or better, with a very strong GPA, would make you at least somewhat competitive for a doctoral program. Scoring at the 50th percentile or better, also with a strong GPA, would potentially make you somewhat competitive for many master's programs. While your GPA and your GRE scores are the first two things that most schools will look at, there are many other factors that will go into their decision of whether or not to accept you into their program. Based upon your GPA and GRE scores, you will most likely get placed into a "reject" pile or a "maybe" pile.

Based on your GPA and GRE scores, let's assume that the graduate program that you're applying to has now placed you into their "maybe" pile. Now what do they look at? The next thing that most programs will evaluate will be your research experience and your letters of recommendation. While most students applying to graduate programs have strong grades and good GRE scores, what sets many applicants apart is their research experience. If you don't have any research experience, it would be very difficult to get accepted into a doctoral program. A doctoral degree (a Ph.D.) is a research-based degree. Ph.D. programs are going to want individuals who have research experience and who have demonstrated some productivity with this research (i.e., conference presentations, publications, etc.). Master's programs may not technically require research experience, but those who do have research experience are seen as stronger applicants, even for master's programs.

These students are taking their GRE. Their performance on this test has huge repercussions on how competitive they are for graduate school.

The letters of recommendation are also seen as very important. Typically the letters of recommendation will be from professors that you've had as instructors since these individuals have typically been through graduate school, know what graduate school involves, and can attest to your ability to get through such a program. You could also have letters from other individuals who know your work ethic, intelligence, and personality, such as an advisor or supervisor. For example, your supervisor at your job or from an internship site would be an appropriate reference, but you'll probably want to have more professors, if possible. Professors whose classes you've been enrolled in and that you, presumably, performed very well in, make good references. The better these individuals know you, the better they can speak to your abilities as a student, your work ethic, your personality, your ability to work with others, your ability to handle stress, as well as many other characteristics. However, if you were simply in their class, but they don't know you, then you wouldn't expect as strong of a recommendation from them. Each year I'll have students who have performed very well in my classes ask me for a letter of reference. I'm happy to do so, but if I don't know them well, I tell them that I can really only attest to the fact that they were enrolled in my class, that they attended my class on a regular basis, and did very well in the class. While this is fine, a stronger letter would be better. Typically, the strongest letters that you can receive are letters from someone who really knows you and can speak to various aspects of your abilities. This strongest letter typically comes from someone that you've conducted research with. For example, I have several students who serve as my research assistants. Many of these individuals also take some of my courses, but I really get to know them from their work in my laboratory. I get to know how motivated they are, their intelligence level, their writing abilities, their speaking abilities, their ability to learn new skills, their personality, their resourcefulness, how well they work with others, their ability to work independently, their punctuality, their dependability, as well as various other aspects or skills. Additionally, I can specifically address their ability to handle graduate school because the work that they do in my laboratory (the research) is similar to the tasks that they'll be doing in graduate school, in addition to their coursework. So, not only is gaining research experience helpful for the sake of showing your ability to conduct research, but it can also be extremely helpful for the endorsement that you can obtain from your research supervisor.

One final part of the application process that many schools require is the personal statement, statement of purpose, or letter of intent. The personal statement is your opportunity to discuss your fit with the program that you're applying to. While you have a significant amount of freedom to discuss anything that you'd like in your personal statement, you may want to address your short-term and long-term academic or professional goals, why you'd like to attend the program that you're applying to, and how your interests fit with that program. The personal statement also provides you with an opportunity to discuss any additional experiences that you've had that make you particularly suited to the particular program or other things that you'd like to discuss that aren't stated elsewhere in your application materials. The personal statement can also give you the opportunity to mention or explain certain aspects of your application. For example, imagine that your GPA was only a 3.14, which might be a bit on the lower side for individuals applying to graduate school. However, you'd like to point out to the admissions committee that you had a very difficult first year, but then your performance was much better during your last three years. You could say this by pointing out that your first year GPA was far below the standards that you set for yourself as you adjusted to college. However, once you settled into college and decided what area of study that you wanted to pursue, your GPA for your last three years was a 3.78. This isn't really an opportunity for you to make excuses, but for you to point out something that the admissions committee might miss. You're simply providing this information and pointing out to them who you really are and what is more representative of the type of work that you do.

There is one additional part of your application that we'd like to mention here. While not every graduate program requires this item, some do require it and many are impressed if you have one to submit. This additional item is your vitae or CV (curriculum vitae). Vitae comes from Latin and translates to "life." Thus, your **curriculum vitae** (or curriculum vita) is your academic life. It's similar to a resume (which is French for "summary), but the vitae is typically longer and includes a much more complete list of your experience, education, accomplishments, achievements, and skills. Typically a resume is expected to be a one page summary of your work experience, regardless of how much experience you have or how long you've been working. For a vitae, it may start out that way, but it will gradually grow. The more experience the person has, the longer it will be. Many professors have a vitae that's over 20 pages long. While your vitae probably won't be that long, you can (and should) start making your vitae now. You'll then want to continually add to it to document your education, achievements, accomplishments, and experience as they occur. As you begin your undergraduate career, you may feel like you really don't have much to put in it, but if you really consider many of the things that you do, you may change your mind. For example, you're currently attending school and working towards your degree. Therefore, you've got an item to place in your educational experience section. If you're working in a professor's lab, you're gaining experience as a research assistant; this would be great for professional or work experience. If you do volunteer work, especially if it's related to psychology or the type of graduate program that you'd like to pursue, include that as related work experience. If you have attended any conferences or presented research at a conference or if your name is on research that was presented at a conference, that's very valuable experience. These could be international, national, regional, or even local presentations. For most of these conferences, in order to attend or present, you probably had to become a student member. That's a professional membership or affiliation that should be on your vitae. Maybe you've worked as a teaching assistant or scored data for a professor for pay, include this too. If you've received good grades and made the Dean's list or the President's list at your school, that's an accomplishment that you'd want to include. Any scholarships or awards that you've received should be listed on your vitae as well. Sometimes people may put specific skills that they have that might be valuable. For example, if you are proficient in SPSS (the statistics software program) or you can program in E-prime or have proficiency in something else, put that down as a skill that you have. You can even add other relevant experiences or activities that you're engaged in to help them better understand who you are.

There are a few general guidelines to making a vitae. First, make sure that you've identified the specific categories of information that you'd like to include and then generate the different items for each of those categories. As we mentioned above, there are certain categories that should probably be included (i.e., education, relevant experience, publications/presentations, etc.). Second, make sure that your vitae is organized and that it's easy for the reader to find the relevant information. Using boldface headings for each of the categories is advisable. This allows the reader to easily find the important information. You can also change the order of the headings depending on what you'd like to really showcase. So organize your headings in order of importance. If you're applying to an internship then your education and relevant experience might be the most important areas. If you're applying to graduate school, your education (especially if you'd like to showcase your GPA), your relevant experience, and your publications/presentations are all important. Additionally, put the categories in the order of your strengths so that they see your strengths first. Third, make sure that you're not too wordy in your descriptions. Feel free to use bullet points to highlight your accomplishments for each item. If you'd rather include a short paragraph, make sure that it's very short and to the point. Don't add a bunch of extra information that isn't pertinent just to make it longer. Brevity is key but make sure that you've covered the important items. Finally, this is your vitae – you're academic life. If you have accomplishments or experience that are valuable, make sure that they know what you did. You'll most likely be using this for a job or graduate school, so you're making this to impress. Don't be afraid to really showcase your accomplishments and strut your stuff!

We've provided a sample vitae in Appendix 3. Take a look at it and feel free to use it as a guide to get you started. To get other examples of vitae formats, ask one of your professors for a copy of theirs so that you can model yours after what they have. Most academic departments at your school probably also post the faculty vitae on their department website. There isn't really a right or wrong format, so take a look at different ones until you find one that you really like.

While all graduate programs may not specifically require you to submit a vitae if you apply to their program, you should have one in case they do want one. Most programs don't require a vitae because most undergraduate students don't have one or don't even know what it is. If you do have one or you submit one even without them requesting it, you may impress them with your knowledge of how academia works and your training to know why the vitae is important. If possible, submit your vitae when you apply to graduate programs, research assistant positions, or even jobs as it really does provide a nice summary of your academic life.

Before moving on to the next section, it's important to note that applying to graduate school isn't cheap. I'm not talking about tuition, but of the costs associated with simply *applying* for graduate school. Of course you're probably aware that taking the GRE costs money. At the time of writing this textbook, the fee for taking the general GRE test was $205 and the fee for taking the psychology subject GRE was $150. In addition to these fees, most graduate programs also charge an application fee. This application fee varies fairly widely, but is typically between $50 and $100. While this may not sound like a lot, it is definitely something worth keeping in mind as you apply since you'll probably be applying to numerous programs. In order to be successful, you'll want to apply to "dream" programs, good programs, and some potentially weaker programs. If your goal is to get admitted into a doctoral program, you may also want to apply to a couple of master's-level programs, just in case. At $100 apiece, applying to 10 programs would be $1000. Most successful students apply to 10–15 programs.

Types of Psychology Programs

If you know what type of graduate program that you'd like to pursue, then you probably don't need to know about the various graduate programs in psychology. However, most undergraduate students either don't know what they want to do or aren't aware of the various areas of study within psychology. If you're looking to pursue graduate studies in psychology, I'd strongly recommend purchasing the book that is published by the American Psychological Association called *Graduate Study in Psychology*. This book is published each year and provides extensive information for more than 600 graduate programs in the United States and Canada. The information provided is invaluable for individuals applying to the various programs. First, it lists all of the different programs as well as the admissions criteria for each program. It also provides the degrees that each school offers, how many applicants they receive each year, how many individuals were accepted into the program, the average GPA of those accepted, the average GRE scores for those accepted, as well as the tuition and stipend amounts among other information. For anyone looking at different graduate programs, it's a very helpful source of information.

As you decide what area of study you'd like to pursue, you'll also need to determine what type of degree you'd like to obtain. Your choices of graduate degrees are a master's degree (M.A. or M.S.), Ph.D., or PsyD. Most master's degree programs are structured so that you can complete your degree in two or three years, although attending programs on a part-time basis is a possibility for some programs. Of course, part-time attendance would extend this completion time. Doctoral programs (both Ph.D. and PsyD) typically take 4–6 years. While most can be completed in 4–5 years, some may take a little longer due to dissertation requirements or internships. Another degree that is becoming more common in certain areas is the specialist degree. For example, in school psychology the specialist degree is becoming more common. The specialist degree requires more education than a master's degree but less than a doctoral degree.

If a master's degree is what you desire then you'll need to know a few things about master's programs. While master's programs can still be very competitive and the workload is typically much greater than what you experience at the undergraduate level, they work similarly to undergraduate study. The admission process to a master's degree is unlike getting into an undergraduate program. You apply for a master's program and, depending on the program, most people will be rejected. For example, the clinical program that I direct typically gets over 90 applications each year. Our program is actually a fairly large program and due to that fact, we can accept up to 16 students each year. While this may not seem like a lot of students, this is a lot. Many programs, especially at the doctoral level, can only accept eight or so students per year. However, if you do get accepted into a master's program then you pay tuition in a similar way as most undergraduate programs. There are some scholarships or other types of financial assistance, but the majority of students end up taking out loans to pay for their graduate education. You should look into sources of funding and even see if there are scholarships, teaching assistantships, research assistantships, or even faculty grants that might help you to pay for your educational costs. Your coursework also works in a similar way as undergraduate programs, except that you can expect a much heavier workload. Because of this, full-time enrollment consists of either 9 or 12 credit hours, whereas full-time status for most undergraduate programs is 12–15 credit hours. If you have future goals to attend a doctoral program sometime later, then a master's program might be a good step in that process. Many students who don't have the research experience or who might not otherwise be competitive for a doctoral program, first enroll in a master's program to show that they can handle the workload and get additional research experience. You can also beef up your vitae by getting research experience, serving as a teaching assistant, teaching a course, or even having individuals who can write you even stronger letters of recommendation. However, some students want to obtain the master's degree because this is the degree that is necessary for them to obtain the type of job that they desire. For example, many students obtain the master's degree in clinical psychology or counseling psychology so that they can work as an LPC or licensed professional counselor. LPCs can provide therapy to clients with various issues and ages. Other individuals may want to teach psychology at the community college level or would like to serve as a part-time or adjunct professor at a university. In most states, a master's degree would allow one to do this as well. In fact, 18 hours of graduate work in a particular area may allow one to be able to teach at the college-level, although obtaining a master's degree would make you more competitive for these types of positions.

If you have a choice (i.e., you can get into either a master's or doctoral program) then my strong bias is that you attend a doctoral program. Keep in mind that I said IF you have a choice. The main limiting factor for doctoral programs, particularly Ph.D. programs, is that they are extremely competitive. For many doctoral programs they receive in excess of 150 applications per year and can only accept about eight students. Some larger schools may receive twice this number, but still only accept eight to nine students. So, IF a doctoral program is an option for you, there are numerous reasons why this would be advantageous. The two primary factors are time and money. As for the time factor, many of the classes that you take in a master's program may transfer into a doctoral program. However, there's a good chance that they won't all transfer in. Some classes that are very unlikely to transfer in would be practitioner-based courses. Those courses where you receive hands-on training regarding how to be a therapist don't typically transfer in. When you take additional practitioner courses in a doctoral program, you'll be working under the license of the instructor of the course or your on-site supervisor (if you have an internship placement). Since you're working under his or her license, he or she needs to attest to the skills that you have as a therapist and that you've been properly trained. These individuals are very unlikely to do this if you've been trained elsewhere since they have little control over that training and since they weren't part of that training. Thus, you would typically need to receive this sort of training at the doctoral program before they'd allow you to work under their license. As for money, master's programs are more expensive for the student than doctoral programs. Ph.D. programs typically provide two very big incentives for students to enroll in their programs and both involve money. If you are accepted into a Ph.D. program, you will typically receive a tuition waiver. This means that you wouldn't pay for tuition. You may pay some of the university fees that many universities love to charge students, but not tuition. This would be paid for you, unlike an undergraduate or master's degree. Additionally, the vast majority of Ph.D. programs also provide you with a stipend. Ph.D. programs do not want you to work another job while you're enrolled in their program. Because of this, they also pay you a stipend to serve as a teaching assistant or a research assistant. You are typically required to work up to 20 hours a week in order to receive this stipend. While you won't get rich on this stipend, it is typically enough money to live on so that you can complete your studies, pay your living expenses, books, etc. without taking out additional loans.

You may or may not have noticed that I mentioned the money incentives (i.e., tuition waivers and stipends) in the previous paragraph as being something that Ph.D. programs offer. However, I didn't mention these incentives for PsyD programs. I didn't forget about PsyD programs; they just don't typically offer those same incentives. PsyD programs usually work in a similar way to master's programs. If you are accepted, you'll be paying your full tuition yourself and the funding is very limited. There are a couple of primary reasons for this. First, PsyD programs accept many more students than Ph.D. programs each year. Thus, it is quite a bit easier to get into most PsyD programs. As such, they aren't able to provide financial support for all the students that they accept. The second reason that PsyD programs don't typically provide tuition waivers or stipends is because PsyD programs are typically found at for-profit universities. Most state and private universities are nonprofit organizations. While there are a very few PsyD programs in state or nonprofit private universities, most PsyD programs are at for-profit universities such as University of Phoenix or Argosy University, and they are very expensive. For example, Argosy University's master's program is a 50-hour program, and their PsyD program is 98 hours. So how much would it cost you. According to Argosy's website, the tuition for two semesters when enrolled for 6 hours per semester is $25,996 for their master's program and $28,636 for their doctoral program. That's about $2166 per credit hour and $6500 per three-hour course at the master's level and $2386 per credit hour and $7159 per three-hour course at the doctoral level. The total cost for a master's degree in psychology would be approximately $108,300, while the PsyD degree would cost about $233,828 (this does not include room and board, but only tuition and fees). According to their website, the PsyD program will take you approximately 5 years to complete, although only 24% of students complete the program in 5 years. One final note regarding PsyD programs is that they don't typically focus on the science of psychology. Most PsyD programs focus on the practitioner; in other words, on being a good therapist, but not necessarily being a good scientist. As a result, the research focus on PsyD programs, while there are a few exceptions, is fairly weak. Because of this lack of a focus on the scientific aspects of psychology, many psychologist look down on PsyD programs as being inferior to Ph.D. programs.

Another distinction that you may see in most Ph.D. and master's programs is whether the program uses a mentor model or not. A mentor model refers to the fact that when a student is accepted into the program, they are assigned a mentor. Oftentimes the mentor selects them into the program so that the student can work with a specific mentor. Individuals may see this mentor model as either a good or bad characteristic. The nice aspect of a mentor model is that when you are accepted into a program, you have a faculty member that you will be assisting with research. It doesn't require you to go and find a faculty member willing to work with you. In essence, you walk into the program with a research home. The potentially negative aspect of this is that you are assigned to a particular individual. The research that you engage in is expected to be with this individual, and you are oftentimes not allowed to work with other professors as that would take away time from the work you should be doing with your mentor. My graduate program was a mentor model, and it worked out well for me because I really liked my mentor and got along with him very well. However, I had classmates who were stuck with a mentor that they didn't get along with and had to suffer through the program. Nonmentor model programs don't have these same expectations. In nonmentor model programs, you don't enter the program with an assigned mentor. The negative aspect of this is that this means that you'll have to find someone willing to work with you and take you on as a mentee. However, you have a lot of control over who you work with, and there's typically not the same possessiveness that is seen in mentor-model programs. Students in nonmentor model programs are typically free to work with whomever they'd like and typically do work with more than one individual at a time. If you're given the opportunity to interview or ask someone about the program, inquiring about whether they have a mentor model might be helpful in gaining insight into the program.

This student attended a PsyD program. While she has her degree, she's also left with a huge amount of student loans.

What to Expect in Graduate School

Assuming that you were able to get accepted into a graduate program, what can you now expect? We already touched on the mentor-model aspects of finding a mentor to conduct research with. What about the rest of graduate school? Well, it's going to be more difficult than anything that you've experienced as an undergraduate. As previously mentioned, the course load will be less, that is, 9 or 12 hours instead of 12 or 15+. However, the workload in each class will be much greater, the content of the courses will be more difficult, and there will be a LOT more reading. The stakes are a little higher also. As an undergraduate, the minimum GPA is a 2.0. In graduate school, you can't have a GPA lower than a 3.0. If your GPA falls below this, you will be placed on probation where you have one semester to increase your GPA to at least a 3.0. If you're unable to do this, you'll be automatically dismissed from the program. If you receive a grade of a C in a course, you may be placed on probation. If you receive another C, you may be dismissed from the program. If at any time you receive a failing grade in a class, you'll be automatically dismissed from the program. One of the reasons that graduate programs require higher GPAs in order to get accepted is because the programs want to make sure that the students who are accepted are the students who can perform at this much higher level. So, if you can't perform at a 3.0 level as an undergraduate, why would the graduate program expect you to perform better than this when the courses get much more difficult?

Another decision that you'll have to make is whether you'd like to conduct a thesis or not. Some programs require you to complete a master's thesis, some don't have a thesis, and still others allow you to select a thesis or nonthesis option. A master's thesis is a fairly involved research project that you conduct mostly independently, but with some guidance from your mentor. The thesis is typically a year-long project, but it may take longer depending upon the complexity of the study, your motivation, the quality of your mentor, and various other factors that may be beyond your control. A similar project, but one that is expected to be more complex and conducted pretty much independently is a dissertation. The thesis is conducted at the master's level and the dissertation is conducted at the doctoral level. Both of these are huge research projects and take an extensive amount of effort from you. We previously mentioned the importance of research experience in getting into a graduate program. One of the reasons for this focus on research is that individuals in thesis master's programs and doctoral programs WILL be engaged in research whether it's research with a faculty member, a master's thesis, or a dissertation.

Most master's programs also have some sort of exit exams. These exams are typically taken as you're finishing up the program, usually in your final semester or the semester before your final semester. The purpose of these exams is to make sure that you know the information that you should know or for you to demonstrate that you have the skills that you're supposed to have before you graduate from the program. These exams take many different forms depending upon the program, but they are usually fairly intense. If you are taking an exit exam for a clinical psychology program, you might be asked to write about or present a specific clinical case in front of a committee of clinical faculty. You may be

© Syda Productions/Shutterstock.com

Following your exit exams or preliminary exams, many graduate students may be required to defend their answers to their committee members.

asked to diagnose the individual, interpret assessment results for the individual, and come up with a treatment plan for the individual. If you were in a nonpractitioner program, you might be required to answer numerous questions to demonstrate your expertise on various topics. This exam could be written or verbal and could be closed notes or open notes, depending upon the program. For individuals in a doctoral program, similar examinations are required at the end of the program. There are also some additional exams that are called preliminary exams as you complete the master's-level coursework and move into the doctoral-level coursework. These exams are to verify your expertise and knowledge prior to "officially" becoming a doctoral student.

One final note regarding graduate programs, specifically practitioner-based programs, is the internship requirement. In a clinical psychology or school psychology or counseling psychology program (i.e., practitioner-based programs), students complete all of the coursework. This may take them two or more years to complete the coursework. They then, during a final year of the program, go on internship. This internship requires them to get a certain amount of hands-on experience and practice hours in order to fully complete the program. Once they have completed their internship and pass the internship requirements they are then allowed to graduate from the program.

Concluding Remarks

At this point you may be asking yourself, why would anyone want to go through all of this? Well, it's a good question. It's a question that I asked myself many times during graduate school. Understandably, many people don't want to go through this and decide that they'd rather get a job or switch their major to something else. Quite honestly, this is the time for you to make this decision. If psychology is what you love or what you're really interested in, that's great! BUT, keep in mind that it will probably require some advance work beyond an undergraduate degree to work in psychology. I will tell you that most of my graduate students are typically surprised at how quickly their graduate education goes by. I think it may have something to do with them really focusing on the work that they do and their classes that they don't realize how quickly the time passes.

End of Chapter Quiz

1. True or False: You must obtain a master's degree before being accepted into a doctoral program.

___2. What are the two primary indicators that graduate programs use for admissions purposes?
   a. GPA and publications
   b. GPA and GRE scores
   c. GRE scores and publications
   d. conference presentations and publications
   e. letters of recommendation and GPA

___3. Which of the following individuals would be the best person to write you a letter of recommendation?
   a. A family friend who has known you for your entire life and can speak to your abilities.
   b. A professor whose class you performed really well in.
   c. A professor whose lab you worked in for the last couple of years.
   d. You parents who can attest to your abilities and "specialness."
   e. Your boss at Chipotle, where you've worked each summer for the past 4 years.

___4. What is the name of the publication that is published by the American Psychological Association that has extensive information on each graduate program in the United States and Canada?
   a. *Graduate Study in Psychology*
   b. *Applying to Graduate School for Dummies*
   c. *How to Get In: Graduate School Guide*
   d. *Psychological Graduate Programs Guide*

___5. What kind of course load can you expect each semester in graduate school?
   a. 6 hours   b. 12 hours   c. 18 hours   d. 21 hours

___6. Approximately how many individuals are accepted into an average-sized doctoral program each year?
   a. 2   b. 4   c. 8   d. 16   e. 30

___7. In most graduate programs, what happens if you receive a failing grade in a course?
   a. Nothing happens as long as your GPA is still above a 2.0
   b. You would be given two more attempts to retake the course and receive a passing grade. If you don't pass the class on the third attempt, you can be dismissed from the program.
   c. You can be placed on academic probation, but you'd need to make up the class the following semester.
   d. You will be automatically dismissed from the program.

___8. In most graduate programs, what happens if you receive more than two grades of C?
   a. Nothing happens as long as your GPA is still above a 2.0
   b. You would be given two more attempts to retake the course and receive a passing grade. If you don't pass the class on the third attempt, you can be dismissed from the program.
   c. You can be placed on academic probation, but you'd need to make up the class the following semester.
   d. You will be automatically dismissed from the program.

___9. What is one of the main differences between a master's program and a doctoral program?
  a. time to complete the program
  b. amount of funding offered
  c. cost of the program per semester
  d. all of the above
  e. only A and B
  f. only B and C

___10. What is a reason given in this chapter that many individuals don't consider PsyD programs?
  a. less prestige for the PsyD degree
  b. amount of funding offered
  c. cost of the program per semester
  d. all of the above
  e. only A and B
  f. only B and C

Homework Assignment #1

Identify five graduate programs that have the type of program that you'd be interested in pursuing. Make a matrix that has at least five characteristics of each of these programs that would allow you to compare the programs. Feel free to use any information that you'd like that might help you to differentiate these programs such as cost, funding availability, location, required GRE scores, GPA requirements, location of program, internship placement rates, research interests of faculty, etc. For each of these characteristics, provide a rating compared to the other programs. Feel free to use the matrix below for your comparisons.

School/Program					

Appendix 1

Sample APA Manuscript

This Appendix provides a sample of a complete APA-style professional manuscript. This sample manuscript is especially useful as a quick reference and provides a quick look at what each section of the manuscript should look like. Other sample manuscripts are available on the APA Style website (https://apastyle.apa.org).

Faces Like Me: Effects of Multiple In-Group Categories on Face Recognition Bias

Jeffrey S. Anastasi[1], Amber M. Giacona[2], and Jessica R. Lee[3]

[1] Department of Psychology, Francis Marion University

[2] Department of Psychology, University of Arkansas

[3] Department of Psychology, Sam Houston State University

Author Note

Jeffrey S. Anastasi (iD) https://orcid.org/0000-0003-3784-6045

Jessica R. Lee (iD) https://orcid.org/0000-0002-1922-0033

Jeffrey S. Anastasi is now at the Department of Psychology, Sam Houston State University.

The authors would like to thank Duncan MacLeod and Kogan James for their assistance with data collection. We have no known conflicts of interest to disclose.

Correspondence concerning this article should be addressed to Jeffrey S. Anastasi, Department of Psychology, Sam Houston State University, Huntsville, TX 77341-2447. Email: jeff.anastasi@shsu.edu

Abstract

In the current study, we evaluated the impact of manipulating more than one in-group/out-group dimension on face recognition accuracy. Both Black and White participants evaluated same- and other-race students and police officer faces. Results indicated that the own-race bias was eliminated in some conditions. Results also showed an additive effect of dimensions such that discriminability was predicted by the number of in-group dimensions shared by participants and faces. Higher discriminability was found when participants shared both dimensions with the faces and the lowest discriminability when the faces were out-group on both dimensions. Results are discussed in terms of Sporer's (2001) in-group/out-group model (IOM) of facial processing and categorization.

Keywords: own-race bias, face recognition, in-group/out-group

Faces Like Me: Effects of Multiple In-Group Categories on Face Recognition Bias

The own-race bias occurs when one demonstrates better recognition of faces from one's own race than faces from another race (Meissner & Brigham, 2001). This bias is of obvious importance for forensic settings but also has significant repercussions any time that remembering a face is necessary. While researchers have yet to come to a consensus regarding an explanation of the own-race bias (Meissner & Brigham, 2001; Sporer, 2001), one of the most popular theoretical explanations for the own race bias is predicated on social categorization.

Sporer's (2001) In-Group/Out Group (IOM) model of face processing postulates that one's memory for faces is dependent upon the amount of processing that a face receives. Each face that we encounter is initially categorized as an in-group or out-group face. Out-group faces are categorized based upon generic, category features resulting in relatively shallow, non-individuating processing that hinders discriminability. However, in-group faces, after the initial categorization as in-group faces, are processed further for additional individuating features facilitating memory for such faces.

While IOM was initially proposed to explain the own-race bias, it can also explain other in-group/out-group biases. For example, Bernstein et al. (2007) demonstrated that faces categorized using a relevant social group can result in similar biases. Using faces obtained from a database, they randomly assigned faces to serve as "Miami" or "Marshall" University students. They showed that Miami University students better remembered faces of other Miami University students compared to students from a rival university (i.e., Marshall University). Further, Rule et al. (2007) demonstrated an own-sexual orientation bias such that homosexual males better remembered homosexual male faces better than heterosexual male faces, while heterosexual males showed better memory for heterosexual faces.

IN-GROUP CATEGORIZATION ON FACE RECOGNITION   4

Overall, IOM has been very successful in explaining studies such as these where a single social dimension has been manipulated. However, predictions from IOM are somewhat less clear when more than one social category is manipulated. For example, Ray et al. (2010) manipulated multiple social dimensions by crossing political party (i.e., Republican or Democrat) with abortion stance (i.e., pro-life or pro-choice). They evaluated face memory of White, pro-choice Democrats for faces identified as pro-choice Democrats, pro-life Democrats, pro-choice Republicans, and pro-life Republicans. It could be argued that in-group faces on both dimensions would be remembered best, while faces that were categorized as out-group on any dimension would be recognized less accurately due to out-group categorization of these faces. Alternatively, one might predict an additive effect of category membership. For example, faces sharing both in-group dimensions would be recognized the most accurately, whereas faces that share a single in-group dimension would be recognized moderately well, with out-group faces on both dimensions showing the poorest discriminability. Results of their study indicated that discriminability was significantly better for faces sharing two in-group dimensions than for faces sharing one in-group dimension. Additionally, recognition for faces sharing no in-group dimensions was equivalent to those sharing a single in-group dimension. Thus, their results indicated no additive effect based on the number of social dimensions shared with participants.

While Ray et al. (2010) manipulated more than one in-group category, only a single study has evaluated the impact of multiple category membership on the own-race bias. Shriver et al. (2008; Experiment 2) evaluated White, Miami University students' ability to remember Black and White students depicted as either Miami University students or as rival students from Marshall University. Results indicated that discriminability was well-predicted by the number of dimensions the faces shared with the participants. Specifically, participants showed superior discriminability for faces sharing two dimensions (i.e., own-race, own-university) followed by faces sharing a single dimension (i.e., own-race, other-university faces), and the poorest discriminability for faces sharing no dimensions (i.e., other-race, other-university). However, contrary to expectations, performance for the other-race, own-university faces (i.e., single dimension) was equivalent to faces that shared no in-group dimension. While these findings are interesting, they provide only partial support for an additive effect. Thus, it is unclear if manipulation of multiple in-group dimensions would lead to an additive or non-additive effect.

Similar to previous studies (Ray et al., 2010; Shriver et al., 2008), we manipulated more than one affiliation dimension in the current study. In our study, similar to the Shriver et al. (2008) study, we manipulated the race of the faces presented by using photographs of both White and Black individuals. Based on pilot testing to determine what other affiliation dimensions would be meaningful to college students, we used photographs of police officers and students as the additional affiliation dimension. One potential limitation of the previous studies that manipulated more than one affiliation was that they only tested White participants. Thus, in the current study, we evaluated the face recognition performance of both White and Black participants for White and Black faces of college students and police officers.

Based upon the previous literature (see Meissner & Brigham, 2001, for a review), we expected to find an own-race bias such that White participants would exhibit better discriminability for White than Black faces, and Black participants would exhibit better discriminability for Black than White faces. We also expected better discriminability for student faces than police officer faces. Finally, we expected discriminability to be predicted by the number of in-group dimensions that the faces share with participants (i.e., an additive effect). Thus, we expected the best discriminability with same-race student faces (two shared dimensions), moderate performance for other-race student faces and same-race police officer faces (both share one dimension with participants), and the poorest performance for other-race police officer faces (no shared dimensions).

Method

Participants

Participants in the current study consisted of 120 Sam Houston State University (SHSU) students who participated in exchange for extra credit or as part of a class requirement for research participation. All participants were between the ages of 18-26 years and consisted of 60 White (M_{age} = 20.23 years, SD = 2.10) and 60 Black (M_{age} = 21.03 years, SD = 2.06) individuals. Participants were tested individually or in groups of up to six individuals.

Design

The design of the current study was a 2 (Participant Race: Black, White) x 2 (Photograph Race: same-race, other-race) x 2 (Photograph Affiliation: student, police) mixed-factor design with participant race treated as a between-subjects variable and photograph race and photograph affiliation manipulated within-subjects. The dependent variable was discriminability (d') scores.

Materials

Each of the 24 faces at encoding depicted a "student" or a "police officer" with a neutral (non-smiling) expression. The majority of the faces used in the current study were taken from the face database developed by Minear and Park (2004). However, due to an inadequate number of Black faces, additional photographs were collected of individuals from the Houston area. As a result, the photographs consisted of an equal number of White and Black faces, each with half males and half females, and showed the head and shoulders of each individual. Photographs of police officers in uniform were taken from various internet websites. These photographs were altered using Adobe Photoshop by placing our face stimuli into the photographs, making sure

that the uniform was visible. Each photograph served equally often in the student and police

officer conditions.

Other materials used in the current study included a rating sheet used at encoding as well

as a recognition test sheet. The rating sheet included a 5-point, similarity rating scale where "5"

corresponded to a rating of "very similar" and "1" corresponded to a "very dissimilar" rating.

The sheet had 24 spaces for participants to indicate their rating for each of the photographs

presented during the encoding phase of the study. The recognition test sheet was made up of 48

items. Participants were to use this recognition test sheet to indicate if they remembered each

presented photograph by circling either the "yes" or "no" next to each item number.

Procedure

For the encoding phase, participants were instructed that they would be shown 24

photographs of SHSU students or police officers one-at-a-time for 8 s each using Microsoft

PowerPoint. They were also informed that the student pictures would have an orange border and

the police officers would have a blue border. Participants were then instructed to rate each

photograph on how similar each individual was to their current social group using a 5-point

similarity scale with 5 being "very similar" and 1 being "very dissimilar."

Following the encoding phase, participants were given a 5-min unrelated filler task.

After completing the filler task, participants we informed that their memory for the faces would

be tested. A total of 48 faces were used for the recognition test and each of the photographs was

altered using Adobe Photoshop so that each photograph had a white background and so that only

the head and neck were visible. Following the recommendation of Sporer (2001), alternate pose

photographs were employed so as to test face recognition rather than picture identification (i.e., recognizing an idiosyncratic feature in a picture of a target rather than the target itself). Thus, the photographs presented on the recognition test depicted individuals with a smiling facial expression. Half of the individuals had been studied and half were lures. Participants were instructed to indicate whether they recognized each individual by circling "yes' on their test sheet if they recognized the individual or "no" if they did not recognize the person. Photographs were presented using Microsoft PowerPoint at a 5-second rate. Once the recognition test was completed, participants were debriefed.

Results

A 2 (Participant Race: White, Black) x 2 (Photograph Race: same, other) x 2 (Photograph Affiliation: student, police) mixed-factor ANOVA was used to analyze the discriminability scores. Table 1 displays discriminability (d') data for Black and White participants for photographs from each of the photograph conditions. The analysis revealed that discriminability did not differ by participant race, $F(1, 118) = 2.78$, $p = .098$, $\eta^2_p = .02$. As expected, discriminability was higher for same-race faces than for other-race faces, $F(1, 118) = 37.41$, $p < .001$, $\eta^2_p = .24$, and was higher for student faces than police faces, $F(1, 118) = 22.90$, $p < .001$, $\eta^2_p = .16$. However, none of the interactions were significant. Specifically, results indicated no Participant Race x Photograph Race interaction, $F(1, 118) = 0.66$, $p = .701$, $\eta^2_p = .01$, Participant Race x Photograph Affiliation interaction, $F(1, 118) = 1.66$, $p = .201$, $\eta^2_p = .02$, Photograph Race x Photograph Affiliation interaction, $F(1, 118) = 2.22$, $p = .139$, $\eta^2_p = .03$, or Participant Race x Photograph Race x Photograph Affiliation interaction, $F(1, 118) = 1.27$, $p = .661$, $\eta^2_p = .01$.

Planned comparisons were conducted in order to determine the impact of combining multiple affiliation dimensions on face recognition. Figures 1 and 2 graphically depict these comparisons for White and Black participants, respectively. As predicted, planned comparisons indicated that White participants showed the highest discriminability for same-race student faces

(two shared dimensions) compared to other-race students (one shared dimension), $t(59) = 3.78$, p

$< .001$, $d = .64$, same-race police officers (one shared dimension), $t(59) = 3.70$, $p < .001$, $d = .66$,

and other-race police officers (no shared dimensions), $t(59) = 6.52$, $p < .001$, $d = 1.06$. They also

showed better discriminability for same-race police officers (one shared dimension) and other-

race students (1 shared dimension) compared to other-race police officers (no shared

dimensions), $t(59) = 2.43$, $p = .018$, $d = .43$ and $t(59) = 2.14$, $p = .036$, $d = .36$, respectively. Also

as predicted, White participants showed no difference in discriminability for other-race students

and same-race police officers, $t(59) = 0.16$, $p = .88$, $d = -.03$, as both of these conditions shared

one in-group dimension with participants.

Black participants also showed higher discriminability for same-race student faces (two

shared dimensions) compared to other-race student faces (one shared dimension), $t(59) = 2.58$, p

$= .012$, $d = .39$, same-race police officers (one shared dimension), $t(59) = 4.20$, $p < .001$, $d = .77$,

and other-race police officers (no shared dimensions), $t(59) = 5.09$, $p < .001$, $d = .92$. As

predicted, Black participants showed better discriminability for other-race students (one shared

dimension) compared to other-race police officers (no shared dimensions), $t(59) = 2.63$, $p = .011$,

$d = .46$, and equal discriminability for other-race students (one shared dimension) and same-race

police officers (one shared dimension), $t(59) = 1.73$, $p = .09$, $d = .30$. However, contrary to

predictions, they did not demonstrate better discriminability for same-race police officers (one

shared dimension) compared to other-race police officers (no shared dimensions), $t(59) = 1.03$, p

$= .31$, $d = .19$.

Discussion

Based on results from the current study, it seems that the ORB can be reduced or even eliminated for faces categorized into an out-group other than race. For example, Black participants showed an own-race bias for student faces, but did not show an own-race bias for faces of police officers. Thus, it appears that the own-race bias can be eliminated in certain conditions when participants are focusing on some other out-group membership dimension.

In evaluating the impact of multiple in-group/out-group dimensions, results of the current study provide evidence for an additive effect. Participants showed the highest discriminability when they shared two category memberships with the faces, moderate discriminability when they shared a single category membership with the faces, and the poorest discriminability when they shared no category membership with the faces. These findings can be explained by Sporer's IOM of face processing (Sporer, 2001).

According to this model, faces are initially categorized as either an in-group or out-group member. Processing for out-group faces concludes with a basic out-group categorization, resulting in poorer discriminability, while in-group faces are further processed for additional individuating features, resulting in better memory for such faces. By extension, faces that are very similar to one's self (i.e., those sharing two dimensions) are processed more fully than those that share only a single dimension, whereas faces that share no dimensions receive only a cursory level of processing. One potential limitation of IOM is that it is unclear which category dimension (i.e., race or affiliation) would take precedence for this initial categorization. This limitation, of course, has fairly important repercussions for the amount of processing conducted for each face. For example, it is unclear if participants initially categorized the faces by race or by affiliation (students or police officers). As this initial categorization was hypothesized to be an automatic process by Sporer, perhaps one is able to effortlessly categorize on multiple social

dimensions at one time. Thus, faces sharing two dimensions would be then processed more fully

than faces sharing a single dimension. This level of processing would then predict an additive

effect of social dimensions, as was found in the current study.

The current findings have significant implications for the legal system when the

possibility of identification errors is likely (e.g., Barkowitz & Brigham, 1982; Brigham &

Malpass, 1985; Meisner & Brigham, 2001; Sporer, 2001). For example, prior research has shown

that out-group biases can lead to eyewitness misidentification when witnesses must identify

individuals of a different race (Barkowitz & Brigham, 1982; Brigham & Malpass, 1985; Meisner

& Brigham, 2001). Other studies have shown similar biases with age (Anastasi & Rhodes, 2005,

2006; Bäckman, 1991; Bartlett & Leslie, 1986; Fulton & Bartlett, 1991; List, 1986; Perfect &

Harris, 2003; Wright & Stroud, 2002) or by using other social categories (Bernstein et al., 2007;

Ray et al., 2010; Rule et al., 2007; Shriver et al., 2008). The current findings indicate that, while

the match between the race of the witness and race of the perpetrator is important to consider,

one must also consider the similarity of the witness and perpetrator on other social categories

when evaluating an individual's ability to remember previously seen faces.

References

Anastasi, J. S., & Rhodes, M. G. (2005). An own-age bias in face recognition for children and older adults. *Psychonomic Bulletin & Review, 12*(6), 1043-1047. https://doi.org/10.3758/BF03206441

Anastasi, J. S., & Rhodes, M. G. (2006). Evidence for an own-age bias in face recognition. *North American Journal of Psychology, 8,* 237-252.

Bäckman, L. (1991). Recognition memory across the adult life span: The role of prior knowledge. *Memory & Cognition, 19*(1), 63-71. https://doi.org/10.3758/BF03198496

Barkowitz, P., & Brigham, J. C. (1982). Recognition of faces: Own-race bias, incentive and time delay. *Journal of Applied Social Psychology, 12*(4), 255-268. https://doi.org/10.1111/j.1559-1816.1982.tb00863.x

Bartlett, J. C., & Leslie, J. E. (1986). Aging and memory for faces versus single views of faces. *Memory & Cognition, 14*(5), 371-381. https://doi.org/10.3758/BF03197012

Bernstein, M. J., Young, S. G. & Hugenberg, K. (2007). The cross category effect: Mere social categorization is sufficient to elicit an own-group bias in face recognition. *Psychological Science, 18*(8), 706-712. https://doi.org/10.1111/j.1467-9280.2007.01964.x

Brigham, J. C., & Malpass, R. S. (1985). The role of experience and contact in recognition of face of own- and other-race persons. *Journal of Social Issues, 41*(3), 139-155. https://doi.org/10.1111/j.1540-4560.1985.tb01133.x

Fulton, A., & Bartlett, J. C. (1991). Young and old faces in young and old heads: The factor of age in face recognition. *Psychology and Aging, 6*(4), 623-630. https://doi.org/10.1037/0882-7974.6.4.623

List, J. A. (1986). Age and schematic differences in the reliability of eyewitness testimony.

Developmental Psychology, 22(1), 50-57. https://doi.org/10.1037/0012-1649.22.1.50

Meissner, C. A., & Brigham, J. C. (2001). Thirty years investigating the own-race bias in

memory for faces: A meta-analytic review. Psychology, Public Policy, and Law, 7(1), 3-

35. https://doi.org/10.1037/1076-8971.7.1.3

Minear, M., & Park, D. C. (2004). A lifespan database of adult facial stimuli. Behavior Research

Methods, Instruments & Computers, 36(4), 630-633. https://doi.org/10.3758/BF03206543

Perfect, T. J., & Harris, L. J. (2003). Adult age differences in unconscious transference: Source

confusion or identity blending? Memory & Cognition, 31(4), 570-580.

https://doi.org/10.3758/BF03196098

Ray, D. G., Way, N., & Hamilton, D. L. (2010). Crossed-categorization, evaluation, and face

recognition. Journal of Experimental Social Psychology, 46(2), 449-452.

https://doi.org/10.1016/j.jesp.2009.12.001

Rule, N. O., Ambady, N., Adams, R. B., & Macrae, C. N. (2007). Us and them: Memory

advantages in perceptually ambiguous groups. Psychonomic Bulletin & Review, 14(4),

687-692.

Shriver, E. R., Young, S. G., Hugenberg, K., Bernstein, M. J., & Lanter, J. R. (2008). Class,

Race, and the face: Social context modulates the cross-race effect in face recognition.

Personality and Social Psychology Bulletin, 34(2), 260-274.

https://doi.org/10.1177/0146167207310455

Sporer, S. (2001). Recognizing faces of other ethnic groups: An integration of theories.

Psychology, Public Policy, and Law, 7(1), 36-97.

https://doi.org/10.1037/1076-8971.7.1.36

IN-GROUP CATEGORIZATION ON FACE RECOGNITION   14

Wright, D. B., & Stroud, J. N. (2002). Age differences in lineup identification: People are better

with their own age. *Law and Human Behavior, 26*(6), 641-654.

https://doi.org/10.1023/A:1020981501383

Table 1

Average Discriminability Scores (d') for White and Black Participants

	White Participants		
Photograph Affiliation	Same-Race Face	Other-Race Face	Mean
Student Faces	1.44 (0.73)	0.97 (0.74)	1.20 (0.73)
Police Faces	0.99 (0.62)	0.73 (0.60)	0.86 (0.61)
Mean	1.21 (0.67)	0.85 (0.67)	

	Black Participants		
Photograph Affiliation	Same-Race Face	Other-Race Face	Mean
Student Faces	1.51 (0.62)	1.23 (0.79)	1.36 (0.70)
Police Faces	1.01 (0.68)	0.87 (0.76)	0.94 (0.72)
Mean	1.26 (0.65)	1.05 (0.77)	

Note. Standard deviations are in parentheses.

Figure 1

Average Discriminability Scores (d') for White Participants for Each Face Condition

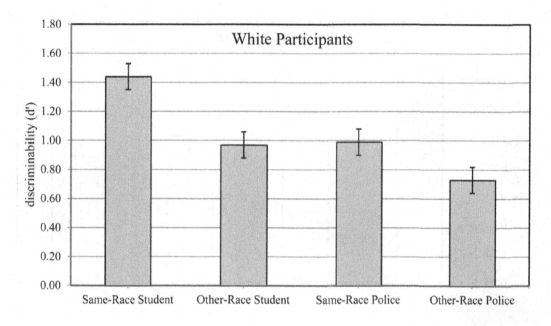

Figure 2

Average Discriminability Scores (d') for Black Participants for Each Face Condition

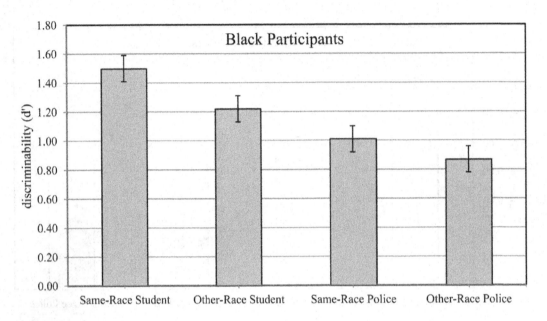

Appendix 2
Sample Journal Cover Letter

WAU Western Aldabra University
A Member of The Sechelles University System
DEPARTMENT OF PSYCHOLOGY AND HERPETOLOGY

June 16, 2020

Editor, *Animal Perceptual Sciences*
Stephen J. White, Ph.D.

Dear Dr. White,

I am attaching a manuscript entitled "An own-species bias: Facial processing biases in cats and

tortoises" that my co-authors and I would like you to consider for publication in *Animal Perceptual*

Sciences. We believe that the topic has broad appeal to others in psychology (e.g., cognitive, social,

developmental, and individuals with an interest in psychology and law) and that it will make a

substantial contribution to the animal face processing literature. The word count for the body of the

manuscript is 4,876 words. This manuscript has not been published and is not under consideration for

publication elsewhere. Additionally, the rights of all animal participants were protected, and the

applicable APA ethical guidelines were followed. Thank you for your assistance, and we look forward

to hearing from you in the near future.

Sincerely,

Jonathan M. Tortuga

Department of Psychology and Herpetology
Western Aldabra University
Victoria, Aldabra Atoll 01341
(344) 294-3049
Email: jon.tortuga@wau.edu

Victoria, Aldabra Atoll 01341-2447   •   1.344.294.1174   •   Fax 1.344.294.3798

Appendix 3

Sample Curriculum Vitae

Marcus T. Snowman

19 Sunny Maple Lane
Huntsville, TX 77341-2447
(936) 555-3049
Email: MTS022@shsu.edu

Education

2020   **Bachelor of Science in Psychology**, Sam Houston State University.
Cumulative GPA – 3.73, Psychology GPA – 3.89

2017   **Associate of Arts in Counseling**, Lone Star College.

Professional Experience

Fall 2019 to Present

Teaching Assistant, Sam Houston State University, Huntsville, Texas.
Serve as a teaching assistant for the psychology research methods course under the supervision of Dr. Jessica Lee. Assisted in all facets of the course and was responsible for grading assignments and lectures in the laboratory component of the course.

Spring 2018 to Present

Research Assistant, Sam Houston State University, Huntsville, Texas.
Work in the laboratory of Dr. Jeff Anastasi. Conducted several independent research projects involving human information processing including topics such as false memory, eyewitness memory, and hypermnesia.

Spring 2017 to Spring 2018

Human Factors Associate, South Texas Human Factors Associates, Galveston, TX
Worked as a member of a design team developing new radar, sonar, and tactical data transfer systems for current Naval aircraft. Performed a task analysis contrasting a completely new system and a system implementation using existing hardware capabilities and made recommendations involving advantages and disadvantages of each system.

Publications

Lee, J. R., Anastasi, J. S., **Snowman, M. T.**, & (2020). Hypermnesia in chipmunks in a speeded response task. *Cognition & Memory, 46*, 48-56. http://doi.org/10.53301/c&m20.5678.321

Conference Presentations

Snowman, M. T., Lee, J. R., Anderson, J. H., & Anastasi, J. S. (2020). Own-age bias in cats: The impact of fur color and age in facial processing. Research presented at the Annual Meeting of the Psychonomic Society, San Juan, Puerto Rico, November 18-21, 2020.

Snowman, M. T., DeLeon, M. A., Sims-Rhodes, N. E., & Anastasi, J. S. (2020). The effects of time travel on the production of false memories. Research presented at the Annual Meeting of the Southwestern Psychological Association, Frisco, TX, August 27-30, 2020.

Anderson, J. H., **Snowman, M. T.**, & Anastasi, J. S. (2019). Own-age face recognition bias: The effects of encoding processing. Research presented to the Annual Meeting of the Association for Psychol gical Science, Washington, DC, May 26-29, 2019.

Wesley, J. L., Wooderson, R. L, **Snowman, M. T.**, & Lee, J. R. (2019). The own-age bias in tortoises: Evaluating attentional-based processing. Research presented to the Annual Meeting of the Association for Psychological Science, Washington, DC, May 26-29, 2019.

Anastasi, J. S., Lee, J. R., & **Snowman, M. T.** (2018). Hypermnesia: Evaluating the effect of repeated testing in tortoise food choice. Research presented at the Annual Conference of the Southwesterr Psychological Association, May, 5-8, 2018.

Awards & Recognition:

Spring 2020	Received the 2020 SHSU Outstanding Teaching Assistant Award. Sam Houston State University, Huntsville, TX.
Spring 2020	Made the President's List for having a 4.0 GPA
Fall 2019	Nominated for the 2019 SHSU Outstanding Teaching Assistant Award. Sam Houston State University, Huntsville, TX.
Fall 2019	Made the President's List for having a 4.0 GPA
Spring 2019	Received the Best Undergraduate Research Presentation Award. Sam Houston State University, Huntsville, TX.
Spring 2017 to Summer 2019	Made the Dean's List for having a GPA of at least 3.50 for six consecutive semesters.

Professional Affiliations

Fall 2020 – Present	Student Member of the Psychonomic Society
Spring 2019 – Present	Student Member of the Association for Psychological Science (APS)
Spring 2018 – Present	Student Member of the Southwestern Psychological Association (SWPA)
Fall 1999 – Present	**President**, Psi Chi Chapter at Sam Houston State University

Other Relevant Activities

Summer 2017 to Present	**Certified Pet Therapy Team**, Logan's Angels, Conroe, TX Obtained pet therapy certification with my dogs, Kenzie and Gambit, from the Delta Society. Volunteer with Logan's Angels to provide pet therapy for abused and at-risk children in Conroe, Texas.
Spring 2019 to Present	**Assistant Soccer Coach**, Texas Gold Rush Soccer, Conroe, Texas Served as an assistant coach for an U-12 soccer team.
Spring 2019 to Summer 2019	**Volunteer**, Special Olympics, Huntsville, TX Served on a steering committee to organized the athletic events for 600 athletes, 25 event sponsors, and 400 volunteers for the Special Olympics Spring Games.
Fall 2018 to Spring 2020	**Psychology Club Webmaster**, Huntsville, TX Designed and maintain the SHSU Psychology Club Web Page.

Glossary

Across-Subjects Counterbalancing	A technique for controlling carryover effects in which each participant is given only one of the various treatment orders obtained by counterbalancing in order to control the progressive error across all participants
Alpha Level	A predetermined level of certainty that indicates the probability of rejecting the null hypothesis and is also known as the Significance Level
Alternative Hypothesis (H_1 or H_A)	A general statement that indicates that there is a statistically significant difference between the different conditions (see also Experimental Hypothesis)
Analysis of Variance (ANOVA)	A parametric statistical method used to test for differences between two or more independent variables as well as the interaction between those variables.
Anonymity	The idea that any data collected from a participant during a study cannot be linked back to the participant
Anthropomorphizing	The attribution of human traits, emotions, or intentions to non-human entities such as animals or objects (ex: "my computer hates me")
Archival Research (Archival Data)	A research approach that is conducted with data or data sets that have already been collected
Assent	A term used to express willingness to participate in research by persons who are too young to formally provide informed consent but who are old enough to understand the proposed research in general, its expected risks and possible benefits, and the activities expected of them as participants
Assignment Bias	Something that occurs when the groups of participants are assigned to the different conditions and are not equivalent due to a faulty or biased process of placing them into these groups
Authorship Ethics	This describes the various ethics involved when giving proper credit to those who worked on a project, presentation, or publication. Authorship should be based on the contribution provided by each author who has made a significant scientific contribution to a study
Balanced Latin-Square Counterbalancing	An across-subjects counterbalancing technique which ensures that each treatment appears once in each treatment position or order and precedes and follows each treatment an equal number of times
Between-Groups Error Variance	The error variance that is due to individual differences or variance between the different groups or conditions
Between-Subjects Design	A research design where all independent variables (IVs) are manipulated between-subjects

347

Between-Subjects Manipulation	Describes a manipulation of the independent variable where each participant receives only one level of the independent variable (IV)
Block Randomization	A subject-by-subject counterbalancing technique in which each participant receives several blocks of orders across multiple trials; can be either complete or partial
Carryover Effects	When the effects of your treatment or manipulation carry over from one condition and affect another subsequent condition
Case Study	A research approach that collects extensive data about a single individual in order to describe their behavior
Causal Claims	Any assertion that invokes causal relationships between variab. s
Causal Statement	The ability of a researcher to say that one variable caused a spec. ic effect (e.g., the drug caused Jessica's headache to go away).
Change in Instrumentation	Any change in the measuring instrument over time that may impac performance from pretest to posttest
Citation	A way of referencing a published or unpublished source of information in order to give someone credit for their work or idea.
Closed-Ended Questions	A question for which a researcher provides research participants with options from which to choose a response (e.g., "yes" or "no")
Compensatory Equalization	When the untreated group learns about the treatment group and demands equal treatment
Compensatory Rilvary	When the untreated group learns about the treatment group and tries even harder
Complete Counterbalancing	A counterbalancing technique in which each participant receives all of the treatment orders that are being used for counterbalancing. Can be used for either subject-by-subject or across-subjects counterbalancing.
Conceptual Replication	When a replication study investigates the same conceptual or general topic or hypothesis, but may use different independent variables (IVs) or dependent variables (DVs)
Concurrent Validity	A type of validity that evaluates the extent to which scores on your measurement correspond to scores on an established measurement that looks at the same construct
Confidentiality	The idea that any data collected during a study cannot be given to or discussed with any other individual outside of the study.
Confound Variable	An extraneous variable that varies with the manipulation
Construct Validity	A type of validity that evaluates if the study is measuring what you think it is measuring
Constructive Replication	When a replication study investigates the same topic or hypothesis (either exact or conceptual) but adds an additional independent variable (IV), level of the independent variable (IV), or an additional dependent variable (DV)
Control Condition	The group or condition that is not exposed to the treatment, but is otherwise treated identically as the experimental group
Control Observation	An observational approach that allows one to control or manipulate a particular behavior once the cause of a certain behavior has been determined
Converging Evidence	Using various research findings to reach a conclusion
Correlation Coefficient	A calculated number that provides a measure of the strength and direction (positive or negative) of the relationship between two variables. It is denoted by r

Correlational Research (Correlation)	A research approach that evaluates the relationship between two behaviors or types of data and can be used to reliably predict one behavior once the other behavior is known
Counterbalancing	A method used to control order effects in within-subject (or repeated-measure) designs by altering the orders that treatments are presented to participants
Criterion-related Validity	A type of validity that evaluates the ability of a measure to produce similar results to another measure
Cross-Sectional Approach/Study	A research approach that is used to study developmental changes in behavior by assessing different groups of participants at the same time who are of different ages in order to determine age-related changes
Curriculum Vitae	A detailed and comprehensive description of one's academic life and includes a summary of one's education, experience, and achievements
Debriefing	The process of discussing the general purpose of the study and its implications with participants at the conclusion of the study
Deception	A term used to describe when participants are misled or wrongly informed about the aims of the research study, typically in order to reduce subject reactivity
Dependent Variable (DV)	The behavior or item that the researcher is measuring
Descriptive Observation	An observational approach that focuses on the systematic and unbiased description of observed characteristics or behaviors
Descriptive Statistics	Summary statistics that are used to quantitatively summarize and describe the data
Differential Attrition	When participants quit or drop out of the study groups at different rates
Diffusion of Treatment	When participants discuss the experiment, become aware of the other conditions, and behave differently because they know which condition they're in
Directional *t*-Test (One-Tailed *t*-Test)	A hypothesis test that determines whether there is a statistically significant difference between two groups or conditions in a specified direction (i.e., one group is higher than another)
Directionality Problem	The issue in a correlation when you cannot determine whether variable A leads to variable B or if variable B leads to variable A
doi Number (Digital Object Identifier)	A unique alphanumeric string that identifies journal articles and some books in order to provide a link to more easily locate the source
Double-Blind Procedure	When both the participant and the researcher are unaware of which condition the participant is in
Effect Size	A measure that quantifies the strength or magnitude of the effect of the manipulation
Empirical Approach	An approach to understanding behavior through direct observation and testing
Enduring Effect	When your treatment permanently changes the participant (e.g., brain lesion)
Environmental Variable	Any variable that is related to the environment that participants are being tested in that could have an effect on the results (e.g., temperature or lighting of the room, noise levels)
Exact Replication	When a researcher replicates a study by using the same type of individuals and follows the exact same methodology to study the same construct
Experimental Bias	A potential problem that could occur where the researcher could bias the results because the researcher is aware of the experimental hypothesis or which condition the participant is in

Experimental Condition	The group or condition that is exposed to the treatment
Experimental Hypothesis	A general statement that indicates that there is a statistically significant difference between the different conditions (see also Alternative Hypothesis)
Experimental Variance	The variance that occurs as a result of the independent variable or the manipulation
Explanation/Explanatory Observation	An observational approach that allows one to determine the actual cause of a certain behavior (used with true experiments)
External Validity	Looks at the extent to which the results can be generalized to other settings and to other participant populations (see also, Generalizability)
Extraneous Variable	A variable, other than the independent variable (IV), that could influence the results (see also Subject Variable, Task Variable, and Environmental Variable)
Face Validity	A type of validity that evaluates how well a measure seems to evaluate what it is designed to measure
Factorial Design	A study that has more than one independent variable (IV)
Fatigue Effects	Exposure to a prior test that decreases or harms performance on a second test
File Drawer Effect	This term describes an issue that occurs when results not supporting the hypotheses of researchers or results that are not thought to be significant often end up in researchers' "file drawers", leading to a bias in published research which would only show the studies that have found significant findings.
Generalizability	Looks at the extent to which the results can be generalized to other settings and to other participant populations (see also, external validity)
Hanging Indent	An indentation of a paragraph in which all lines except the first line are indented from the left margin
History	Any outside even that occurs during the time of the study that may impact performance from pretest to posttest
Homogeneous Participant Utilization	A technique that attempts to minimize the individual differences in the study by utilizing participants with only certain characteristics (e.g., only females, only children)
Independent Variable (IV)	The experimental treatment that the researcher manipulates
Independent-Samples *t*-test	An inferential statistical test that determines whether there is a statistically significant difference between the levels of a between-subjects independent variable
Inferential Statistics	Statistics that allow you to make predictions ("inferences") from that data using probabilities and allow you to determine if your groups/conditions are different
Information Carryover Effect	When participants are provided with information in the first test that carries over to the second test and allows the individual to perform better due to this information
Informed Consent	A process for getting permission before conducting an experiment which clarifies the role of the researcher and the participant and lets the participant know of their rights and any risks involved with participating in the study.
Institutional Review Board (IRB)	A committee that protect the rights and welfare of human research participants by reviewing the methods proposed for research to ensure that they are ethical

Interactions	Part of an ANOVA that determines if each independent variable (IV) has an effect on another independent variable (IV)
Internal Validity	Looks at the extent to which changes in the dependent variable (DV) can be attributed to the manipulation or independent variable (IV)
Interrater Reliability	The extent to which two or more raters (or observers, coders, etc.) agree
Interval Scale	A scale that provides rank ordering such that the difference between the scale units is equal (e.g., Celsius, Fahrenheit)
Interviewer Bias	When the interviewer acts or behaves in a way that alters the responses of the participants
Keywords	Words, phrases, or acronyms that describe the most important aspects of your research that are placed at the end of the Abstract and can be used as potential search terms for your paper
Laboratory Observation	An observational research approach that focuses on observing participants in a laboratory or well-controlled setting (used with both non-human animal research and human research)
Latin-Square Counterbalancing	An across-subjects counterbalancing technique which ensures that each treatment appears once in each treatment position or order
Levels of the Independent Variable	The specific manipulations used for a given independent variable (IV)
Literature Review	This describes an extensive overview of the relevant previous research that critically evaluates and compares what has already been published on a particular topic
Longitudinal Study	A research approach that is used to study developmental changes in behavior by assessing the same group of participants at multiple times in order to determine age-related changes
Main Effect	Part of an ANOVA that determines if there are differences between the levels of a single independent variable.
Manipulated Variable	A variable that the researcher is able to manipulate such that participants can be randomly assigned to a condition (e.g., drug conditions, training groups)
Matching Subjects (Matched-Group Design)	A research approach that is used to help ensure that the different groups are equal to one another by controlling individual differences by matching individuals on certain measures and then randomly assigning them to the different groups.
Mean (Average)	A number expressing the central value in a set of data and is calculated by dividing the sum of the values in the data set by the number of items in the data set
Measures of Central Tendency	A single computed value that describes a set of data by identifying the central position of those data. Central tendency could be measured with the mean, median, or mode
Measures of Dispersion	The extent to which a distribution is spread out
Median	A number expressing the central value in a set of data and is calculated by finding the middle score of the ranked distribution.
Meta-Analysis	A procedure in which researchers statistically combine the data from previous research studies so that an evaluation of all of the previous studies can be conducted.
Mixed-Factor Design	A research design where when the independent variables (IVs) are manipulated using a combination of between-subject and within-subject manipulations
Mode	A number expressing the central value in a set of data and is calculated by finding the value that appears most often within the data set

Naturalistic Observation	A observational research approach that focuses on observing participants in their natural setting (used with both non-human animal research and human research)
Negative Correlation	A relationship when the two variables move in the opposite direction, one variable increases as the other decreases (e.g., grades increase as drug use decreases)
Nominal Scale	A scale that consists of categories that do not have a natural order or ranking, but are simply different in name (e.g. freshman, sophomore, junior, senior)
Nondirectional t-Test (Two-Tailed t-Test)	A hypothesis test that determines whether there is a statistically significant difference between two groups or conditions but not in a specified direction (i.e., it only determines if the groups are different, rather than determining which group had the higher score)
Non-Systematic Group Variance (Error Variance)	The variance that occurs as a result of random, nonsystematic factors such as measurement imprecision or individual differences and is not attributable to the independent variable or counfounding variables
Normal Distribution (Gaussian Distribution or Bell-Shaped Curve)	A symmetrical frequency distribution of scores from a data set such that the mean, median, and mode are equal.
Null Hypothesis (H_0)	A general statement or default position that states that there was no effect of the independent variable (IV)
Observational Research	A research approach that focuses on systematically observing and recording of behavior
Observer Bias	When the expectations of the observer or researcher distorts or influences their observation
Open-Ended Questions	A question that cannot be answered with a "yes" or "no" response, or with a static response. Open-ended questions are phrased as a statement which requires a response.
Ordinal Scale	A scale that provides rank information; where the order matters but not the difference between values (e.g., 1st place vs. 2nd place)
Oricid iD (Open Researcher and Contributor ID)	A nonproprietary alphanumeric code to uniquely identify scientific and other academic authors and contributors
Outlier	A data point that differs significantly from other scores in the data set
Paired Samples t-test	An inferential statistical test that determines whether there is a statistically significant difference between the levels of a with-in-subjects independent variable
Paper Presentation	A method of presenting research at a conference that involves an oral presentation in which you share your research details with conference attendees in an abbreviated presentation
Partial Counterbalancing (also Randomized Partial Counterbalancing)	A counterbalancing technique in which participants only receive some of the possible treatment orders. Can be used for either subject-by-subject or across-subjects counterbalancing
Participant Observation	When a researcher becomes an active participant in the group or situation they are studying
Participant Replication	When a study is replicated by investigating the same hypothesis but uses different participants
Pearson Product-Moment (Pearson's r) Correlation	A statistic that provides the linear correlation between two variables that are measured using either interval or ratio scales
Peer Review	The process that is used to evaluate a manuscript for a journal such that the manuscript is evaluated by individuals who are experts on the given topic (i.e., peers) in order to make sure that the research should be published

Personal Statement	An essay that is typically written when applying to graduate or undergraduate programs or scholarships that typically provides information about your career aspirations, qualifications, and interest in the program or scholarship.
Phi Coefficient	A statistic that provides the linear correlation between two variables that are measured using dichotomous scales
Plagiarism	The practice of taking someone else's work or ideas and passing them off as one's own.
Point-Biserial Correlation	A statistic that provides the linear correlation between two variables, either of which is measured using a nominal scale
Positive Correlation	A relationship when the two variables move in the same direction, either both increasing or decreasing (e.g., incidence of lung cancer goes up with an increase in smoking)
Poster Presentation	A method of presenting research at a conference that involves presenting your research details in the form of a poster that conference attendees may view
Practice Effects	Exposure to a prior test that improves performance on a second test
Predictive Observation	An observational approach that focuses on using data, events, or conditions to predict a specific behavior (typically used by correlational and quasi-experiments)
Predictive Validity	A type of validity that evaluates the ability of a measure to predict some future behavior
Pretest/Posttest Design	The most common type of within-subjects design, this is an experiment where measurements are taken both before and after a treatment
Professional Paper	This describes a professional paper is a manuscript that is intended for publication in a research journal
Pseudoscience	An area of study that is thought to be similar to an established science, but doesn't hold up to the scrutiny of scientific testing
PsycINFO	An extensive database of research studies that have been conducted in the field of psychology
Quasi-Experiments	A research approach that uses subject variables to place participants into groups or conditions, similar to a true experiment except that it lacks a researcher manipulated variable
Random Assignment	Refers to the way that participants are assigned to groups to ensure that each participant has an equal chance of being assigned to any given group or condition
Range	A number expressing the dispersion of a set of data and is calculated by finding the difference between the lowest and highest values
Ratio Scale	A scale that has all the properties of an interval variable, and also has a true or absolute zero (e.g., weight, length)
Rational Approach	An approach to understanding behavior through reason, intuition, and logic
Regression to the Mean	The tendency of extreme scores to regress or return to the average over repeated tests
Repeated-Measures Design	When all independent variables (IVs) are manipulated within-subjects (see also, Within-Subjects Designs)
Replication	The ability to reproduce or duplicate the findings
Resentful Demoralization	When the untreated group learns about the treatment group and puts in less effort (i.e. gives up)
Reverse Counterbalancing	A subject-by-subject counterbalancing technique in which each participant receives the different treatments in order followed by the reverse order (e.g., ABCCBA)

Running Head	An abbreviated version of the title of the manuscript that appears at the top of every page in the header and has a maximum length of 50 characters
Scatterplot	A graphical depiction of the two variables in a correlation such that the x-axis depicts the value of one variable and the y-axis depicts the value of the second variable.
Secondary Citation	This describes a citation where the author is citing research that has been cited and discussed by another author. This would be used when you are unable to track down the original research document, but would still like to discuss the cited work.
Single-Blind Procedure	When the participant is unaware of which condition they are participating in
Single-Factor Design	A study that has only one independent variable (IV)
Spearman Rank-Order Correlation	A statistic that provides the linear correlation between two variables, either of which is measured using an ordinal scale
Standard Deviation	A number expressing the dispersion of a set of data and is calculated by finding the average distance that each score deviates from the mean
Standard Score	A standardized score that indicates the number of standard deviations your score is above or below the mean
Statistical Power	Refers to the likelihood that a study will detect an effect of the IV when there is an effect to be detected
Stratified Random Sampling	A method of sampling from a population that accurately reflect the sub-populations from which participants are drawn (e.g., if the population is made up of 50% White, 30% Blacks, and 20% Hispanics then the sample would consist of these same percentages).
Structured Interviews	An interview that involves a standard set of questions asked in the same manner and order to all of the participants
Student Paper	This describes a student paper is written for classroom work (e.g., essays, reaction papers, literature reviews) but is not intended to be published in a professional journal
Subject Attrition	This occurs when participants quit or drop out of the study
Subject Bias	A potential problem that could occur where the participant could bias the results because the participant is aware of the experimental hypothesis or which condition they are in
Subject Maturation	When participants do better on a subsequent testing simply because they are getting older or maturing
Subject Reactivity	When participants alter or change their behavior when they know that they are being observed
Subject Variable	A variable that the researcher is not able to manipulate such that participants are placed into groups or conditions based on some pre-existing characteristic of the participants that cannot be changed or cannot ethically be changed or manipulated (i.e., sex, race, religion)
Subject-by-Subject Counterbalancing	A technique for controlling carryover effects in which each participant receives all of the treatment orders used in the experiment in order to control for the progressive error within each participant
Surveys	A research approach that provides a snapshot of opinions, attitudes, beliefs, and reported behaviors (includes interviews and questionnaires)
Systematic Group Variance	The variance that occurs as a result of predictable means such as the experimental manipulation or due to confounding variables.

Task Variable	Any variable that is related to the specific task that could have an effect on the results (e.g., number of words to remember, amount of time to study)
Testing Effect	When participants perform better (or worse) on a second test compared to the first test due to their previous experience with the test
Third-Variable Problem	A variable or factor, other than the variables being evaluated, that provides an indirect link to the variables in a correlation
Title Block	For a professional APA paper, the title block consists of the title of the manuscript, the names of the author(s), and the author(s) affiliation(s) on the title page
Title Case	Title case describes the capitalization format where major words (e.g., nouns, verbs) are capitalized, and most minor words (e.g., conjunctions, articles) are lowercase.
t-Test	A parametric inferential statistic that allows you to compare two groups or conditions to determine if they are different from one another
Type 1 Error	When a decision is made to reject the null hypothesis when the null hypothesis is actually true (a false positive)
Type 2 Error	When a decision is made to accept the null hypothesis when the null hypothesis is actually false (a false negative)
Uncontrolled Carryover Effect	A carryover effect that, despite your best efforts, cannot be controlled using any counterbalancing techniques
Unobtrusive Measures	Measures that are made when participants are unaware that they are being observed or studied
Unstructured Interviews	An interview in which there is no specific set of predetermined questions such that different participants may receive different questions, although the interviewers usually have certain topics in mind that they wish to cover during the interview
Variance	A number expressing the dispersion of a set of data and is calculated by determining the average of the squared deviations from the mean
Vividness Effect	When "evidence" like testimonials are seen as more influential than the actual scientific evidence by individuals
Within-Groups Error Variance	The error variance that is due to individual differences or variance within a group or condition
Within-Subjects Design	A research design where all independent variables (IVs) are manipulated within-subjects (see also, Repeated-Measures Designs)
Within-Subjects Manipulation	Describes a manipulation of the independent variable where each participant receives all levels of the independent variable (IV)
Z-Score	The most common standard score that indicates the number of standard deviations your score is above or below the mean.

Index